Mormonism at the Crossroads of Philosophy and Theology

Mormonism at the Crossroads of Philosophy and Theology

Essays in Honor of David L. Paulsen

Edited by Jacob T. Baker

GREG KOFFORD BOOKS
SALT LAKE CITY, UTAH
2012

Copyright ©2012 Greg Kofford Books, Inc.
Cover design copyright © 2012, 2016 Greg Kofford Books, Inc.
Cover design by Loyd Ericson

2nd printing, 2016

All rights reserved. No part of this book may be reproduced in any form or by any means without permission in writing from the publisher, Greg Kofford Books. The views expressed herein are the responsibility of the author and do not necessarily represent the position of Greg Kofford Books, Inc.

2015   14   13   12   11   5   4   3   2   .

Greg Kofford Books, Inc.
P.O. Box 1362
Draper, UT 84020
www.gregkofford.com
facebook.com/gkbooks

Library of Congress Cataloging-in-Publication Data

Mormonism at the crossroads of philosophy and theology : essays in honor of David L. Paulsen / edited by Jacob T. Baker.
 pages cm
 Includes index.
 ISBN 978-1-58958-192-0
 1. Church of Jesus Christ of Latter-day Saints--Theology. 2. Mormon Church--Theology. 3. Church of Jesus Christ of Latter-day Saints--Doctrines. 4. Mormon Church--Doctrines. I. Baker, Jacob T., editor of compilation. II. Paulsen, David L. (David Lamont), 1936- honoree.
 BX8635.3.M67 2012
 230'.93--dc23
                                    2012020905

Contents

Introduction, ix
   Jacob T. Baker

David Lamont Paulsen: A Life, xxv
   Daniel S. Barron and *Jacob T. Baker*

1. Classifying Mormon Theism, 1
   Carl Mosser

2. Collision, Division, Conversation: When Mormon Scholars and Christian Theologians Talk, 35
   Donald W. Musser

3. "Faith Seeking Understanding": Mormon Atheology and the Challenge of Fideism, 47
   Brian D. Birch

4. Restoration or Rebirth: Mormon and American Options of Authenticity, 69
   Douglas J. Davies

5. Mormonism, Natural Law, and Constitutional Democracy: Reflections on the Romney Candidacy, 95
   Francis J. Beckwith

6. The Enigma of Mormonism: Ruminations of an Anglican Friend and Critic, 109
   Paul Owen

7. Pursuing Truth, Justice, and Dialogue: A Primer on Liberation Theology Toward an Intra-Christian Dialogue, 131
   Joseph L. Price

8. The Messiah and Prophet Puzzle: Explaining Jesus Christ and Joseph Smith, 147
   Lyndsey Nay and *John W. Welch*

9. Is Evangelical Mormonism a Viable Concept for the Near Future? 171
   Craig L. Blomberg

10 Conceptual Metaphor Theory and the Mormon Understanding of God, 193
    John E. Sanders

11 David Paulsen on Divine Embodiment, 211
    Stephen T. Davis

12 Does Divine Passibility Entail Divine Corporeality? 227
    Clark H. Pinnock

13 Transascendence: Transcendence in Mormon Thought, 235
    James E. Faulconer

14 "We Shall Be Like Him": Explorations into the LDS Doctrine of Deification, 255
    Robert L. Millet

15 Kalam Infinity Arguments and the Infinite Past, 277
    Blake T. Ostler

16 Lehi's Opposition Theodicy, 309
    Dennis Potter

17 All's Well that Ends Well: Evil, Eschatology, and Love in F. W. J. Schelling and David L. Paulsen, 319
    James M. McLachlan

Appendix: List of Publications, 345

Contributors, 349

Subject Index, 353

Scripture Index, 365

Dedicated to Clark Pinnock (1937–2010),
who saw Mormonism in Christ and Christ in Mormonism

Introduction

Jacob T. Baker, *Brigham Young University*

In January 2007 several Mormon graduate students gathered socially for the first time in the shadow of the Kresge Chapel on the campus of Claremont School of Theology (now Claremont Lincoln University) in Claremont, California. They were a somewhat unusual group—young Mormons who chose to pursue a professional life studying and teaching religion outside the purview of official LDS religious and higher education.[1] Each of them had a distinctive background and contrasting academic interests concerning the academic study of religion. Several of them intriguingly discovered, however, that they had in common one particular teacher who had encouraged them to study religion professionally, and who was also a significant factor in deciding to pursue a degree in Claremont: David Paulsen, a professor of Philosophy at Brigham Young University. Thus was born the idea for this volume.

David Paulsen has been and continues to be a well-known defender and explainer of the Mormon faith, as evidenced by his considerable published oeuvre. However, his longest-lasting legacy will likely be seen in his separate, though related roles as both a student mentor and a dialogue partner with scholars from more traditional Christian communities. Dozens of students have served as research and teaching assistants for David's writing projects and classes. It is particularly noteworthy that many of his publications are co-authored with a student.[2] While few of these students go on to graduate school to teach philosophy and religion, his influence on students for generations to come is sure to be fairly widespread. In fact, two of the contributors here—Blake Ostler and Dennis Potter—are former student assistants of David, who

---

1. None of the LDS institutions for higher learning currently include religious studies or any academically related subject as part of their curricula. Instead, Religious Education, a devotional, ecclesiastical structure focused on inculcating specifically Mormon teachings and values, is required of all students who attend these schools. The Church Education System oversees and implements religious instruction for young people under 18 (seminary) and for young adults under the age of 30 (Institute).

2. See the many publications that David co-authored with his students in the appendix.

themselves have gone on to become academics and published authors in their own right. At a time when Mormonism is slowly and visibly emerging from intellectual obscurity, David's impact on his students might prove to be just as much a contributing factor as his publications pertaining to his own involvement in this developing phenomenon.

There have been several anthologies or published dialogues concerning Mormonism and Christian thought, and Mormonism and Evangelical dialogues in particular.[3] However, this anthology—though for the most part broadly ecumenical—differs from other similar volumes in two notable ways. First, many of the essays here are arguably as or more *philosophical* in nature than previous collections of Mormon-themed essays. Though theology figures prominently in this collection, many of the essays are more strictly classified as philosophical. This is significant inasmuch as Mormonism has usually been considered within the structure and worldview of Christian theology and has therefore been normally investigated and presented theologically instead of philosophically. Sterling McMurrin's original study of the "philosophical foundations" of Mormon theology[4] has only occasionally—and usually unsystematically—been pursued and responded to.[5] Mormonism as an ontology, or as a rigorous philosophical perspective on the nature of reality and the structures of human and nonhuman existence, has yet to be widely and recognizably explored on a large scale. As Truman Madsen wrote in his 1959 review of McMurrin's essay, "If one can more or less accurately discern an ontology in the Mormon literature, what then of other matters: a distinctive theory of knowledge, an ethic, a philosophy of language, of history, of education, of aesthetics, of science? Much clarification, comparison, and integration (which is to say,

---

3. See, e.g., David's own volume, edited with Donald W. Musser, *Mormonism in Dialogue with Contemporary Christian Theologies* (Macon, Ga.: Mercer University Press, 2007); Craig L. Blomberg and Stephen E. Robinson, *How Wide the Divide? A Mormon and An Evangelical in Conversation* (Downers Grove, Ill.: InterVarsity Press, 1997); Robert L. Millet and Gerald R. McDermott, *Claiming Christ: A Mormon-Evangelical Debate* (Grand Rapids, Mich.: Brazos Press, 2007).

4. Sterling McMurrin, *The Philosophical Foundations of Mormon Theology* (Salt Lake City: University of Utah Press, 1959).

5. See, for example, Truman Madsen, *Eternal Man* (Salt Lake City: Deseret Book Co., 1966); Blake Ostler, *Exploring Mormon Thought: The Attributes of God* (Salt Lake City: Greg Kofford Books, 2001); James Faulconer, *Faith, Philosophy, and Scripture* (Provo, Utah: Neal A Maxwell Institute, 2010). As far as being "systematic" in nature, only Ostler's work might be classified here as such.

much understanding and appreciation) might well result from such topical analyses of Mormonism—topics which underly and overly the theology and religion."[6] Indeed, one might wonder if Mormon literature, aesthetics, ethics, etc., are even possible in the absence of a Mormon ontology, or a description of the foundations of a "Mormon world." Though the nature of this collection alone prevents such a careful and systematic undertaking, it is hoped that some of the essays in this volume might contribute in some small way to that task of a Mormon philosophy.

Second, the essays here are not strictly written dialogues between and among disparate authors as many Mormon-Christian volumes are.[7] Nevertheless, they are dialogical in nature, products of a consistent and patient exposure and imaginative working out of the subject matter, in conversation with others sharing the same general concerns. This is particularly significant considering that some of the authors here first encountered Mormon thought combatively and somewhat antagonistically. Though not converted to the Mormon faith by any means, they nevertheless developed over time the hard-won ability to carefully articulate, explore, and criticize Mormon theological teachings in a constructive and charitable manner—not an easy task, even for Mormons raised in the faith. I have heard David similarly describe his own spiritual and intellectual journey in seeking to understand and charitably express the views of his mainline Christian interlocutors. Such a process is, I might suggest, exemplary of the introspective and contemplative practice of repentance, a gifted grace that might be viewed as providing one with the ability to extend charity and benevolence to the views of others as well as to one's own perspectives and beliefs. Such a charitably penitent process softens the heart and the mind without weakening the integrity of either. It allows one to see redemption and retrieval everywhere—no belief or doctrine is wholly unsalvageable; there is always something that can be gleaned, extracted, and deployed in some productive manner to the benefit of someone. Careful, sophisticated, and non-caricatured readings of others' views requires experience with imagination and creativity, and the essays here lack for none of these. To engage in intellectual tasks—particularly where those tasks oblige us to fairly represent views that we

---

6. Truman G. Madsen, "Review of Sterling McMurrin's *The Philosophical Foundations of Mormon Theology*," *BYU Studies* 2, no. 1 (Autumn 1959–Winter 1960): 105.

7. All of the volumes in note 3 are essentially written in this format, as are other publications in the Mormon-Christian genre.

are opposed to—with repentant charity requires the willingness to "play around" in foreign worlds by dipping one's toes in exotic waters and exploring the terrain of alien lands. None of these activities requires more than the bestowal, at most, of an honorary citizenship; there is no need to become a permanent resident. What counts is that one realizes that one cannot have enough friends in a dangerous, uncertain, and fallen world, and friendships are created, first and foremost, in the act of seeking mutual understanding. We must be willing to change our minds about one another on an ongoing and never-ending basis. Then and only then does theology approach that chief Christian virtue, charity, and only as charity can theology do its most rigorous and effective work.[8]

One final note is in order. An image of Danish writer and philosopher Søren Kierkegaard subtly graced the the cover of the first printing of this book. At first glance this may appear somewhat odd; though a giant in the world of philosophy and literature, Kierkegaard can only tentatively be assigned the title of "theologian," and of course he was in no way a Mormon. Furthermore, (and regrettably) none of these essays directly address Kierkegaard's work.

Kierkegaard has been, however, a central figure in David Paulsen's own academic career. It is well-known among David's students and colleagues how much he has treasured Kierkegaard's writings. For many years he taught upper division seminars on some of Kierkegaard's most influential works. He has also published an article on Mormon and Kierkegaardian thought,[9] as well as co-authoring an essay on the one known Mormon encounter with a Kierkegaard (Søren's older brother, Peter).[10] It seems only fitting, then, that one of David's most cherished thinkers graces the cover of a book created in his honor.

But perhaps we might infer a broader symbolism in placing Kierkegaard's image on the cover of a volume that explores so-called Mormon philosophy and theology. Kierkegaard intersects philosophy and theology in anything but a linear fashion. His writings were as

---

8. On theology as charity I've benefitted from Adam Miller's insights on the subject in his *Rube Goldberg Machines: Essays in Mormon Theology* (Salt Lake City: Greg Kofford Books, 2012).

9. David L. Paulsen, "What Does it Mean to Be a Christian? The Views of Joseph Smith and Søren Kierkegaard," *BYU Studies* 47, no.4 (2008): 55–100.

10. Julie K. Allen and David L. Paulsen, "The Reverend Dr. Peter Christian Kierkegaard's 'About and Against Mormonism' (1855)," *BYU Studies* 46, no. 3 (2007): 101–56.

much literature, poetry, and autobiographical memoir as they were philosophical or theological. We cannot simply and all-sufficiently label Kierkegaard a philosopher or theologian; his thought immerses itself in both fields at various times, but often inchoately, and certainly complicatedly. Similarly, Mormonism, which has so often been described as concerned more with praxis than dogmatic theology, and in which there is no theological magisteria or developed institution for rigorous thought, might seem to appear only hesitantly at the interstices of philosophy and theology before it frustratingly moves on to another locale of human experience. Though scholars such as David Paulsen and those who contribute to this volume have made deep and impactful inroads into serious philosophical and theological examinations of Mormon thought, perhaps there is something at Mormonism's core that resists insertion into the Christian philosophico-theological tradition—something that insists, like Kierkegaard, in being a critique or re-evaluation of Christianity from the inside. One might rightly say of David Paulsen himself that his capacity to examine Mormonism philosophically and theologically is a loving re-evaluation of the faith he has so loved and defended.

More than merely a collection of essays from Mormon and non-Mormon scholars writing about Mormon philosophy and theology, this collection is a symbolic gift in honor of a scholar who has personally and professionally contributed an exceptional mind and an exceptional life to what, in the end, is the central cause of Christ: that we love one another even as he loved us (John 13:34). And so, to David: for whom theology became nothing more or less than charity.

Following a biographical essay on David Paulsen's life and academic accomplishments by Daniel Barron and Jacob Baker, Carl Mosser begins the volume with his essay, "Classifying Mormon Theism." Here, Mosser inquires how Mormonism might be theologically classified: is it a species of Christian theism? Atheism? Polytheism? Monotheism? Mormon and non-Mormon scholars have variously assigned Mormonism to each of the above categories. Mosser provides detailed reasons for Mormonism's problematic classification. First, it is not the case that the above terms create a comprehensive taxonomy. Mosser shows that it is so often supposed that these terms are sufficiently comprehensive because of mistaken assumptions regarding their meanings and etymologies. Thus, there is no straightforward way to classify Mormonism. However, Mormon theism itself is complex enough to affirm metaphysical and theological positions that place it under archetypical examples of each of these taxonomies. Nevertheless, there are too many dissimilarities with each of the taxonomies for Mormon theism to simply be a species of just one of them. In the end, Mormonism may stand apart from any current theistic classification, but if one must be provided, Mosser argues that the term *Anglo-American finitism* might best describe Mormon thought.

In his essay, "Collision, Division, Conversation: When Mormon Scholars and Christian Theologians Talk," Donald Musser directly addresses the work of dialogue and conversation between Mormons and mainline Christians. Historically, heterodox Christian faiths like Mormonism have collided (often violently) with traditional Christianity. In recent years, however, the situation can be more accurately described in terms of "divisions" rather than "collisions"; some bridges have been built and for the most part the violence has dissipated. Yet, disunity remains the norm. Consequently, Musser wants to explicitly consider how we can move beyond divisiveness and mere lack of violence and into a mode of "conversation"—respectful and inclusive dialogue that does not shy away from conflict and debate but honestly considers all aspects of the faiths engaged within a framework of trust and mutuality. For his part, as a Christian theologian, Musser finds an aid in creating such a conversational mode in the theology of Paul Tillich. Tillich advocated a dialectic of acceptance and rejection on the part of the Christian theologian, claiming that Christianity is indeed particular—in that it makes exclusive truth claims. But it is not inherently insular. Christianity is by nature an ever-reforming revelation. This is because what constitutes a faith is both its encounters with other faiths and its encounters with itself. Traditional Christian and Mormon faiths are inherently (though in different ways) open to novelty, and both have the resources to rethink their own traditions (though these are not always deployed). These two elements provide real promise for the possibility of engaging in genuine conversation.

In "Faith Seeking Understanding: Mormon Atheology and the Challenge of Fideism," Brian Birch explores Mormonism's uneasy relationship with the practices and methods of theology. Though some early Mormon thinkers (such as Parley and Orson Pratt) willingly adopted accepted forms of theological language and terminology in their defenses of the Mormon faith, expressions of modern Mormonism have largely lacked formal and traditional theological articulation. In fact, modern Mormon scholars have often described theology proper as antithetical to Mormon thinking and practice, thus making Mormonism, in a way, "atheological." This of itself makes it theoretically more difficult to identify how Mormons might more deeply examine and expound their faith in a wider cultural and social context. Equally intriguing, however, is that Birch sees Mormonism's epistemic practices (its methods and means for identifying and obtaining knowledge) as strongly fideistic, or, in other words, as more dependent on faith and revelation than on the dictates of reason and logic—notwithstanding intermittent assertions from Mormon scripture and Church authorities that reason complements and buttresses faith. Birch argues that rational evidence in the Mormon realm inconsistent with so-called orthodoxy is usually treated in one of three ways: (1) rejected outright as inconsistent with belief, (2) deferred until further evidence is provided, or (3) such inconsistent evidence becomes the object of cognitive dissonance. Thus, the compelling question becomes how Mormonism can or should negotiate this unique relationship between faith and reason.

In "Restoration or Rebirth: Mormon and American Options of Authenticity," Douglas Davies addresses the Latter-day Saint resistance to the traditional Christian language of being "born again" through an investigation into a uniquely Mormon way of understanding grace and spiritual rebirth. Some Mormon scholars have suggested that one reason for this resistance is because of the customary Latter-day Saint theological emphasis on works over grace, an emphasis that many of these same scholars have in recent years attempted to soften. However, Davies believes that the resistance has less to do with theology *per se* and more to do with a unique (Mormon) way of understanding divine grace, the root of which is the effort to establish and experience religious authenticity. Davies argues that, where Evangelicals, for example, gain authenticity via spiritual rebirth (being "born again"), Mormons, by contrast, gain a sense of authenticity through the notion of "restoration," accessed through ritual-symbols. Davies explores how Mormon patriarchal blessings in particular (as one of these symbols) encompass a number of key Latter-day Saint themes that provide the authenticity that other Christians seek through spiritual rebirth.

In "Mormonism, Natural Law, and Constitutional Democracy: Reflections on the Romney Candidacy," Francis Beckwith maintains that religious beliefs of any political candidate are subject to legitimate inquiry. Nevertheless, in order to genuinely understand and represent Mormonism in the political sphere there are three mistakes that should be avoided by any Mormon presidential candidate, political commentator, or non-Mormon Christian: 1) the Kennedy Mistake; 2) the Pundit's Mistake; and 3) the Confessional Mistake. The Kennedy Mistake is the inclination to believe that theology could not in principle be counted as legitimate knowledge and therefore must be kept private. Further, by claiming that her beliefs do not influence her politics, a candidate might lose the support of those whose very different beliefs influence their politics in the same direction, i.e., traditional Christians. A Mormon candidate could instead demonstrate that *because* of her theological beliefs, rather than in *spite* of them, she is deeply committed to shared principles and values. The Pundit's Mistake is to assume that there is no room in Mormon thought for a binding universal, natural morality grounded in natural law because the Mormon God is a finite being who is merely co-existent with the rest of the universe. According to this reasoning, Mormons remain inextricably and narrowly bound to morals and values as expounded by their human prophets, and therefore Mormons are ultimately incapable of appealing to a broader, universal, and shared morality. On the contrary, argues Beckwith, the Mormon concept of God implies that God is indeed circumscribed by unchanging moral law and that such law is found in the eternally existing cosmos instead of emanating from God's very Being. Finally, the Confessional Mistake occurs when a citizen believes that the planks of his or her creed or theological confession (e.g., the Nicene Creed or the Westminster Confession) are the best standard by which to judge the suitability of a candidate who is running for public office. Christendom's most important creeds and confessions not only pre-date the existence of liberal democracies, but their subject matter bears no relation to assessing those attributes that we consider essential to the leadership of a political regime.

In "The Enigma of Mormonism: Ruminations of an Anglican Friend and Critic" Paul Owen looks at Mormonism from the perspective of one who has undergone a significant personal pilgrimage of faith.

This pilgrimage has influenced both how Owen approaches issues that produce divisions between and among faiths in general, and the practice of dialoguing with Mormons in particular. Here, Owen wants to carefully rethink the doctrinal content of the Book of Mormon as well as Mormon and Christian approaches to the Trinity, thereby demonstrating how such careful rethinking might work in practice. Regarding the Book of Mormon, Owen sees plenty of evidence for the book of scripture being produced at least in part through Joseph Smith's own religious novelty. However, he argues that the Book of Mormon can nevertheless be viewed as evidence of Smith's prophetic character or as a valid testimony from heaven—though one that stands outside the boundaries of traditional Christianity and is not binding canonically on other Christians. The Book of Mormon may be viewed by non-Mormon Christians as a legitimate witness to Jesus Christ that arose out of a particular religious and historical need in Smith's time. In fact, Smith's prophetic narrative in general may have real value for Christians as one more witness of the saving Gospel (and one that has biblical precedents)—though, again, not in a way that lays binding claim on the Christian world in general. Concerning Mormon encounters with the Trinity, Owen considers various Mormon scriptural accounts as well as sayings of Joseph Smith in order to point out that there is potentially genuine space within Mormon thought for affirming classical formulations of the Trinity. Nevertheless, many other teachings of Joseph Smith, as well as more recent discussions of Mormonism as "social Trinitarianism," make it difficult to affirm one formulation over another. In the end, Owen contends that thinking more carefully about topics such as these can help Mormons and Christians grow together in mutual understanding.

In "Pursuing Truth, Justice, and Dialogue: A Primer On Liberation Theology Toward Intra-Christian Dialogue," Joseph Price sees liberation theology—a political theology that interprets the Christian gospel as liberation from unjust economic, social, and political conditions—as a unique method in which to engage dialogue among the disparate faiths of Christianity. As a relatively new theological method with a particular history that has determined its shifting parameters, Price argues that liberation theology is accommodating enough to the theological complexities of the various wings of Christianity to potentially serve as a means of stimulating new forms of dialogue between

Mormons and other Christians around the foundational liberation concept of justice. Consequently, Price summarily outlines liberation theology's tumultuous history, pointing out that its emphasis on praxis lends itself to a new way for Christians to talk to other Christians with distinct histories and theological backgrounds: instead of focusing on rational systematization of doctrinal truths, liberation theology asks Christian faiths to begin with justice, and hence to mutually create praxes of justice in finding common ground around liberating those who live in unjust conditions and circumstances. Thus, fundamental differences with regard to doctrinal claims need not prevent a meaningful and productive dialogue from occurring. Instead, liberation theology makes possible a dialogue that may produce substantial and material good as a result.

In their jointly written essay, "The Messiah and Prophet Puzzle: Explaining Jesus Christ and Joseph Smith," John Welch and Lyndsey Nay explore various possible connections between the way scholars have attempted to explain the character and phenomenon of Jesus Christ in Christian history and the way scholars have attempted to explain the character and phenomenon of Joseph Smith Jr. Noting that the work of academic scholarship precludes the acceptance of spiritual or supernatural causes, Welch and Nay explore an assortment of theories that have been utilized by various scholars at different times to explain both Jesus Christ and Joseph Smith. Welch and Nay point out that in this particular essay they do not offer explanations for the inexplicable, nor do they compare the relative strengths and weaknesses of these various interpretive explanations for the "Messiah Puzzle" and the "Prophet Puzzle." Instead, they are intrigued to find a high degree of resonance between interpretive theories used to explain Jesus Christ and interpretive theories used to explain Joseph Smith. Does this high level of congruence indicate something about human responses in general to the supernatural? Do Jesus Christ and Joseph Smith share something in common that needs further elaboration? Do these shared patterns shed any light on the "puzzles" that scholars see in their life histories? This essay attempts to build a foundation for more adequately addressing these questions.

In his article, "Is Evangelical Mormonism a Viable Concept For the Near Future?" Craig Blomberg asks if it is possible that there could one day be a minority of Mormons who might be willing to identify themselves as "Evangelical." Citing as precedence other once-heterodox religious groups being gradually accepted into the National Association of Evangelicals, Blomberg inquires about the possibility of Evangelicals coming to new understandings and interpretations about Mormon doctrinal affirmations that might allow some group or groups within Mormonism to be justly categorized as "Evangelical" (Evangelical Mormons, just as there are, for example, Evangelical Catholics). Blomberg points out that after several years of sustained dialogue amongst Mormons and Evangelicals, both groups have discovered that they are more similar to one another than previously surmised. Further, upon analysis of what it means to "be" an Evangelical, or to affirm Evangelical belief, much of Mormonism appears to be quite closely aligned to such a label. The primary obstacles that stand in the way of straightforward acceptance of such an alignment are essentially Mormonism's own creedal affirmations (Latter-day Saints adhere, functionally, to creeds, but do not adhere, significantly, to the creeds of traditional Christianity), as well as a distinct cultural history that is separate from mainline Christians. Nevertheless, if one takes the National Association of Evangelicals' statement of faith as an accurate barometer in accepting one into the Evangelical fold, Mormonism can more or less meet that standard. The category "Evangelical" has been refashioned and broadened over the years and compromise has occurred wherein more and more diverse groups have been identified or have self-identified as Evangelical. Even so, for such an inclusive acceptance of Mormonism to occur there must also be concessions made on the part of the Mormon church. Blomberg asserts that Mormons must make some kind of ecclesiological move that asserts that the true Church of Jesus Christ—as conceived by Latter-day Saints—is more comprehensive than the institutional Church of Jesus Christ of Latter-day Saints.

In "Conceptual Metaphor Theory and the Mormon Understanding of God," John Sanders considers the potential role metaphor theory can play when applied to biblical literalism. Christian scholars are often mired in a debate about how to read the biblical text: which texts are to be read literally, and which are to be read metaphorically? Sanders has been accused by both Evangelical Calvinists and Mormons (in different ways) about not being consistent regarding which texts he believes should be read metaphorically or literally. In response, he utilizes here "conceptual metaphor theory" in order to shed light on how we might reason about the biblical text, and therefore our understanding of biblically derived concepts, like the nature of God. Conceptual metaphor theory is an account concerning how different cultures and societies conceptualize and reason about human experience. Most metaphors are based on the "embodied" nature of human experience; that is, how humans perceive the world in and through bodies. Consequently, descriptions of human experience in the world have this element of "bodilyness," which we apply to abstract concepts in order to better understand them, each culture bodily experiencing the world in distinct ways. Sanders shows that this same phenomenon occurs when applied to scriptural hermeneutics; the concepts we derive from the scriptures are metaphorically interpreted, and therefore "literal" interpretations make no sense. Most Mormon interpretations of scripture appear to be highly literal in nature, and therefore come under particular scrutiny under the conceptual metaphor model.

In an essay entitled "David Paulsen on Divine Embodiment," Stephen Davis directly engages David Paulsen's writings on the philosophical ramifications of, and biblical evidence for, an embodied God. Davis briefly outlines the biblical case for divine immaterialism, or the notion (held by the vast majority of Christians) that the scriptural account of God's nature demonstrates that God does not have a physical body, but is instead an incorporeal spirit. Davis then proceeds to carefully analyze several important contributions Paulsen has made to the philosophical and theological literature regarding the viability of divine embodiment (likely, Davis points out, the topic to which Paulsen has devoted most of his intellectual labors in print). Finally, he offers three philosophico-theological arguments that he believes are sufficiently decisive to show that the Christian God does not have a body. First, the Bible seems to support the idea that God is *inherently* invisible. Second, the Bible presents God as omnipresent. Davis interprets this as implying that God can directly influence all points in time and space without the need for intermediaries. This would seem to necessitate divine immateriality. Finally, only an immaterial God can be said to be a necessary being, one that is not dependent on conditions or laws in the material universe for his existence and therefore one that can truly be omnipotent.

By contrast, in his essay, "Does Divine Passability Entail Corporeality?" Clark Pinnock inquires whether God can be affected by events in the world and, if so, if this entails that God has a bodily dimension that handles sensory and corporeal input. Contrary to the long-accepted orthodox Christian doctrine that God is an immaterial, spiritual being, Pinnock instead argues that if God is passable—if God is capable of loving, feeling, and therefore suffering—then God must be embodied in some way (though not necessarily the way Mormonism articulates divine embodiment). Further, God is a person, and embodiment is essential for personhood. While Pinnock argues that divine embodiment must be qualitatively different from human embodiment, he believes that it is nevertheless essential in order for God to be the personal, loving God that Scripture declares God to be.

In "Transascendence: Transcendence in Mormon Thought," James Faulconer explores the notion of divine transcendence, or the way(s) in which God might be said to go beyond or surpass the world. Traditionally, theologians have interpreted transcendence to mean that God is "beyond being" or, in other words, that God stands ontologically apart from Creation, making his being qualitatively separate from the being of created things. Lithuanian Jewish philosopher Emmanuel Levinas, however, defined divine transcendence, or "beyond being," differently. Levinas said that all that is—being—is a conceptually comprehended totality. God stands outside that totality, and is thus "beyond being." God's being is not something that can be understood through some kind of systematic totality. However, the being of mortal persons is the same. Part of what it means to be a *person* is not to be able to be encapsulated within a totalizing scheme of comprehension. Faulconer points out that the philosophical elucidation of transcendence in Mormonism is problematic because Mormon thought has usually leaned more toward its analogue—immanence—in describing God's relationship to the world and human beings, where God's being and humankind's being is essentially univocal (though the concept of "transcendence" is often employed in more common theological discourse). Faulconer's proposed solution is through an understanding of being and transcendence that Levinas calls "transascendence." Being may be metaphysically univocal in Mormon thought, but God and *every other person* are transcendent in the sense that persons are interrupted by other persons as those who are higher, and to whom they become indebted. Transascendance is a moving upward toward another person, and God is that preeminent Other to whom we transascend in a personal relationship to another.

In "'We Shall Be Like Him': Explorations Into the LDS Doctrine of Deification," Robert Millet examines the concept of *divinization* or *deification* in Mormon thought, or the doctrine that human beings can in some way become like God. Millet explores why such a modernly controversial concept need not be seen as heretical or unorthodox; various biblical scriptures, early Church Fathers, and Eastern Orthodoxy in particular have all affirmed the doctrine of deification in various ways. More recently, popular Anglican novelist and theologian C. S. Lewis attested to the truthfulness of the concept as a Christian one in that the work of God's grace is to turn ordinary people into gods. Millet concludes that when Latter-day Saints pronounce the importance of deification as derived from their scriptures, such a pronouncement is consistent with both biblical teachings and Christian tradition. He points out that many other Christians often misunderstand what this entails for Mormons (Latter-day Saints often misunderstand what is being affirmed as well). He argues that the Mormon doctrine of deification does not assert that Mormons can, by their own efforts, become divine; only God's grace can do this. Neither do Mormons believe that the exaltation of God's children to gods and goddesses in any way removes God the Father and Jesus Christ from their exalted spheres; no matter our state of salvation or exaltation, the Father and the Son are the only Gods worthy of worship.

In his "Kalam Infinity Arguments and the Infinite Past," Blake Ostler has produced an important contribution to the ongoing philosophical discussions revolving around Creation theology. Here, he responds to particular arguments that God (as a personal yet immaterial being) created the universe out of nothing—a consequence of which is that the universe cannot be eternal, and that space-time has a beginning. One of the keys for this line of argumentation is that an actual infinite series is impossible, and that, therefore, the universe began a finite time ago. Ostler replies that these arguments do not respond to the order of infinity involved in an infinite past. He shows that these positions turn on the fallacy of equivocation by utilizing logic that applies to individual members in finite collections instead of infinite sets. None of these arguments apply to the order of infinity involved in the infinite past. Further, Kalam infinity arguments can only be shown as sound when the coherence of Cantor's infinite set logic is shown to be problematic. Ostler then demonstrates how it is at least logically possible that a material universe has always existed without beginning. The necessity of positing a universe created out of nothing—and consequently the need for the kind of God that can and does create out of nothing—is therefore called into question.

In "Lehi's Opposition Theodicy," Dennis Potter analyzes the assertion (well-known in Mormonism) that Lehi makes in the Book of Mormon that it is necessary that there be an opposition in all things. Potter says that such a claim might be marshaled as a possible Mormon response to the problem of evil. The entailment of such a claim might be that it is impossible to have the best possible world without evil also being present in such a world. Potter calls this the *opposition theodicy*. Here, Potter makes it his task to explore potential ways in which the good/evil opposition might be considered necessary, and thus determine if such a theodicy is sound. He concludes that the good/evil opposition is either not, in fact, necessary after all, based on something other than objective reality, grounded in linguistic necessity only, or based on non-linguistic but nevertheless subjective facts. He also considers the possibility that even if this opposition can be based on something objective, it nevertheless becomes reducible to a non-relative opposition, and therefore doesn't involve the kind of necessity with which Mormons (or Christians) would be satisfied. None of these options seem to be tenable, and therefore the viability of something like the opposition theodicy as a response to the argument from evil is called into question.

Finally, in "All's Well that Ends Well: Evil, Eschatology, and Love in F. W. J. Schelling and David L. Paulsen," James McLachlan explores the problem of evil in philosophy through the lenses of German Romantic philosopher Friedrich Schelling, process theology, and Mormon thought—particularly in some of the writings of David Paulsen. Maintaining that classical solutions to the problem of evil do not seem to work, McLachlan considers several of Schelling's works, and shows how Schelling offers real possibilities to Mormons who want to think philosophically about divine power, human freedom, evil, and eschatology. McLachlan utilizes process theology as an example of a relational theology that re-conceptualizes the natures of God and the universe in order to show these natures to be relational instead of discrete and separate. However, one of the consequences of such re-conceptualizations is that the universe becomes a locality of unmitigated risk. In relational theologies (process theology being exemplary here) God's power is not the kind of power that can offer metaphysical guarantees; certain kinds of events cannot be prevented, physical intervention is not possible, and some people cannot be saved. God suffers with us, and the universe just is a place where such suffering will always occur. Mormon theology resonates to a certain degree with this, but in certain important ways it cannot accept a God who is not able to offer some kind of salvific, covenantal promise. McLachlan argues that Schelling offers just such a relational vision that is compatible with Mormon thought, a vision of a God who cannot metaphysically guarantee the rightness of the universe, but who can nonetheless guarantee a final victory in and of love.

Naturally there are many people who must be acknowledged as assisting to bring this volume to fruition, and I am surely forgetting some. The authors themselves must be recognized equally for their contributions as well as their patience with this project over a considerable length of time; Loyd Ericson, my editor at Kofford Books, who significantly improved my own edits in every aspect of the final manuscript; Greg Kofford for accepting the project and encouraging its publication; Lavina Fielding Anderson, who worked on and improved some early drafts of the essays; my sister Holly, herself a graduate student, teacher, and editor, for several insightful comments on several of the chapters; my wife Amanda for her encouragement and personal interest; and finally, David himself—for all the standard reasons as the inspiration behind and the subject of this venture, but also for his patience during its slow completion. It has been a singular pleasure to be able to honor in some small way a human being of his caliber. As is only expected and appropriate, any errors or omissions herein are ultimately my responsibility alone.

Jacob Baker
Provo, Utah
May 2012

David Lamont Paulsen: A Life

Daniel S. Barron and Jacob T. Baker

A quick survey of David Paulsen's office at Brigham Young University might be as good a place as any to frame the story of his life. Hordes of books, journals, old papers, notes, and correspondence, are all stacked and stuffed into a ten by fourteen foot office—a fitting annotation to David's long and distinguished academic career. Blessed with a superb intellect and trained at some of the nation's finest educational institutions, he could have plausibly spent each day polishing his legacy in pursuit of academic immortality. These files, however, tell a different story: carefully written letters to colleagues and fortifying comments to students reveal that David was indeed trying to establish a legacy, albeit a much quieter and more selfless one.

Without losing the good-natured practicality of his small-town upbringing, David refined his intellectual powers over the years, progressively honing an intense interest and capacity to engage in interfaith dialogue—an increasingly productive activity that, even more importantly, produced rich and meaningful interfaith relationships. Though he has excelled at meeting the highest intellectual standards of his profession, the ability to reach across what some have called "the divide" between Mormons and Christians requires more than intellectual engagement and argumentation; such a task also requires persistent, genuine love and care on the part of all involved. Motivated by this love and by an ability to see divergence in belief as an opportunity for conversation instead of accusation, David has been able to foster dialogue and respect among Mormons and mainline Christians.

In the end, we might sum up his professional legacy with two observations: (1) David's influence as a mentor to countless students over nearly four decades of teaching, and (2) his labors in establishing mutual understanding between Mormonism and traditional Christianity. Consequently, much of this all-too-brief and inadequate sketch of David's life will focus on these two significant aspects of a momentous and influential life, a life that is justly recognized and celebrated in this volume, composed of essays written by some of these very same students and fellow laborers in interfaith pursuits.

Childhood

David Lamont Paulsen was born on November 13, 1936, to (George) Ray and Helga Mae Peterson Paulsen in Ephraim, Utah. As part of a small agrarian town working through the Great Depression, David and his four siblings spent their childhoods struggling to eke a livelihood out of their family's small farm. In addition to small bimonthly checks afforded them by milk they sold to the local Ephraim Creamery, the family usually earned about $300 to $400 for wool every May and $1,000 to $1,300 every fall for lambs.

Though burdensome, the hard work put food on the table and clothes on their backs—quite an accomplishment in a time when the majority of the country struggled to make ends meet. In addition to the chores of the day, the family always found time to read and study. At age thirty-eight, Ray suffered a recurrence of rheumatic fever that left him with severe heart damage and the inability to perform demanding farm labor. Undeterred, he tenaciously sold some of his land and completed what might be considered an educational *blitzkrieg*. In rapid succession, he passed the GED exam, received an Associate of Science degree at Snow College, a Bachelor of Science degree at Brigham Young University, then earned a secondary school teaching certificate in social studies and history, followed by a Master's degree in guidance and counseling, also from BYU. The money obtained from the sale of their land was supplemented by aid from the Utah State Division of Vocational Rehabilitation and from the LDS Church Welfare program; however, in order to keep the family afloat during their father's schooling David and his brothers often hired themselves out to local farmers for 25 cents an hour. For three years, David worked for a local sheep man, Willie Larsen, who didn't flinch when repeatedly telling David, "You're the dumbest kid I ever knew." David, however, did flinch.

Military and Mission

Though Ephraim was far from a cosmopolitan metropolis, there were opportunities for David to receive an education. After graduating from high school, he enrolled in Snow College where he earned an Associate's degree in English in 1957. As part of a rural, almost entirely Mormon community, David never once had occasion to discuss religion with non-Mormons. This, however, would change when he began a tour of active duty with the United States Army Reserve.

During basic training at California's Fort Ord, David bunked across the aisle from a young man from the University of California who was a lapsed member of the Reorganized Church of Jesus Christ of Latter-day Saints (now the Community of Christ) and was working towards a doctorate in Physics. As they cleaned their rifles and polished their boots, David was surprised to hear someone so bright passionately challenge beliefs he had long taken for granted. Among other things, this young man asserted that there was no compelling basis in either reason or in experience for believing in God and challenged the historicity of the Book of Mormon. A bit astonished by his atheist friend and not knowing how to respond, David sent an "SOS" letter home to his father. In answer to his son's concerns regarding the viability of faith and reason, Ray sent him statements by prominent scientists who found evidence for God in the causal and teleological order of the world. Ray also sent him a copy of Hugh Nibley's *An Approach to the Book of Mormon*.[1] Though David made little headway in convincing his friend, he came away from the experience with a conviction that would become the foundation of his life's work in apologetics: faith challenged can become faith defended.

Shortly after returning from his tour of active duty, David was asked to serve as a full-time missionary in the Northern States Mission, headquartered in Chicago, Illinois. Like his service in the Army, David's two years of missionary service continued to challenge him as well as providing additional opportunities for interfaith dialogue. One of the tasks assigned to him as a missionary was to promote an accurate representation of the history and doctrines of the Church of Jesus Christ of Latter-day Saints. Public curiosity coupled with inaccurate and sometimes deliberately misguided statements about the Church had created many misconceptions; David's job was to clear up these misconceptions and to set the record straight. He was directed to supplement—or, if possible, even replace—books in local libraries that misrepresented the

---

1. Hugh Nibley, *An Approach to the Book of Mormon* (Salt Lake City: Deseret Book Co., 1988).

Church's beliefs and history. Among the books that David introduced to local libraries in Illinois were: *Essentials in Church History*,[2] *Jesus the Christ*,[3] *Articles of Faith*,[4] and *A Marvelous Work and a Wonder*,[5] in addition to copies of the Book of Mormon and Doctrine and Covenants. At one library, the director was more than happy to replace *The Crimes and Mysteries of Mormonism*;[6] *Mormonism, the Islam of America*;[7] and *No Man Knows My History*[8] for these Mormon-authored texts.

The questions raised in these latter books concerning the doctrines and history of the Church were initially painful for David, but they also served to expand his own views. He recalls, "The books posed objections to the truth of the restored gospel for which I had no ready answers. This was troubling. But their impact was not to leave me with serious doubts. Rather they drove me to intense study and prayer."[9] In response to his prayers for help, David was blessed with certain sacred experiences that would remain the bedrock of his faith and the impetus for his work in explaining and defending Mormon thought, not only during his mission but for the rest of his life. Though his missionary service helped him learn to articulate and defend his beliefs through reason, he nevertheless felt reason was a supplement to faith, not its substance.

BYU and University of Chicago

Following his missionary service, David enrolled at Brigham Young University with the intent of preparing for law school. He had no previous experience with political science, but when advised that it was *the* pre-law major on campus, he enrolled in his first courses,

---

2. Joseph Fielding Smith, ed., *Essentials in Church History*, (Salt Lake City: Deseret Book Co., [1922], 1979).

3. James E. Talmage, *Jesus the Christ* (Salt Lake City: Deseret Book Co., [1915], 2004).

4. James E. Talmage, *The Articles of Faith* (Salt Lake City: Deseret Book Co., [1899], 1990).

5. LeGrand Richards, *A Marvelous Work and a Wonder* (Salt Lake City: Deseret Book Co., [1950], 2007).

6. J. H. Beadle, *Life in Utah, or the Mysteries and Crimes of Mormonism* (Kessinger Publishing [1870], 2004).

7. Bruce Kinney, *Mormonism: The Islam of America* (Kessinger Publishing, [1912], 2004).

8. Fawn McKay Brodie, *No Man Knows My History: The Life of Joseph Smith*, 2nd ed. (New York: Vintage Books, [1945], 1995).

9. David L. Paulsen, interview with Daniel Barron.

including a class taught by Professor Louis Midgley. Though listed as "political philosophy," David recalls, "The course content was often skewed toward Mormon apologetics. Indeed, Midgley had a passion for apologetics which proved contagious. No doubt, in due time, his influence helped shape the course of my academic career."[10] Ironically for David, Midgley often expressed his distrust of philosophy, which he considered anti-religious because of his belief that early and modern Christians had too often bowed to classical philosophical paradigms.

In 1961 the "dumbest kid Willie Larsen ever knew" graduated from BYU in political science as valedictorian of his class. Following graduation, David returned to Illinois where he was a National Honors Scholar at the University of Chicago Law School. Just as with his missionary service, Chicago presented a rich array of religious beliefs and personalities that continued to whet his appetite for interfaith dialogue and apologetics. His classmates represented a collage of religious backgrounds: Orthodox, Conservative, and Reformed Jews; Roman Catholics; Protestants of all stripes; agnostics; and atheists. Such diversity produced interesting and challenging theological discussions in the cafeteria, at weekly wine mess, and especially in his residence hall lounge. These conversations became so popular they earned David's residence hall, Linn House, the nickname "Linn Theological Seminary." Students from other halls often came to join the discussions. Serving as the unofficial host of these pseudo-conferences, David developed the personality and the patience necessary to moderate fruitful discussions over a sometimes-sensitive subject.

During his third year of law school, David's local church leaders noticed his enthusiasm for talking about and teaching LDS doctrine. His ability to relate to and inspire interest in others made him an ideal instructor for an early morning seminary class held for high school-age youth. David arose each morning at 4:30 and drove through Chicago's south side to the local church building, picking up students along the way for a 6:00 A.M. class. After class, he dropped several students off at their high schools, returning home just in time for a quick breakfast and classes of his own. David's interpersonal teaching style allowed his students to vocalize many of their questions about Church teachings and life experiences. Though the discussions occasionally veered a little off-topic, such deviation was always a delight to respond to. However,

---

10. David L. Paulsen, interview with Daniel Barron.

when asked questions about other faiths, David was sometimes unsure how to respond. Instead of speculating, he organized field trips to the services of that faith, staying after with religious leaders for question and answer sessions.

On the last day of class, the students presented David with a new Bible, his name engraved on the front cover. Inside the cover, all 11 students had signed their names below a thank you note. Among other things, they wrote, "This past year of Seminary is an experience we will treasure throughout our lives. We'll always remember the Seminary banquet attending other churches, our 6:00 A.M. breakfast parties, the night we were in charge of sacrament meeting ... every day brought a new experience."

Marriage

Upon graduation from the University of Chicago Law School in 1964, David accepted a position at the Salt Lake City firm of Parsons, Behle, Evans and Latimer, and later accepted an offer from Kirton and Bettilyon, the firm that, at the time, represented the Church of Jesus Christ of Latter-day Saints. Always a social person, he dated frequently. One Friday night, May 5, 1967, he agreed to go on a blind date with Audrey Lucille Lear, a case worker for LDS Social Services. That evening, after dropping off Audrey at her apartment, David called home and informed his mother he had just met the girl he was going to marry. It took Audrey a little longer. What might have been a lengthy courtship accelerated when Audrey received a marriage proposal from another suitor who proposed on July 14. David acted quickly and also proposed a week later on July 21. Audrey accepted, and they married on September 1, 1967. On the night of their engagement, Audrey and David, eager to make plans for their future, set two goals: seven children and a Church mission together upon retirement.[11] They even discussed possible names for their children. However, while family and Church service had been principal *foci* from the beginning, David's resumption of his education was not part of the engagement package.

---

11. The Paulsens have succeeded (very nearly to the letter) in accomplishing both these early goals. They would come to welcome six children into their family (just one short of the original goal of seven) and have been blessed to be the grandparents of eighteen grandchildren. David and Audrey have since been called to serve in the Copenhagen Denmark Mission.

Return to School

Prior to his marriage, David attended a University of Utah singles ward, where he taught the Sunday gospel doctrine class. Some of David's students were enrolled in philosophy courses at the university and often raised issues and questions they were encountering. To better answer the questions his students were asking, David decided to enroll in evening courses in philosophy at the University of Utah. Professors such as Peter Appleby, Sterling McMurrin, Richard Henson, and Waldemer Read taught subjects in process philosophy, ethics, philosophy of religion, early Christian thought, and history of philosophy. David was so stimulated by his exposure to philosophy (particularly how it pertained to religion) that he knew almost immediately that this would come to be his professional course in life.

University of Michigan

Though he was able to resist academia's tug for some time, four years of tugging proved more than he could bear. In 1968 David gave up practicing law and embarked on another academic adventure at the University of Michigan, returning to the Great Lakes region to pursue a doctorate in philosophy. Though well-acquainted with the rigors of post-graduate education, this time he had to balance his studies with a growing family. When the Paulsens moved to Ann Arbor, they had already been blessed with one child, six-week-old David Erik (July 1968). In September 1969, Trinyan joined them. Before David finished his dissertation, their family of four would become a family of seven with the additions of Kjrsten (1970), Ntanya (1972), and Leif (1975).

Returning to a graduate school lifestyle with a wife and children was not easy. David and his family struggled to make ends meet, a difficult transition after having lived much more comfortably in Salt Lake City as a lawyer. Still, supported by his loving companion and driven by his passion for the subject, David found Michigan to be a taxing yet valuable experience.

Ann Arbor bore fruits of enduring friendships and a challenging education that David valued in precisely that order. Studying the writings of Anselm, Augustine, and Aristotle came second to developing interests in and admiration for devout men and women of other faiths: George Mavrodes, Robert and Marilyn Adams, and Abraham Kaplan, among others. While scholars often see religious convictions as something to be outgrown through intellectual maturity, and many believers are apprehensive to examine their convictions too closely, David discovered men and women who proved through example that religion was something that could and should be examined with all the powers of the intellect, that one could be both highly intellectual and deeply devout.

Return to Brigham Young University and Family

David's interest in apologetics (reasoned arguments and writings in justification of religious doctrines) developed early on. After completing his required courses in 1972 he began work on his dissertation, entitled, "Comparative Coherency of Mormon (Finitistic) and Classical Theism," which he successfully defended in 1975 while teaching full-time at Brigham Young University. In his dissertation David argued that Mormon theism provides a more coherent and illuminating framework than classical theism for understanding and explaining humankind's experience of evil, teleological arguments for God's existence, moral experience, and evolutionary process. Though never published *in toto*, a substantial portion of his published work is an outgrowth of ideas he first advanced in that dissertation.

While finishing his dissertation and preparing for the courses he was teaching, David was called to serve as branch president and later as bishop (when BYU branches were converted into wards) of the BYU 65th Ward. He served in this position until 1979. In addition to his ecclesiastical and university responsibilities, David's family welcomed another son, Patrick (1979), making the Paulsen family eight members strong. Notwithstanding the pressures of his new teaching assignments combined with the gauntlet of defending his dissertation, he still consistently found ways to make time for his primary priority—his family.

While in Ann Arbor, one of the Paulsen family's favorite pastimes was exploring the miles of orchards and forests surrounding the city. Coming home from a long day at school, David would signal the occasion by singing: "Are we going for a ride in the countryside?" After hiking and exploring, they would finish their outing at a favorite orchard, sipping fresh-pressed apple cider. David thoroughly enjoyed his role as father. In addition to the flute, piano, and other musical concerts he attended, David—an avid fan of sports—also coached his sons' football, basketball, and soccer teams. Whenever a break allowed, the family would load up their secondhand station wagon and explore the country, from San Francisco to Plymouth Rock. To this day family members still remember these trips with fondness.

Society of Christian Philosophers

Though BYU was to become David's permanent academic residence, he kept in close contact with friends he made in Michigan—some of whom were among the founders of the Society of Christian Philosophers (SCP), established in 1978. Unlike some Christian organizations that extend membership only to persons who subscribe to the ecumenical Christian creeds, the SCP adopted a more inclusive criterion. To join the SCP, one needed only *to consider oneself* both a philosopher and a Christian. Without hesitation, David joined the society, much to the astonishment of many of its members. In an interview with *Modern Reformation*, David later clarified his interest in the SCP:

> Faithful Latter-day Saints put their trust in, believe in, and worship the New Testament Godhead. They accept Jesus Christ as Lord and Savior. They love him and seek to follow him and keep his commandments. By these standards, the earliest saints were known as Christians. By these same standards, Latter-day Saints are also Christians, as well as faithful members of evangelical and many other Christian Churches.[12]

David enjoyed working and conferencing with members of the SCP, often presenting papers at regional meetings throughout the United States. These gatherings were times of engaging, exciting dialogue and of catching up with old friends. On one such occasion, David noted that an intermountain region of the SCP had yet to be organized. With encouragement from George Mavrodes, David's Dissertation Chair at the University of Michigan and SCP president at the time, David became the founder of the intermountain region of the SCP and served as regional chairman for the next seven years.

---

12. "Are Mormons Trinitarians?" *Modern Reformation* 12, no. 6 (November/December 2003): 40–43.

SCP's Intermountain Region and BYU

In 1991 and 1993, BYU hosted the first two meetings of the Intermountain Region of the SCP, later known as the Mountain/Plains region. As the coordinator for both meetings, David invited, coordinated, and hosted the many presenters and arranged for the traditional ecumenical worship service held in conjunction with the meetings. The inaugural worship service was held in the Provo LDS Tabernacle, with a local Episcopal pastor conducting the service and delivering the sermon. Despite some minor hiccups typical to planning such a large event, the BYU-hosted meetings went exceptionally well. Years later George Mavrodes, who delivered the keynote address at the inaugural meeting, remarked, "I was cordially received there. . . . [W]e had good and open discussions with the philosophical faculty there and the students. And frankly, I came away with a substantially more optimistic view about Mormonism."[13]

The first criticism of the events surfaced some months after the inaugural meeting with the appearance of Francis Beckwith's article entitled, "What Does Provo Have to Do with Jerusalem?"[14] In the article, Beckwith claimed a paper he had submitted to the BYU-held SCP meeting ("Mormon Theism and the Argument from Design") had been rejected because it was critical of Mormon theology and would expose the LDS Church's non-Christian status.

Soon thereafter, certain SCP members successfully sought election to the SCP Executive Committee and, once elected, persuaded board members to pass a resolution stating that SCP regional meetings should not be held at or subsidized by any private institution professing to be Christian while at the same time subscribing to a doctrinal position directly contradicting the ecumenical creeds. Upon asking for clarification of the resolution, William Craig advised David that although the purpose of the resolution was "not directed specifically at BYU or any LDS institution," the committee worried that "holding meetings

---

13. E-mail message from George Mavrodes to David Paulsen, October 25, 2000. Used with permission.

14. The essay can be found in an appendix to Francis J. Beckwith and Stephen E. Parrish, *See the Gods Fall: Four Rivals to Christianity* (Joplin, Mo.: College Press Publishing, 2000).

at places like BYU might be interpreted as lending legitimacy to LDS claims ... to be Christian [or] ... a legitimate Christian alternative."[15]

Given his significant efforts in cultivating a meaningful dialogue between Mormons and Evangelicals, the SCP resolution left David heartsick and perplexed. Though ostensibly directed at preventing the illusion of SCP-extended legitimacy to Mormon contributions, it instead established an SCP-approved method of determining illegitimacy. Over the next month, David sent out scores of e-mail messages to members of the SCP—including all of the previous SCP presidents—inquiring what they thought of the resolution. Many of the SCP members were surprised to learn of it, nearly all expressing disapproval and doubt as to why it would have passed, especially given the SCP's self-identification requirements for membership. Previous SCP presidents Marilyn Adams, Robert Adams, and Nicholas Wolterstorff jointly wrote the SCP Executive Committee and other prominent members, outlining in detail their protest of the resolution based on its incoherence in relation to the SCP's history and regarding the nature of the resolution itself. Rebutting Craig's comments to David, they wrote, "In relation to the LDS, we find the executive committee resolution multiply objectionable. . . . LDS philosophers have self-identified as Christians because they believe in Christ." Later in the same memo, they commended David for his initiative to found the Mountain Province SCP, comparing him and his colleagues at BYU to Justin Martyr, Clement of Alexandria, Origen, and Augustine as they strove to philosophically articulate their beliefs in the midst of considerable opposition.[16]

At the following SCP Executive Meeting, the resolution was rescinded and replaced by a vague political statement with the same qualitative effect, recommending that meetings not be held at sites that are likely to be considered objectionable by a substantial number of members of the Society. Though still not an ideal situation, David's campaign had borne some fruits of change. Subsequently, however, for reasons independent of the BYU controversy, the SCP dissolved the Mountain-Plains Regional Meetings.

---

15. E-mail message from William Craig to David Paulsen, September 14, 2000. Used with permission.

16. Memo from Adams, Adams, and Wolterstorff, October 17, 2000. In possession of David Paulsen, used with permission.

In resolution of the personal conflict between David and Francis Beckwith, after the 2002 AAR meeting in Denver Francis approached David and, while not ignoring his feelings of conflict over what he still considered a "legitimate grievance," he apologized for the "incendiary and conspiratorial language" he had employed while attacking both David and BYU in his published complaint.[17] Since their conversation in Denver, David and Francis have developed a strong personal and professional friendship; Dr. Beckwith, in fact, is a generous contributor to this festschrift.

Richard L. Evans Chair for Christian Understanding

Shortly after assisting in the organization of the SCP's Intermountain Region, David was appointed Richard L. Evans Chair for Christian Understanding,[18] a position formed in the early seventies by Lowell Berry, a California industrialist, in memory of the passing of his dear friend, Richard L. Evans, who had spent his life cultivating interfaith understanding. The principal objectives of the Evans Chair were to correct mutual misconceptions between Latter-day Saints and other Christians and to promote mutual understanding, respect, friendship, and cooperation.

David greatly enjoyed being able to officially promote and engage in interfaith dialogue—he had already had quite a bit of practice. His first project as chair was to organize a series of mini-seminars wherein he invited theologians to come to BYU and lecture on contemporary Christian thought. Though he had many responsibilities as Chair, his most memorable experiences were personally hosting non-LDS scholars and theologians. Though he made sure to take each to Salt Lake City and give them a tour of historic Temple Square, David also enjoyed catering to their particular interests. When inviting someone to BYU for a conference or a lecture, he would do a little probing to discover if there were something in particular they would like to do while in Utah.

The first guest lecturer David hosted was Donald Musser, a Baptist pastor and theologian at Stetson University in Florida. After learning Donald had grown up in Pittsburg and, as a boy, had been an ardent admirer of Mormon baseball player Vernon Law (who had pitched for

---

17. Email message from Francis Beckwith to Jacob Baker, December 30, 2009. Used with permission.

18. The name of the chair has since been changed to "Richard L. Evans Chair for Religious Understanding."

the Pittsburg Pirates for sixteen seasons), David arranged for boy and boyhood hero to meet at the Cougar Club in the BYU football stadium where they chatted for quite some time. Donald returned to Florida not only with warm memories of BYU and of Utah, but with several autographed baseballs for his mantle.

In 1996, David invited Don McKim, a Presbyterian pastor who, at that time, was teaching at the Memphis Theological Seminary, to come to Provo and lecture on Karl Barth. Don accepted and brought along one of his graduate assistants to share the experience. After an enjoyable lecture series, David took Don and his assistant to an open house tour of the Mount Timpanogos Temple led by apostle and former BYU President Elder Jeffrey R. Holland. Both Don and his student were deeply touched. David remembers Don commenting, "This is the most beautiful place I have ever been in."

Another guest, Dennis McCann, was interested in his family history. When he came to BYU to lecture on Reinhold Niebuhr, David guided him through Temple Square and brought him to see the Church film, *Legacy*. They subsequently visited the Family History Library, where a specialist in Irish genealogy helped Dennis find information about many of his ancestors. Dennis, then President of the Society for Christian Ethics, was so impressed with Temple Square that he proposed—albeit unsuccessfully—that the Society hold their annual meeting in the nearby Little America hotel.

Soon after Professor McCann's visit, David invited Joseph Price, a professor of religious studies at Whittier University, to lecture on Paul Tillich. During lunch, Joseph told everyone that though he was the son of a Protestant pastor and grew up in the South, his family always enjoyed listening to the Mormon Tabernacle Choir broadcasts. In addition, during his time as a divinity student at the University of Chicago, Joseph had sung with the famed Rockefeller Chapel Choir, but his lifetime dream had always been to sing with the Mormon Tabernacle Choir. Following lunch, David contacted Temple Square and made arrangements for Joseph to sing with the Choir the following evening during their Thursday night rehearsal. Naturally, Joseph was ecstatic.

These and many other visiting scholars came to BYU during David's tenure as Evan's Chair. David formed lasting friendships with many of them, friendships that have remained long after formal and sustained academic discourse have ceased.

Academic

David's published legacy is impressive. Over the course of his nearly 40 year career he has published dozens of articles and reviews in prominent academic journals, presented papers on Mormon philosophy and theology at prestigious academic conferences all over the world, and continues to author and co-author books on various aspects of Mormon thought even in retirement. Always interested in Mormon apologetics, David has compared Mormon thought to Trinitarian theology, Process and Openness Theology, and to famous thinkers and philosophers such as Origen, Anselm, Augustine, William James, and Søren and Peter Kierkegaard.

One presentation, however, has had a particularly significant and lasting effect on students, colleagues, and David personally. On September 21, 1999, he gave an address entitled, "Joseph Smith and the Problem of Evil" at BYU's weekly devotional forum where 30,000 students and faculty gathered to listen. In a somber introduction, David spoke of the shocking and heart-wrenching tragedies of the day, including the Oklahoma City bombings and the Columbine shootings, and of more distant horrors such as the Holocaust. He concluded his introduction by posing the anguished and often asked question, "Why, God? Why?" Noting this plea forms the ultimate basis for the logical, soteriological, and practical problems of evil, over the next hour David drew upon the writings of Joseph Smith, B. H. Roberts, and C. S. Lewis, as well as scholars less familiar to the LDS community such as John Hick, Thomas Morris, Stephen Davis, and Anthony Flew. The paper sought to show that Mormon teachings (principally through the teachings and revelations of Joseph Smith) offered a unique, reasoned, and inspiring response to philosophical theology's most perplexing and devastating problem. The paper had a profound impact on students and faculty alike, evidenced by the many grateful letters and phone calls that poured in afterwards. In fact, within an hour of the presentation, he received a phone call from John Welch, editor of BYU Studies (and a contributing author in this volume), asking if David would publish his address; the article appeared in the next issue as well as two more subsequent issues.[19]

---

19. The original publication was published in BYU Studies as "Joseph Smith and the Problem of Evil," *BYU Studies*, 39, no.1 (2000): 53–65. The address was republished twice in 2005: "Joseph Smith and the Problem of Evil," *BYU Magazine*, October 2005, 37–38; and "Joseph Smith and the Problem of Evil,"

Because of its strongly apologetic nature and its unique approach in responding to a centuries-old philosophical and theological dilemma, David's paper caught the attention of non-LDS scholars as well when he presented it at three SCP meetings—including the Pacific Regional meeting hosted by Biola University in California, which proved to be a particularly memorable experience. As the chair was closing a lively Q&A session following David's presentation, a participant—a young man probably in his mid-twenties—stood up and said, "I have one more question: Is it possible to be a Mormon and be intelligent?" David smiled and answered: "You've been listening to one for forty-five minutes; you'll have to answer your own question." Several people in the audience who would likely not have agreed with David's religious views were clearly disturbed by the disrespectful nature of the question. During the closing prayer, the man offering the prayer expressed the hope that all in attendance would seek to be more like Christ and less an obstacle to those seeking to genuinely follow God. A conciliatory and friendly atmosphere prevailed.

At some of these meetings David would receive questions similar to the following, posed by an SCP conference attendee in Seattle: "If God is not omnipotent (as classically defined), how can you be certain that he can save us?" To this David would issue a reply nearly identical to one he often gave his own students: "Because he's told us that he can. My faith in God is grounded in his self-disclosures, not in logical inferences from philosophically constructed premises."[20]

Mormon Evangelical Consultation

In 2001 Robert Millet, a professor of religious education at BYU, and Richard Mouw, then President of Fuller Theological Seminary, initiated a Mormon-Evangelical Consultation at the American Academy of Religion with the aim of fostering dialogue and better relations between these two religious communities. At one such consultation in

---

Praise to the Man: Fifteen Classic BYU Devotionals about the Prophet Joseph Smith, 1955–2005 (Provo, Utah: BYU Publications, 2005), 151–67. The paper was revised and expanded with Blake Ostler for a chapter in Truman G. Madsen's *festschrift*, "Sin, Suffering, and Soul-Making: Joseph Smith and the Problem of Evil," in *Revelation, Reason, and Faith: Essays in Honor of Truman G. Madsen*, ed. (Provo, Utah: Foundation for Ancient Research and Mormon Studies, 2002), 237–84.

20. David L. Paulsen, interview with Daniel Barron.

Denver, Carl Mosser asked David to participate on a pre-publication panel responding to *The New Mormon Challenge*,[21] an anthology that openly challenged Mormon faith claims that Mosser edited along with Francis Beckwith and Paul Owen. David accepted the invitation by responding to the authors' self-stated aims and assessing how well those aims had been met. David's responses to the book are particularly notable because they serve as an example both of his conciliatory attitude in such situations, as well as his analytical ability to evaluate philosophical propositions and truth claims.

David began his assessment by optimistically stating that a book critical of Mormonism, he would score *The New Mormon Challenge* "near the top of its class." However, in response to the book's aims, David delicately stated his confusion of how a declaration and pursuit of all-out war on another's faith could generate good will and genuine conversation. "Nevertheless," he added, "I personally hope that this warfare doesn't diminish dialogue between our two Christian communities."[22] Regarding the book's aim to state Mormon beliefs as accurately as possible, David pointed out that this meant they would have to state Mormon beliefs to the satisfaction of Mormons themselves. David considered this "a major failing in the book" based on the authors' "failure to set out our LDS Christology, soteriology, and doctrine of the trinity while nonetheless attempting to convince their readers that our faith cannot be considered Christian 'in any theologically significant way.'" Concerning the book's goal of respectfully and charitably treating LDS beliefs, David lamented how LDS members and beliefs had been described in the book as "parasite," "pagan," "cult," "pitiable," "poppycock," and "a fairy tale." Courteously, David stated, "Given your aims, would you please help me understand why these descriptions of my faith remain in your book? . . . This is certainly not the kind of respect I have for my Evangelical friends. I respect them as valued allies standing together with us in the cause of Christ against his real enemies." Significantly, four of the authors and contributors to *The New Mormon Challenge* appear in this volume honoring David's legacy, all remaining close friends and colleagues to the present time.

---

21. Francis Beckwith, Carl Mosser, and Paul Owen, eds., *The New Mormon Challenge: Responding to the Latest Defenses of a Fast-Growing Movement* (Grand Rapids, Mich.: Zondervan, 2002).

22. From David Paulsen, unpublished remarks, copy in author's possession.

Mormonism in Dialogue

In 2007, David and his co-editor Donald Musser, published what they hope will serve as a model for genuine interfaith dialogue: *Mormonism in Dialogue with Contemporary Christian Theologies*.[23] The nearly 600-page book boasts eleven dialogues treating diverse theologians and theologies, each dialogue originating from a series of mini-seminars David had hosted as the Richard L. Evans Chair for Religious Understanding. In his introductory overview, David reflects, "The relationship between Mormonism and other Christian traditions in regard to theological discussion has been tenuous at best. Historically, polemics, proselytizing, and prejudice have dominated interaction rather than genuine attempts to understand and learn from one another through dialogue."[24] Always confident in the potential for improvement, he explains his hope that *Mormonism in Dialogue* will be used as a model for future dialogues wherein both sides are afforded a voice to articulate their own views while allowing for responses, rejoinders to responses, and replies to rejoinders, thus providing respectful yet "thought-provoking and challenging" critiques that prompt both sides to "rethink and refine" their respective ideas.[25] In one such dialogue with David himself, Clark H. Pinnock acknowledged, "I appreciate interacting with Dr. Paulsen very much, both in person and in print, and am the richer for it as a theologian and as a person. There is a good deal of room in both LDS and evangelical thinking about God to make a dialogue between us worthwhile.... [T]he intellectual and cultural distance between us is considerable and the evangelical/LDS dialogue is at an early stage. We are not going to get things altogether right the first time round, and the best thing for us to do is just to get on with it."[26]

---

23. Donald W. Musser and David L. Paulsen, eds., *Mormonism in Dialogue with Contemporary Christian Theologies* (Macon, Ga.: Mercer University Press, 2007).

24. David L. Paulsen and Donald W. Musser, "Introduction," in *Mormonism in Dialogue with Contemporary Christian Theologies*, ed., David L. Paulsen and Donald W. Musser (Macon, Ga.: Mercer University Press, 2007), 10.

25. Clark H. Pinnock and David L. Paulsen, "A Dialogue on Openness Theology," in *Mormonism in Dialogue with Contemporary Christian Theologies*, ed., David L. Paulsen and Donald W. Musser (Macon, Ga.: Mercer University Press, 2007), 546.

26. Ibid., 542–43.

Work with Students

Though not as recognizable and quantifiable as his accomplishments in writing and interfaith dialogue, perhaps when all is said and done David Paulsen's greatest achievement will have been serving as a teacher and mentor to thousands of students. Before he finished his dissertation, David had begun teaching introductory courses in philosophy and the philosophy of religion at Brigham Young University, courses he continued to teach throughout his career. Of particular note were his recurring upper division philosophy of religion seminars on Søren Kierkegaard, William James, and Mormon theology. No matter the subject, whenever David hosted guests, he always invited his students to attend the guests' lectures on campus, and often encouraged guests to teach a portion of a class and answer students' questions.

In addition to classroom hours, David often invites students to assist him in his research. Since 1972, he has published approximately 30 articles and worked with more than 45 different student assistants listed as co-authors or significant contributors. In the final years before his retirement in 2011, virtually all of his publications were produced with the assistance of students. Meeting with his assistants weekly, David was always interested in discussing their individual lives and their research assignments (in that order). Blessed by their interaction with David, these assistants gained a more profound appreciation for David's work and profited greatly from his personal mentorship.

As of the time period of the publication of this volume in David Paulsen's honor, Mormonism is poised on the cusp of emerging, likely for the last time, from the shadows of obscurity, 182 years after its founding. The consequences and effects of Mormon Republican candidate Mitt Romney's highly publicized presidential campaign will be far-reaching, though little understood, at least for some time. No longer, for better or for worse, will Mormonism be considered in public channels and venues as a little known, barely-understood backwater of a religious movement. Now and likely far, far into the future Mormonism will grow and adapt to the glare of the national and international spotlights that have been thrust upon it.

Yet Mormonism does not step under the bright lights unprepared or without allies and friends. People like David have done much significant work in preparing both Mormons and non-Mormons for the advent of a Mormonism to come, a Mormonism that could legitimately take its place amongst other great religious and cultural bodies as an intelligent, profound, and genuinely novel way of considering the world and its peoples. David's preparatory academic and pedagogical work can genuinely be seen in this light, but when we magnify and enlarge the picture we have of the landscape of his life we see that, as with so many human beings who have touched and influenced others for good, it has been the relationships and bonds David has established with students and colleagues, non-Mormons and fellow Mormons, that have and will continue to have the most profound influence, and provide the truest and longest lasting depiction of his life's legacy.

1

Classifying Mormon Theism

Carl Mosser, *Eastern University*

Introduction

David Paulsen commenced his academic career in 1975 with a doctoral dissertation that compares the philosophical coherence of Mormon and classical theism.[1] David was not the first Latter-day Saint to present serious philosophical arguments for Mormon theism over and against classical theism. Early in Mormonism's history the self-taught Pratt brothers and B. H. Roberts pioneered this area with impressive skill. Neither was David first to bring to the task a professionalism developed in the course of pursuing a Ph.D. in philosophy. In this he followed the path of individuals such as William Chamberlin, Sterling McMurrin, and Truman Madsen.[2] Nonetheless, David's dissertation marked an important milestone in the maturation of Mormon thought. David was able to collate the insights of his predecessors and bring Mormon thought into dialogue with contemporary philosophy of religion. Moreover, by utilizing the tools of the analytic method, David presented arguments for Mormon theism that were more sophisticated and rigorous than those of his predecessors.

In subsequent scholarship David has shown himself to be an admirably shrewd apologist. Whether addressing the problem of evil, divine embodiment, or Social Trinitarianism, David is always concerned to defend and commend a distinctively Mormon theism. For example, in one of his early articles David discusses the question of whether God must

---

1. "Comparative Coherence of Mormon (Finitistic) and Classical Theism" (Ph.D. diss., University of Michigan, 1975).

2. Due to poor health, Chamberlin suspended his doctoral studies at Harvard, never to resume them.

be incorporeal.³ To the uninformed reader this looks like the sort of piece a philosopher writes to explore a question merely because it is interesting. Mormonism is nowhere mentioned. Nonetheless, David's intent is to demonstrate that the LDS commitment to divine embodiment is philosophically tenable. His related articles on divine embodiment in Origen and Augustine might be taken as the work of a dilettante patrologist.⁴ Ever the lawyer,⁵ he is calling these Church Fathers to the witness stand to give reluctant testimony to the existence of a key Mormon teaching among the early Christian communities.⁶ Similarly, another of David's articles appears to be an analysis of William James's critique of the God of the philosophers and a description of James's alternative.⁷ In reality the article is a critique of traditional Christian theism and a defense of Joseph Smith's conception of God.

David has produced several clear explanations of what he considers to be the basic metaphysical tenets of Mormon theism: eternalism, pluralism, theological finitism, and materialism. This has usually been done in the course of comparing and contrasting alternative concepts of God. For example, his earliest expositions identified significant points of similarity with the views of William James, John Stuart Mill and Edgar Sheffield Brightman. Subsequent work has identified points of commonality with Process Theism, Open Theism, and various other movements within contemporary theology. On the other side of the

---

3. "Must God be Incorporeal?" *Faith and Philosophy* 6, no. 1 (1989): 76–87. A subsequent essay of the same title appeared in *Mormon Identities in Transition*, ed. Douglas Davies (London: Cassell, 1996), 204–10.

4. "Early Christian Belief in a Corporeal Deity: Origen and Augustine as Reluctant Witnesses," *Harvard Theological Review* 83, no. 2 (1990): 105–16; "Reply to Kim Paffenroth's Comment," *Harvard Theological Review* 86, no. 2 (1993): 235–39; and (with Carl W. Griffin), "Augustine and the Corporeality of God," *Harvard Theological Review* 95, no. 1 (2002): 97–118.

5. Prior to pursuing his Ph.D., David earned a J.D. from the University of Chicago Law School.

6. The apologetic argument is made explicitly in "The Doctrine of Divine Embodiment: Restoration, Judeo-Christian, and Philosophical Perspectives," *BYU Studies* 35, no. 4 (1996–97): 7–94 and "Divine Embodiment: The Earliest Christian Understanding of God," in *Early Christians in Disarray: Contemporary LDS Perspectives on the Christian Apostasy*, ed. Noel B. Reynolds (Provo, Utah: FARMS and BYU Press, 2005), 239–93.

7. "The God of Abraham, Isaac, and (William) James," *The Journal of Speculative Philosophy* 13, no. 2 (1999): 114–46.

coin, David has frequently argued that Mormon theism is biblically and philosophically preferable to classical Christian theism, especially with respect to the problem of evil. This comparative method is illuminating, but it also raises an important question: How should we classify Mormon theism with respect to broader theistic categories? David's work lays important groundwork for an answer but does not develop one.

It is popularly assumed that all theological systems can be classified according to a taxonomy in which the highest-level categories are atheism, monotheism, and polytheism. The question before us is how to properly classify Mormonism. The apparent simplicity of this question is betrayed by the fact that scholars have variously placed Mormonism in each of the above categories. The reasons for these incommensurate conclusions are simple. First, these terms simply do not form a comprehensive taxonomy—at least not in the manner that many people suppose. The supposition that they do is based on mistaken assumptions about the meanings and etymologies of these words. Second, traditional Mormon theism affirms significant metaphysical and theological positions comparable to those found in paradigm examples of atheism, monotheism, and polytheism. However, in each case significant dissimilarities also exist that make it both unhelpful and misleading to categorize Mormon theism simply as a species of atheism, monotheism, or polytheism. I will suggest that Mormon theism is *sui generis*, but if a single category is needed, then *Anglo-American finitistism* may be the most useful option. In order to reach that conclusion we will need to first make our way through an etymological bramble patch.

I. Problems with *-theism* Terms

Everyone believes in no gods, one god, or more than one god.[8] This grounds the popular assumption that all theological systems can be grouped into primary *taxa* determined by the number of gods they postulate. On this view all systems that reject belief in any gods are versions of atheism; those that affirm belief in only one god are species of monotheism; and those that affirm belief in more than one god are types of polytheism. Terms built on the same etymological pattern are em-

---

8. In the sense used here, agnostics and atheists both believe in no gods. The difference is that the atheist asserts the improbability that any god exists while the agnostic merely withholds belief.

ployed to refer to supposed subcategories (e.g., henotheism as a genus of polytheism and pantheism as a genus of monotheism). However, such taxonomy proves inadequate given the variety of actual religious beliefs. The problem is partly relieved by employing supplemental categories such as deism, dualism, monism, polydaemonism and totemism. Even so, some religions cannot be classified according to strictly quantitative criteria without causing distortion and confusion. Mormonism is one of those religions, or at least such is the proposition that I will argue.

The Etymological Objection

It might seem counterintuitive that counting gods cannot establish whether a theological tradition qualifies as atheistic, monotheistic, or polytheistic. Indeed, some people are quick to offer a rejoinder that appeals to the etymology of the terms. The Greek word for 'god' is *theos* (θεός). The compound word formed when *theos* is prefixed with the alpha privative refers to belief in "no god." The compound word derived from *monos* and *theos* refers to belief in "one god." Similarly, the compound of *polus* and *theos* refers to belief in "many gods." As stated above, every theological system affirms belief in no gods, one god, or more than one god. Thus, we should be able to classify any theological system as a species of atheism, monotheism, or polytheism by counting gods because the *meanings* of these words correspond to this acknowledged fact. On the surface this rejoinder appears cogent but it ultimately fails. There are three reasons for this. First, it depends upon a fallacious appeal to etymology. Second, it is uninformed by the history of actual usage. Third, it fails to sufficiently consider the concepts to which these words refer.

Etymological Fallacies

The etymological fallacy comes in at least two distinct forms. The first form assumes that a word's "real" or "true" meaning is the earliest meaning that can be documented for it and that this original meaning is somehow retained in all subsequent usage. An example of this is the assertion that "the word 'silly' comes from the Old English word 'selig,' and its literal definition is 'to be blessed, happy, healthy and prosperous.'"[9] The second form of the fallacy assumes that the real meaning of a word

---

9. Zig Zigler, *Over the Top*, rev. ed. (Nashville: Thomas Nelson, 1997), 98.

can be determined by analysis of its constituent parts (etymons). We see this when we are told such things as "Whenever you say 'Good-bye' to someone you are literally telling her 'God be with you.'"

The etymological objection commits the second form of the fallacy. Both forms fail because they treat word meaning as if it is natural and stable rather than conventionally determined and mutable.[10] However, word meaning must be determined by the immediate context of any particular occurrence, current patterns of usage in the language at large, and by usage in older texts that continue to be read by people outside the philological disciplines. This does not deny that etymology can occasionally help determine the meaning of a word, but it is frequently an unreliable guide.

In this case appeal to etymology does not reliably inform us about meaning. In addition to an inappropriate appeal to etymology, the objection takes the meaning of the etymons to be self-evident—at least if one knows some Greek. However, even if the meanings of *atheism*, *monotheism*, and *polytheism* could be determined merely by analysis of their etymologies, establishing those meanings would not be as simple as the rejoinder assumes. This is because of two things. First, *theos* has had a very broad semantic range over the course of its history. Second, atheism, monotheism, and polytheism are early modern terms coined by French and English intellectuals. When we trace the history of these terms, we find that they were coined to emphasize qualitative notions and that this usage has endured alongside etymologically inspired definitions. It will take a few pages to trace these histories, but doing so will supply important background information that informs my argument.

What is (a) theos?

Every first-year Greek student is taught that *theos* simply means "god" or "deity." Furthermore, it has been frequently assumed that *theos* (plural *theoi*) is related to the Latin word *deus* and its Indoeuropean cousins.[11] This is incorrect. *Theos* was coined from a different root and did not

---

10. There is a non-conventional connection between the meaning of an onomatopoeic word and the thing it signifies, but even here convention plays an important role in determining meaning. This can be seen in the variations between onomatopoeic words in different languages that refer to the same thing (such as animal sounds).

11. The *prima facie* plausibility of this assumption stems from (1) their synonymy when designating deities and (2) the fact that in Indoeuropean languages

begin its career as a noun that simply refers to deities. It is unclear why a new word was coined or how it came to displace words stemming from the Indoeuropean *dieu/deiw* root.[12] What is clear is that the word's meaning in antiquity was never as restricted as the English words *God* and *god* or their modern European equivalents. Indeed, it was used in highly equivocal ways that doom any simplistic appeal to etymology.

Walter Burkert has argued that *theos* is built on the *thes-* root and thus unrelated to the Latin *deus*. He observes that in Homer and other early writers *theos* is closely associated with several words clearly built on the *thes-* root. These words usually point to extraordinary experiences, "especially to smells, noises, and voices encountered in the range of seers and singers."[13] Burkert notes that *theos* could be used to refer to such things as good luck, impersonal powers and forces, and even the recognition of friends. It could also express reaction to certain situations and sudden surprise. From the classical period onward *theos* was used as an attributive term expressing such qualities as immortality, glory, incorruptibility, blessedness, and sublimity.[14] This usage probably predates its employment as a substantive, and persisted throughout antiquity.

---

d, *th*, and *t* are often equivalent in cognate words. For example, the following words all have the same root and meaning: *thugatēr* (Greek), *tochter* (German) and *daughter* (English).

12. The *dieu/deiw* root appears in numerous words referring to the day, daylight, and the sky. Most notably, it appears in the name of the great sky-god, Father Sky—*Diespiter/Juppiter* (Latin), *Zeus pater* (Greek). This seems to reflect an original association between the major divinities and the bright daylit sky. Walter Burkert suggests that a new word was coined because the Greeks moved away from associating their gods with the sky. See his "From Epiphany to Cult Statue: Early Greek *Theos*," in *What Is a God? Studies in the Nature of Greek Divinity*, ed. Alan B. Lloyd (London: Duckworth, 1997), 15–16.

13. Burkert, "From Epiphany to Cult Statue," 19.

14. Illustrative examples can be found in: Walter Burkert, *Greek Religion*, trans. John Raffan (Cambridge: Harvard University Press, 1985), 271–72; W.H.S. Jones, "A Note on the Vague Use of ΘΕΟΣ," *The Classical Review* 27 (1913): 252–55; Ivan M. Linforth, "ΟΙ ΑΘΑΝΑΤΙΖΟΝΤΕΣ (Herodotus iv. 93–96)," *Classical Philology* 13 (1918): 23–33 (esp. p. 26); Hermann Kleinknecht, "θεός," in *Theological Dictionary of the New Testament*, eds. Gerhard Kittel, Gerhard Friedrich, and Geoffrey W. Bromiley, 10 vols. (Grand Rapids, Mich.: Wm. B. Eerdmans Publishing Co., 1985), 3:70; Arthur Darby Nock, *Essays on Religion and the Ancient World*, ed. Zeph Stewart, 2 vols. (Oxford: Clarendon, 1972), 144–45, 260–61.

As a substantive, *theos* referred to various beings associated with the infra- and supramundane realms, especially divinities credited with the inspiration of oracles or the governance of some aspect of nature or human society. The connection between the gods and their corresponding phenomena was never fully abandoned, but the gods took on more personal and more human traits. It was widely thought that gods and humans were the same basic kind of being, but the gods occupied a higher level in the order of being. Whereas human beings were weak and subject to death, the gods were immortal and possessed extraordinary powers within their particular spheres of authority that could be used to assist or afflict human beings. Thus, the gods were worshipped in order to secure their favor. The noun *theos* could also refer to the cult statue that was variously thought to represent the deity, be indwelt by it, or be the location from which the deity's power emanated.

Theos was employed euhemeristically of heroes who had been granted immortality and elevated to the pantheon in recognition of their great deeds or personal virtues. In the Hellenistic era kings were also honored in this manner, a practice that was later adopted by the Roman Emperors.[15] These divinized humans became the objects of cults.

Over time a pronounced skepticism about the traditional gods developed in philosophical circles. Skeptics formulated arguments to show that the kind of embodiment and sentience attributed to the gods was incompatible with imperishability and immortality, hallmark properties of the truly divine.[16] Thus, philosophers appropriated *theos* to refer to the ultimate principle of organization or movement in the cosmos (i.e., that which constituted the cosmos as a universe rather than a multi-verse or pluri-verse) despite its evident multiplicity. Many schools of thought went further and described this principle as transcendent, personal (or quasi-personal), and the proper object of worship

---

15. A great deal of literature has been published on this topic. A state-of-the-art discussion can be found in Hans Josef-Klauck, *The Religious Context of Early Christianity* (Edinburgh: T&T Clark, 2000), 250–330 or Ron C. Fay, "Greco-Roman Concepts of Deity," in *Paul's World*, ed. Stanley E. Porter (Leiden and Boston: Brill, 2008), 51–79.

16. See A. A. Long, "Scepticism about Gods in Hellenistic Philosophy," in *Cabinet of the Muses: Essays on Classical and Comparative Literature in Honor of Thomas G. Rosenmeyer*, ed. Mark Griffith and Donald J. Mastronarde (Atlanta: Scholars Press, 1990), 279–91. Available online: http://repositories.cdlib.org/ucbclassics/ctm/festschrift19 (accessed April 16, 2012).

that providentially governs the universe. Whatever else might be said of this *theos*, it was unlike the anthropomorphic, immoral, and capricious *theoi* of Homer and Hesiod.[17] It was a different sort of *theos* altogether.

A few philosophers advocated abandoning the traditional cults, but most either considered the gods to be manifestations of the one *theos* or took the view that a person could worship the one *theos* through the guise of worshipping the traditional *theoi*. This view became influential enough among some writers that the grammatical distinction between the singular *theos* and the plural *theoi* became practically meaningless.[18] They could refer to the *theos* or the *theoi* collectively with no apparent difference in meaning.

After Hellenism spread under Alexander and his successors, Greek-speaking Jews employed *theos* to refer to their national deity, pagan deities, cult statues, and, in rare contexts, human beings.[19] Something could be identified as a *theos* because it was a heavenly being, exemplified divine attributes like immortality, or served as the object of cultic devotion. Worship was the most basic criterion for whether something was a *theos* in the sense of deity. It was irrelevant whether Jews considered the object of worship to be the one God, a secondary heavenly being, a demon, a cult statue, or a figment of the imagination. These were all *theoi*, but equivocation allowed Jews to also assert that theirs was the only true *theos* without contradiction.[20] While Gentiles could insist that people should worship only their own nation's deities, Jews universalized their insistence that Israel's God is the only proper object of worship. All na-

---

17. For an accessible overview, see Malcom Schofield, "Theology and Divination" in *Greek Thought: A Guide to Classical Knowledge*, ed. Jacques Brunschwig and Geoffrey E. Lloyd (Cambridge, Mass.: Harvard University Press, 2000), 498–510. More detailed treatment can be found in Werner Jaeger's classic, *The Theology of the Early Greek Philosophers* (Oxford: Oxford University Press, 1947) and Lloyd P. Gerson, *God and Greek Philosophy: Studies in the Early History of Natural Theology* (London: Routledge, 1990).

18. R. J. Zwi Werblowsky, "Polytheism," in *The Encyclopedia of Religion*, ed. Mircea Eliade, 16 vols. (New York: Macmillan, 1987), 11:439.

19. Illustrative examples can be found in Marianne Meye Thompson, *The God of the Gospel of John* (Grand Rapids: Eerdmans, 2001), 17–55. The chapter is titled "The Meaning of 'God.'" For discussion of Jewish texts that use *theos* in reference to human beings, see Norman Russell, *The Doctrine of Deification in the Greek Patristic Tradition* (Oxford: Oxford University Press, 2004), 53–78.

20. For illustrations, see Michael Frede, "Monotheism and Pagan Philosophy in Later Antiquity," in *Pagan Monotheism in Late Antiquity*, eds. Polymnia Athanassiadi and Michael Frede (Oxford: Clarendon, 1999), 58–67.

tions should exclusively worship this God because he is the all-powerful and sovereign creator of all reality.²¹ As such he was in a class of his own, metaphysically unlike anything else that might be referred to as a *theos*.²² Thus, Israel's national deity was considered the only true *theos* to whom all nations would ultimately give their devotion.²³

In the Patristic era, Christians largely followed Jewish usage. But in soteriological contexts they sometimes used *theos* in reference to the final state of redeemed human beings. First-century Christians had proclaimed a notion of salvation in which the redeemed would be resurrected immortal, incorruptible, glorious, and blessed by virtue of their union with Christ in his death and resurrection.²⁴ Because each of these attributes could be synonymous with the attributive use of *theos*, it was natural for native Greek-speaking Christians to summarize redemption in terms of being made *theos* (attributive) or a *theos* (substantive).²⁵ Later Hellenistic philosophers also spoke about the elevation of human beings to immortality, incorruptibility, etc., and thus to the level of *theos*

---

21. Jews like Philo of Alexandria expressed this in the language of Greek metaphysics. Most Jewish texts, however, identify the God of Israel by a variety of other means that forcefully make many of the same points. See Richard Bauckham, *Jesus and the God of Israel* (Grand Rapids: Eerdmans, 2008), 6–13 (reiterated and expanded upon in various ways on pp. 114–16, 152–64, 233–34).

22. There is currently a healthy discussion about the nature of early Jewish monotheism, especially as it relates to the Christology of the New Testament. A few scholars go so far as to argue that Second Temple Judaism was not monotheistic or that it was monotheistic only in a qualified sense. These claims will be briefly described below.

23. The eschatology of the Old Testament already anticipates a time when Gentiles would worship God in his temple and when Gentile nations would become God's own people. See Ps. 96:7–10; Isa. 2:2–4; 19:21–25; 25:6–8; 56:6–7; 66:23; Jer. 3:17; Amos 9:11–12; Micah 4:1–5; Zech. 2:11; 14:16. Several of these texts tie the sovereignty of Israel's God over Gentiles to the fact that he is creator of "the heavens and the earth."

24. Matt. 5:2–11, 13:43; John 17:22; Rom. 2:7, 5:2, 6:5, 8:18–30; 1 Cor. 15:42–55; 2 Cor. 3:18; Philip. 3:21; 2 Thes. 2:14; 2 Tim. 1:10; Heb. 2:10; 1 Peter 1:3–4, 23. Cf. Dan. 12:3.

25. The significance of this terminology is discussed in Carl Mosser "The Earliest Patristic Interpretations of Psalm 82, Jewish Antecedents, and the Origin of Christian Deification," *The Journal of Theological Studies* 56, no. 1 (2005): 30–74. The way some Mormons have misunderstood its significance is addressed on pp. 41–46.

through the exercise of virtue or by various theurgic means.[26] These Christian and philosophical usages differ from the euhemeristic elevation of heroes and kings in that the human who becomes *theos* is not an object of worship or veneration (i.e., he or she is not a deity).

Throughout antiquity *theos* had a broad semantic range. Even when restricted to its most common usage ("god," "deity"), it was used in highly equivocal ways. The gods of the Greek pantheon, the various first principles of the philosophers, and the God of Jews and Christians were all understood to be objects of worship, but they did not necessarily refer to the same type of thing. Yet, there was little chance of confusion. In this respect *theos* was similar to our word *love*. For example, in one breath a man can profess love for God, his wife and his neighbor, but he will be in deep trouble if he loves them all in the same sense. He may also love his job, his car, Beethoven's symphonies, and pepperoni pizza. In each case he "loves" in highly equivocal senses but few fluent English speakers would confuse the different meanings employed.

Finally, the semantic range of *theos* narrowed due to the influence of Christian theology during the Byzantine and Modern eras. Earlier synonymies fell out of use so that the word is now used in Modern Greek almost exclusively to refer to deities and as an element in certain idiomatic constructions—much like the contemporary English words *God* and *god*.

It should now be clear that defining atheism, monotheism, and polytheism etymologically is not as straightforward as people tend to think. This is due to the fact that their common etymon has functioned for much of its history as a polyseme, a word with multiple related meanings. This being the case, we must ask whether the etymon functions within these three words univocally or equivocally. In the next section I will argue that it has always functioned equivocally. That explains why these terms cannot function as a set of coordinate first-level *taxa* by which all religious or theological systems can be classified, at least not in the strictly quantitative manner that many people assume.

The Invention of -theism Terms & the Taxonomy of Religions

To begin, it should be observed that the words atheism and monotheism do not have any equivalents in ancient Greek. Though built on

---

26. E. R. Dodds, *Pagan and Christian in an Age of Anxiety* (Cambridge: Cambridge University Press, 1965), 74–101.

Greek roots, they are not Greek words. Polytheism has an ancient Greek equivalent (*polytheos, polytheia*), but it is really a modern reinvention that can convey nuances that *polytheia* did not. All three are modern words coined during the sixteenth and seventeenth centuries as terms of art. This is an example of the modern tendency to coin words built on Greek and Latin roots in order to create special terms with precise meanings or referents. A great deal of medical, scientific, theological, and philosophical jargon consists of such words.

In ancient Greek texts the adjective *atheos* and the noun *atheotēs* mean such things as *without the gods, denying or neglecting worship to the gods, abandoned by the gods, impious* and *godlessness*.[27] They can also be used in reference to those who deny the gods of a city or nation. This can take the form of denying the existence of all gods or denials that we would not consider atheistic. For example, one could be considered *atheos* for preferring another nation's gods to those of one's own people. Jews and Christians were often labeled atheists because they refused to participate in the cults of the Greek and Roman pantheons, and because there was no cult statue in the Jerusalem Temple (pre-70 C.E.) or in synagogues and churches. By common Greco-Roman standards, they did not worship any *theos* and were thus *atheos*. While there were people who denied the existence of any sort of deity, there were no Greek terms quite equivalent to *atheism* or *atheist*. According to the *Oxford English Dictionary*, atheism was derived from the French *athéisme* in about 1587. The French terms *athéisme* and *athée* (atheist) had themselves just been coined in the previous decade. The modern term began with a meaning roughly equivalent to the Greek *atheotēs*. However, this meaning was soon supplanted and *atheism* became a designation for belief systems that deny the existence of God—in particular, the God of the monotheistic religions.

The *Oxford English Dictionary* attributes the first use of *monotheism* to the influential Cambridge Platonist Henry More in 1660.[28] More

---

27. Cf. Henry George Liddell and Robert Scott, *Greek-English Lexicon with a Revised Supplement*, rev. and augmented by Henry Stuart Jones (Oxford: Clarendon, 1996).

28. *An Explanation of the Grand Mystery of Godliness*... (London, 1660), 61–62. A search of the Thesaurus Linguae Graecae and standard lexicons finds no occurrences of the expected Greek equivalent, *monotheotēs*. The related term *monotheia* is found in two texts. The first is an odd work misattributed to Julias Africanus, *Events in Persia after the Birth of Christ* (ANF 6.127–30; PG 10.97–108). There

coined the word to distinguish between ancient pagan views that equate the one God with the material world from the proper understanding of God's oneness. This was part of a larger project in which he develops a typology of religions in which monotheism and atheism are antonyms.[29] Ultimately all religions and theologies qualify as versions of one or the other. Judaism and the philosophical monotheism of the Greek philosophers are corrupt versions of monotheism. Pantheism, on the other hand, pretends to be a version of monotheism but is actually a form of atheism. Polytheistic religions are likewise classified under atheism.

It might seem odd that a religion that affirms belief in many gods and another that affirms belief in only one God can both equally qualify as atheistic. While belief in one God is necessary for monotheism, it is not sufficient if the purported God does not share the basic qualities More finds in his paradigmatic examples. Clearly, the *number* of deities postulated or worshiped is not the central question. Rather, More is concerned with the *kind* of deity that is affirmed. Quantity plays a role only in that the type of *theos* found in monotheistic religions is such that there can only be one. God is necessarily unique. Thus, metaphysically God is not in the same category as the *theoi* of polytheistic religions. Polytheistic religions affirm the existence of deities, but they are forms of atheism because they do not affirm the existence of a *theos* of the sort that monotheistic religions affirm. Similarly, metaphysical differences between the *theos* of monotheism and that of pantheism are so great that the latter cannot be taken as monotheistic despite the affirmation that only one *theos* exists.

Three characteristics of More's typology should be noted. First, the typology has only two first-level *taxa*: monotheism and atheism. All

---

monotheia is used once in the sense of 'singular divinity' (PG 10.101). The word is next found in the fourteenth-century *Historia Romana* by Byzantine historian Nicephorus Gregoras. It occurs in a single passage comparing one party's position in the Barlaamite Controversy with unitary views of God found among Jews and Persians (969.4).

29. In what follows I depend on the descriptions of More's taxonomy in Nathan MacDonald, "The Origin of 'Monotheism,'" in *Early Jewish and Christian Monotheism*, ed. Loren T. Stuckenbruck and Wendy E.S. North (London and New York: T&T Clark, 2004), 204–15 and by R. W. L. Mowberly, "How Appropriate is 'Monotheism' as a Category for Biblical Interpretation?" in *Early Jewish and Christian Monotheism*, eds. Loren T. Stuckenbruck and Wendy E.S. North (London and New York: T&T Clark, 2004), 216–34.

other-theism terms are subordinate categories. Atheism does not necessarily deny the existence of all deities. Rather, it is the specific denial that any God exists like the one affirmed by classical Christianity, Judaism, and Islam in the early modern period. It is the negation of what we today refer to as classical theism. Second, the *theos* etymon equivocates between various -theism terms by referring to different kinds of beings. Third, the three main -theism terms with quantitative prefixes (*a, mono, poly*) are not really quantitative designations. They are qualitative designations that assume particular criteria derived from paradigm examples.[30]

The characteristics of More's typology have been retained in subsequent usage alongside the tendency to give simple etymological definitions.[31] A nice example is found in *The Oxford Dictionary of the Jewish Religion*. The editors tell us that the composition of the word monotheism "indicates that monotheism is a form of theism, that is, belief in a personal divine being, but biblical monotheism differs from polytheistic paganism *not only quantitatively* in the number of gods professed but also *qualitatively in its understanding of God* as absolutely above nature and in complete mastery of it."[32] The definition of theism included here excludes some forms of pantheism because they deny that the divine being is personal. Though postulating the existence of exactly one deity, they are not monotheistic since monotheism is taken to be a variety of theism (in the narrow sense).

Emphasis on primarily qualitative rather than quantitative criteria accounts for the distinction between *God* and *god* in the traditional English lexicon. *God* is used to refer to the deity of classical Jewish, Christian, and Islamic faith while *god* is used in reference to deities associated with the pantheons of ancient Greece, Egypt, Scandinavia, etc. This distinction reflects the fact that metaphysically different types of deities are in view. It also implies a theological judgment: *God* refers to

---

30. MacDonald does not appreciate the significance of this when he apparently agrees with Gregor Ahn that the language of polytheism and monotheism "prioritizes one particular question, that of the number of deities" ("Origin of 'Monotheism,'" 212). In More's case, at least, that is certainly not the case.

31. I deliberately pass over appropriations of *monotheism* and related terminology that arose between the sixteenth century and today (e.g., in the literature of the Deists and Unitarians). For my argument it is sufficient to illustrate that the terms continue to be used in something like More's sense.

32. R. J. Zwi Werblowsky and Geoffrey Wigoder, eds., *The Oxford Dictionary of the Jewish Religion* (Oxford: Oxford University Press, 1997), 477; emphasis added.

the one true deity of classical theism while *god* refers to any of the false deities of mythology.

While this might look like a mere capitalization convention for a polysemous word, it is arguably the case that linguistically *god* and *God* are different words. They are partially synonymous homonyms. Both refer to supramundane beings that are objects of cultic devotion. Every God is a god in that sense, but most gods are not a God. Unlike *god*, there is no true plural for *God*. A God is understood to be the absolute creator of all reality and metaphysically such that only one can exist. A god, on the other hand, is understood to have such a nature that more than one can exist and no god can be described as the absolute creator. Furthermore, *God* can function as a proper name whereas *god* cannot. It refers to a particular divine person with particular attributes. When discussing certain non-classical theisms, *God* is employed analogically (e.g., Process Theism) or as a rigid designator for the God of the Bible (e.g., Mormonism). In recent usage, however, some academic and religious writers intentionally conflate the two words for methodological or ideological reasons. Thus, some people treat *God* and *god* as homonyms with overlapping semantic ranges while others treat them as a single polysemous or even univocal word.

Summary

In this section I have attempted to demonstrate that it is not unproblematic to define *atheism*, *monotheism*, and *polytheism* etymologically. While the meaning of the quantitative prefix in each word is straightforward, *theos* has had a broad semantic range throughout its history and could be used in highly equivocal ways. Moreover, though based on Greek roots, these terms were coined or reinvented in the early modern period in an attempt to classify religions and theological belief systems. *Atheism*, *monotheism*, and *polytheism* were coined as qualitative designations and only the first two functioned as first-level taxonomic categories. This usage has persisted alongside the more recent tendency to treat these words as quantitative designations.

I will now illustrate how quantitative definitions cause confusion within scholarship. Furthermore, I will argue that etymological definitions lead to absurd results if they are consistently applied without consideration of qualitative criteria. We will then be in a position to classify Mormon theism in an informed and hopefully enlightening manner.

II. The Inadequacy of Quantitative Definitions

Confusion among the Scholars

The terms we have been discussing play an important role within religious studies, history of religions, biblical studies, and the philosophy of religion. But within each discipline there are scholars who find this terminology inadequate and use it only in combination with various modifiers. Some scholars go further and suggest that it be abandoned while others defend its propriety. A great deal of the confusion has been generated by etymological definitions emphasizing quantity. Rather than abandon the terminology, it would be more helpful for scholars to employ it with clear qualitative definitions. Since much of the discussion has centered on monotheism, I will illustrate the point by making some observations about the debate surrounding its usefulness for the study of early Judaism and Christianity.[33]

Scholars frequently identify monotheism as one of the key commitments that distinguished and unified Jewish identity in the Greco-Roman world.[34] A handful of scholars, however, have argued that it is inaccurate to describe early Jewish beliefs as monotheistic.[35] While Jews and Christians insisted on the exclusive worship of Israel's national deity, they did not consistently deny the existence of all other divine be-

---

33. For a summary of the main positions, see James F. McGrath, *The Only True God: Early Christian Monotheism in Its Jewish Context* (Urbana: University of Illinois Press, 2009), 1–22. Essays representing the main positions in the debate can be found in Loren T. Stuckenbruck and Wendy E.S. North, eds., *Early Jewish and Christian Monotheism* (London and New York: T&T Clark, 2004).

34. See, for example, E. P. Sanders, *Judaism: Practice & Belief 63 BCE–66 CE* (Philadelphia: Trinity Press International, 1992), 242–47; James D. G. Dunn, *The Partings of the Ways Between Christianity and Judaism and their Significance for the Character of Christianity* (Philadelphia: Trinity Press International, 1991), 19–21; and N. T. Wright, *The New Testament and the People of God* (Minneapolis: Fortress, 1992), 248–59.

35. Most notably, Peter Hayman, "Monotheism—a Misused Word in Jewish Studies?" *Journal of Jewish Studies* 42 (1991): 1–15; and Margaret Barker, *The Great Angel: A Study of Israel's Second God* (London: SPCK, 1992).

ings. In fact, it is easy to find Jewish and Christian texts in which words like *theos* and *elohim* refer to such beings in ways that presuppose their existence. If monotheism is the belief that precisely one *theos* exists, then the authors of these texts were not monotheists. Rather, as Paula Fredriksen says, "ancient monotheists were polytheists."[36] Because of this, she suggests that *monotheism* should face mandatory retirement.

Other scholars working with the same texts continue to find *monotheism* to be a necessary category. William Horbury, for example, retains its use but makes a distinction between "exclusive monotheism" and "inclusive monotheism."[37] Exclusive monotheism denies the existence of all divine beings except Israel's God. Inclusive monotheism, on the other hand, affirms the existence of various kinds of supramundane beings but places the God of Israel above them all and reserves worship for him.[38] Richard Bauckham, however, finds Horbury's qualifications unnecessary. Bauckham observes that "such beings have been considered creatures, created by and subject to God, no more a qualification of monotheism than the existence of earthly creatures is."[39] Along similar lines, Larry Hurtado insists that "monotheism does not involve denying the *existence* of such beings, only that they properly cannot be compared with the one deity in status and significance, and even in nature."[40]

---

36. Paula Fredriksen, "Mandatory Retirement: Ideas in the Study of Christian Origins Whose Time Has Come to Go," in *Israel's God and Rebecca's Children: Christology and Community in Early Judaism and Christianity*, ed. David B. Capes, et al. (Waco, Texas: Baylor University Press, 2007), 37.

37. William Horbury, "Jewish and Christian Monotheism in the Herodian Age," in *Early Jewish and Christian Monotheism*, eds. Loren T. Stuckenbruck and Wendy E.S. North (London and New York: T&T Clark, 2004), 16–44.

38. Though not created with this particular debate in mind, philosopher George Mavrodes has developed a more extensive and useful set of distinctions between different types of monotheism and polytheism. But as with many biblical scholars, he begins by assuming that *monotheism* and *polytheism* on their own must refer to quantitative concepts. See George I. Mavrodes, "Polytheism," in *The Rationality of Belief and the Plurality of Faith*, ed. Thomas D. Senor (Ithaca, N.Y.: Cornell University Press, 1995), 261–86; and George I. Mavrodes, "Monotheism," in *Routledge Encyclopedia of Philosophy*, ed. Edward Craig, 10 vols. (London and New York: Routledge, 1998), 6:479–83.

39. Bauckham, *Jesus and the God of Israel*, 108.

40. Larry Hurtado, "Monotheism," in *The Eerdmans Dictionary of Early Judaism*, eds. John J. Collins and Daniel C. Harlow (Grand Rapids, Mich.: Eerdmans, 2010).

The scholars mentioned above who reject the use of *monotheism* are implicitly defining it etymologically. This is why they assess whether texts are monotheistic on the basis of whether words like *elohim* and *theos* are used to refer to beings other than Israel's God. If this usage is found, then it is evidence of polytheism or henotheism.[41] In contrast, scholars like Bauckham and Hurtado do not see monotheism as a thesis about how many beings exist that happen to be called "gods." In the very same texts that others deem problematic for Jewish monotheism, they find important conceptual distinctions drawn between the God of Israel and all other divine beings.[42] This makes it clear to them that exclusive monotheism was the norm among early Jews and Christians. The analysis of Bauckham and Hurtado presupposes that monotheism should be understood qualitatively. It is also sensitive to the equivocal ways in which *theos* and cognate terms were used in antiquity.

The disparate ways in which scholars understand monotheism render some of their disagreements more apparent than real. Sometimes what one scholar identifies as an example of monotheism another identifies as polytheism or henotheism with no significant difference between their phenomenological descriptions. This serves to muddy the waters and make it difficult to always discern where real disagreements are found. The confusion this generates is one of the reasons that Paula Fredriksen would like scholars of early Judaism and Christianity to abandon *monotheism* altogether. But in one passage Fredriksen unwittingly suggests a more fruitful corrective. She states:

> What do we mean by 'monotheism?' In the modern context of its origin, the word denotes belief in a single god who is the only god. When modern scholars transpose the term to antiquity, the definition remains constant. And that is a large part of the problem.[43]

Fredriksen is correct to identify the root problem as a particular definition of monotheism inadequate to describe ancient patterns of belief. If monotheism is determined simply by counting the number of

---

41. In evolutionary models of religious development, henotheism represents a transitional stage between polytheism and monotheism. Henotheism is commonly defined as the belief that many deities exist but worship is rendered to only one.

42. Especially see Bauckham, *Jesus and the God of Israel*, 107–26; and Larry W. Hurtado, *Lord Jesus Christ: Devotion to Jesus in Earliest Christianity* (Grand Rapids, Mich.: Eerdmans, 2003), 29–52.

43. Fredriksen, "Mandatory Retirement," 35.

beings someone identifies as gods, then it applies to no ancient belief system. But she seems unaware that the word can also be used with qualitative definitions amenable to the combination of emic as well as etic perspectives.[44] This is clear when Fredriksen mistakenly identifies the quantitative definition as the original. The proper corrective is not to abandon monotheism as a useful category, but to abandon dubious quantitative definitions derived from the word's etymology.

What kinds of gods count? What sort of belief?

Up to this point my discussion has focused on the definition, history, and use of *atheism*, *monotheism*, and *polytheism*. I wish now to focus on atheism, monotheism, and polytheism more directly as concepts. My contentions are simple. Despite the etymologies of the terms, belief in the existence of one god is not a sufficient criterion for a religion to be classified as monotheistic. Likewise, belief in the existence of multiple gods is not sufficient for a religion to be classified as polytheistic. Perhaps most astonishing, atheism is not necessarily incompatible with the belief that one or more gods exist. If I am correct about these contentions, then important implications follow for how we classify Mormonism and a few other religions.

For example, let's imagine that Mack and Sam each believe in the existence of one god but no others. Mack is convinced that the Great Blue Ball is the only god that exists. He has no doubt about its existence; he regularly watches it float near the ceiling of his apartment. Friends tell Mack that his god is really a helium balloon, but he pays them no mind. The Great Blue Ball is an object of sublime beauty and Mack derives satisfaction from worshipping it. Is Mack a monotheist? He is according to a strictly etymological definition of monotheism but it is pretty clear that Mack's theology does not really conform to the *concept* of monotheism. The concept does not cover belief in the existence of any sort of entity that one might identify as a god. It presupposes belief in a particular sort of deity. In other words, the concept of monotheism entails a particular *conception* of God.

---

44. Emic perspectives are those that would be acceptable given the categories and perceptions of someone within the culture being studied. Etic perspectives employ concepts and categories external to the culture being studied that are useful to scholars conducting the investigation.

Sam's god, on the other hand, is a rational and very powerful being who can accomplish astonishing feats. When Sam prays to his god sometimes things happen that convince him that his prayers were answered. Sam is also convinced that his god is responsible for many things that happen for which he did not pray. When Sam watches the evening news he can discern the handiwork of his god in some of the reported events. Sam insists that he believes in the one true god and that all other "gods" are psychological projections or mythological characters.

On first blush it appears that Sam is a monotheist. However, there is an idiosyncrasy in Sam's "monotheism"—he believes that Hermes is the one true god. Just as in the Olympian myths, Hermes is a precocious trickster and thief.[45] With his magical staff he causes people to sleep or wake at will, creating opportunities that he uses for good or malice. He is a magnificent communicator but not always trustworthy. He is usually benevolent to those who render worship, but he has a capricious vengeful streak as well. Because of this Sam is usually scrupulous to offer the sacrifices Hermes demands. But if Sam watches the news and detects Hermes' handiwork in a foreign country, he saves himself the expense because it is unlikely that Hermes will find out. After all, even the one true god cannot be in two places at the same time.

As with Mack, Sam is not a monotheist. The reason is simple: Hermes does not exemplify some of the key moral and metaphysical attributes one finds in the paradigm examples of monotheism. The monotheist does not merely believe in the existence of one deity of some sort or other. He believes in the existence of a particular sort of God, one who is the self-sufficient, necessarily good, unchangeable, trustworthy, all-powerful, omnipresent, and all-knowing Creator upon whom all things depend for their existence. One might argue for the inclusion of additional attributes or question how we should understand those that are listed, but these are the basic parameters of the concept. Furthermore, the monotheist understands the nature of God to be such that there could not possibly be more than one deity of this sort. The *monos* is entailed by the nature of the *theos*.

In like manner, the concept of polytheism also presupposes deities with particular moral and metaphysical attributes derived from paradigm examples. Mack could believe in the existence of several Great

---

45. My description of Hermes draws upon the sketch found in Burkert, *Greek Religion*, 156–59.

Blue Balls but that would not make him a polytheist. Sam, however, might be plausibly classified as a polytheist despite believing that only one god exists. That would certainly be the correct classification if in Sam's theology Hermes happens to be the one true god because, for example, he deprived the rest of the Olympians of their immortality by means of some chance discovery.

Now let's take the thought experiment one step further. The Smithsonian arranges to exhibit the world's ten most valuable gemstones in a single case. To protect the exhibit, a new security system is installed that incorporates several very advanced technological features never before seen. One day the security system is tripped and there, caught in the act of stealing the gems, is Hermes himself. Though very powerful and clever, Hermes is unable to free himself. Everyone is compelled to believe in the existence of Hermes, but does this disprove monotheism and atheism in favor of polytheism? Not necessarily. It could turn out that something like Erich von Däniken's ancient astronaut theory or the plotline of the television show *Stargate SG1* is true. In that case, everyone would "believe in" the god Hermes, but not in the relevant sense. Monotheists and atheists would continue to reject the Olympian worldview and classify Hermes as a member of an advanced species from elsewhere in the universe and not a deity worthy of worship. Both atheism and monotheism are compatible with the existence of any number of such gods.

Here is the upshot of this thought experiment. The concepts designated by the terms we have been discussing are not really concerned with linguistic trivialities about how many entities happen to be called "god." They are instead concerned with a set of claims about the existence of particular sorts of deities and, by implication, the nature of the cosmos. Monotheism and polytheism each presuppose that the deities they affirm possess particular moral and metaphysical attributes drawn from paradigmatic examples. Furthermore, when speaking of how many gods are "believed in," mere "belief in the existence of" is not the whole picture. The more pertinent sense of belief is "devotion and cultic reverence for worship." Thus, before classifying a religion or system of belief as monotheistic or polytheistic, we should consider not just the number of gods it postulates, but also the nature of those gods, their relationship to the cosmos, and whether those gods are objects of worship. When doing so a few religions may turn out to be neither polytheistic nor monotheistic, but something else. In such cases we should resist the temptation to pigeon-hole.

III. Mormon Theism

Mormonism in its traditional form makes a number of metaphysical and theological claims that set it apart from the paradigm examples of atheism, monotheism or polytheism. Paradoxically, Mormonism also exemplifies characteristics found at the core of each concept. These can be summarized under the following headings.

1. *Eternalism.* The universe and its basic constituents have always existed in some form. The doctrine of creation *ex nihilo* is rejected along with the understanding of the universe's contingency entailed by that doctrine.
2. *Metaphysical Pluralism.* There are several ultimate entities or principles. These include the uncreated, chaotic matter from which this world was fashioned (D&C 93:33; Abr. 3:24, 4:1); eternally existing intelligences at various stages of progression;[46] and eternal laws or principles that regulate the universe. Each of these things self-exists and their most basic properties and potentialities are brute facts.
3. *Theological Finitism* is entailed by eternalism and pluralism. God is a highly developed intelligence who exists within an environment that he neither made nor transcends in the manner affirmed by classical theism. Though very powerful within the cosmos, what he is capable of fashioning and doing is limited by the uncreated natures of matter, intelligences, and principles.
4. *Eternalism and Finitism* entail an odd form of *Naturalism*. That is, there is no "supernatural" realm or being transcending the uncreated natural realm of matter, energy, intelligence

---

46. The nature of intelligences has been debated within Mormonism, but this is the view that became dominant within the tradition. See Blake T. Ostler, "The Idea of Pre-Existence in the Development of Mormon Thought," *Dialogue: A Journal of Mormon Thought* 15, no. 1 (1982): 59–78, "The Idea of Preexistence in Mormon Thought," in *Line Upon Line: Essays on Mormon Doctrine*, ed. Gary James Bergera (Salt Lake City: Signature, 1989), 127–44; and Charles R. Harrell, *"This Is My Doctrine": The Development of Mormon Theology* (Salt Lake City: Greg Kofford Books, 2011), 211–12.

and eternal law. Mormonism's naturalism is an odd form of naturalism because it does not entail denial of the existence of deities, angels and demons, nor does it preclude the occurrence of unusual events that defy what seems to be possible given our current scientific understanding of the world and its laws (i.e. miracles). Rather, traditional Mormonism affirms the existence of each of these but defines them in ways that differ significantly from the classical tradition.

5. *Plurality of Gods*. Authoritative Mormon texts such as the Book of Abraham and Joseph Smith's later sermons explicitly teach that many Gods exist. These Gods rule over other worlds and are not objects of worship for the inhabitants of this world.

6. *Divine-human nature*. All intelligences, spirits, human beings, angels, demons, and Gods share the same metaphysical nature. They are members of the same species at differing stages of development.

7. *Eternal Progression and Exaltation*. The God with whom we have to do has not always been God. He was once an intelligence and later lived as a man on another world. He was exalted to Godhood by following eternal principles, developing in his moral character, and obeying the God above him.[47] We too can be exalted by following his example. "God," then, is an honorific title.[48]

8. *Embodiment, Gender, and Sexuality*. God the Father possesses a gendered, glorified physical body.[49] His counterpart and wife is Heavenly Mother.[50] Official statements of the First Presidency

---

47. Recently some Mormon thinkers have questioned whether this view is compatible with the LDS Standard Works or entailed by statements made in Joseph Smith's King Follett Discourse. Especially see Blake T. Ostler, *Exploring Mormon Thought: Of God and Gods*, (Salt Lake City: Greg Kofford Books, 2008), 17–26.

48. Paulsen, "Comparative Coherency," 71.

49. This kind of embodiment is *not* analogous to the orthodox Christian doctrine of the Incarnation. Within Mormon theism, embodiment is a natural stage in the development of intelligences as they progress toward Godhood and an expression of the single metaphysical nature that all sentient beings share. Within Christian theology the second Person of the Trinity takes on a human nature in addition to his intrinsic divine nature. Embodiment is natural to his humanity but not to his divinity.

50. David Paulsen discusses this distinctive notion in "Are Christians Mormon? Reassessing Joseph Smith's Theology in His Bicentennial," *BYU Studies* 45, no. 1 (2006): 96–102.

suggest that God the Father and Heavenly Mother procreate spirit children through sexual union. Though not commonly mentioned today, earlier LDS writings frequently defend the idea that Jesus was begotten on earth by God and Mary in the same manner.[51]

9. *Moral Goodness and Mutability*. Gods are exemplars of moral goodness and virtue that work together in harmony. However, it is (theoretically) metaphysically possible for a God to cease being supremely good and thus fall from his status as a God.[52]

Mormonism and Monotheism

Authoritative LDS texts affirm that there is one God (1 Ne. 13:41; Alma 11:26–29; Ether 2:8; D&C 20:19). This God is the Supreme Creator (Alma 30:44; cf. Alma 11:22; D&C 107:4). He is omnipotent (Mosiah 3:5, 17–18, 21; 5:2, 15; D&C 61:1); all-knowing (2 Ne. 27:10; Alma 40:8; Ether 3:25–26); eternal and unchangeable (Morm. 9:19; Moro. 8:18; D&C 20:17, cf. v. 28); and infinitely good and merciful (2 Ne. 1:10; Mosiah 5:3; Hel. 12:1; Moro. 8:3; Mosiah 28:4). Though no longer included in the Standard Works of the LDS church, the *Lectures on Faith* contain a similar theology. God is described as "the only supreme governor and independent being in whom all fulness and perfection dwell. He is omnipotent, omnipresent, and omniscient, without beginning of days or end of life."[53] These texts appear to straightforwardly establish Mormon theism as a variety of classic monotheism. However, studying Mormon theology—like studying Christian theology generally—would not be very interesting if it was a simple matter to establish Mormon doctrine!

All of these passages were written early in Joseph Smith's prophetic career. Smith's later teachings introduced a number of notions that would bear upon the LDS understanding of the divine attributes affirmed in

---

51. Douglas J. Davies very diplomatically describes the belief that Jesus is taken to be the Son of God "in the most direct sense of God the Father engaging with Mary to engender his Son." Douglas J. Davies, *An Introduction to Mormonism* (Cambridge: Cambridge University Press, 2003), 69.

52. See further Carl Mosser, "Exaltation and Gods Who Can Fall: Some Problems for Mormon Theodicies," *Element* 3, no. 1–2 (2007): 45–67.

53. Lecture 2:2 in Larry E. Dahl and Charles D. Tate, eds., *The Lectures on Faith in Historical Perspective* (Provo, Utah: BYU Religious Studies Center, 1990), 39.

these texts. These notions include the idea that God works within an environment comprised of uncreated matter, intelligences, and laws or principles. God did not create our world out of nothing but from preexisting chaotic matter. God's nature is progressive (He was not always God); other Gods exist in addition to the God of our world; and human beings possess the same nature and potential as God. Smith was murdered before he had a chance to reconcile his earlier and later teachings about God. The task was left instead to Brigham Young and second-generation Mormon intellectuals like B. H. Roberts and John Widtsoe.[54] In their works Smith's later teachings serve as the hermeneutical lens through which to interpret statements about God's attributes found in the Book of Mormon and early sections of the Doctrine & Covenants. The result is a unique cosmology that leads Mormon intellectuals to redefine omnipotence, omniscience, unchageability, etc. within the context of Mormon theology.[55] It also leads Mormons to speak of God in ways that are distinctive enough that one LDS philosopher has devoted an entire chapter to "The Meaning of 'God' in Mormon Thought."[56]

---

54. Eugene England narrates key moments of the process in "Progression and Perfection: Two Complimentary Ways to Talk about God," *BYU Studies* 29, no. 3 (1989): 31–47.

55. Examples include: John A. Widtsoe, *Rational Theology* (Salt Lake City: Signature Books, 1997), 9–15, 23–24, 61–65; B. H. Roberts, *The Truth, The Way, The Life, An Elementary Treatise on Theology: The Masterwork of B. H. Roberts*, ed. Stan Larson (San Francisco: Smith Research Associates, 1994), 472–83, cf. 373–83; Sterling McMurrin, *The Philosophical Foundations of Mormon Theology* (Salt Lake City: University of Utah Press, 1959); Sterling McMurrin, *The Theological Foundations of the Mormon Religion* (Salt Lake City: University of Utah Press, 1965); Truman Madsen, *Eternal Man* (Salt Lake City: Deseret Publishing, 1966); Paulsen, "Comparative Coherency," 64–81; Kent E. Robson, "Time & Omniscience in Mormon Theology," *Sunstone* 5, no. 3 (1980): 17–23; Blake T. Ostler, "The Mormon Concept of God," *Dialogue* 17, no. 2 (Summer 1984): 57–84; Blake T. Ostler, *Exploring Mormon Thought: The Attributes of God*, (Salt Lake City: Greg Kofford Books, 2001); Robert L. Millet, "The Supreme Power over All Things: The Doctrine of the Godhead in the Lectures on Faith," in *The Lectures on Faith in Historical Perspective*, eds. Larry E. Dahl and Charles D. Tate (Provo, Utah: BYU Religious Studies Center, 1990), 223 n. 1. A dissenting view is registered by Stephen D. Robinson in Matthew R. Connelly, Stephen E. Robinson, and Craig L. Blomberg, "Sizing Up the Divide: Reviews and Replies," *BYU Studies* 38, no. 3 (1999): 175–76.

56. Ostler, *Exploring Mormon Thought: The Attributes of God*, 1–25.

Mormon cosmology requires an understanding of God that is ultimately finitistic and progressive. Because of this, Mormon teachings represent a parting of the ways from the paradigm examples of monotheism.[57] Traditional Mormon theism is not monotheistic in either the qualitative or quantitative sense.

Beginning with Orson Pratt, there have always been some Mormons who dispute whether the predominant theological synthesis (or elements of it) accurately represents the teachings of Joseph Smith. This has been echoed by at least one non-Mormon scholar.[58] Recent years have seen an increasing number of LDS intellectuals suggest that Smith's later teachings should be interpreted through the lens of the earlier writings included in the Standard Works. Whether this will lead to a viable form of Mormon monotheism remains to be seen.

Mormonism and Polytheism

The LDS Standard Works mention the existence of Gods other than the God that should be worshipped by this earth's inhabitants (Abr. 4–5; D&C 121:32; D&C 132:18–20, 37). Joseph Smith also spoke openly about a plurality of Gods in his King Follet Discourse and Sermon in the Grove. Ever since, critics have charged Mormonism with polytheism. A common statement of the charge says that Mormonism is more polytheistic than Hinduism. Whereas Hinduism postulates 300 million gods, Mormonism postulates an infinite number of deities. More charitable students of Mormonism have also described Mormon beliefs as polytheistic. Rarely, though, does one come across a Latter-day Saint who describes Mormon theology as polytheistic.

---

57. For two reasons I have deliberately not discussed the nature of unity within the Godhead in this section. First, the focus is on the question of monotheism as such, not Christian monotheism in particular. Second, too often Latter-day Saints respond to the claim that Mormonism is not monotheistic by arguing that the LDS understanding of the Godhead qualifies as social trinitarianism. While unity in the Godhead is relevant to the question, it is secondary. Even if social trinitarianism is an appropriate way to describe Mormon teachings (I do not believe it is), establishing that leaves more important issues unaddressed.

58. See Paul Owen, "Monotheism, Mormonism and the New Testament Witness," in *The New Mormon Challenge*, eds. Francis J. Beckwith, Carl Mosser and Paul Owen (Grand Rapids, Mich.: Zondervan, 2002), 468 n. 2

Whether presented as an accusation or merely a description, the idea that Mormonism is polytheistic depends entirely on the etymological definition of polytheism and its sole concern with quantity. We should keep in mind that *polytheism* was coined to refer to a type of religious beliefs and practices found in ancient Mesopotamia, Egypt, Greece, Rome, and Scandinavia. No belief system should be classified as polytheistic unless it bears significant similarity to these paradigmatic examples. Of course, polytheistic religions display a great deal of variety. This makes it impossible to identify a single common denominator other than the fact that several gods are objects of cultic reverence. But, "some basic and characteristic features are discernible, even though not all of them may be present in each and every case."[59]

Polytheistic religions generally consider their deities to be gendered and metaphysically finite.[60] Each has authority over specific areas of nature or society such as fertility, war, love, healing, and the underworld. Gods can also have authority over specific trades. Each deity is accorded distinct cultic devotion appropriate to his or her position in the pantheon and importance to a society's needs. Polytheistic gods are not always exemplars of moral virtue and can have rivalries with one another. Often the gods that are worshipped are second or third generation gods who have assumed their positions upon defeating a preceding generation in primordial combat. The ordering of the world and humanity's creation is sometimes explained as the result of such combat. These characteristics are common but some are not found in certain polytheistic religions. One idea that does seem to be universal is that the basic elements of the world have always existed in some form. As a result, no god is omnipotent in the traditional sense. Many religions also count forces like fate and magic among the primal elements and see even the gods subject to them.

Both ancient and contemporary polytheistic religions display a tendency to develop forms that posit some kind of unity between the gods. Sometimes the gods of the pantheon are considered parts of an organic whole analogous to the human body composed of individual parts with distinct functions. More often the gods who are worshipped

---

59. Werblowsky, "Polytheism," 11.435–39.

60. This and the following paragraph are adapted from Carl Mosser, "Polytheism," in *New Dictionary of Christian Apologetics*, eds. W. C. Campbell-Jack and Gavin McGrath (Leicester: Inter-Varsity Press, 2006), 558.

are considered manifestations of a hidden high god, an impersonal divine reality or a philosophical principle. Because of this some scholars reclassify these religions as monotheistic. However, there remain significant differences between an omnipotent creator and a very powerful god who may be behind the gods. Even when high gods are praised as creators of the world they are in reality mere craftsman; invariably they fashion the world from uncreated materials. Moreover, the unity attributed to the gods does not lead to unity of devotional practice. The various gods continue to be objects of distinct cultic reverence.[61]

If we focus narrowly on metaphysical issues, it would be hard to deny that there are some striking similarities between polytheistic and traditional Mormon cosmologies.[62] This might justify classifying Mormonism as quasi-polytheistic. But there are also some very significant differences. These include:

1. Polytheistic worship is distributed between many gods. Latter-day Saint worship is reserved only for the Godhead who rules over this world.[63]
2. Many polytheistic gods are personifications of nature or associated with specific aspects of nature or society. Mormonism's Gods have power over all aspects of nature and society within the worlds that they rule.
3. Whereas polytheism is idolatrous in the strict sense of the term, Latter-day Saints do not even use images in their liturgy and prayers.
4. Mormonism's Gods are exemplars of moral virtue; polytheistic gods often (though certainly not always) look more like exemplars of vice.
5. Polytheistic gods often compete with one another and sometimes engage in combat. Mormonism's Gods are united in

---

61. Additional features of polytheistic beliefs about the gods are summarized nicely in Theodore M. Ludwig, "Gods and Goddesses," in *The Encyclopedia of Religion*, ed. Mircea Eliade, 16 vols. (New York: Macmillan, 1987), 6:59–66.

62. See Jim W. Adams, "The God of Abraham, Isaac, and Joseph Smith? God, Creation, and Humanity in the Old Testament and Mormonism," in *The New Mormon Challenge*, eds. Francis J. Beckwith, Carl Mosser, and Paul Owen (Grand Rapids, Mich.: Zondervan, 2002), 179–90.

63. To keep focus on polytheism as traditionally understood rather than tritheism, questions about the nature of unity within the Godhead will be passed over.

their purposes. Any God who breaks this unity falls (in theory) from his status as a God.[64]
6. In polytheistic religions the sexuality of the gods is regularly displayed in promiscuity, fornication, and adultery. Sexual activity of the LDS God is expressed (if at all) within the moral boundaries of marriage and family life.[65]

There are very significant differences between paradigmatic forms of polytheism and Mormonism. It is inappropriate to classify Mormonism as a polytheistic religion. To do so conveys highly misleading connotations.

Mormonism and Atheism

In recent literature the word *atheism* has been variously defined as disbelief in the existence of any deities, lack of belief in any deities, and denial of the existence of God. As with *monotheism* and *polytheism*, there has been a tendency to define the word strictly on the basis of its etymology. But we should remember that this modern word began its career in the sixteenth century as a way of saying "godlessness" or "impiety." In both senses of the phrase, that is the word's etymological meaning. But as noted earlier, this meaning was quickly eclipsed and it became widely used as a designation for belief systems that deny the existence of God. Particularly in view is the God of classic Judaism, Christianity, and Islam. This remains to be the most widespread sense in which *atheism* is used.

The modern concept of atheism is comprised of disbelief regarding the existence of the classical God complemented by the affirmation of naturalism. It is usually assumed that this entails disbelief in any sort of deity, but that is not quite right. As we have already seen, while most atheists would gladly endorse that disbelief, atheism is compatible with the existence of any deity that can fit within a naturalistic understanding of the cosmos. The God of traditional Mormon theism appears to be that sort of deity. The Mormon God is not an absolute creator (i.e., He does not create all reality out of absolute nothingness); He does not transcend

---

64. See further Mosser, "Exaltation and Gods Who Can Fall."

65. It is not entirely clear whether this is limited to marriage with a single Mother in Heaven or to multiple wives. The latter view was predominant in the nineteenth and early twentieth century.

the cosmos; and his power is limited by eternal principles, natural laws, the innate properties of matter, and other uncreated entities.

In this light, it comes as no surprise that many LDS philosophers find several arguments designed to establish atheism congenial to their apologetic efforts. These Latter-day Saints simply agree with the majority of atheists on several key issues in metaphysics. The apologetic strategy is three-pronged. The first prong is to appropriate the strongest available atheistic arguments to prove that the God of classical theism does not exist. The second is to show that the Mormon concept of God is immune to these arguments. Finally, arguments for God's existence that undermine classical theism are deployed. The goal is to establish the philosophical superiority of Mormon theism vis-à-vis both classical theism and atheism.

A few scholars have gone so far as to classify Mormonism as a sophisticated form of atheism, most notably A. A. Howsepian in a 1996 article.[66] One LDS scholar, Daniel Peterson, charged that Howsepian's "breathtakingly audacious" claim depends on "lexical imperialism" and "terminological trickiness" in place of rigorous analysis.[67] The ground for these charges is the fact that Howsepian defined *God* in broadly Anselmian terms. Peterson found this to be an "idiosyncratically restrictive definition" that renders Howsepian's arguments irrelevant.[68] But most troubling was the way in which Howsepian repeatedly used *atheism* and *atheist*.[69] Howsepian's use of these terms, Peterson observes, are not merely idiosyncratic; they entail that every polytheistic religion to ever exist should also be classified as a sophisticated form of atheism.[70] Peterson seems to think that this reduces Howsepian's argument to absurdity. The fact, however, is that Howsepian's usage is far from idiosyncratic; he has nearly 350 years of precedent in its favor.

My earlier discussion about More's taxonomy of religions shows that Howsepian's use of *atheism* and *atheist* was current no later than 1660. It also provides an example of someone explicitly drawing the conclusion about polytheism implicit in Howsepian's use of these

---

66. A. A. Howsepian, "Are Mormons Theists?" *Religious Studies* 32 (1996): 357–70.

67. Daniel C. Peterson, "Editor's Introduction," *FARMS Review of Books* 10, no. 2 (1998): v–xx.

68. Ibid., xiii.

69. Ibid., viii.

70. Ibid., ix, xi.

terms. More's precedent is significant because of his role in shaping the modern understanding of monotheism and atheism. But precedent is not limited to seventeenth-century examples or contemporary Christian writers who might be motivated to exclude Mormonism from Christianity. Contemporary atheists use this terminology in much the same sense when they take *theism* and *atheism* to be the two primary *taxa* under which to classify religious views. This becomes clear when we observe that contemporary philosophers define *theism* in precisely the sense that More ascribed to *monotheism*.

For example, consider J. L. Mackie's highly regarded *Miracle of Theism*. Mackie begins by identifying theism as the doctrine that there is a god "as conceived in the central tradition of the main monotheistic religions, including Judaism, Christianity, and Islam."[71] Following Richard Swinburne, Mackie takes the primary doctrines of theism to be that there is a god who is "a person without a body (i.e., a spirit), present everywhere, the creator and sustainer of the universe, a free agent, able to do everything (i.e., omnipotent), knowing all things, perfectly good, a source of moral obligation, immutable, eternal, a necessary being, holy, and worthy of worship."[72] Atheism is the denial that such a person exists. Subsequent atheist philosophers like Nicholas Everitt and Graham Oppy take a similar approach.

Everitt identifies theism with the monotheistic understanding of God shared by mainstream Christianity, Judaism, and Islam. He explicitly indicates that the term *theism* does not apply to religions that are not monotheistic.[73] Graham Oppy similarly understands the debate between theism and atheism to be about the existence of a god like the one described in orthodox monotheism. The fact that there are arguments for the existence of non-monotheistic gods is only mentioned in order to then be dismissed as irrelevant to the debate.[74] According to Oppy, "a *theist* assigns a probability to the claim that an orthodoxly conceived monotheistic god exists that is vague over an interval that is bounded below by 50 percent; an *atheist* assigns a probability to the claim that

---

71. J. L. Mackie, *The Miracle of Theism: Arguments for and against the Existence of God* (Oxford: Clarendon, 1982), 1.

72. The definition is taken from Richard Swinburne, *The Coherence of Theism* (Oxford: Clarendon, 1977), 2. Also found on page 2 in the 1993 revised edition.

73. Nicholas Everitt, *The Non-Existence of God* (London: Routledge, 2004), 14.

74. Graham Oppy, *Arguing about Gods* (New York: Cambridge University Press, 2006), 2.

an orthodoxly conceived monotheistic god exists that is vague over an interval that is bounded above by 50 percent."[75] Everitt makes the same point more succinctly: an atheist is "someone who thinks it at least more likely than not that God does not exist."[76]

Lest there be any doubt about the relevant understanding of God, Everitt offers a definition. God "is the creator and preserver of everything, a being who is omnipotent, omniscient, and perfect. He is in some sense a conscious or minded being, in that he is the subject of various psychological predicates. . . . He is eternal, and omnipresent; and he is without bodily parts. Finally, he is an appropriate object of worship."[77] Everitt anticipates objections like Peterson's. "Why should anyone accept this definition, and what should be said to objectors who say 'That's just your definition of God. Who is to say that yours is the right one? I have my own different definition.'" Everitt's response is that his definition "can claim historical and linguistic accuracy. A huge tradition of people over the last two millennia who have declared a belief in God have understood 'God' in substantially the sense defined." (Observe that Everitt's definition does not require a specifically Anselmian understanding of God.) While agreement has not been universal, there is a broad consensus about the properties that God has even if those properties have sometimes been understood in different ways. Of course, a person can define *God* differently if he chooses. After all, says Everitt, "Anyone is free to be a linguistic deviant."[78]

Though Oppy and Everitt are aware that some religions do not meet the criteria they list for theism, it is doubtful that they intend to include any of them under the umbrella of atheism. But if atheism is simply the belief that it is unlikely that an orthodoxly conceived monotheistic God exists, then it follows that all forms of pantheism, polytheism, etc. are forms of atheism. The only significant difference between More's seventeenth-century taxonomy and this one is that More explicitly states the implications for these religious types.

Taken at face value, the definitions of *God*, *theism*, and *atheism* put forward by Mackie, Everitt, and Oppy also entail that Mormonism qualifies as a form of atheism. It is unlikely that many atheists are

---

75. Ibid., 37.
76. Everitt, *Non-Existence of God*, 14.
77. Ibid., 15.
78. Ibid., 16.

familiar enough with Mormon theology to know this, though. So no one can accuse these philosophers of redefining the terms in order to exclude Mormonism from any desirable group or category. To the contrary, they have inadvertently included Mormonism in the group that they consider most desirable.

Of course, there is something odd about calling someone an atheist who affirms the existence of some sort of deity. It seems that there is an appropriate sense in which one can refer to such people as theists even if they are not theists in the sense pertinent to the atheism/theism debate. William Rowe maintains that some religious beliefs can be classified as atheistic in the sense above but still be considered theistic in another sense without contradiction. In an influential essay on the problem of evil, Rowe helpfully distinguishes between a narrow and broad sense of *theist* and *atheist*. It is worth quoting him at length on this point.

> By a "theist" in the narrow sense I mean someone who believes in the existence of an omnipotent, omniscient, eternal, supremely good being who created the world. By a "theist" in the broad sense I mean someone who believes in the existence of some sort of divine being or divine reality. To be a theist in the narrow sense is also to be a theist in the broad sense, but one may be a theist in the broad sense—as was Paul Tillich—without believing that there is a supremely good, omnipotent, omniscient, eternal being who created the world. Similar distinctions must be made between a narrow and a broad sense of the terms "atheist" and "agnostic." To be an atheist in the broad sense is to deny the existence of any sort of divine being or divine reality. Tillich was not an atheist in the broad sense. But he was an atheist in the narrow sense, for he denied that there exists a divine being that is all-knowing, all-powerful and perfectly good.[79]

When we apply Rowe's distinctions to traditional Mormonism, Mormonism turns out to be a form of atheism in the narrow sense but a form of theism in the broad sense.

---

79. William Rowe, "The Problem of Evil and Some Varieties of Atheism," *American Philosophical Quarterly* 16, no. 4 (1979): 335–41, reprinted in William Lane Craig, ed., *Philosophy of Religion: A Reader and Guide* (Edinburgh: Edinburgh University Press, 2002), 317–18; additionally, see 317–27.

Mormonism and Anglo-American Finite Theism

If traditional Mormonism is theistic in the broad sense but it is not a form of monotheism or polytheism, what kind of theism is it? Here David Paulsen points the way. In his doctoral dissertation David classified Mormon theism as a form of theistic finitism alongside the theologies of John Stuart Mill, William James, and Edgar Sheffield Brightman.[80] Elsewhere he and other LDS philosophers have described significant similarities between Mormon and process theism, another position commonly classified as finite theism.

Some years ago Frank Dilley published an article that pleads for philosophers to reconsider finite theism. He describes three finite theologies that he thinks deserve serious consideration: David Ray Griffin's version of process theism; Brightman's personal idealism; and the Platonic version of theism presented in the *Timaeus*. Dilley identifies three core features common to these views: "creation is not *ex nihilo*; that the world is co-eternal with God; and that God only has limited power to deal with the problem of evil since there are aspects to the created order that God did not deliberately create and which operate independently of the divine will."[81] In addition, Dilley contends that for any finite theism to be religiously adequate, God cannot be limited in goodness.[82] In this regard finite theism retains genuine similarity with monotheistic conceptions of God. According to Dilley's criteria, Mormonism is quite clearly a form of finite theism.

In his recent work David avoids using the term *finite* to describe the LDS understanding of God. He does not think it is inappropriate if properly understood. He is concerned that it is too easily misunderstood and can be rhetorically inappropriate.[83] Indeed, the term *finite theism* can be easily misunderstood. But the problem can be mitigated if we give the designation greater specificity. Consequently, that is what I propose we should do.

It is fairly clear that, with the exception of the Platonic version, finite theisms arose in England and America during the nineteenth and

---

80. Paulsen, "Comparative Coherency," 3–90.

81. Frank B. Dilley, "A Finite God Reconsidered," *International Journal for Philosophy of Religion*, 47 (2000): 29–30.

82. Ibid., 34.

83. David L. Paulsen and R. Dennis Potter, "How Deep the Chasm? A Reply to Owen and Mosser's Review," *FARMS Review of Books* 11, no. 2 (1999): 236.

twentieth centuries. All are motivated by a desire to avoid the perceived shortcomings of Judeo-Christian monotheism. They share important beliefs about the nature of God, creation, and the cosmos. If we want a category of theism in the broad sense that will allow traditional Mormonism to be placed alongside theologies with which it bears deep family resemblances, at least in terms of its cosmology and metaphysical assumptions, we can do no better than *Anglo-American finite theism*.

Within Anglo-American finite theism we can distinguish species of singular finitism and plural finitism. However, we should not pigeon-hole any of them into the categories of monotheism or polytheism.[84] Instead, we should let finite theism stand as a category of its own.

---

84. In any case, the previous discussion establishes that "finitistic monotheism" would be an oxymoron and "finitistic polytheism" a neoplasm.

2

Collision, Division, Conversation: When Mormon Scholars and Christian Theologians Talk

Donald W. Musser, *Stetson University*

The title of this essay is taken from three significant volumes (discussed below) pertinent to the challenge and the promise of fruitful conversations among scholars of two of the Abrahamic faiths; namely, 1) the Church of Jesus Christ of Latter-day Saints, which traces its history from the covenant of God with the Hebrew patriarch Abraham; and 2) other churches in the lineage of Abraham, especially Protestant Christians emerging from the reformations of the sixteenth century. This essay will refer to these thinkers as "Mormon scholars" and "mainline theologians," respectively. One could include in this discussion, of course, figures from Judaism, Islam, the Mandaeans, and the Community of Christ (formerly known as the Reorganized Church of Jesus Christ of Latter Day Saints), and possibly others. However, this study focuses only on the largest body of the Restoration stemming from Joseph Smith in the nineteenth century and ecumenical Protestants, those who, for the most part, are members of churches associated with the National Council of Churches of Christ in the USA, as well as a number of Roman Catholic theologians.

Though modest in scope, I believe that the focus of this essay has implications for the limits and depths of relations between these faiths at the nexus of interfaith and ecumenical encounters. The first of the title words, "collision," references the primary characteristic of their relations, beginning with Joseph Smith's claims of latter-day revelations around 1830. This historical narrative about relations between the Latter-day Saints, and especially ecumenical Protestants, can be written in terms of riots, rancor, and retribution. But, more specifically, the word "collision" alludes specifically to a recent work, the first of the volumes mentioned above, *When Faiths Collide*.[1] Authored by Martin E. Marty, this important volume treats both the perils and possibilities of interchanges of oft-colliding faiths, but it does so within the framework of an overarching commitment to mutual hospitality, a critical component of interfaith exchanges. Marty proclaims hope for historic antagonists in the light of the scriptural advocacy of reconciliation, even in the face of often seemingly unfathomable differences.

If "collide" is an apt verb to describe the historic situation, "division" is a pertinent noun for describing the present state of these churches and their thinkers. Although some bridges have been constructed, thereby bringing Mormons and mainliners together on some common causes, disunity, rather than unity, has been the norm. The fine volume by Evangelical scholar Craig L. Blomberg and Mormon scholar Stephen E. Robinson, *How Wide the Divide?* was a significant contribution toward a civil exchange on biblical and theological issues, and it opened possibilities for future encounters.[2] However, although it bridged the chasm in important respects, *How Wide the Divide?* also displayed significant conceptual, historical, and revelatory obstacles between Mormons and Evangelical Protestants.

The third word in the title of this essay, "conversation," embodies what Blomberg and Robinson initiated—respectful dialogue without rancor. The word "conversation" also appears in the title of another volume that provides specific background for this essay, the book of conversations titled *Mormonism in Dialogue with Contemporary Christian Theologies*, edited by myself and David Paulsen.[3] How this book came about, was organized, and the arduous story of a long decade that brought it to print, all inform my thinking presented here. The word "conversation" evokes similar words, like "discussion" and "consultation," neither of which necessarily carry the meanings of debate nor conflict, although conversation may concern differences and disputes, and result in contestation.[4]

---

1. Martin E. Marty, *When Faiths Collide* (Malden, Mass.: Blackwell Publishing, 2005).
2. Craig L. Blomberg and Stephen E. Robinson, *How Wide the Divide? A Mormon and an Evangelical in Conversation* (Downers Grove, Ill.: Intervarsity Press, 1997).
3. Donald W. Musser and David L. Paulsen, ed., *Mormonism in Dialogue with Contemporary Christian Theologies* (Macon, Ga.: Mercer University Press, 2007).
4. The concept of "contestation" is delineated and clarified by Peter Berger in *The Heretical Imperative* (New York: Anchor Press, 1980), 143–72.

Before I proceed it will be necessary to outline the context within which I've arrived at my conclusions. In that regard, I reference Langdon Gilkey's mature book of pungent essays, *Blue Twilight*, in which he reflects on the topic of "American Theology Since Niebuhr and Tillich."[5] In this volume Gilkey delineates the most pertinent issues in contemporary theology as twofold: (1) the declining sense of "the objectivity of revelation" and (2) the concomitant increase of theological relativism that has ensued in its wake.[6] Gilkey then turns to the problem and promise of "religious pluralism."[7] He cites the decline of "the predominance and so-called superiority of Christianity" which has resulted in a new religious "balance of power" among the world religions that has led to "some sort of 'rough parity'" between them.[8] Gilkey further claims that this softening of Christian (and Western) superiority has opened paths of "genuine dialogue" with other claims of belief and practice across the globe, especially with regard to personal piety. He finally notes the turn inward in the West, especially to mystical practices such as Zazen and yoga.[9] Although Gilkey does not reference them, one might also include the recovery of "spiritual gifts" and the rise of ecstatic experiences (such as speaking in tongues) within Western Christianity.

From my decade long engagement with practitioners of the Mormon faith, I have found little that would lead me to think that Latter-day Saints have been consciously focused on—to say nothing of eager about—the situation that Gilkey describes. The objectivity of revelation, and the superiority of the Christianity restored by Joseph Smith, have been, and continue to be, core elements of Latter-day Saint thought. Mormons hold to an objective priestly and prophetic core of revelation that they believe was evident in the earliest decades of the apostolic period, subsequently lost in The Great Apostasy, and not recovered until the Restoration of the nineteenth century. In addition, because apostolic authority was restored exclusively with Joseph Smith, and continued through the prophetic offices of the Mormon authorities to this day, Mormons es-

---

5. Langdon Gilkey, *Blue Twilight* (Minneapolis: Augsburg Fortress Press, 2001), 109–18.
6. Ibid., 110.
7. Ibid.
8. Ibid., 111.
9. Ibid.

chew any notion that their truths and practices are less-than-absolute. Thus, any claim of relativity to those tenets and sacraments is generally not tolerated. Further, the veracity of those authorities—in the sense of the church's official views being a restoration of the faith-once-delivered by Jesus in the first century and, therefore, the standard by which all other Christians and non-Christians claims are judged—is unquestioned. If this description of Latter-day Saints is at all correct, then Langdon Gilkey's conclusions about the loss of objective revelation, the relativity of all religious truth-claims, and the inward journey of many Christians into personal and mystical experiences, away from objective beliefs, may mirror nothing more than the delusions of one who has not been baptized into the world of the latter-day Restoration.

But is this the entire story? Is the divide between Mormon theology and the Christian theology Gilkey espoused an uncrossable abyss? My work with David Paulsen may provide perspectives from which to answer this question. In the remainder of this essay I wish to reflect on my experiences and encounters with Professor Paulsen and other scholars who joined us for more than a decade in academic interchanges. As a Christian believer who finds Gilkey's picture of the contemporary religious situation persuasive (at least in its broadest strokes), and as one who enjoys the adventure of exploring other ways of faith and practice, I was excited to receive an invitation in 1997 to participate in a program sponsored by David Paulsen, then in his position as the Richard L. Evans Professor of Religious Understanding at Brigham Young University. Despite the cautions of my professional acquaintances that I must be wary of being drawn into a Mormon public relations operation, staged to enhance public acceptability of the Latter-day Saints in the non-Mormon world, I embraced this challenge with relish.

On my several visits to Provo during the last years of the twentieth century, I came to appreciate the life and thought of faithful Mormons, especially Professor Paulsen and his colleagues, in ways that both informed and revised my previous and often distorted view of Mormons. In an atmosphere of gracious hospitality, we engaged in a series of dialogues on core beliefs and practices. One tangible result was our co-edited volume, mentioned above. A second result—and one that became professionally and personally important to me—was my commitment to pursue and advocate a dialogue between contemporary Christian theology and Mormon thought as I closed the seventh decade of my life. Thus, this modest essay is penned with great appreciation for David Paulsen, a friend, fellow-laborer, and companion scholar. I will reflect autobiographically here in the light of the "context" in which these conversations will take place (or, more accurately, my perceived understanding of the context) and provide a perspective about the promise of a Mormon dialogue with mainline Christians, especially in the light of Paul Tillich's thinking about the relationships of different faiths.

My many personal experiences with Mormons testify to the power of the Benedictine principle of hospitality to make possible serious conversations, genuine friendships, and profound respect.[10] "The Rule of St. Benedict," of which I was not fully aware, was enacted between David and me and, I expect, most of the scholars who entered the conversations during those years. Like Benedict's wayfarers in need of food and shelter, the Latter-day Saints welcomed us with care. Although strangers, and "from afar" in certain beliefs and practices, we were treated as honored and valued guests. We were welcomed and affirmed, and in keeping with the monastic tradition, we, for our part, abided by the mores and traditions of our hosts.[11] Although I suspect that some viewed us as strangers, I, for one, seldom had the notion that I was merely being "tolerated." Grace and kindness prevailed.

I must admit, however, that I occasionally felt as though I was being viewed as a prospect for witness, as an "outsider" in need of spiritual restoration. At the Salt Lake City Tabernacle, for example, my guide was intent on sharing her testimony with great enthusiasm. Presenting her faith fervently, she seemed unwilling to engage in casual conversation. I was irritated and disappointed, but having once zealously

---

10. In this regard I am grateful to Professor Martin E. Marty, who graciously introduced David and I and who is to be credited with enabling our conversations. It was in Marty's book, *When Faiths Collide*, that I found the idea of Benedictine hospitality expounded, and it was then I concluded that we had been enacting this monastic impulse, doing what Benedictines do by following the rule: "Let all guests be received as Christ."

11. To satisfy my addiction to caffeine, I was pleased that the local motel served aromatic coffee, and I always had an extra cup before spending a day on campus! I also found that dessert is an important element of Mormon meals, even at lunch, and I indulged myself with the consumption of more ice cream than I had in years. When I was told that Utah has the highest per capita sales of ice cream, I mused to myself that sugar must be a substitute stimulant for the caffeine that is generally not ingested by the Latter-day Saints.

witnessed to others as a fervent Baptist, I tolerated what I viewed as a presumptuous intrusion from my perspective and experience. Even though I became aware that personal witness is part and parcel with Mormon faith, I believe that genuine dialogue is damaged by the sense that either party is on a mission to proselytize.

That lived imperative—which I only inchoately understood when I inaugurated the conversations with a series of lectures at Brigham Young University in 1998[12]—enabled me to respond to what often is THE conversation-ending question (on both sides) that a Mormon can ask a non-restorationist Christian. That question initiated the period of questions and answers that followed my lectures, and if I recall the situation with clarity, it caused a pall to fall over our gathering. I learned later that the questioner was a senior citizen from the Provo community. Hers was the first hand I saw and I immediately called on her. She rose, and solemnly asked, "Do you think Mormons are Christians?" I suppose I should have expected someone to ask me this question. But, frankly, at that time I had no idea how important it was to Latter-day Saints.

In the light of this question, then, I want to explore "relations" between the Latter-day Saints and mainline Christians. The latter grouping (although I am not fully satisfied with the term "mainline") is both my personal affiliation as an ordained theologian and also where I find my intellectual home. Let me start with a major issue, one that connects directly with the question put to me at Brigham Young University: "Do you think Mormons are Christians?" Both the Latter-day Saints and Christians of every variety, for the most part, have historically considered our faith as an exclusive one; that is, as "the true faith," the one way. With that, we have excluded other ways because they are incomplete, heretical, erroneous, or apostate. To make the situation more problematic, Protestants have either officially, or unofficially, considered Mormons theologically perverse. As I stated earlier, "we" understand that Mormons have historically considered us apostates, having departed from the Gospel and, thus, no longer recipients of God's revelation. If this belief is generally the case, how can we possibly expect hospitality from one another on matters of our faith? I believe that help may come from an unlikely source, namely, Paul Tillich.[13] Despite

---

12. See Musser and Paulsen, *Mormonism in Dialogue*, 2–9, for what I said in those presentations.

13. For a succinct introduction to Tillich, see Donald W. Musser and Joseph L. Price, *Paul Tillich* (Nashville, Tenn.: Abingdon Press, 2009).

critiques from Mormon scholars[14] and others in the wider Christian world of Tillich's thought on both theological and ethical grounds, his voice remains helpful to understand the basis for a hospitable theological dialogue.

At the first glance, Tillich does not appear as a promising guide because he often sounds like an exclusivist. He held, on Christological grounds, that only Christianity can claim validity as the decisively true faith. Indeed, as a Christian Tillich adamantly avers that the one and only criterion by which one can measure the veracity of an authentic commitment to divine reality is by the criterion of Jesus-as-the-Christ. In an incisive and seemingly ultra-exclusive statement, Tillich claims:

> The final revelation, the revelation in Jesus as the Christ, is universally valid, because it includes the criterion of every revelation and is the *finis* or *telos* (intrinsic aim) of all of them. The final revelation is the criterion of every revelation which precedes or follows. It is the criterion of every religion and of every culture, not only of the culture and religion in and through which it has appeared. It is valid for the social existence of every human group and for the personal existence of every human individual. It is valid for mankind as such, and, in an indescribable way, it has meaning for the universe also. Nothing less than this should be asserted by Christian theology. If some element is cut off from the universal validity of the message of Jesus as the Christ, if he is put into the sphere of personal achievement only, or into the sphere of history only, he is less than the final revelation and is neither the Christ nor the New Being. But Christian theology affirms that he is all this because he stands the double test of finality: Uninterrupted unity with the ground of his being and the continuous sacrifice of himself as Jesus to himself as the Christ.[15]

Thus, the Christian theologian is to explore and evaluate all traditions, including one's own, from this seemingly exclusivist perspective. Some theologians—Tillich especially notes Karl Barth in this respect—and many Christians throughout history have interpreted the Christian priority in an absolutist way, as not one way but the only way to spiri-

---

14. See Musser and Paulsen, *Mormonism in Dialogue*, 123–59, for a rather contentious interchange between Joseph L. Price and late Mormon philosopher Truman G. Madsen.

15. Paul Tillich, *Systematic Theology*, vol. 2 (Chicago: University of Chicago Press, 1951), 137.

tual truth. Additionally, like Barth, they have denounced other faiths as false, incomplete, and essentially untrue revelations.[16]

Unlike Barth, however, Tillich maintains a dialectical focus between Christianity and other faiths, both rejecting them when they contradict Christianity, but also accepting and embracing some of their forms, claims, and practices.[17] In fact, Tillich argues that the dialectic of rejection and acceptance was the predominant Christian view until the eleventh century, when an absolute exclusivism gained prominence for mostly political and polemical reasons. In a study of Israel's relationship to pagan faiths, the Gospel teachings of Jesus, Paul's mutual rejection and acceptance of aspects of paganism and Judaism, and the early *Logos* theology at Alexandria, he finds evidence of the "preparatory character of [other] religions," namely, Judaism and paganism, emphasizing how they asked questions from a nescient intimation of truth.[18] Thus, rather than being exclusive, Tillich finds early Christianity more appropriately inclusive, rejecting other ways, but, at the same time, modifying and adapting Jewish and pagan traditions and content within the kerygma of Christian faith. From an "astonishing universalism," based on the *Logos* doctrine that posited the entire universe's grounding in God, Tillich claims Christianity is particular, but not insular; confessional, but open to other ways of thinking; or, as he says frequently, reformed, yet ever reforming.[19]

Tillich illustrates some ways that Christianity has adapted parts of other traditions, for example, the Old Testament (the texts of Judaism), Stoic-based ethics in Paul, worship forms from the Gnostics and mystery religions, and the language and concepts of the Greco-Roman Empire. Christianity was also self-critical, hearing and responding to the polemics of other ways; for example, the criticism from Judaism that Christianity rejected monotheism and the pagan critique that Christianity had profaned the natural world.[20]

The dialectical acceptance and rejection of other ways, based on what Tillich calls "the Protestant principle," may be a persuasive precept

---

16. Paul Tillich, *Christianity and the Encounter of the World Religions* (New York: Columbia University Press, 1963), 44–45. Although Tillich strongly disagrees with Barth here, he commends Barth's absolutist stand against the quasi-religious Nazi threats of his time.
17. Ibid., 28–30.
18. Ibid., 33–34.
19. Ibid.
20. Ibid., 85–87.

of a Mormon-Christian dialogue. By this standard, each faith is in an encounter with another faith, and, at the same time, an encounter with itself. Tillich finds copious evidence of this interactive movement in the Hebrew prophets' attack on Israel's religious and political leaders; in Jesus' appeal to a "higher law" (the law of love); and the Reformation's critique of church authority and ritual.[21] If religions would enter into mutual external criticism and internal critique, Tillich believes they would create "a community of conversation which will change both sides of the dialogue."[22] It seems to me that this position provides promise for conversations between Mormon scholars and mainline theologians because both are theoretically open to new revelations and insights (albeit in distinctly different ways) and because both have the ability to rethink and reconfigure ideas and practices of their historic traditions.

This position is entirely commensurate with Tillich's ecclesiology, that the church is both the recipient of absolute revelation, and a finite and social institution that is both fallible and ambiguous. Thus, the early church set the tone for what Tillich believes should be the normative position of Christianity with respect to the world religions: that of critical inclusivism. Because God is the ground of being, and therefore the ground of everything in finite existence, God can in principle be known by all people. Tillich agrees that all persons who seriously respond to objects, events, or persons whom they perceive as vehicles of the sacred are in communion with the heart of reality, with Being, with God, and, in principle, inchoately but not directly, with the universal revelation in Jesus as the Christ. Such a position is not peculiar to Christian history, but reflects impulses found in the Gospel of John, the Epistle to the Colossians, patristic thinker Justin Martyr, recent Roman Catholic theologian Karl Rahner, the declarations of the Second Vatican Council, and the French Jesuit theologian of the mid-twentieth century, Pierre Teilhard de Chardin.

From Tillich's position with regard to the possible relations between faiths, and from reflecting on Langdon Gilkey's description of the historic "situation" in which we live our faith, and finally from the perspective of Martin Marty's call to hospitality between faiths, let me close with some suggestions that appear necessary, to me, for fruitful conversations that may bridge wide divisions of the expressions of truth claims.

---

21. Ibid., 89–92.
22. Ibid., 95.

Both Gilkey and Tillich recognize our increasing awareness that faiths collide with one another in a world of diverse claims, beliefs, and practices. A plurality of faiths is an empirical fact. In this situation, Tillich and Gilkey seek to avoid two commonly held positions: those of dogmatic isolation (claiming the absolute veracity of one's own faith and the falsehood or inadequacies of all others), and, the opposite, that of universal convergence (concluding that all faiths, despite their particular differences, are, at their core, seeking the same outcome, however their "plans of salvation" seem to conflict). Both Gilkey and Tillich eschew both these options, considering both rationally indefensible. Yet, at the same time, they seek a position that mediates between the extremes and gives credence to elements of both. Both hold, for example, that Christianity, as a matter of faith, is the pre-eminent faith of all faiths. At the same time, they recognize that other faiths pronounce certainty about their claims, thus creating the puzzling dilemma of an inherent relativity in the face of a particular faith's claim of being the one and only valid way. Thus, they conclude that all truth claims must be considered preliminary, subject to revision, and fallible. Nevertheless, both aspire to a position of mellow conviction in a pluralistic world, thinking out of a position that claims that Jesus as the Christ is the revelation of God, but recognizing that all such claims about that revelation are finite expressions of fallible humans who witness to a truth that ever remains in its essence as mystery. This position is ever-reforming, and is open to "rumors" of transcendence in all finite entities, including, especially, other faiths.[23] If one takes this position with regard to Mormons vis-à-vis others who name Christ, conversations surely become possible, even necessary, with the promise of understandings that will enrich and advance our comprehension of divine revelation on both sides.

The usual simplistic positions must be rejected, or significantly modified. A rigidly dogmatic view that one way of faith is the only complete and historic way, and that all other ways are false, inadequate, distorted, or incomplete must be set aside. Equally, a position that diminishes or rejects particular faith claims and historical traditions of revelation that are espoused and celebrated for an elusive and undefined center that all faiths inhabit, also must be discarded.

For conversations to have real promise, participants must embrace an epistemic humility that may be difficult, even forbidden, given the

---

23. Here, I am obliquely referencing Peter L. Berger's *A Rumor of Angels* (Garden City, N.Y.: Doubleday, 1969).

historic divisions, frequent collisions, and disparate theological traditions. Such humility requires openness to possible truth, goodness, and value in the Other. More importantly, both sides must risk the possibility that some might modify their views, espouse ideas from the other, question beliefs of their own faith, or become heretics or apostates. These risks are real, and possibly frightening, and thus threatening to conversations. But, these fears do not necessarily silence our conversations, as long as we believe in a universal truth that transcends all finite truths, and which, further, beckons us to walk and talk together in the grace of humility and hospitality.

If these reflections bear consideration in a Mormon-mainline Christian dialogue, both sides will need to eschew the way of entrenched dogmatism or tepid relativism, the notion that one way—my way—is the only way; or, the view that all ways are true or can be reduced to a common core. Humility seasoned with hospitality must infuse any dialogue. Participants must learn, to the extent possible, to indwell the other's views and positions empathetically.[24]

If these thoughts have any historic precedent by being rooted in the common past we share, I suggest that Abraham himself, as Genesis narrates his story, is a representative ideal. He lived in a time of astonishing religious diversity. His experience convinced him that a particular and peculiar God to whom he prayed to understand had encountered him. When called to leave on a journey that was barely defined, he followed his heart, in faith. As the book of Hebrews reminds us, "By faith Abraham obeyed when he was called to set out for a place that he was called to receive as an inheritance, and he set out not knowing where he was going" (Heb. 11:8).

I thus invite my Mormon brothers and sisters, and my mainline Christian colleagues, as children of Abraham, and joint heirs with Jesus Christ to the promises made to Abraham, to walk and dialogue through the arid desert together, despite the struggle and the danger, toward a better land, a place of promise, and ultimately toward the God we conjointly serve.

---

24. Michael Polanyi, *The Tacit Dimension* (Garden City, N.Y. Anchor Books, 1966).

3

"Faith Seeking Understanding": Mormon Atheology and the Challenge of Fideism

Brian D. Birch, *Utah Valley University*

Fides quaerens intellectum[1] has been among the most durable and oft quoted mottos in the western intellectual tradition. In the nine centuries since Anselm coined the phrase, it has been utilized in a variety of ways and invoked to support a variety of positions in the relationship between the life of mind and the life of the spirit. Anselm, of course, self-consciously situated his theologizing within the devotional life of Christianity, and is most clearly evidenced in the *Proslogion*, written as an extended prayer.[2]

Theology, however, has not comfortably remained within the confines of worship. Modernist thinking, for example, gave rise to questions regarding the very foundations of knowledge, which prompted a variety of responses, including skepticism and fideism. Theologians were forced to reconsider their enterprise within their contemporary social and intellectual landscape. Christian movements sprang up that openly questioned theological authority and which began to favor individual piety and practice over adherence to creeds, confessions, or concords and the theology upon which they were based. This is especially evident in American religious culture, which has been resistant to the intellectualizing of Christianity. For historian Brooks Holifield it was the "disdain for the 'metaphysical' that gave impetus to the cult of 'common sense' in American theology, and after the great controversy

---

1. This paper is largely a revision of two papers presented at the Annual Meeting of the Society for Mormon Philosophy and Theology, "Rethinking Atheology" (University of Utah, 2008) and "Reformed Epistemology, Mormonism, and the Question of Fideism" (Westminster College, Salt Lake City, 2006).

2. The *Proslogion* famously contains what eventually came to be known as the Ontological Argument for the Existence of God.

over deism, common sense would begin to define the very meaning of theological rationality."³

Mormon Atheology

As "an American original," Latter-day Saints exemplify many of these cultural characteristics of including common sense, pragmatism, and a distrust of intellectualism in religious matters.⁴ Church President John Taylor (1808–87) opined, "I consider that if ever I lost any time in my life, it was while studying the Christian theology," referring to it as "the greatest tomfoolery in the world."⁵ Though almost assuredly an exercise in hyperbole, this statement captures the widespread sensibility among Latter-day Saints that Mormon doctrine and practice are at odds with the theological enterprise that has shaped Christian thought across the centuries. As R. Douglas Phillips puts it in the forward to Hugh Nibley's *The World and the Prophets*, "it is abundantly clear that the whole philosophical theological enterprise, however well-intentioned, is incompatible with the existence of continuing revelation."⁶

---

3. E. Brooks Holifield, *Theology in America: Christian Thought from the Age of the Puritans to the Civil War* (New Haven, Conn.: Yale University Press, 2003), 56.

4. See, for example, Davis Bitton, "Anti-Intellectualism in Mormon History" *Dialogue: A Journal of Mormon Thought* 1, no. 3 (Fall, 1966): 111–40; Davis Bitton, "Mormon Anti-Intellectualism: A Reply" *FARMS Review of Books* 13, no. 2 (2001): 59–62; and Terryl Givens, *People of Paradox: A History of Mormon Culture* (New York: Oxford University Press, 2007), 3–19, 65–99, 195–240.

5. John Taylor, *Journal of Discourses*, 26 vols. (London and Liverpool: LDS Booksellers Depot, 1854–86), 5:240.

6. R. Douglas Phillips, "Foreword" in *The World and the Prophets*, eds. John W. Welch, Gary P. Gillum, and Don E. Norton, Collected Works of Hugh Nibley 3 (Salt Lake City: Deseret Book Company, 1987), xii. Resistance to theology takes various forms in LDS discourse. See M. Gerald Bradford, "On Doing Theology," *BYU Studies* 14 (1974): 345–58; Louis Midgley, "Prophetic Messages or Dogmatic Theology? Commenting on the Book of Mormon: A Review Essay" *FARMS Review of Books* 1, no. 1 (1989): 47; Louis Midgley, "Directions That Diverge: 'Jerusalem and Athens' Revisited," *FARMS Review of Books* 11, no. 1 (1999): 27–87; Louis Midgley, "Theology" in *Encyclopedia of Mormonism*, ed. Daniel H. Ludlow, (New York: MacMillan Publishing Company, 1992), 1475–76; Daniel C. Peterson, "What Has Athens to Do With Jerusalem? Apostasy and Restoration in the Big Picture," FAIR: The Foundation for Apologetic Information and Research, http://www.fairlds.org/fair-conferences/1999-fair-conference/1999-what-has-athens-to-do-with-jerusalem-apostasy-and-restoration-in-the-big-picture, (accessed April 30, 2012); and James L. Siebach, "Response to Professor Tracy," in *Mormonism in Dialogue with Contemporary Christian Theologies*, eds. Donald W. Musser and David L. Paulsen (Macon, Ga.: Mercer University Press, 2007), 462–67.

Such a view was not always the case in Mormon thought. Early in the Church's history, Parley P. Pratt published his *Key to the Science of Theology*, which offers an expansive and integrative account of the relationship between reason, scientific learning, and revealed religion. John Widtsoe published his *Rational Theology* in 1915 for use as a manual of study for the Church's Priesthood, and it was subsequently reproduced in six editions and translated into seven languages between 1915 and 1952. Widtsoe describes his project as "based on fundamental principles that harmonize with the knowledge and reason of man."[7]

In recent literature, however, the word "theology" has all but disappeared from the Mormon intellectual vocabulary. One can scarcely think of a work within the orbit of LDS-approved publications with the term in its title or subtitle. Observers of Mormonism have puzzled over this antipathy. Martin Marty, for example, has openly wondered about Latter-day Saints who "note and sometimes even brag that they do not have a theology. Though he acknowledges the need for a "slightly broader definition" for reference to Mormon doctrinal discourse, Marty concludes that Latter-day Saints nonetheless have a theology and make theological statements.[8] The Reformed Christian philosopher Stephen Davis identifies three reasons for Mormonism's "aversion" to theology: (1) Mormonism has always been oriented more toward the down-to-earth problems of life and practice than to theoretical or academic concerns. (2) Mormon scriptures have always been taken as far more important than any theology. (3) Mormonism's insistence on continuing revelation makes systematic theology largely useless.[9] Davis goes on to articulate the ways in which philosophical theology *could* assist Latter-day Saints to move toward greater clarity on points

---

7. John A. Widtsoe, *A Rational Theology* (Salt Lake City: Signature Books, 1997), iii. Other examples include B. H. Roberts' *Seventy's Course in Theology* and *The Way, the Truth, and the Life: An Elementary Treatise on Theology*. Noteworthy as well is the fact that the once canonized "Lectures on Faith" were also referred to as the "lectures on theology." It must be acknowledged that Pratt and Widtsoe employed the term in peculiar fashions, and I would certainly agree with those, like Louis Midgley, who maintain that the term meant something particular to each of these thinkers; but I would argue that this actually supports my point.

8. Marty E. Marty, "Forward" in *Mormonism in Dialogue with Contemporary Christian Theologies*, eds. Donald W. Musser and David L. Paulsen (Macon, Ga.: Mercer University Press, 2007), vii.

9. Stephen T. Davis, "Philosophical Theology for Mormons: Some Suggestions from an Outsider," *Element: The Journal of the Society for Mormon Philosophy and Theology* 3, no. 1&2 (Spring and Fall, 2007): 104.

of doctrine, particularly in response to criticisms and in contexts of comparative exchange.

This project has been taken up by David Paulsen, whose writings are perhaps the finest example of Mormon attempts to utilize philosophy and theology to clarify and lend support to Latter-day Saint beliefs. He has demonstrated that substantive and sustained dialogue with Christian theologians can be mutually enriching and cast Mormon thought in a new light in relation to alternative approaches. His efforts to defend the coherence and consistency of Latter-day Saint beliefs in response to critics is Mormon apologetics at its finest, and I am confident his work will be increasingly valuable in coming years as Mormons seek a deeper level of engagement with other faith traditions.

The issues raised by Marty and Davis are especially significant in light of the renewed openness toward the academic study of Mormonism on the part of the Church of Jesus Christ of Latter-day Saints. On November 2, 2007, the Church offered a commentary statement entitled "Mormon Studies and the Value of Education," with the purpose to express warm encouragement for emerging Mormon Studies programs such as those at Claremont Graduate University and Utah State University. Of particular interest for this investigation is the following statement: "The Church encourages a deeper and broader examination of its theology, history and culture on an intellectual level, and this is a wonderful opportunity to expand open dialogue and conversation between the Latter-day Saints and various scholarly and religious communities."[10] Two months later, the Church released another commentary entitled "A Mormon Worldview," which intended to give observers a taste of the "collective spiritual experience" of the Latter-day Saints. The document ends with an intriguing assertion: "Getting at the heart of Mormonism is best undertaken not by narrowly focusing on controversy and getting mired in esoteric theological debates, but through a more imaginative examination of the worldview that inspires its members."[11]

In reflecting upon the application of these two documents, the question naturally arises as to what it means to undertake a "deeper and broader examination of Mormon theology." Can this be done with-

---

10. See "Mormon Studies and the Value of Education," LDS Newsroom, http://newsroom.lds.org/ldsnewsroom/eng/commentary/-mormon-studies-and-the-value-of-education (accessed April 30, 2012).

11. See "A Mormon Worldview," LDS Newsroom, http://newsroom.lds.org/ldsnewsroom/eng/commentary/a-mormon-worldview (accessed April 30, 2012).

out engaging in "esoteric theological debates"? How is the esoteric to be distinguished from the imaginative? Can one explore deeply and avoid the mire? The outcome of these questions, I believe, will have profound consequences for the academic study of Mormonism in the years to come.[12] With these questions in mind, we can turn our attention toward a more refined understanding of how theology operates both within and outside Mormonism.

Within Latter-day Saint discourse, one frequently observes the term "theology" referenced in contradistinction to some other category of the Mormon doctrinal lexicon (e.g., theology vs. revelation, theology vs. prophetic teaching, or theology vs. theophany). In a "living gospel" regulated by continuing revelation, theology has become a metaphor for a rootless Christianity in desperate search for truth. LDS writer Louis Midgley sums up this position nicely in his aphorism that "theology involves arguments about God and not encounters with God."[13]

However, in our attempt to penetrate beyond the rhetorical volleys between Mormons and their critics, it is vital to acknowledge the range and diversity within theological discourse. This is an obvious and essential first step toward identifying the intended meaning of the term as a target of criticism. So how do influential contemporary theologians define and utilize the term? A useful place to start, I believe, is with David Ford's *Theology: A Very Short Introduction*, which defines theology "at its broadest as *thinking about* questions raised by and about the religions."[14] This definition is, of course, easy for Mormons to accept. Like those of many other faiths, Latter-day Saints think about questions raised by and about their religion with great frequency.

---

12. I am among those who have resisted systematic theology as the most appropriate means of capturing Mormon doctrinal discourse. My theoretical leanings tend toward narrative and other post-liberal theologies influenced by philosophical hermeneutics and the later Wittgenstein. On the other hand, I find myself resistant to the culture of dismissiveness regarding theological inquiry and the critical engagement with LDS scripture and teaching. See Brian D. Birch, "Theological Method and the Question of Truth: A Postliberal Approach to Mormon Doctrine and Practice," in *Discourses in Mormon Theology: Philosophical and Theological Possibilities*, eds. James M. McLachlan and Loyd Ericson (Salt Lake City: Greg Kofford Books, 2007), 103–31.

13. Louis Midgley, "No Middle Ground: The Debate over the Authenticity of the Book of Mormon," in *Historicity and the Latter-day Saint Scriptures*, ed. Paul Hoskisson (Provo, Utah: Religious Studies Center, Brigham Young University, 2001), 165.

14. David Ford, *Theology: A Very Short Introduction* (Oxford: Oxford University Press, 2000), 3; emphasis added. Ford holds the prestigious Regius Professorship in Divinity at Cambridge University.

A more robust definition, however, comes from the famed Catholic theologian and cardinal Avery Dulles, who describes theology as "a *methodical inquiry* into the meaning and grounding of what, in faith, is taken to be the word of God."[15] Depending on how one understands the term "methodical," Dulles's description is not at all alien to a Latter-day Saint self-understanding. Mormons believe themselves to be divinely instructed to carefully study their faith in the attempt to gain a deeper understanding of what they take to be the revelations of God.

Finally, let us consider Shubert Ogden, certainly one of the most influential American theologians of the last half-century. For Ogden, theology is more demanding and constitutes the *"fully reflective understanding* of the Christian witness of faith as decisive for human existence." Of course the operative term here is "fully reflective," by which he means that theology "ought to exhibit at least some of the formal marks of any 'science,' including the methodological pursuit of its questions and the formulation of its answers in a precise conceptuality."[16] This is the point at which Latter-day Saints begin to get uncomfortable. The attempt to obtain a fully reflective understanding of LDS doctrine is said to be precluded by the doctrine of continuing revelation expressed in the Article of Faith that reads "we believe that He [God] will yet reveal many great and important things pertaining to the Kingdom of God" (A of F 9). A Mormon theology thus leaves things incomplete and perhaps untidy. Because there is more to know, there cannot be (at least in our present state) a complete system of doctrine. This is articulated well by James Faulconer:

> Since Latter-day Saints insist on continuing revelation, they cannot have a dogmatic theology that is any more than provisional and heuristic, for a theology claiming to be more than that could always be trumped by new revelation. Dogmatic theology, however, tempts us to think we have found something more. As a rational system, it gives the appearance of being complete.[17]

---

15. Avery R. Dulles, *The Craft of Theology: From Symbol to System* (New York: Crossroad Publishing, 1992), 105; emphasis added.

16. Shubert M. Ogden, *On Theology* (New York: Harper & Row Publishers, 1986), 2; emphasis added. Ogden does not speak here of a complete system; rather, he talks about the methodological *pursuit* of doctrinal questions.

17. James E. Faulconer, "Rethinking Theology: The Shadow of the Apocalypse," *FARMS Review of Books* 19, no. 1 (2007): 179. Faulconer wants to make clear that by dogmatic theology he means "pertaining to doctrines/teachings," not "asserting . . . opinions in an

As an advocate of the "atheological" character of Mormonism, Faulconer nevertheless proceeds to effectively delineate the kind of theology he thinks most appropriate to Latter-day Saint thought, what he calls *prophetic revelation theology*: "Unless one insists that all theology be systematically rational, and I know of no one who does, it makes sense to call prophetic revelation theology. Indeed, revelation is *the* Latter-day Saint theology."[18]

Faulconer's suggestion here is valuable and productive. The expanding body of truths that Mormons consider revelation plays an authoritative role similar in some respects to that of dogmatic theology in other Christian traditions. However, the key difference, as we have seen, is that Latter-day Saints are not reflecting upon, nor attempting to articulate, a body of revelation that is complete. Thus the effort to bring systematic coherence to Mormon doctrines is said to be misguided in part because rational systems imply the presence of at least a kind of completeness.

It is worthwhile, however, to acknowledge an important response to this approach. Stephen Davis maintains that systematic theology is possible despite an expanding set of truths. "I don't see why the words of Mormon theologians or even official church-sanctioned theological statements cannot be indexed to a certain time. The point could be made or implicitly understood that any such statement is subject to revision by later revelation or authoritative interpretation."[19] For Davis, Latter-day Saints are still "on the hook" of rational justifiability just to the extent they claim their teachings are consistent at any given time.[20]

Benjamin Huff extends these considerations and argues in favor of what he calls a "modified systematic approach" to theology. He attempts to address the concerns of Mormons over system building without giving up on the quest for rational consistency. In doing so, he distinguishes between *monosystematic* and *polysystematic* approaches to theological discourse; the former is the attempt to fit all knowledge into a single system, while polysystematic approaches

---

authoritative, imperious, or arrogant manner."

18. Ibid., 180.
19. Davis, "Philosophical Theology for Mormons," 104.
20. Similar points are raised by the Anglo-Catholic theologian Paul Owen in "Can Mormon Theology be Systematic?" in a paper delivered at Yale University as part of a March, 2003 conference on "God, Humanity, and Revelation." Paper in author's possession.

are necessarily provisional and expect to be superseded by more adequate systems in light of additional revelation.[21] Huff writes, "If one set of concepts is inadequate, then we should work toward a better set. The new set may also be inadequate, yet still be an improvement. To refuse to think through one's understanding systematically at all, I suggest, is to risk simply consigning oneself to confusion."[22]

This approach is not altogether different from contemporary Catholic dogma, which acknowledges the provisional and evolutionary character of theology. The Second Vatican Council made this point explicit in the "Dogmatic Constitution on Divine Revelation." Though the Catholic community "awaits no further public revelation," they do affirm an ongoing "living tradition, whose wealth is poured into the practice and life of the believing and praying Church." Moreover they acknowledge that there is a "growth of understanding of the realities and words which have been handed down."[23] Avery Dulles sharpens the point: "Every theological system is deficient, but some systems are better than others, especially for making the faith intelligible to a given cultural group at a given period in history."[24]

Louis Midgley, among the most outspoken Mormon critics of theology, acknowledges that Latter-day Saint teaching is "rationally structured, coherent, and ordered." While explicitly rejecting philosophical, dogmatic, and speculative theologies, he nevertheless maintains that Mormonism "does allow room for reason as a tool for attaining coherence and for working out implications in the revelations."[25] Midgley's colleague and protégé, Gerald Bradford, maintains further that "it is *required* that the theologian present his ideas in a clear and cohesive manner. His reflections must be carried out in a consistent and systematic fashion. His arguments must be valid according to the rules of logic, theology being as dependent on logic as any other scholarly discipline. The

---

21. See Benjamin Huff, "Theology in Light of Continuing Revelation," in *Mormonism in Dialogue with Contemporary Christian Theologies*, eds. Donald W. Musser and David L. Paulsen (Macon, Ga.: Mercer University Press, 2007), 485.

22. Ibid., 487. See also Jacob T. Baker, "The Shadow of the Cathedral: On a Systematic Exposition of Mormon Theology," *Element: The Journal of the Society for Mormon Philosophy and Theology* 4, no. 1 (Spring 2008): 23–57.

23. "Dogmatic Constitution on Divine Revelation," (paragraphs 4, 7, 8), Vatican: the Holy, http://www.vatican.va/archive/hist_councils/ii_vatican_council/documents/vat-ii_const_19651118_dei-verbum_en.html (accessed April 30, 2012).

24. Dulles, *The Craft of Theology*, 10.

25. Midgley, "Theology," 1475.

emphasis would be on theological clarification not theological system-building or speculation."[26] The crucial consideration for Bradford here lies in the distinction between systematic thinking and *system-building*. The major target for Midgley, Bradford, and other LDS apologists have been theological projects that introduce philosophical concepts, categories, or distinctions that could serve to displace scripture and authoritative teaching. "No doubt one who undertakes to do theology ought to see his job primarily as one of exposition or description of what is taken to be the revealed word of God."[27] These arguments reflect conventional wisdom in LDS scholarship. The earlier and more daring works in Mormon thought have given way to compendia, expositions, and commentaries, a persistent theme of which has been the conscientious effort to avoid any hint of theological adventurism.

This naturally leads us to consider the extent to which these works have succeeded (or indeed can succeed) in this regard. Though these self-described expositions and commentaries *appear* to be theoretically modest, this approach can be misleading. From the absence of theoretical language it does not follow that substantive theological claims are not being made. Though the theological impact is more tacit in these cases, the implications may be every bit as dramatic and potentially problematic as that of the speculative theologian decried in the literature.

In reviewing Robert Millet and Joseph Fielding McConkie's *Doctrinal Commentary on the Book of Mormon,* Midgley compares their work to that of the "revisionists" who subject the Book of Mormon to "the categories of Secular Fundamentalism":

> Though Millet is clearly opposed to speculation about a radical "reconstruction of Mormon doctrine," unfortunately both he and McConkie share basically the same understanding of "doctrine" as do the Revisionists, for they also think in terms of a complex network of dogmas answering a host of different questions. They are therefore prepared to say exactly what Mormon doctrine is on the nature of God and man, and numerous other theoretical questions. They differ from the Revisionists by holding that the vast array of statements and beliefs that Latter-day Saints have entertained on various questions must be winnowed, and the doctrines of what they call "true religion" (1:369; 2:102, 107, 115) or even "revealed religion" (1:369;

---

26. M. Gerald Bradford, "On Doing Theology," *BYU Studies* 14, no. 1 (Spring 1974): 352.
27. Ibid., 353.

2:115) then ascertained, harmonized, and taught authoritatively. A commentary thus provides the occasion for setting forth an elaborate and detailed creed, at least partially explicated in terms of categories quite foreign to the scriptures, upon which assent is thought to be mandatory for salvation. Labels like "true religion" and "revealed religion," like "theology," are categories foreign to the scriptures, but common to our post-Enlightenment, secularized world.[28]

Midgley's point here is important and well expressed. Doctrinal commentaries indeed can engage in a form of implicit dogmatic theology. Ironically, however, he goes on to offer an alternative reading of the message of the Book of Mormon that is every bit as theological as he accuses Millet and McConkie's work of being. He argues that doctrinal commentary ought to be replaced with forms of narrative and practical theology (though he does not refer to them as such), and both of these approaches have solid places in the Christian theological tradition.[29] I too argue in favor of a narrative approach to scripture and doctrine; but to maintain that this is an *alternative* to theology is misleading. The claim that the "living gospel," "prophetic teaching," or "continuing revelation" *overcomes, supersedes, or replaces* theology is a classic case of a false dichotomy; and though these invocations are often intended to serve as "conversation-stoppers" in LDS discourse, they ought to function as the opening act in theological reflection as to what these statements mean and how they fit and cohere with other ideas.[30]

---

28. Louis Midgley, "Prophetic Messages or Dogmatic Theology?" 48. See also Robert L. Millet and Joseph Fielding McConkie, *Doctrinal Commentary on the Book of Mormon*, 3 vols. (Salt Lake City: Bookcraft, 1991).

29. See, for example, Hans W. Frei, *The Eclipse of Biblical Narrative: A Study in Eighteenth and Nineteenth Century Hermeneutics* (New Haven, Conn.: Yale University Press, 1974); George A. Lindbeck, *The Nature of Doctrine: Religion and Theology in a Postliberal Age* (Philadelphia: Westminster Press, 1984); Stanley Hauerwas and L. Gregory Jones, eds., *Why Narrative? Readings in Narrative Theology* (Eugene, Ore.: Wipf & Stock Publishers, 1997); George W. Stroup, *The Promise of Narrative Theology: Recovering the Gospel in the Church* (Eugene, Ore.: Wipf & Stock Publishers, 1997); and William C. Placher, *Unapologetic Theology: A Christian Voice in a Pluralistic Conversation* (Louisville, Ky.: Westminster John Knox Press, 1989)

30. James Faulconer does nuance his description of theology in making his argument for the "atheological character" of Mormonism: "As I use the word 'theology' here, it begins with belief and uses of the methods of rational philosophy to give support to that belief: dogmatic, systematic, or rational theology." Recognizing the variety of methods and approaches to theology, he goes on to claim that "since rational theology is what most Latter-day Saints first think of when they think of theology, since dogmatic (in other words, church-sanctioned) theologies, are rational, and since I think at least some of what I say of rational or systematic theology may also apply to other theologies, I think it reasonable to

Whichever side one takes in the debate over the value of systematic accounts of Mormonism, there is agreement that all reflective inquiry must take account of the claim of ongoing revelation. Nevertheless, there is a vast theological literature on the very nature of revelation, and there are a variety of views within Mormonism regarding the necessary and sufficient conditions for LDS prophetic revelation, each of which could form the basis of a distinct "prophetic revelation" theology. Settling the question as to which of these options is most preferable may depend on the very sources under consideration.[31] For some, this circularity is vicious and thus unacceptable. For others, however, it comes part and parcel with the affirmation of continuing revelation.

The Challenge of Fideism

The last point leads us to consider the dynamics of religious belief in relation to our question of "faith seeking understanding." The debate over faith, reason, and revelation has been revitalized in recent years

---

focus on rational theology." James Faulconer, "Why a Mormon Won't Drink Coffee But Might Have a Coke: The Atheological Character of the Church of Jesus Christ of Latter-day Saints," *Element: The Journal of the Society for Mormon Philosophy and Theology* 2, no. 2 (Fall 2006), 21–22. Despite this qualification, the use of atheological language has been both helpful and a challenge for scholars of religion from other faith traditions who do not have an understanding of the theological landscape.

31. See Dulles, *Models of Revelation*; H. Richard Niebuhr, *The Meaning of Revelation* (New York: MacMillan Publishing Co., 1941); Kern Robert Trembath, *Divine Revelation: Our Moral Relation with God* (New York: Oxford University Press, 1991); Ronald F. Thiemann, *Revelation and Theology: The Gospel as Narrated Promise* (Notre Dame, Ind.: University of Notre Dame Press, 1985); John Baille, *The Idea of Revelation in Recent Thought* (New York: Columbia University Press, 1961); and William Abraham, *Divine Revelation and the Limits of Historical Criticism* (New York: Oxford University Press, 2000). Regarding Latter-day Saint approaches to revelation and doctrinal authority, see Nathan Oman, "A Defense of the Authority of Church Doctrine," *Dialogue: A Journal of Mormon Thought* 40, no. 4 (Winter 2007), and "Jurisprudence and the Problem of Church Doctrine" *Element: The Journal of the Society for Mormon Philosophy and Theology* 2:2 (Fall 2006); Loyd Ericson, "The Challenges of Defining Mormon Doctrine" *Element: The Journal of the Society for Mormon Philosophy and Theology* 3, no. 1&2 (Spring and Fall 2007): 69–90; Robert L. Millet, "What Do We Really Believe? Identifying Doctrinal Parameters within Mormonism," in *Discourses in Mormon Theology: Philosophical and Theological Possibilities*, eds. James M. McLachlan and Loyd Ericson (Salt Lake City: Greg Kofford Books, 2007), 265–81; Dallin H. Oaks, "Reason and Revelation," in *The Lord's Way* (Salt Lake City: Deseret Book Company, 1991), 45–76; and Janice Allred, "Do You Preach the Orthodox Religion?" in *God the Mother and Other Theological Essays* (Salt Lake City: Signature Books, 1997), 1–19.

and in directions that have implications for the way Latter-day Saints reflect on their beliefs.

At the heart of this debate has been the challenge of fideism, which can be broadly described as the position that religious understanding is ultimately grounded in faith and not on rational argument or scientific knowledge.[32] It is typically contrasted with rationalism, which can be described in its strongest form as the position that religious belief must be provable according to commonly accepted standards of rationality. The most influential form of rationalism is *evidentialism*, which argues that the justification for religious belief lies in proportioning one's belief to the evidence for or against a given proposition.[33] Antony Flew, in his landmark essay, "The Presumption of Atheism," states that if one wishes to establish that God exists, then "we have to have good grounds for believing that this is indeed so. Until and unless some such grounds are produced we have literally no reason at all for believing."[34] For Flew, these "good grounds" would be evidential in nature. Fideism, by contrast, maintains that religious belief is appropriately grounded in ways of understanding that are religious by nature.

The term *fideism* has been used to characterize a variety of specific positions, which vary in both form and strength. For this reason, it is important to properly identify and delineate the type of fideism I am interested in applying to certain Mormon epistemic practices. First, there is *radical fideism*, which is the position that faith is somehow *con-*

---

32. The *Compact Oxford English Dictionary* defines fideism as "the doctrine that knowledge depends on faith or revelation." The Blackwell Companion to the Philosophy of Religion describes fideism such that "faith does not need the support of reason, and should not seek it." Philip L. Quinn and Charles Taliaferro, *A Companion to Philosophy of Religion* (Oxford: Blackwell Publishers, 2000), 376. Michael Peterson, et al., describe fideism as "the view that religious belief-systems are not subject to rational evaluation." Michael Peterson, et al., *Reason and Religious Belief* (New York: Oxford University Press, 2003), 45.

33. Aquinas, following Aristotle, states that all knowledge is based upon either self-evident propositions or propositions that are what he calls "evident to the senses." Both classes of propositions are known immediately and are the foundation for all mediate knowledge. Mediate knowledge or *scientia* consists of either self-evident propositions or a body of propositions that are logically deduced from self-evident propositions. Locke states that the mark of a rational person lies in "not entertaining of any proposition with greater assurance than the proofs upon which it is built will warrant." Finally, Hume holds that a "wise man proportions his belief to the evidence."

34. Antony Flew, "The Presumption of Atheism," in *Contemporary Perspectives on Religious Epistemology*, eds. R. Douglas Geivett and Brendan Sweetman, (New York: Oxford University Press, 1992), 25.

trary to reason. One form of this approach is that reason is not merely irrelevant to justifying religious belief, but that its use is a positive barrier to gaining religious understanding.[35] Thinkers such as Tertullian, Kierkegaard, and Bayle, for example, have maintained that "Christian proclamations, most notably those of the Incarnation and the Trinity, do not merely look paradoxical but must genuinely be so, and that the believer must knowingly brush aside the claims that reason makes when faith confronts it."[36] This position may be contrasted with *moderate fideism*, which merely rejects the requirement to justify religious belief on rational grounds. Thus the reliance on any kind of natural theology or evidentialist apologetics is rendered unnecessary. Under this general category stand two well-known contemporary approaches to religious belief: Reformed epistemology and so-called Wittgensteinian fideism.[37] While both resist the fideist label, they do seek to demonstrate the misleading, incoherent, and question-begging nature of evidentialism as it applies to religious belief.

Reformed Epistemology and Fideism

To put the broad agenda of Reformed epistemology in its most simple terms, the movement seeks to demonstrate that Christians are justified in believing in God without being required to formulate arguments, cite evidence, or otherwise give their beliefs over to the demands of science. Of course they are responding to critics, who, as we noted above, point out the lack of evidence for religious claims and

---

35. I am relying on the work of Terrance Penelhum for these distinctions and characterizations. See his *Reason and Religious Faith* (Boulder, Co.: Westview Press, 1995), *God and Skepticism* (Dordrect: Reidel, 1983), and his essay on fideism in *A Companion to Philosophy of Religion*, eds. Philip L. Quinn and Charles Taliaferro (Oxford: Blackwell Publishers, 2000), 376–82.

36. Penelhum, *Reason and Religious Faith*, 379.

37. See Ibid., 376. Notable examples of these arguments are found in Alvin Plantinga, "Reason and Belief in God," in *Faith and Rationality: Reason and Belief in God* (South Bend, Ind.: University of Notre Dame Press, 1984); Alvin Plantinga, *Warranted Christian Belief* (New York: Oxford University Press, 2000), William Alston, *Perceiving God: The Epistemology of Religious Experience* (Ithaca, N.Y.: Cornell University Press, 1991); D. Z. Phillips, *Faith After Foundationalism* (Boulder, Co.: Westview Press, 1995); *Religion Without Explanation* (New York: St. Martin's Press, 1976); Nicholas Wolterstorff, *Reason Within the Bounds of Religion* (Grand Rapids, Mich.: Wm. B. Eerdmans Publishing Company, 1976); and Peter Winch, "Understanding a Primitive Society," in *Religion and Understanding* (Oxford: Blackwell, 1967).

yet demand firm and unshakable belief. These critics often characterize religious belief as irrational adherence to a cultural artifact. Over the past two decades or so, philosophers such as Alvin Plantinga, William Alston, and Nicholas Wolterstorff have been responding to these criticisms in very interesting ways that have implications, I believe, for how Latter-day Saint scholars could reflect on the dynamics of faith and belief in their tradition.[38] I will focus here on the work of Alvin Plantinga, as his writings present the most sustained argument against evidentialism. I'll concentrate my attention on those aspects of his argument that have the most relevance to the charge of fideism.

Beginning with his 1981 essay "Reason and Belief in God," Plantinga argues that theistic belief may be foundational for a person and justifiably so. By foundational, he means that, in the set of beliefs a person holds, certain beliefs are more firmly rooted and serve as the basis for others. These are what Plantinga calls "basic beliefs."[39] Obviously it is the case that millions of people believe in God in a basic way. The question is whether these beliefs are *properly* basic, whether a person is justified in maintaining them. In the philosophical tradition of foundationalism, candidates for properly basic beliefs are those that are either (1) logically self-evident, or (2) perceptually incorrigible. Since beliefs about God meet neither of these criteria, it is argued, they are

---

38. Though there has been some exceptionally rich and valuable work done by Latter-day Saints on the epistemology of religious belief, there remains, nevertheless, a considerable unevenness in the quality of the writings being produced. The literature in Reformed epistemology is much more developed, and for this reason I will focus on these arguments. To the extent Mormon treatments on faith, reason, and revelation are structurally similar to that of Reformed epistemology, they will share the strengths and weaknesses of the position. For further reading in the LDS literature, see Donald W. Parry, Daniel C. Peterson, and Stephen D. Ricks, eds., *Revelation, Reason, and Faith: Essays in Honor of Truman Madsen* (Provo, Utah: FARMS, 2002); Paul Y. Hoskissen, ed., *Historicity and the Latter-day Saint Scriptures* (Provo, Utah: Religious Studies Center, Brigham Young University, 2001); Robert L. Millet, ed., *"To Be Learned is Good If..."* (Salt Lake City: Bookcraft, 1987); Susan Easton Black, ed., *Expression of Faith: Testimonies of Latter-day Saint Scholars* (Provo, Utah: FARMS, 1996); Boyd K. Packer, "The Mantle is Far Far Greater Than the Intellect," *BYU Studies* 21, no. 3 (Summer 1981): 259–71; Dallin H. Oaks, *The Lord's Way* (Salt Lake City: Deseret Book Company, 1991); Sterling McMurrin, *Religion, Reason, and Truth: Historical Essays in the Philosophy of Religion* (Salt Lake City: University of Utah Press, 1982).

39. More precisely, Plantinga calls this set of beliefs one's "noetic structure" and defines it as follows: "A person's noetic structure is the set of propositions he believes, together with certain epistemic relations that hold among him and these propositions." Plantinga also introduces the term "depth of ingression" to describe the relative strength of noetic beliefs in relation to each other. See "Reason and Religious Belief," 48, 50.

not properly basic. Plantinga challenges this stringent requirement and argues that certain religious beliefs may be no more unjustified than those of memory or sense perception. On what basis should these receive exclusive priority in a person's belief structure? Even philosophers believe all sorts of things in a basic way that are neither self-evident nor incorrigible such as the existence of other minds, the existence of the past, and certain propositions based upon testimony. Hence, according to Plantinga, classical foundationalism is too restrictive and cannot live up to its own strictures in practice.[40]

Citing the Dutch theologian Herman Bavinck, Plantinga argues that "we cannot come to a knowledge of God on the basis of argument"; the Christian believer "should *start* from belief in God rather than from the premises of some argument whose conclusion is that God exists. What is it that makes those premises a better starting point anyway?"[41] Furthermore, why couldn't a person maintain that these basic beliefs about God originate from an innate awareness of divinity? Plantinga employs two concepts from the Calvinist tradition that resonate with Latter-day Saints. The first is called the *sensus divinitatis*, which was introduced by Calvin to describe "an instinct, a natural human tendency, a disposition . . . to form beliefs about God under a variety of situations."[42] In the *Institutes*, Calvin describes it as follows:

> There is within the human mind, and indeed by natural instinct, an awareness of divinity. This we take to be beyond controversy. To prevent anyone from taking refuge in the pretense of ignorance, God himself has implanted in all men a certain understanding of his divine majesty. . . . Since from the beginning of the world there has been no region, no city, in short, no household that could do without religion, there lies in this a tacit confession of a sense of deity inscribed in the hearts of all.[43]

---

40. Even more strongly, Plantinga argues that classical foundationalism is "self-referentially incoherent" because the proposition that *only self-evident and incorrigible beliefs are properly basic* is neither self-evident nor incorrigible.

41. Alvin Plantinga, "Reason and Belief in God," in *Faith and Rationality: Reason and Belief in God*, ed., Alvin Plantinga and Nicholas Wolterstorff (South Bend, Ind.: University of Notre Dame Press, 1984), 65.

42. Plantinga, *Warranted Christian Belief*, 171.

43. *Institutes of the Christian Religion*, I, iii, 1. See also Paul Helm, "John Calvin, the Sensus Divinitatis, and the Noetic Effects of Sin," *International Journal for Philosophy of Religion* 42, no. 2 (April 1998): 87–107.

Hence, the *sensus divinitatis*, being properly basic, is similar to perception, memory and other human constitutive faculties. Consequently, the argument goes something like this: "If belief in God is unjustified, then, so too with perceptual, memory, and *a priori* beliefs. But since these are all *evidently* rational, then so too with belief in God."[44]

As a form of general revelation, the *sensus divinitatis* compares in interesting ways with the LDS concept of the Light of Christ, which is a universal endowment described by Parley P. Pratt as the "intellectual light of our inward and spiritual organs, by which we reason, discern, judge, compare, comprehend, and remember the subjects within our reach."[45] In recent years, the Light of Christ has been described in terms of the innate human ability to recognize good and evil than as a cross-cultural awareness of divinity.

Plantinga's second concept is the *internal instigation of the Holy Spirit*, which functions according to intervening divine grace to produce beliefs, the propositional content of which are the central truths of Christianity, including trinity, incarnation, resurrection, and eternal life. Referring to this as a "special kind of cognitive instrument," Plantinga maintains that it is "not part of our constitution as we came from the hand of the Maker, but instead part of a special divine response to our (unnatural) sinful condition."[46] Applied to a Latter-day Saint context, the central truths in this set would include the restoration of the fullness of the gospel, continuing revelation through a living prophet, the truth of the Book of Mormon, etc. According to Plantinga, these two cognitive mechanisms form a "model" for human understanding that is no more unjustified than a model that views humans as rational animals that acquire knowledge exclusively by means of "perception and reflection."[47] But the question then remains: Why aren't belief in God and the central teachings of Christianity more widespread? In a word: *sin*, which is itself a component of the model described above. Plantinga states:

> Calvin's claim, then, is that God has created us in such a way that we have a strong tendency or inclination toward belief in him. This tendency has been in part overlaid or suppressed by sin.... This is the

---

44. Imran Aijaz, "An Assessment of Alvin Plantinga's Reformed Epistemology: A Review of *Warranted Christian Belief*," unpublished manuscript in the author's possession, 5.
45. Parley P. Pratt, *Key to the Science of Theology* (Salt Lake City, 1979), 25.
46. Plantinga, *Warranted Christian Belief*, 180.
47. He calls this model the "Aquinas/Calvin model." See ibid., 167–241.

natural human condition; it is because of our presently unnatural sinful condition that many of us find belief in God difficult or absurd.[48]

Why could this not be the guiding narrative for understanding the nature of human belief? It accounts for why some people so naturally believe in God and some do not. Plantinga attempts to place the burden of proof back onto the critic of religious belief to demonstrate in a non-question-begging way that a Christian model of human understanding is inferior to some species of rationalism.

Given this approach, one could articulate an analogous Latter-day Saint model of human understanding, which would include the Light of Christ, Gift of the Holy Ghost, faith, sin, etc. and adopt the structure of Plantinga's arguments as being applicable to these truths of the restored gospel of Jesus Christ. However, to the extent one accepts his arguments, one must accept the implications of his position and be open to the criticisms that follow.

Analysis of Reformed Epistemology

As might be expected, Plantinga's position has generated a tremendous amount of discussion and debate in both the theological and philosophical communities. The most interesting criticisms for our purposes center on the charge that Plantinga's Reformed epistemology is subject to the three aforementioned charges, namely: intellectual isolation, lack of mutual standards of rationality, and immunity from rational criticism. In the interest of brevity, we will focus attention on the criticism most relevant to our purposes, namely the possibility of rationally undermining or rebutting the central claims of Christianity.

By way of review, it can be said that because theistic belief can be properly basic, it can be rational, and because it can be rational, it can be justified. So in one obvious sense Plantinga's position is not fideistic precisely because it claims *rationality* for religious belief. Furthermore, he acknowledges there can be what he calls "defeaters" to Christian beliefs, which he describes as rational reasons for giving up a belief.[49]

---

48. Plantinga, "Reason and Belief in God," 66.
49. More specifically, a "defeater for a belief b, then, is another belief d such that, given my noetic structure, I cannot rationally hold b, given that I believe d." See Plantinga, *Warranted Christian Belief*, 361.

Suppose someone accepts belief in God as basic. Does it follow that he will hold this belief in such a way that no argument could move him or cause him to give it up? Will he not hold it come what may in spite of any evidence or argument with which he could be presented? Does he not thereby adopt a posture in which argument and other rational methods of settling disagreement are implicitly declared irrelevant? Surely not.[50] But has not Plantinga already eliminated the genuine possibility of defeaters given his description of the *sensus divinitatis* and internal instigation of the Holy Spirit? Given his own description, *no* amount of evidence or argument will defeat these beliefs when a conflict arises because, on Plantinga's own account, a person is justified in siding with the Holy Spirit, come what may from reason. "Probability with respect to public evidence," he states, "is neither necessary nor sufficient for warranted Christian belief."[51] Furthermore, it is not the case for him "that the theist and atheist agree as to what reason delivers, the theist then going on to accept the existence of God by faith; there is, instead, disagreement in the first place as to what are the deliverances of reason."[52]

At this point one may reasonably ask of Plantinga: given this approach, what could *possibly* count as a "counterargument or counterevidence" to these beliefs? It appears that he has cut the feet out from under his denial of fideism such that evidence and argument may have no relevance to a religious belief despite the possibility of widespread consensus that the belief is irrational to maintain. One may respond, as Plantinga does, that consensus as to what counts as a rational defeater may differ depending on which group (or individual) you are considering. Of course—but in order for his openness to counterargument or counterevidence to make any sense, he has to appeal to a concept of rationality that is broader than that of the religious community that holds

---

50. Plantinga, "Reason and Belief in God," 82; emphasis added. In response to the Great Pumpkin Objection, Platinga states that "there is the claim that if belief in God is really properly basic with respect to warrant, then arguments and objections will not be relevant to it; it will be beyond rational scrutiny and will be insulated from objections and defeaters. . . . But obviously objection and argument are relevant to theistic belief: therefore, it isn't warrant-basic. . . . So it is not true, in general, that if a belief is held in a basic way, then it is immune to argument and rational evaluation; why, therefore, think it must hold for theistic belief?" Plantinga, *Warranted Christian Belief*, 343–44.

51. Alvin Plantinga, "Rationality and Public Evidence: A Reply to Richard Swinburne," *Religious Studies* 37, no. 2 (June 2001): 221.

52. Plantinga, "Reason and Belief in God," 90.

the belief in question.⁵³ Consider the example of biblical scholarship to demonstrate the point.

Plantinga maintains that, because Christians can know the truth of what really happened in the Bible through the internal instigation of the Holy Spirit, the results of critical biblical scholarship may ultimately be inconsequential. An argument familiar in Mormon apologetic circles is that because Christian belief and higher criticism begin from different presuppositions, the outcomes will inevitably be different and often incompatible; and because Christian presuppositions are based upon basic beliefs about God and his workings in the world, they are not subject to counterargument or counterevidence.⁵⁴ Furthermore, since skeptical scholars disagree among themselves, their arguments are open to doubt and their assumptions are questionable, which is all the more reason to reject them in favor of beliefs grounded in the Holy Spirit.⁵⁵ Consider the following quote from Plantinga:

> [T]here is available a source of warranted true belief, a way of coming to see the truth of these teachings, that is quite independent of historical study: Scripture/the internal instigation of the Holy Spirit/ faith. . . . By virtue of this process, an ordinary Christian, one quite innocent of historical studies, the ancient languages, the intricacies of textual criticism, the depths of theology, and all the rest can nevertheless come to know that these things are, indeed true. . . . Neither the Christian community nor the ordinary Christian is at the mercy of the expert here; they can know these truths directly.⁵⁶

---

53. Plantinga does make this appeal in his statement that "[y]ou give me a defeater in the relevant sense only if you propose to me a belief which is such that a rational sophisticated believer . . . would accept it upon being presented with it." Plantinga, *Warranted Christian Belief*, 366. However, my point is that he has undercut the very appeal to the "rational sophisticated believer."

54. See for example, Robert Millet, *A Different Jesus: The Christ of the Latter-day Saints* (Grand Rapids, Mich.: Eerdmans, 2005).

55. See Aijaz, "An Assessment of Plantinga's Reformed Epistemology," 10. Furthermore, couldn't someone argue that because there is so much disagreement regarding central elements of the faith within the Christian community that are said to come from the Holy Spirit, that we have reason to reject the internal instigation of the Holy Spirit as a method for finding truth? If Plantinga can appeal to the inconclusive nature of biblical scholarship as a means to reject the method upon which it is based, then the same could be said of the method upon which he relies to the extent that it is inconclusive.

56. Plantinga, *Warranted Christian Belief*, 374.

It appears then that the Christian may reject any possible rational defeater that is in conflict with what is perceived to come by way of the Holy Spirit. Despite this, Plantinga does not eliminate the possibility of defeaters when he states in the same chapter that

> [I]t is possible, at any rate in the broadly logical sense, that just by following ordinary historical reason, using the methods of historical investigation endorsed or enjoined by the deliverances of reason, someone should find powerful evidence against central elements of the Christian faith; if this happened, Christians would face a genuine faith-reason clash.[57]

However, because evidence of this sort has not emerged, Christians need not worry (at least at this point) about having to face a conflict between the deliverances of the Spirit and powerful evidence to the contrary. At least two questions emerge here. First, based upon his own account of direct confirmation by way of the Holy Spirit, why couldn't someone reject *any* evidence that came by way of "ordinary historical reason"? If one's very conception of "the deliverances of reason" ultimately comes by way of the Holy Spirit (including that the Bible is authoritative and that the Holy Spirit has guided the Christian church ensuring that its central teachings are true), then *any* evidence that conflicts with the teachings of the Bible may be rejected out of hand.[58] Thus I would argue that Plantinga has, on the one hand, effectively eliminated the *condition* for the possibility of *genuine* defeaters to Christian belief, while on the other hand, maintaining their real possibility. If I am correct about this inconsistency, it has serious implications for his project as a whole.

In short, on the one hand Plantinga maintains that reason could come up with arguments or evidence that would defeat religious belief, but on the other hand he appears to eliminate the need for a religious believer to entertain possible defeaters due to the spiritual grounding of beliefs. His position seems to imply that "defeaters provide no problem for those who are convinced of the truth of Christian theism, even if all the evidence goes against it. Thus, Plantinga's contention of the falsifiability of Christian theism, and his criticisms of various defeaters, seems to be only a pretense."[59] In this way, he can keep central religious beliefs immune from criticism while maintaining that he is not a fideist.

---

57. Ibid., 420.
58. Ibid., 380.
59. Aijaz, "An Assessment of Plantinga's Reformed Epistemology," 8.

This kind of fideism is best revealed, I believe, by Nicholas Wolterstorff, in the following passage:

> From the fact that it is not rational for some person to believe that God exists it does not follow that he ought to give up that belief. Rationality is only *prima facie* justification; lack of rationality, only *prima facie* impermissibility. Perhaps, in spite of its irrationality for him, the person ought to continue believing that God exists. Perhaps it is our duty to believe more firmly that God exists than any proposition which conflicts with this, and/or more firmly than we believe that a certain proposition *does* conflict with it. Of course, for a believer who is a member of the modern Western intelligentsia to have his theistic convictions prove nonrational is to be put into a deeply troubling situation. There is a biblical category which applies to such a situation. It is a *trial*. May it not also be that sometimes the nonrationality of one's conviction that God exists is a trial, to be endured?[60]

Here Wolterstorff gives voice to one way in which arguments against Christian belief are subsumed under religious categories. One need not recognize a defeater as such because one is justified in holding religious beliefs more firmly than one holds to scientific evidence or logical argument. Thus, religious convictions may trump rational evidence in cases of conflict. If certain evidence does come to place a person's religious faith in doubt, there are religious narratives and categories to deal with this situation as well.

If this analysis is correct, then Plantinga's Reformed epistemology does not escape the fideistic label. In the end his approach appears to be susceptible to the traditional criticisms described above, namely intellectual isolation, lack of mutual standards of rationality, and immunity from rational criticism. The possibility of defeaters and the *prima facie* status of justification, though given lip-service, does not need to be taken seriously by Christians who have had the truths of the gospel confirmed by the Holy Spirit.

Implications for Latter-day Saint Epistemology

I believe that the way in which Plantinga wrestles with these issues and tensions is instructive for Latter-day Saint philosophy and theol-

---

60. Nicholas Wolterstorff, "Can Belief in God Be Rational?" in *Faith and Rationality: Reason and Belief in God*, eds. Alvin Plantinga and Nicholas Wolterstorff (Notre Dame, Ind.: University of Notre Dame Press, 1983), 177.

ogy. For example, the mantra "seek learning, even by study and also by faith" is often utilized to argue in favor of something like the *complementarity thesis*, namely that faith and reason work effectively together in the acquisition of knowledge.[61] A careful observation, however, of some of Mormonism's central epistemic practices reveals strong fideist tendencies. Reason, argument, and evidence are ultimately subsumed under religious categories in nearly *all* cases of perceived conflict. Evidence inconsistent with perceived orthodoxy is very often (a) rejected out of hand as irrelevant to belief, (b) held in abeyance in anticipation of subsequent evidence that will resolve the conflict, or (c) the object of cognitive dissonance.

These observations are not meant to imply that Mormons should give themselves over to some form of rationalism. Instead we should focus our attention on the set of epistemic practices that informs *how* the faith/reason or reason/revelation split is negotiated. Merely to say that Mormons value both reason and faith is theoretically uninteresting. What is interesting and relevant, however, is how, in practice, this relation is negotiated in cases of perceived conflict. These practices show what rationality comes to in these contexts. Latter-day Saints cannot, on the one hand, claim to share with some broader community the same conception of reason, and then, on the other hand, under pressure of criticism, appeal to an idiosyncratic conception of rationality to preserve doctrinal orthodoxy. We see this dynamic at work in Plantinga's philosophy and, I believe, in our own tradition as Mormons wrestle with what it means to be rational beings while maintaining theologically "scandalous" beliefs.

---

61. Dallin Oaks, in *The Lord's Way*, however, argues that reason can never trump revelation. Fair enough, but this is very nearly a truism. The real question is a Lockean one: whether something is indeed a revelation. Once it is established that something is a revelation from God, who is going to argue except the most promethean among us?

4

Restoration or Rebirth: Mormon and American Options of Authenticity

Douglas J. Davies, *University of Durham, UK*

It is a personal pleasure to contribute to David Paulsen's *festschrift*. Our friendship commenced when, under the auspices of the Richard L. Evans Chair in Religious Understanding, he hosted me at Brigham Young University more than a decade ago. While I neither want to embarrass our subject nor exaggerate the case, the topic pursued here—authenticity—is one that aptly reflects the man we celebrate. It also pinpoints a significant issue within religious studies that facilitates a partial response to David Paulsen and Cory Walker's extensive critique of my *Mormon Culture of Salvation*[1] in their article in the *FARMS Review of Books*.[2] Grateful for their appreciative attention to my work in general, I have decided to respond not to their major criticism of my understanding of grace but to the issue they raise over my evaluation of spiritual rebirth in Mormonism. In so doing, I focus on patriarchal blessings as a condensation and personalization of key LDS themes that furnish a sense of authenticity that obviates any necessity for Latter-day Saints to engage in born-again language.

Paulsen and Walker argue, "Even if some Latter-day Saint authors avoid or have, in the past, avoided such locutions as *saved* or *born again*, such avoidance is merely nominal, not conceptual."[3] I think it more conceptual than nominal. Still, they qualify their assertion with both the note that Mormons and Evangelicals may well not "mean the same thing by them,"[4] and by

---

1. Douglas J. Davies, *The Mormon Culture of Salvation: Force, Grace, Glory* (Aldershot, England: Ashgate, 2000).
2. David L. Paulsen and Cory G. Walker, "Work, Worship and Grace," *The FARMS Review of Books* 18, no. 2 (2006): 83–177.
3. Ibid., 110; italics in the original.
4. Ibid., 111.

saying that they do not wish to "imply that such locutions are commonplace amongst Latter-day Saints."[5] Indeed, they add, "Most would probably resist explaining their spiritual experiences as experiences of being 'born again.'"[6] Why might that be? This question might prompt others to ponder why some contemporary Latter-day Saints, not least BYU professor and former Richard L. Evans Chair Robert L. Millet, are increasingly happy to use "born-again" language in their religious work. Perhaps this chapter will help them see potential solutions to what is obviously a moot point.[7]

I understand that Paulsen and Walker argue as they do in order to emphasize the vitality of grace in Mormon thought; nevertheless, I think there are identifiable reasons for LDS resistance to the "born-again" idiom, reasons that have less to do with theological debates over grace as such and more to do with an alternative route of intimacy with the divine: an intimacy that has its own way of understanding grace. My proposition is that Mormons gain a sense of "authenticity" primarily through the notion of restoration, a notion accessed by ritual-symbols—including patriarchal blessings, the main route explored below. Other routes include vicarious baptism, itself a constraint upon the born-again motif. Protestant Evangelicals, by contrast, gain authenticity through the notion of "The Gospel," accessed via spiritual rebirth. Though necessarily simplified for argument's sake, this exercise continues my long-term descriptive analysis of Mormon factors partnered by a degree of comparative theology which, in context, may contribute to David's more recent work—typified in his jointly edited book with Donald W. Musser—that takes Mormon thought into wider Christian theological traditions.[8]

Authenticity

From a sociological perspective, it is obvious that the notion of authenticity is foundational for much of religious life, while its lineaments often differ from group to group. Gerhard Ebeling makes the point,

---

5. Ibid.
6. Ibid.
7. Robert L. Millett, *Christ-Centered Living* (Salt Lake City: Bookcraft, 1994), 37, 81. See also Robert L. Millet and Gregory C. V. Johnson, *Bridging the Divide: The Continuing Conversation between a Mormon and an Evangelical* (New York: Monkfish Book Publishing Company, 2007), 89–91.
8. Donald W. Musser and David L. Paulsen, eds., *Mormonism in Dialogue with Contemporary Christian Theologies* (Macon, Ga.: Mercer University Press, 2007).

theologically, that "faith cannot be made explicit at all without getting into the issue of diverse conceptions."[9] Indeed, awareness over how authenticity is configured within different religious traditions and academic conventions will foster understanding and help reduce unrecognized prejudice. In American LDS history, for example, the very distinction between "truth" and "conviction" has not always been clear. For example, Bette Norvit Evans, in considering the Supreme Court's judgment in the case of *Davis v. Beason*, argues that "polygamy violated 'the enlightened sentiment of mankind,'" notwithstanding "the pretence of religious conviction."[10] One person's "pretence" is another's obvious reality.

Our brief concern with authenticity must, perforce, ignore sociological issues of trust and psychological-philosophical problems of transparency and opacity in both mutual and self-knowledge[11] while, nevertheless, highlighting the notion of "spirituality," a term I have advocated within Mormon studies since the publication of my volume *Mormon Spirituality*. There, I emphasized "the very human yearning for a quality of experience and fulfillment,"[12] a view sympathetic to Northrop Frye's description of reality as the sense of "otherness, the sense of something not ourselves," without which being human would hardly be possible.[13] For, whatever else authenticity involves, I take it to include just such a "yearning" contextualized by "otherness." This is not to say that religious individuals or groups will always be authentic, nor that some will grieve over their own failures while others continue in duplicity, but it does highlight the emotional force underlying the goals widely desired by religious traditions.

---

9. Gerhard Ebeling, *The Study of Theology*, trans. D. A. Priebe (1975; rpt., London: Collins, 1979), 39.

10. Bette Norvit Evans, *Interpreting the Free Exercise of Religion: The Constitution in American Pluralism* (Chapel Hill: University of North Carolina Press, 1997), 68.

11. See Joseph Luft, *Of Human Interaction* (Palo Alto, Calif.: Mayfield Publishing Corporation, 1969), 14, 36, 138, for issues of sensitivity over mutual knowledge, and S. M. Jourard, *Self-Disclosure: An Experimental Analysis of the Transparent Self* (New York: Wiley, 1971), 53, for differences in self-disclosure amongst different Christian denominations.

12. Douglas J. Davies, *Mormon Spirituality: Latter-day Saints in Wales and Zion* (Nottingham, Eng.: University of Nottingham Press, 1987), 18.

13. Northrop Frye, *The Secular Scripture: A Study of the Structure of Romance* (Cambridge, Mass.: Harvard University Press, 1976), 60. See also Douglas J. Davies, *Anthropology and Theology* (Oxford, Eng.: Berg, 2002), 29, 48, 50, for "inner-otherness."

American Authenticity

Culturally speaking, the desire for authenticity has been a significant force within American religious history from its inception, long concretized in the Puritan "city on a hill" motif and evident in the Great Awakenings. The Second Awakening's emphasis on "the intentional making of a life through the self-determining power of the will," when "Calvinism was transformed into evangelical Arminianism," and "choice" replaced "the sovereignty of God," offers a valuable background against which to consider both authenticity and the emphasis of an emerging Mormon spirituality upon personal agency.[14] So, too, with sacred scriptures and the dramatically important role of "faith in reading," with the "textual piety" of nineteenth- and twentieth-century American Protestants accentuated in Mormonism's Standard Works.[15] LDS authenticity was also inextricably grounded in individual proofs, or "testimonies," of the truth of the Book of Mormon and its root prophetic source, Joseph Smith. The "sure text" of Protestant desire was not only replicated in the Book of Mormon but also complemented by a living prophet.[16] The dynamic of this pattern of authenticity tended to render spiritual rebirth a marginal category.

Concerning this issue of authenticity of identity, we must not "ignore the subtlety" inherent in notions such as rebirth nor, indeed, of revivalism, as George Thomas has quite properly argued in accounting for "the millennial ideal of the Kingdom of God" as the "common bond of North American Christianity."[17] Part of the subtlety demanding attention is the fundamental question of why so many early and contemporary Americans in revivalist and general Evangelical circles claimed to be "born-again" while most Mormons did not make such claims. This is especially tantalizing when Mormonism is held to be the quintessential

---

14. Julius H. Rubin, *Religious Melancholy and Protestant Experience in America* (New York: Oxford University Press, 1994), 131.

15. Pamela E. Klassen, "Textual Healing: Mainstream Protestants and the Therapeutic Text, 1900–1925," *Church History: Studies in Christianity and Culture* 75, no. 4 (2006): 810.

16. See Norman O. Brown, *Love's Body* (New York: Random House, 1966), 192–95, for Protestant literalism and *"die feste Schrift."*

17. George M. Thomas, *Revivalism and Cultural Change* (Chicago: University of Chicago Press, 1989), 74.

American religion or an "American original."[18] Part of the answer lies in Thomas's understanding of "citizens reborn as moral agents," whose "personal rebirth is associated with the rebirth and empowering of the nation within the world system." However, his application of this for Latter-day Saints is weak and too group-introverted.[19] This born-again motif is, for example, relatively irrelevant as a social marker for most European or other Europe-derived societies, except for restricted moments of revivalism. This suggests that spiritual rebirth affords a potential medium for authenticity of the self in societies undergoing rapid growth or dramatic social change, or in rootless individuals. The consequential issue is why Mormons have very largely avoided the rhetoric of rebirth. My tentative answer is that Mormons prefer alternatives that affirm the Restoration while ensuring a distinctive identity against its Protestant matrix. Space precludes discussion both of whether Mormons are atypically or quintessentially American in their attitude towards being born-again and of US fundamentalism, which is radically related to rebirth motifs but also involves religious-political issues that are marginal to this chapter.[20]

Re-birth Spirituality

The idea of spiritual rebirth, especially in its familiar motif of being born-again, has long held a prized place within Evangelical spirituality.[21] Bebbington places it first as conversionism, followed by activism, Biblicism, and crucicentrism within the "quadrilateral of priorities that is the basis of Evangelicalism."[22] Often aligned with revivalism and, for example, with the rise of Methodism and the "campaign" style of evangelism in the early nineteenth century, spiritual rebirth often served as a

---

18. Paul K. Conkin, *American Originals: Homemade Varieties of Christianity* (Chapel Hill: University of North Carolina Press, 1997). See also Harold Bloom, *The American Religion: The Emergence of the Post-Christian Nation* (New York: Simon and Schuster, 1992), 81.

19. Thomas, *Revivalism and Cultural Change*, 159.

20. Philip Melling, *Fundamentalism in America: Millennialism, Identity, and Militant Religion* (Edinburgh: Edinburgh University Press, 1999), 104–34.

21. See Leslie Reynolds, *Mormons in Transition* (Salt Lake City: Gratitude Press, 1996), 68–70, for an Evangelical convert seeking to convert Mormons to Evangelical Christianity.

22. David W. Bebbington, *Evangelicalism in Modern Britain: A History from the 1730s to the 1980s* (London: Routledge, 1989), 3.

prime mark of authenticity of religious identity, marked by explicit forms of experience and of social acknowledgement in and through testimony meetings. It was grounded in a theology of the Fall that yielded a negative identity for sinners, whose access to divine grace was only through Christ's substitutionary atonement, made effective by the indwelling of the Holy Spirit. The feeling-states associated with this process involved a sense of freedom from sin and guilt, and an entry into a "new life." It mattered little who the preacher might be or, indeed, within which religious denomination this message was accepted. The Holy Spirit, as such, knew no denominational boundaries, itself a logical correlate of the Reformation's protest against Catholicism's possessive control of absolution and grace. Even so, there was something of an American undercurrent that prompted Protestants "to find their self-identification in their denomination rather than in the broader Christian community,"[23] a factor classically criticized by theologian Richard Niebuhr.[24]

Classically, Protestant Evangelicalism speaks of the Holy Spirit or, sometimes, of Jesus Christ as transforming an essentially worldly person who, in Pauline terms, "lives according to the flesh" (Rom. 8:13) to one who will "walk by the Spirit" (Gal. 5:25). A significant stream of Pauline and Johannine thinking is driven by this idea, with believers' very bodies being viewed as temples in which God's Spirit dwells (Gal. 5:16, 1 Cor. 3:16). One is reborn through the Spirit just as one is born physically through the waters of the womb (John 3:5–6). In John's Gospel, believers have the Spirit "breathed out" upon them and are promised the Holy Spirit as their teacher (John 20:22, Luke 12:12). Protestant appropriation of this style of theological discourse emphasizing re-birth is often aligned with a new sense of life-experience that re-evaluates the past life as "old," "sinful," or unregenerate. Protestant culture history has often interpreted the re-birth language of the Bible through the conversions narrated in the lives of great leaders such as Augustine, Luther, and Wesley, and has sought a similar metamorphosis of self by preaching conversion experience to its youthful members.[25]

---

23. William E. Nawyn, *American Protestantism's Response to Germany's Jews and Refugees* (Ann Arbor: University of Michigan Research Press, 1981), 185.

24. H. Richard Niebuhr, *The Social Sources of Denominationalism* (New York: Harper and Row, 1929).

25. See Bebbington, *Evangelicalism in Modern Britain*, for the mean age of conversion of U.K. teenagers between 1780 and 1900.

But Mormonism, emerging amidst much conversionist rhetoric, did not take this avenue. Its use of conversion-language became rare, its absence constituting one expression of boundary maintenance against its Protestant background. Early LDS emphasis lay not upon instant transformations of the self by a miraculous intervention of the Holy Spirit but upon a process of change both in this life and beyond. While firmly retaining the language of faith, repentance, baptism, and the conferral of the Holy Ghost by the laying on of hands, faith was stressed as an internal alertness of what was, after all, the eternal intelligence of a person. Such alertness allowed the LDS believer to heed the religious message of the Restoration and see it as a gospel of wide import, including a series of rites—the ordinances of the Gospel—that would lead one through life, death, and resurrection into an eternity of exaltation. While often using language of salvation or being saved, the word "salvation" itself was transformed so that a Mormon's goal should be that of "exaltation" as a progressively divine being within a "celestial kingdom." The faith involved in that progression necessitated a firm, ongoing dedication to ethical practice and a growing knowledge of God through LDS principles. Just how a sense of the miraculous entered this process is significant when comparing Mormonism and Protestant Evangelicalism. Practically speaking, Christ's most significant coming was not to individual hearts but in his presence at Joseph Smith's First Vision. The authenticity of salvation lay precisely in that matrix of the Restoration, and was reinforced as such when the Second Coming, anticipated in earliest Mormonism, did not materialize.

Mormonism developed a kind of pragmatism concerning the dynamics of faith. Just as young Joseph sought after the truth and the "true church," so should all others. Faith engages the competence of an eternal intelligence now "finding" itself in this probationary period of mortality. While the individual may encounter "miracles, healings, tongues, interpretations of tongues"[26]—as with Joseph and his visions—such supernatural events are contextualized as of secondary importance. The prime miracle is the Church itself. In comparison to Protestant discourse on the body as a temple of the Holy Spirit—a concept perfectly consonant with spiritual rebirth—the LDS view not only advocated a practical-ethical care of the body through its Word of Wisdom texts but also added the literal dimension of concrete temples that were holy

---

26. Articles of Faith, 7; Doctrine and Covenants 46: 11–27.

to the Lord and in which the devotee could enhance personal religious experience. The existential process of the "finding of self" was, for early Mormonism, allied with its discovery of a place of refuge and flourishing, enshrined in the notion of Zion and symbolized by its temples, priesthoods, and ordinances. The notion of Zion responded to what William Dean posed as "the problem for Americans," namely, how "to recognize and respond to the openness of their situation" and how to "subdue the openness of American space."[27] Temples brought all space within sacred walls. One sharp alternative to this form of the finding of self lay precisely in the act of Protestant rebirth: to be born-again was one means—albeit more fragile—of responding to the openness of a wide world as the Savior of all comes to "me" personally. Again, the Restoration is relevant here, for it brings Christ to America in one of his resurrection appearances.

Consequently, as far as Mormonism and its American world of origin—and, indeed, the America of today—is concerned, the concept of spiritual rebirth is of particular importance for understanding the relationships among Mormon, Protestant Evangelical, and other forms of Christianity. For most Catholic-sacramental traditions, rebirth is aligned with the rite of baptism. The initiate turns from evil and the devil, is washed from sin, symbolically dies with Christ in the watery-grave of baptism, and rises to newness of life, reborn by the Spirit. Theologically speaking, the act of confirmation—a partner rite of baptism—expresses that gift of the Holy Spirit. In such traditions, there is no expectation of an immediate and emotional sense of changed experience. The Catholic Church brings people to Christ and embraces them within the community of grace and salvation; further sacraments await them as they progress in faith in love. That image is quite different from the often-used image of being "born-again," which, in many Protestant-Evangelical worlds, assumes an emotional experience associated with repentance and an awareness of gaining a personal relationship with the resurrected Jesus Christ practically irrespective of ecclesial rites.

Here, as in many other contexts, Mormons resemble Catholics more than they do Protestants, as evident in the language of Christ "coming into the heart," or becoming someone's "personal Savior." While Nancy Ammerman sees the goal of this form of evangelism as

---

27. William Dean, *The Religious Critic in American Culture* (Albany: State University of New York Press, 1994), 178.

being "central to the way Conservative Protestants describe themselves" and aligns it with the funding of LDS missionary work, real caution is needed in the nuanced understanding of "mission" in each case.[28] Not only so, for the "born-again" motif can also carry other associations, as in some later twentieth-century African-American and other Evangelical circles in which to have a sense of being "born-again" is identified with "rights and privileges" of "personal empowerment" respecting health and wealth. Milman Harrison identifies this sense of religious privilege as not unlike the more "secular forms of transition ideologies" embedded within American notions of progress and manifest destiny.[29] Certainly, the early "white" American sense of being in a favored covenant with God was much enhanced within the LDS ideology of the Restoration of primal religious truth that long ante-dated the Founding Fathers (taking itself back to the biblical Patriarchs), but it did not develop in terms of any "prosperity gospel" idioms applied at a more personal level. Nor was this privileged access founded on spiritual rebirth. Latter-day Saints were more likely to speak of being blessed by God when they faithfully practiced paying their tithing, but the basis for this was more that of faithfulness to the overall organization and leadership of the Church than to any personal born-again status.

More recently, though Mormons might to a degree align themselves with the "Moral Majority" fostered by the "new right" in American Evangelicalism in the late 1970s and 1980s, this too was because of elements of family likeness grounded in a strong opposition to secularism, in support for Israel and the Jews, and in a commitment to conservative ethics, rather than in any shared sense of spiritual rebirth.[30]

Psychological Issues

In its day, William James's text on religious experience provided an influential psychological documentation of religious conversion.[31]

---

28. Nancy Taton Ammerman, *Pillars of Faith: American Congregations and Their Partners* (Berkeley: University of California Press, 2005), 138.

29. Milman F. Harrison, *Righteous Riches: The World Faith Movement in Contemporary African American Religion* (Oxford: Oxford University Press, 2005), 148, 157.

30. R. J. Neuhaus and Michael Cromartie, *Piety and Politics: Evangelicals and Fundamentalists Confront the World* (Washington, D.C.: Ethics and Public Policy Center, 1987), 81, 88.

31. William James, *The Varieties of Religious Experience* (London: Longmans, 1902).

His differentiation between the "once-born" and the "twice-born" individual, or between the "religion of healthy mindedness" and the "religion of the sick soul," offered a useful means of distinguishing between more Catholic and Protestant forms of interpreting rebirth. However, the "twice-born" or "born-again" category remains deeply problematic as a phrase whose familiarity may be deceptive to the casual reader. In many respects, this concept of spiritual rebirth is profoundly strange, so much so that it is understandable that religious people have often interpreted it as near miraculous—and certainly supernatural—in origin. Here, methodology becomes important, especially when it can account for the reasons why people in particular groups or contexts should wish to be born again. Because this question has received much less social-scientific theoretical attention than it merits, I will offer a tentative but brief comment grounded in the fact that life experience, especially of pain and loss, has often engendered a sense of dissatisfaction, driving self-conscious and morally aware persons to ask if there is not a better world than this one.

Creative religious founders have produced their own depiction of just what that world might be in ideas of "salvation," integrating theological-philosophical rationality with intuitive capacities of insight-generation to yield a type of wisdom in life. Inherently human problem-solving capacities or discovery procedures help humanity adapt to physical and moral environments and yield a sense of transcendence over a world deemed imperfect.[32] The fact that different cultures achieve this in varying ways is to be expected, but as a method of inquiry it helps to relate phenomena that are otherwise seen as distinct. The Buddhist sense of the bitterness of life that may lead to an enlightenment and sense of freedom from attachments to causes of distress, or the Hindu and Sikh notions of the illusoriness of the world and the potential for gaining release from its bonds, reflect this process. The Jewish, Christian, and Islamic hope for some form of righteous Kingdom of God set against the unrighteousness of human life offers another set of similar possibilities. So, too, numerous tribal societies initiate young people—often men but sometimes women—into adulthood by teaching the duties and mysteries of life's hardships and the means of coping with them. To discuss the idea of re-birth without acknowledging its potential similarity to the dynamics

---

32. C. D. Batson and W. L. Ventis, *The Religious Experience* (Oxford, England: Oxford University Press, 1982).

of change and the gaining of transformative insight in other traditions would be reprehensible.[33] Here, Wilhelm Dupré's definition of religion as "an achievement through which man becomes capable of bearing the burden of existence" is germane.[34]

Mormon Experience

Joseph Smith's engagement with the burden of existence began with the available language of Protestantism concerning sin and redemption, developed into Adventist apocalyptic, and flourished in a mystical ritualism, but it did not embrace the rhetoric of rebirth. Book of Mormon references to rebirth—as cited by Paulsen and Walker[35]—echo biblical usage and reflect the deep influence of John's Gospel on Joseph Smith, especially on his earlier thought.[36]

That individual spiritual transformation was appreciated by early Latter-day Saints is exemplified in the case of Willard Richards. Joseph Smith's partner in jail when Joseph was killed, Richards later became an Apostle and died a decade later. His obituary speaks of one who had been refused admission to the Congregational Church and had even believed that he had "committed the unpardonable sin." It also tells of a "change that swept over him" upon becoming a Saint, which "showed forth the reality of a new birth personified in his subsequent life,"[37] but such a reference is unusual amidst LDS accounts of changes that brought about an emotional sense of the truth of the Church's message and organization. Here, two dimensions of change need comment: one

---

33. Douglas J. Davies, *Meaning and Salvation in Religious Studies* (Leiden, Netherlands: Brill, 1984), 69–76.

34. Wilhelm Dupré, *Religion in Primitive Culture: A Study in Ethnophilosophy* (The Hague, Netherlands: Mouton, 1975), 47.

35. Paulsen and Walker, "Work, Worship and Grace," 110–11, 163–77. Their fourteen-page appendix on references to being "saved" is largely irrelevant to the "rebirth" motif.

36. That background is, I think, also far more persuasive than Clyde Forsberg's assertion that "all the talk in the Book of Mormon concerning the 'new birth' can also be seen as Masonic," a proposition I cannot explore here as an alternative root of authenticity. See Clyde Forsberg Jr., *Equal Rites: The Book of Mormon, Masonry, Gender, and American Culture* (New York: Columbia University Press, 2004), 148.

37. Orson Spencer, *Latter-day Saints' Millennial Star* 16, no. 23 (June 10, 1854): 354.

concerning individual identity and organization, and another dealing with corporate identity and boundary marking.

Individual Identity and Organization

The classification of personal change depends upon whether stress is placed upon the institution framing change or upon the experience itself. Catholic and Orthodox Churches favor the former, and many Protestant and especially Evangelical churches favor the latter. Traditionally speaking, the Catholic Church sees itself as the primary vehicle for salvation, established by Christ and maintaining authority through its apostolic succession. While the religious experiences of members—not least of mystics, martyrs, and saints—help to validate the organization and confer upon it a sense of authenticity, it is that church's teaching authority, validity of priesthood, and sacraments that ensure the grace of salvation. By contrast, the experience-focused pattern of individual experience evident in some Protestant forms of spirituality gives the life of the individual before God prior claim over that of any church organization. This would be clear, for example, in the best known of twentieth-century Protestant evangelists, Dr. Billy Graham, whose message of repentance, faith, and personal commitment to Christ was not tied to membership in any specific church. While, doubtless, he would have preferred it to be Evangelical in nature, his prime concern was with individual rebirth and Christ and not with denominational adherence.

Latter-day Saints have followed the Catholic and not the Protestant pattern. Mormon missionaries, for example, are highly unlikely to be unconcerned over any convert's subsequent denominational allegiance. Indeed, LDS missionary experience itself has been described as emphasizing the "transience of persons and the priority and continuity of Church officers and roles."[38] The very historical emergence of Mormonism resulted through Joseph Smith's primal religious experience (which later came to be identified and canonized as the First Vision) and took shape amidst issues of Church authenticity. Indeed, Joseph's "conversion experience" was not documented as a "new-birth" but as a vision that led to the birth of a new church organization.

---

38. Keith Parry, "The Missionary Companion," in *Contemporary Mormonism: Social Science Perspectives*, eds. Marie Cornwall, Tim B. Heaton, and Lawrence A. Young (Urbana: University of Illinois Press, 2001), 200.

At the heart of that church was the notion of priesthood, held not simply as an ideology but as an organizational practice, which, after Joseph's death, took precedence over the charisma of any particular individual. This phenomenon is clearly exemplified in Orson Hyde's[39] powerful speech responding to Sydney Rigdon's efforts to become the legitimate successor of Joseph Smith. Hyde affirmed the priesthood as "the same to this church" as is "the government to the nation." It "emanated wholly from God" and was "destined to rule all the nations;" it "holds the keys of death and hell." The priesthood pertained to all of life and overcame any spiritual-temporal divide. Just as going to the polls is integral to politics, so was going to prayer meetings in the Church. In contrast to this portrayal of ultimacy—indeed of fundamental authenticity—he described Rigdon as "subject to peculiar ebbings and flowings," to gusts of passions and flights of fancy, occasionally "beyond the bounds of time and space," and, sometimes, "completely in the jaws of despair." Though he may have "watered" and refreshed the Saints, he is no "star to guide." Hyde recounts how Rigdon reckoned to have had a vision of Joseph in heaven, at the "head of this kingdom," arguing that prayer went "first to him—from him to the apostle Peter—from Peter to Christ, and that Christ presented them to the Father."[40] Hyde had long known Rigdon in their mutual pre-Mormon days and had been baptized by him. Hyde's final judgment, however, was grounded both in experience of the man and in an understanding of a system in which priesthood was central, and he came down on the system rooted in priesthood.

Hyde's contemporary, Parley P. Pratt, also explained the priesthood when discussing how God—with a body and, therefore, a physical location—might influence the cosmos. He said, "How or in what sense can an organized intelligent being be everywhere present?" His answer, "not in person but in influence or representation," was exemplified by analogy with Queen Victoria who, as Empress of India, possessed effective representatives across the globe. For God, too, it was through the delegated authority of the priesthood—"of the order of his son"—that

---

39. Orson Hyde, *Speech of Elder Orson Hyde Delivered before the High Priests' Quorum in Nauvoo April 27th, 1845 upon the Course and Conduct of Mr. Sydney Rigdon and upon the Merits of His Claims to the Presidency of the Church of Jesus Christ of Latter-day Saints* (Liverpool, England: James and Woodburn, 1845).

40. Ibid., 4–12.

his work was achieved, work that God would do if present. Pratt complements this argument with a typical Mormon notion of a "principle" and speaks of "a proceeding principle which emanates from him to fill the immensity of space, which principle is light." It is the "law by which they live and move and have a being."[41] This complementarity expresses the depth of significance of priesthood as the authentic functioning basis of the LDS Church in a fashion that other churches might find hard to grasp, especially those that locate authenticity in personal conversion or in biblical texts.

Corporate Identity and Boundary Marking

Such differences among churches highlight the second reason for considering re-birth motifs: that of boundary marking between Joseph's church—self-defined as a Restoration movement—and pre-existing churches reckoned to be part of an apostatized Christianity.[42] The Restoration was of God's divinely ordained Church that had in various ways existed from the beginning of time. Its distinctive nature lay both in the priesthoods conferred on its leaders by Jesus and key apostles, and in the rites it brought back to humankind that would ensure eternal progression. It was entry into that organization, ordination into those priesthoods, and faithful obedience in reception of the ordinances of this Gospel that counted. Because other churches did not possess those things they could serve to demarcate boundaries of truth and fields of authenticity. Certainly, individuals should feel led by the Spirit and might perhaps gain experiences of a re-birth type in connection with sin, repentance, and faith, but the crucial fact was that they should, as LDS language came to express it, "gain a testimony" of the truthfulness of this particular church as God's own Church and of Joseph as God's prophet. Individuals who gained a testimony of the truthfulness of the Book of Mormon would reflect "The Testimony of Three Witnesses" and "The Testimony of Eight Witnesses" who, at the outset, validated

---

41. Parley P. Pratt, *An Appeal to the Inhabitants of the State of New York, Letter to Queen Victoria, The Fountain of Knowledge, Immortality of the Body, and Intelligence and Affection* (Nauvoo, Ill.: John Taylor Printer, n.d. [but letter dated 1841]), 32.

42. Conkin, *American Originals*, 176–77, sees Joseph Smith as a "restorationist ... with a vengeance, incorporating Pentecostal, Adventist and millenarian themes, but with his 'original' beliefs and ordinances emerging shortly before his death."

the Book of Mormon and the existence of the plates from which Joseph derived the English text. Such testimony demarcated Mormonism from other churches, and that was more important than stressing experiences that might resemble what was happening in other churches when many in Protestant America stressed the born-again motif.

Authenticity via Restoration, Not Rebirth

The LDS focus of "authenticity," then, lay on the Church, its priesthoods, its prophet, and its book. Whereas Evangelicals might testify to having been born-again, Mormons testified of the "true Church" and their discovery of it. Restoration replaced Rebirth in the authenticity stakes. Implicit in this distinction is a certain direction of religious attention, with LDS energies being largely outward-looking towards their Church and Evangelical conversionism inward-looking to the reborn self. That Mormon spirituality came to invest a great deal of significance in the emotional sensations of individuals is evident; and because this is frequently aligned with belief in the activity of the Holy Ghost, it is clear that Mormonism's long avoidance of rebirth language is not due to any avoidance of Holy Ghost-experience.[43] It is the preferred theological framing of experience that turns it in the direction of testimony to the Church of Jesus Christ of Latter-day Saints than to a private inner-conversion.

But the inner-life did play a significant part in LDS spirituality as an arena within which divine and human figures interplayed. The imagery of light, for example, often marked such an experience, as in Joseph's First Vision; sometimes other sensory references also touch the emotional base of life. For example, one account of Joseph's early visions, published by the Reorganized Church, tells of a "light that bursts into the room ... as though (a) consuming fire" and how a "calmness and serenity of mind, and an overwhelming rapture of joy, that surpassed understanding" attended the angelic vision dated as September 21, 1823,[44]

---

43. Grant Wacker, *Heaven Below: Early Pentecostals and American Culture* (Cambridge, Mass.: Harvard University Press, 2001), 180, 256, refers to Protestant resistance against ideas of early LDS glossolalia, and yet notes how Mormons helped generate widely held ideas of "latter times prophecy."

44. Oliver Cowdery, "Letter to W. W. Phelps from Oliver Cowdery," *Latter Day Saints' Messenger and Advocate* 1 no. 5 (February 27, 1835): 79.

the day before Joseph visited the site of the buried plates. Two decades later, when Joseph addressed the deeper mysteries of God in his King Follett Discourse, he spoke of "tasting" the sweet truthfulness of the doctrine, a clear expression of his sensory power of awareness.

The role of visions in Joseph's life accorded them wider significance within Mormonism, not least in patriarchal blessings, as in William McBride's to Amanda Ellena, daughter of James and Ann Webb Pace, born 1869 and blessed in 1879. She is told that she "will have dreams and visions"; indeed, the Angel of the Lord is to be with her and converse with her "face to face as we converse with each other."[45] It is to such blessings that we now turn as one clear medium of LDS authenticity that helped render the "rebirth" route redundant. As a ritualized narrative form, these blessings brought many LDS ideas to a single focus within an individual's life.

Patriarchal Blessings and Authenticity

Patriarchal blessings furnished one distinctive medium of an LDS authenticity that is ascribed by another rather than achieved by the self.[46] Patriarchal blessings provided individuals with goals and rooted their future-directedness in a person's ancestral membership in one of Israel's tribes and, occasionally, even in his or her pre-mortal status. Just as Protestants might look back to the day of conversion, to the blessed time when he or she was "saved," the LDS person is also granted a significant past whilst bidden to look from the present moment of blessing into a future in which all needs to be realized.[47]

---

45. James Pace, *A Biographical Sketch of the Life of James Pace*, 122, FAC 510, n.d., Huntington Library, San Marino, Calif.

46. See Irene M. Bates and E. Gary Smith, *Lost Legacy: The Mormon Office of Presiding Patriarch* (Urbana: University of Illinois Press, 1996) for general history. Just why there should have been a complex situation over naming the early office of Patriarch as "evangelical ministers" (D. Michael Quinn, *The Mormon Hierarchy: Origins of Power* [Salt Lake City: Signature Books with Smith Research Associates, 1994], 47–57), is potentially interesting in the context of "rebirth" in this chapter.

47. See L. Brent Goates, comp., *Harold B. Lee: Remembering the Miracles* (American Fork, Utah: Covenant Communications, 2001), 161–64, for a moving testimony about a patriarchal blessing fulfilled in severe illness.

The cases considered below all derive from the diary of James Henry Martineau,[48] who took four wives in plural marriage, was personally acquainted with Brigham Young, served in the Mormon militia, performed faith healings, and served a mission. His temple work included being sealed to some one hundred deceased women, while his own children numbered over twenty. At age 22, when en route from Montgomery County, New York, to California's gold fields, he stopped at Salt Lake City in 1850 and became an LDS convert. He helped found the new town of Parowan in Iron County and was an early settler of Logan. As a clerk and surveyor, he worked for railroad companies and the Mormon Church, but it is his status as a patriarch and giver of blessings that concerns us here. In his document entitled "Pearls: collected from Church works," an unpublished but extensive work which "commenced in Salt Lake City in 1887," he noted a conference address on the office of patriarch by John W. Taylor, delivered April 6, 1900.[49] Taylor speaks of it as an "eminent" office but one currently "not respected as it should be"; indeed, Taylor asserts, "Ignorance regarding the Patriarchal order is extremely dense among L. D. Saints." Not so with Martineau, who believed that "very few Patriarchal blessings" remained unfulfilled as long as recipients kept God's commandments.[50] He received three blessings during the course of his life: in 1851 when aged 23 and a recent convert; in 1876 when aged 48; and in 1884 when he was 56.[51]

The first was conferred by Patriarch John Smith on March 6, 1851, who laid hands on him "in the name of Jesus of Nazareth," telling him that he had "received the gospel in lieu of gold," which pleased the Lord who had given angels to assist and teach him. In the blessing, he is told that He is "of the blood of Joseph, and a lawful heir to the priesthood" that will "be sealed" on him in due course, teaching him "all the hidden mysteries of the Redeemer's kingdom" and giving him power "to do miracles." He is called "to go to the nations of the earth" to "bring thousands to a knowledge of the truth, and lead them to Zion." He would "see things fulfilled which the

---

48. Donald G. Godfrey, Rebecca S. Martineau-McCarty, eds., *An Uncommon Common Pioneer: The Journals of James Henry Martineau* (Provo, Utah: BYU Religious Studies Center, 2008).
49. Ibid., 468.
50. Ibid., 509–11.
51. Ibid., 128, 209–10, 304, 561

prophets have spoken concerning Zion, and enjoy all the blessings of the redeemer's kingdom for ever and ever Amen."[52]

Here, a profusion of motifs echo a factor that was intimately related to authenticity in Mormon thought, namely, its strong "Jewish" or what might be called "Mormon-Israel" nature, typified here in references to Joseph of Egypt's blood, Zion, and the hosts of Israel amidst which Martineau's future offspring will have their place. Reference to angels is evocative of a Mormon sense of communication with the heavens, just as references to the priesthood stand out as distinctive, given the additional emphasis upon hidden mysteries of the kingdom. The blessing itself furnishes a clear base of authenticity for the believer. In a formal sense, the "blessing" from the Church to the individual mirrors the "testimony" often possessed by the believer to the Church. In terms of comparative symbolism, such a blessing begins to parallel the Evangelical notion of "assurance" of salvation felt by those who are born-again. We shall see how that assurance develops further in later blessings.

Martineau's second blessing, from Patriarch Joel H. Johnson at Bellevue on May 20, 1876, came when he was sick. In it, he is blessed "in the name of Jesus Christ of Nazareth," as "one of the seed of Ephraim." On recovering, he will engage in missionary activity and "hunt thy brethren of the house of Ephraim and Israel from the dens and caves of the earth and fish them from the islands of the sea." He is to "do great work in the temple" in the "center stake of Zion, for the redemption of thy dead" who will "manifest themselves unto thee when the time comes for their redemption." Blessings are sealed upon him as were also given to Abraham, Isaac, and Jacob. Like them, his "seed shall become numerous and multiply and become a great and mighty nation." To this end he will "take more wives and raise up seed unto the Most High." In his missionary work, his words will be "quick and powerful causing the ears of them that hear them to tingle and their hearts to be penetrated." In particular, "thousands of Lamanites" will rejoice at his words.[53] He is "sealed up unto eternal lives to come forth in the morning of the first resurrection with all thy wives and children to inherit glory, immortality and eternal lives." Once more, these blessings are conditional on

---

52. James Henry Martineau, *Book of Pearls* (n.d.), 151–52, taken from original manuscript in Huntington Library archives.

53. "Lamanites" was (and in some ways still is) an early LDS form of reference to Native Americans, derived from the Book of Mormon.

his faithfulness. In this blessing, the Mormon-Israel emphasis is strong and is combined with health, future family growth, and missionary endeavor, as well as with the conquest of death. The frame of authenticity continues to develop. The following year he took his third wife.

His third and final blessing, in July 1884 at the hand of William J. Smith in Logan, followed a rite of further anointing that marked a higher status in what was a developing ritualized Mormonism.[54] Addressed only as "Brother Martineau" and with no initial invocation of the name of Christ, he is told that the Lord loves him for his integrity and "has given his holy angel charge" over him to deliver him from the power of the wicked one and from his enemies. He will have health and the power to perform healings, miracles, and even "to cause the sun and moon to stand still and to move mountains" if the Lord's work requires such. He is to die in old age, as indeed he did at 93, some 37 years after this blessing. A distinctive feature of this blessing lies in a sealing of "the Second Comforter" upon him. This Latter-day Saint use of the "Second Comforter" idiom was generally interpreted not—as in much Christian thought—in association with the Holy Ghost but as Jesus Christ himself. Indeed, the blessing directly says that Martineau will "see and converse with the Savior face to face." Before then, he will bring many souls to Christ and have the ability to learn many languages. The Lord will help him and his family to move both to Arizona and Mexico. This blessing is, then, replete with promises and ideas of fulfillment. The power of God and the divine angels will assist and protect in every way; his enemies will be helpless before him; prison walls will not be able to contain him.[55]

Here is a man who has reached a religious status of note, a point of marked authenticity. His blessing shows a dramatic reduction in conditional elements and ends in a promissory and not conditional fashion: "And thou shalt be faithful to the end of thy life, and be exalted to a throne in the celestial glory. Therefore rejoice and trust in God thy friend. Amen." Even the phrase "trust in God thy friend," reads relationally and not as an imperative. This blessing is essentially LDS in its formulations and reflects his new anointing and his bonding with Jesus Christ. Indeed, it is this sense of intimacy with the divine that pervades

---

54. See David John Buerger, *The Mysteries of Godliness: A History of Mormon Temple Worship* (San Francisco: Smith Research Associates, 1994), 62–68.

55. Here are biblical echoes of Acts 5:19, where an angel frees the apostles from prison.

the blessing and expresses an authenticity that has reached as high a level as might reasonably be expected by an LDS member.

Martineau's first wife, Susan Ellen Johnson, received her first blessing in March 1854 at age 18. Patriarch John Smith sealed on her "in the name of Jesus Christ" the "blessings and priesthood that was sealed upon the daughters of Joseph." She would have her heart's desires, wisdom to conduct her family affairs, and power to heal family sickness. Her numerous children would be "mighty in the priesthood" and "extend their dominions from sea to sea" while she would "live to see the winding up scene of wickedness . . . see and converse with your Redeemer" as well as "inherit all the blessings and glories of his kingdom."[56] A link with Israel is drawn in a parallel between Susan Ellen and "the daughters of Joseph," and the millennial aspect of Mormonism is sharply drawn in the promise that she will witness what is presumably meant to be the coming judgment of God upon wickedness in and through the second advent of Christ. Indeed, she would speak with Jesus. She also received a blessing from her own father, Joel H. Johnson, in June 1881 when she was 45 years old. In the name of Jesus Christ he blessed her "with all the blessings of thy fathers, Abraham, Isaac and Jacob."[57] He names her as an "Ephraimite in whom there is no guile."[58] She is to "share in the priesthood" with her companion, and together they will have power to drive "the Destroyer" from their household. The Spirit of God is to "abide in thy bosom like a well of water springing up to everlasting life,"[59] and she will "know and understand things that appertain" to her "glory and exaltation far beyond" her previous grasp. What is more, some of her "friends from behind the vail (sic)" will visit her in her "vision in the night time" and instruct her "in all things that appertain" to her exaltation and glory. Inasmuch as she is faithful to "words of wisdom and eternal life," she is now sealed up "unto eternal lives, with thy companion and thy children to come forth

---

56. The promise that the faithful would live to see "the winding up scene" was "one of the most prominent promises made by the Elders to those whom they bless." This was related to Joseph Smith's revelation that if he lived until he was eighty-five he would see the face of the Son of Man. That prediction made the year 1890 potentially auspicious. See John Hyde Jr., *Mormonism: Its Leaders and Designs*, 2nd ed. (New York: W. P. Fetridge and Company, 1857), 174–75.

57. Martineau, *Pearls*, 155.

58. An echo of John 1:47 referring to an "Israelite . . . in whom is no guile."

59. Another echo of John 4:14.

in the morning of the first resurrection, clothed with glory, immortality and eternal lives."

Here, the ongoing family factor is strongly evident as her father aligns her with ancient Israel and fore-aligns her with her eternal family. Underlying the blessing is an understanding of ritual sealing and its eternal effect. This, too, marks the authenticity of the believer and, being church-based in ritual, offers a pragmatic context for authenticity that a remembered "born-again" experience need not convey. This is further exemplified when she receives yet another blessing, from Patriarch William J. Smith at Logan on July 28, 1884, when she is 48. She receives it along with her husband following their rite of special anointing mentioned above. As in his so in hers: all is positive and full of life-affirmation. There is no conditionality present in this blessing that seals and "makes sure" the anointing just received. She will have great faith and "great power to heal the sick;" her "counsels shall be full of life and salvation." The Mormon-Israel motif is strong in affirming her as a "mother in Israel" who will "possess numerous posterity . . . mighty in the priesthood." This feature of posterity reflects the ancient Hebrew cultural sense of blessing in numerous offspring.[60] The name that emerges from such a posterity is "honorable in Israel" but also extends in a directly LDS fashion into the afterlife for her "children and all your father's house shall be saved." In the following extract, distinctive Christian-Mormon features are pervaded with strong Mormon-Israel overtones:

> You shall have visions and dreams, and be a prophetess and seeress and shall be taught great and mighty principles by heavenly messengers and shall see and converse with the savior face to face. . . . You shall do a great work in the temples of the Lord, and be a savior to many of thy dead, in acting for them in the ordinances of the Gospel.[61]

Following the higher ordinance of anointing, Susan Ellen, like her husband, is to learn mysteries and, more particularly, is to encounter Jesus "face to face." This reveals something of the intimate connection that had, by this stage of Mormonism's development, emerged between

---

60. "Mother in Israel" was also used in other Protestant groups for "godly women." In LDS contexts, it also fostered an identity with Israel. Such women share "honor among the Saints for their nurturing capacity and their spiritual maturity." Maureen Ursenbach Beecher, ed., *The Personal Writings of Eliza Roxcy Snow* (Logan: Utah State University Press, 2000), 286.

61. Martineau, *Pearls*, 157–58.

the ritual forms of temple activity and relationship with Jesus. It is crucial evidence for an understanding of Jesus in Mormonism in alliance with ritual forms. He is more an "external" reality than one that dwells in the heart. All of this underscores the individual's authentic status, even that of being "a savior" herself.

As for the generation following Martineau, his son Nephi, born March 11, 1862, is blessed in August 1865. He is told that he will have "power to raise the dead, and to do any miracle to forward this kingdom," and that he will "come upon Mount Zion with the 144,000 in their robes of righteousness, and converse with many of the holy prophets face to face." A deep authenticity is marked by the fact that he will "sit in council with Joseph and Hyrum and with your Redeemer." Again, the note of ancestry is struck with him being "of Joseph and a lawful heir to the fullness of the priesthood," while the future promises "wives and a great kingdom on the earth." Concretely, he is told that he will "help to rear a temple in Jackson County" and "help pave the streets around the temple in Jackson County with gold." He is even to "hear the prophet Joseph talking unto you about the New Jerusalem." Here, the recipient's authentic status is asserted and reinforced through a plethora of LDS symbols and motifs. The complex interplay of biblical and Mormon themes emerges as the 144,000 righteous witnesses derived from the biblical Book of Revelation integrate with holy prophets, including the recent Mormon leadership. More telling still is the way the biblical New Jerusalem of the Book of Revelation parallels the anticipated temple in Jackson County, the site of the New Jerusalem in America and of the return of Christ.[62] One significant feature in the reflection on heaven concerns the manner in which the Book of Revelation concept—that the streets of the New Jerusalem descending from heaven are paved with gold—is aligned with the Jackson County Temple of the future. Though the biblical account has no temple in heaven (for God is said to be its temple) (Rev. 21:22), the pragmatic nature of Mormonism at this period could hardly conceive of a renewed earth devoid of a temple; indeed, it was part of the ideology that much temple work would need to be accomplished during the millennial reign of Christ. Here the issue of authenticity is woven into a fabric of biblical and LDS strands of thought.

---

62. See Julius C. Billeter, *The Temple of Promise* (Independence, Mo.: Zion's Printing and Publishing Co., 1946).

Martineau's line of blessings extends still further with those blessings he gave to his grandchildren. Two, given in 1900 and 1903 respectively, draw out a feature absent in those already considered, that of the pre-existence. To his granddaughter Aurelia, he says that she had been "valiant and true in your first estate, and because of this you have been held in reserve to labor in this dispensation which is the last and greatest of all."[63] So, too, with his grandson Lee Edward, born in July 1903 and given his blessing one month later,[64] when Martineau asks that he himself may be "dictated by the holy spirit (sic)" for the event. His grandson is "of Ephraim, a natural heir to all the priesthood, blessings, and promises sealed upon Abraham, Isaac and Jacob." Notably, he is also described as "one of those who were valiant for the truth when Lucifer fell," another reference to the pre-mortal heavenly council, with the faithful who sided with Jesus and the apostates who sided with Lucifer and who became "fallen angels" with him in his negative identity as Satan. Here, there is an indication of the influence of ideas concerning pre-mortal existence that are particularly present in Nephi Anderson's *Added Upon*, a well-known turn-of-the-century piece of Mormon religious fiction depicting the pre-mortal Council events.[65]

Martineau describes his grandson as having "been held in reserve, to live in this dispensation and to assist mightily in the establishment of Zion and in the redemption of the dead," and he undertakes to "seal upon you faith, that it may become in you like unto that of Enoch of old, and that like him you may hold communion with your Father in Heaven, and be filled with the wisdom of eternity." This direct reference to Lee Edward as one "valiant for truth" who supported Jesus against Lucifer in that pre-mortal conflict over the method of the Plan of Salvation is invoked as the reason for the baby's recent birth into a time not only of Zion's establishment but also of the "redemption of the dead." As an expression of personal authenticity few examples could be more persuasive. Rather than being "born again," we have the notion of an individual born at a special time.[66] Having individuals described as

---

63. Martineau, *Pearls*, 167.
64. Ibid., 172.
65. Nephi Anderson, *Added Upon*, 6th ed. (1898; rpt., Independence, Mo.: Zion's Printing and Publishing Co., 1912 [1898]).
66. Lycergus A. Wilson, *Outlines of Mormon Philosophy* (Salt Lake City: Deseret News Publishing Co., 1905), 64.

"choice" is not uncommon in LDS discourse and should not be ignored because it undergirds the very notion of authenticity.[67] The timeliness of the birth of such a special person echoes similar blessings that gave their recipients a distinctive sense of identity as special people in a special time, who have a singular relationship both with Jesus-Jehovah and with his and their Heavenly Father.

Conclusion

This extensive account of patriarchal blessings both exemplifies one significant LDS route of authenticity-conferral and marks out a religious practice unlike anything in Protestantism. In comparative terms, patriarchal blessings in the LDS Church might be seen as resembling the notion of a "sacramental" in Catholic tradition, an event separate from listed sacraments such as baptism or the Eucharist but which conveys a spiritual effect through some other act of the Church.[68] In the Mormon context, the patriarchal blessings cited have served as the form through which key LDS content of authentic identity is manifest by direct guidance of the Holy Ghost to provide spiritual benefit for its recipient. Historically speaking, such blessings set LDS identity firmly in a biblical-Jewish context that helped make sense of the practical covenants enacted between the believer and God and added a distinctive meaning to the oft-cited but not always persuasive motif of the American people as the chosen people.[69] Here, Udall's argument is germane—the Mormon trek to Utah "has a sharp edge that punctures a gaping hole in the Manifest Destiny balloon kept aloft by the puffings of five generations of western writers" precisely because Mormons "were Old Testament folk who believed they were taking part in a pageant of divine destiny." It seems to me that this pageant developed through a cumulatively personal cluster of LDS phenomena, including patriarchal blessings, but not through the phenomenon of spiritual rebirth.

---

67. It also stresses the notion, typical of all religions, of merit. However, this topic lies beyond present interests.

68. F. L. Cross and E. A. Livingstone, *The Oxford Dictionary of the Christian Church* (Oxford: Oxford University Press, 1997), 1436.

69. Fritz Hirschfeld, *George Washington and the Jews* (Newark: University of Delaware Press, 2005), 40, 43. Contrast this with the Puritans' affinity for "Jewish culture" whilst "real-life Jews were anathema" to them.

Howsoever fashioned—whether by blessing or rebirth—we cannot but appreciate those like Martineau and, indeed David Paulsen, who emerge from cultural pageants and serve as exemplars of their own traditions of faith. This is especially true for serious thinkers who engage with the challenging world-views of others. Accordingly, in celebration of David and his work, let me conclude with an insight of one of the greatest nineteenth-century exemplars of religious studies, William Robertson Smith (1846–94). Written when still a student, it remains as germane as ever.

> Intellectual culture, say some, is apt to make a man less spiritual. This supposes the spiritual part of the mind to be a peculiar faculty. In fact the emotional is meant. But a man may as readily err by trusting his own emotions as by trusting his own intellect. Spirituality is not the development of one part of the mind but the development of the whole mind in a special direction.[70]

---

70. J. S. Black and G. W. Chrystal, *The Life of William Robertson Smith* (Edinburgh: A & C Black, 1912), 64.

5

Mormonism, Natural Law, and Constitutional Democracy: Reflections on the Romney Candidacy

Francis J. Beckwith, *Baylor University*

In 2008 and 2012 Mitt Romney was among the Republican candidates vying for his party's presidential nomination. A former governor of Massachusetts (2003–2007), Romney is a devout member of the Church of Jesus Christ of Latter-day Saints.[1]

As has been aptly documented,[2] LDS foundational beliefs are contrary to those historically held by the three major branches of Christianity—Catholic, Orthodox, and Protestant. Mormon theology denies the great creeds of Christendom, including the Apostles' Creed and the Nicene Creed. The LDS Church includes in its canon extra-biblical texts such as the Book of Mormon, the Doctrine and Covenants, and the Pearl of Great Price. Mormonism embraces a doctrine of God that is a significant departure from the classical understanding of God, which creedal Christians have held for nearly two millennia. And yet, the LDS Church claims to be the restoration of original Christianity that had largely vanished from the earth for nearly sixteen centuries un-

---

1. This chapter is a revised and edited version of a paper presented at the conference, "Mormonism and American Politics," Princeton University, 9–10 November 2007. Hosted by Princeton University's Center for the Study of Religion, it was co-sponsored with Princeton University's James Madison Program in American Ideals and Institutions, the Center for Human Values, and the Woodrow Wilson School of Public and International Affairs, as well as Brigham Young University's The Charles Redd Center for Western Studies and the Religious Studies Program at Utah Valley State College (now Utah Valley University). Portions of this chapter are adapted from the essay, "Can a Christian Vote for a Mormon?" *Christian Research Journal* 30.5 (2007).

2. See Francis J. Beckwith, Carl Mosser, and Paul Owen, eds., *The New Mormon Challenge: Responding to the Latest Defenses of a Fast-Growing Movement* (Grand Rapids, Mich.: Zondervan, 2002).

til the arrival in nineteenth-century America of the Mormon prophet Joseph Smith. But unlike the leaders of religious bodies that arose out of the sixteenth-century Reformation and the nineteenth-century restoration movements, Smith claimed the mantle of apostolic succession that re-established true Christian priesthoods, as well as a visible church and hierarchy that issues authoritative theological pronouncements and facilitates the only means by which one can achieve the highest level of posthumous exaltation.

Thus, it was not surprising that some have raised questions as to whether Mitt Romney's theological and ecclesiastical commitments are an impediment to fellow citizens who might consider voting for him, but who may be hesitant to do so because they hail from more conventional Christian traditions.[3] Although one may suggest that such considerations should play no part in the electorate's deliberations about candidates for national office, it seems to me that if we want to take religion seriously there is nothing untoward in exploring a candidate's beliefs and the role those beliefs play in the personal formation of the candidate. That is, the religious beliefs of any candidate are a legitimate subject of inquiry, as would be a candidate's ideas about anything else he or she claims to know in disciplines outside of theology, such as history, business, science, or economic theory.

My purpose in this chapter is to take Mormonism seriously by drawing the reader's attention to three mistakes that should be avoided by any Mormon presidential candidate, secular political commentator, or non-Mormon Christian who wants to think clearly about Mormonism and politics. I have given each mistake a name: (1) *The Kennedy Mistake*, (2) *The Pundit's Mistake*, and (3) *The Confessional Mistake*.

I. The Kennedy Mistake

In 1960, Senator John F. Kennedy, a Catholic, was the Democratic Party's candidate for the U. S. Presidency. He would soon become the first Catholic president in a country whose citizenry had been predominantly Protestant and pugnaciously anti-Catholic since its infancy. Many Protestant Christians were concerned that Kennedy's commitment as a

---

3. See, Albert Mohler Jr., "Mormonism, Democracy, and the Urgent Need for Evangelical Thinking," AlbertMohler.com, October 10, 2011, http://www.albertmohler.com/2011/10/10/mormonism-democracy-and-the-urgent-need-for-evangelical-thinking/ (accessed April 23, 2012).

Catholic to the teaching of his Church's Magisterium on a variety of social, moral, and political issues would serve as his guide for U. S. domestic and foreign policy. In order to assuage Protestant fears, on September 12, 1960, Senator Kennedy addressed the Greater Houston Ministerial Association and assured the attendees that nothing of his Catholic faith would play any role in his judgments as occupant of the White House:

I am not the Catholic candidate for President. I am the Democratic Party's candidate for President who happens also to be a Catholic. I do not speak for my church on public matters—and the church does not speak for me. Whatever issue may come before me as President—on birth control, divorce, censorship, gambling or any other subject—I will make my decision in accordance with these views [i.e., religious liberty and church-state separation], in accordance with what my conscience tells me to be the national interest, and without regard to outside religious pressures or dictates. And no power or threat of punishment could cause me to decide otherwise.[4]

From the vantage point of the early twenty-first century, Senator Kennedy's historic speech reads like a complete acquiescence to American mainline Protestant notions of privatized faith and anticlericalism, with its stereotypical, outdated, and uncharitable ideas about the Catholic hierarchy and the teachings of the Catholic Church. Senator Kennedy could have argued that his Catholicism informed him of certain theological and moral doctrines that would make him a thoughtful and principled president. He could have consulted and mined from the works of Catholic scholars such as philosopher Jacques Maritain or theologian John Courtney Murray, both of whom were able defenders of liberal democracy and the natural law that grounds it. Senator Kennedy's speechwriter, Ted Sorenson, said that while he was writing the speech "he had vetted [it] with ... Murray, ... chief architect of the Second Vatican Council's landmark affirmation of religious freedom." One writer notes that most historians, however, "agree that Murray disapproved of the strident separationism that Kennedy championed."[5] Senator Kennedy's speech was a terrible concession because it played to his audience's anti-

---

4. John F. Kennedy, "Address to the Greater Houston Ministerial Association," September 12, 1960, Rice Hotel, Houston, TX. Available at Quote DB, http://www.quotedb.com/speeches/greater-houston-ministerial-association (accessed April 23, 2012).

5. Colleen Carroll Campbell, "The Enduring Costs of John F. Kennedy's Compromise," *The Catholic World Report*, February 2007, http://www.colleencampbell.com/articles/020107JFK.htm (accessed April 23, 2012).

Catholic prejudices while saying that his religious beliefs are so trivial that he would govern in exactly the same way if they were absent.

A Mormon presidential candidate,[6] in order to pacify critics (including traditional Christians), may be tempted to emulate Senator Kennedy and claim that Mormon thought and practice do not influence or shape his politics. There are at least two reasons why this would be a mistake. First, it would signal to traditional Christians that the candidate does not believe that theology could count in principle as knowledge. This is, however, precisely the view of the secularist who believes that religion, like matters of taste, should remain private. If a citizen has good reason to believe that her theological tradition offers real insights into the nature of humanity and the common good—insights that could be defended on grounds that even a secularist may find plausible—why should she remain mute simply because the secularist stipulates a definition of religion that requires her silence? Why should one accept the secularist's limitations on one's religious liberty based on what appears to many of us to be a capricious and politically convenient understanding of "religion?" If a Mormon candidate were to commit the Kennedy mistake, it would give tacit permission for secularists to call into question the political legitimacy of the Mormon candidate's most likely natural allies: traditional Catholics and Evangelicals.

Second, claiming that her beliefs do not influence her politics could cost the candidate the support of those whose very different beliefs influence their politics in the same direction. While traditional Christians

---

6. Romney did in fact give a speech that addressed his faith. Presented on December 6, 2007, at The George Bush Presidential Library on the campus of Texas A & M University (that included the 41st president in its audience), Romney offered an account of his faith and its relationship to American politics that was far more nuanced and confident than Senator Kennedy's 1960 speech. His emphasis on our common heritage of religious liberty and the American Founders' view of the theistic patrimony of our natural rights was very well done. However, Romney addressed certain concerns in a fashion that, in my judgment, provided legitimacy to popular and superficial understandings of the LDS Church. For example, he states, "Let me assure you that no authorities of my church, or of any other church for that matter, will ever exert influence on presidential decisions. Their authority is theirs, within the province of church affairs, and it ends where the affairs of the nation begin." See "Romney's 'Faith in America' Address," *New York Times*, December 6, 2007, available at http://www.nytimes.com/2007/12/06/us/politics/06text-romney.html?_r=1 (accessed April 23, 2012). Nevertheless, it was generally a good speech and far superior to Kennedy's famous address.

may believe that LDS theology is fundamentally not Christian, it does not mean that traditional Christians cannot see that Mormon thought includes beliefs that they would find defensible or even consistent with their own views. If that is the case, as I believe it is, then the Mormon candidate may be able to argue that *because* of her theological beliefs, rather than *in spite of them*, she is deeply committed to principles of justice and liberal democracy that require that the government protect certain inalienable rights—like those mentioned in the Declaration of Independence and the Bill of Rights. In what follows, I offer a reading of Mormon thought that I believe supports such an understanding.

II. The Pundit's Mistake

In response to the sort of reasoning I have suggested, Damon Linker argues that Mormon theology simply does not have the sort of resources (such as natural law theory) that traditional Christians have at their disposal.[7] In order to understand Linker's argument, we have to first briefly summarize the traditional LDS view of moral law and its relationship to the Mormon understanding of the universe, its purpose, and the place of the divinity in it.

Although LDS writings say little specifically about the nature of moral law, they do say much about the nature of laws and principles that apparently include moral laws. Joseph Smith maintained that laws and principles are eternal and unchanging: "Every principle proceeding from God is eternal and any principle which is not eternal is of the devil. . . . The first step in the salvation of man is the laws of eternal and self-existent principles."[8] In the Doctrine and Covenants Smith states that "there is a law, irrevocably decreed in heaven before the foundations of this world, upon which all blessings are predicated—And when we obtain any blessing from God, it is by obedience to that law upon which it is predicated" (D&C 130:20–21). According to Mormon philosopher Kent Robson, "LDS thought is uncommon in the Christian world in its affirmation that intelligence, truth, the 'principles of element,' priesthood, law, cov-

---

7. Damon Linker, "The Big Test: Taking Mormonism Seriously," *The New Republic*, January 1–15, 2007, http://www.tnr.com/article/politics/the-big-test (accessed April 23, 2012).

8. Joseph Smith Jr., *Teachings of the Prophet Joseph Smith*, Joseph Fielding Smith, ed., (Salt Lake City: Deseret Book Co., 1977), 181.

enants, and ordinances are eternal."[9] Smith seems to affirm a view of government that is in the natural law tradition—that the purpose of government is to promote the common good as well as protect those rights that are grounded in unchanging moral laws. For instance, in section 134 of the Doctrine and Covenants, Smith states:

> We believe that governments were instituted of God for the benefit of man ... We believe that all governments necessarily require civil officers and magistrates to enforce the laws of the same; and that such as will administer the law in equity and justice should be sought for and upheld by the voice of the people if a republic, or the will of the sovereign ... We believe that all men are bound to sustain and uphold their respective governments in which they reside, while protected in their inherent and inalienable rights by the laws of such governments ... and that all governments have a right to enact such laws as their own judgments have best calculated to secure the public interest. (D&C 134:1, 3, 5).

Mormon philosopher Sterling McMurrin writes that "Mormon metaphysics is marked by *value universals*. In the matter of values, particularly moral values, Mormon philosophy assumes an absolutistic character. . . . Truth and goodness in the Mormon view are fixed eternally in the universe and their reality and status do not depend on what men actually think or do."[10] So, for LDS thought the moral law is eternal and unchanging, can be known by human beings, and can be applied to practical matters such as the formation of just governments and just laws. To use the language of jurisprudence, there is an eternal law from which human beings may derive the natural law that may be employed to assess whether the positive law is truly just.

Mormonism teaches that certain basic realities have *always* existed and are indestructible—even by God. In the dominant stream of LDS thought,[11] God, like each human being, is another creature in the universe,

---

9. Kent E. Robson, "Time and Eternity," in *Jesus Christ and His Gospel: Selections from the Encyclopedia of Mormonism*, Daniel H. Ludlow, ed. (Salt Lake City: Deseret Book Co., 1994), 458–61.

10. Sterling M. McMurrin, *The Philosophical Foundations of Mormon Theology* (Salt Lake City: University of Utah Press, 1959), 24–25.

11. See, for example, Gary James Bergera, ed., *Line Upon Line: Essays in Mormon Doctrine* (Salt Lake City: Signature Books, 1989); McMurrin, *The Philosophical Foundations of Mormon Theology*; Sterling M. McMurrin, *The Theological Foundations of the Mormon Religion* (Salt Lake City: University of Utah Press, 1965); Blake

though not merely such, for each has an eternal patrimony integral to the constitution and purpose of the cosmos. Nevertheless, in the Mormon universe God is not responsible for creating or sustaining matter, energy, natural laws, personhood, moral principles, the process of salvation (or exaltation), or much of anything. Instead of the universe being subject to Him (as it is in traditional Christianity), the LDS God is subject to the universe. In the words of McMurrin, "God is not the totality of original being and he is not the ultimate source or the creator of all being. This is a radical departure from the position of traditional theism, whether Christian, Jewish, or Islamic, and the failure to recognize the far-reaching implications of this idea is a failure to come to grips with the somewhat distinctive quality of Mormon theology, its essentially non-absolutistic character."[12]

In light of this, let us carefully look at Linker's argument. He writes:

> The obstacles to Mormons developing a binding moral theory go beyond the church's generalized suspicion of autonomous reason; their concept of God seems to deny the very possibility of such a theory. Unlike the God of Catholics and Protestants—who is usually portrayed as the transcendent, all-powerful, all-good, and all-wise creator of the temporal universe out of nothingness—Smith's God is a finite being who evolved into his present state of divinity from a condition very much like our own and then merely "organized" preexisting matter in order to form the world. As a result of this highly unorthodox revelation, there is simply no room for a natural morality in Mormon theology, since Mormonism tacitly denies that the natural world possesses any intrinsic God-given moral purpose. Everything we know—

Ostler, "The Mormon Concept of God," *Dialogue: A Journal of Mormon Thought* 17 (Summer 1984) 65–93; David L. Paulsen, "Foreword," in B. H. Roberts, *The Mormon Doctrine of Deity: The Roberts-Van Der Donckt Discussion* (Salt Lake City: Signature Books, 1998); David L. Paulsen, *The Comparative Coherency of Mormon (Finitistic) and Classical Theism* (Ann Arbor, Mich.: University Microfilms, 1975); Kent Robson, "Omnis on the Horizon," *Sunstone* 8 (July–August 1983): 21–23; Kent Robson, "Time and Omniscience in Mormon Theology," *Sunstone* 5 (May–June 1980): 17–23; and O. Kendall White Jr., *Mormon Neo-Orthodoxy: A Crisis Theology* (Salt Lake City: Signature Books, 1987), 57–67.

12. McMurrin, *Theological Foundations*, 2. This quote may seem inconsistent with an earlier quote from McMurrin in which he states that the LDS worldview affirms, "in the matter of values, particularly moral values . . . an absolutistic character." See McMurrin, *Philosophical Foundations*, 24. I do not believe, however, that they are inconsistent. In one case McMurrin is saying that Mormonism denies absolutism when it comes to the nature of God, but in the other case McMurrin is saying that Mormonism affirms absolutism when it comes to moral values.

or could ever know—about right and wrong comes entirely from divine commands communicated to humanity by prophets. The idea of appealing to a higher principle against the word of a prophet—the idea, in other words, of using one's own mind to cast moral or intellectual doubt on the veracity of a prophetic pronouncement—therefore makes no sense in the Mormon conceptual universe.[13]

I believe that Linker's argument is flawed in several ways. First, it offers an uncharitable reading of Mormon thought by isolating the office of prophet and the exaltation and authority of God from the essential components of LDS metaphysics. Although the LDS prophet may offer new revelation, his authority is neither boundless nor under his absolute control. His pronouncements are limited by certain eternal principles—such as those articulated by Smith and other Mormon prophets—as well as the moral and religious requirements of the LDS canon of scripture and the numerous teachings of the church's General Authorities. Thus, Linker is simply wrong that the Mormon prophet can say anything because the Mormon God can issue any command. If anything, as we have seen, the LDS universe is shot through with teleology—moral and otherwise. The Mormon God is bound by an unchanging moral law outside himself that is part of the infrastructure of an eternally existing cosmos. The LDS prophet, therefore, has less wiggle-room for theological innovation than the typical mega-church pastor. This, of course, does not mean that one may not raise philosophical questions about the existence of a moral law without a moral lawgiver that is identical to the Good, as C. S. Lewis argued in his book, *Mere Christianity*.[14] Rather, it means that Linker locates the dispute between Mormons and traditional Christians in the wrong place: it is not over whether one can *know* that the natural moral law exists; it is over whether or not that the natural moral law is merely part of the furniture of the universe or ultimately has it origin in the Being of God. As McMurrin puts it, "[T]he typical Mormon view does not account for the absoluteness of values in terms of an unchanging intellect or moral will

---

13. Linker, "The Big Test: Taking Mormonism Seriously," 19–20.
14. See C. S. Lewis, *Mere Christianity* (New York: MacMillan, 1948), chapters 1–5. See also, Francis J. Beckwith, "Moral Law, the Mormon Universe, and the Nature of the Right We Choose," in *The New Mormon Challenge: Responding to the Latest Defenses of a Fast-Growing Movement*, eds. Francis J. Beckwith, Carl Mosser, and Paul Owen (Grand Rapids, Mich.: Zondervan, 2002), 219–41.

of God, the common position in historical Christianity, but interprets the will of God rather as conforming to the demands of morality."[15]

Second, Linker's argument proves too much. If, as he claims, a natural moral law requires a self-existing divine source, then the same criticism can be leveled against atheists, agnostics, and skeptics who defend principles of justice and yet do not believe that these principles are only legitimate if they are grounded in a divine mind that has infused the universe with purpose and its moral agents with natural ends. Thus, if we are to fear the Mormon because his moral principles are allegedly derived from the willfulness of a superior (though less than ultimate) being, then perhaps we should fear the unbeliever who claims to derive his moral principles from something he calls "Reason," which nearly always seems to recommend policy proposals consistent with the unbeliever's own political leanings.

Third, Linker's argument proves too little. For there are traditional theisms—such as some forms of Christianity and Islam—that maintain a divine command theory that suggests that the moral law flows not from God's benevolent nature but is the result of His will and nothing more. This voluntarist understanding of God's moral law is far more capricious than the LDS view depicted by Linker. Thus, he should be just as fearful of Calvinist and Muslim candidates as he is of Mormon ones.

III. The Confessional Mistake

This mistake occurs when a citizen believes that the planks of his or her creed or theological confession (e.g., the Nicene Creed or the Westminster Confession) are the best standard by which to judge the suitability of a candidate who is running for public office. Suppose, for example, a Presbyterian elder voted for one of Romney's primary opponents solely on the basis of Romney's rejection of the Nicene Creed and the Westminster Confession. An elder who did this would not truly understand the purpose of creeds and confessions. Their purpose is to provide a summary of beliefs that one must embrace in order to be considered an orthodox member of a particular church body, not to measure the qualifications of a political candidate in a liberal democracy. Christendom's most important creeds and confessions not only pre-date the existence of liberal democracies, but their subject matter

---

15. McMurrin, *Philosophical Foundations*, 25.

bears no relation to assessing those attributes that we consider essential to the leadership of a political regime.

In practice, most Christians already grasp this truth. For instance, I know of many Evangelicals who in the 1980 presidential election voted for Ronald W. Reagan over Jimmy Carter—even though Carter was clearly more Evangelical in his theology and church participation than Reagan. What was decisive for Reagan's supporters were his policies and not his theology. These Evangelicals likely would have chosen Carter over Reagan to teach Sunday School, but they preferred Reagan in the oval office because they believed that Reagan's policies best advanced the common good.

To briefly illustrate what I mean, consider these scriptural citations that instruct the individual and the state to advance the common good:

A. *Loving One's Neighbor.* Jesus tells us to love our neighbors as ourselves (Luke 10:27), and offers the parable of the Good Samaritan in order to help us to understand that strangers, too, are entitled to be treated as our neighbors (Luke 10:29–37). The Christian is also committed to the Pauline precept, "if it be possible . . . live peaceably with all men" (Rom. 12:18). Thus, the Christian must be careful that the policies she supports are not draconian and that the tone in which she offers them is not disrespectful of the citizens with whom she disagrees.

B. *Helping the Less Fortunate.* The Bible commands us to help the poor, feed the hungry, clothe the naked, and comfort the afflicted (Matt. 25:31–46; James 1:26–27). We can accomplish this through our churches or through government programs. (Some Christians, like Marvin Olasky,[16] emphasize the former, while others, like Jim Wallis,[17] stress the latter.)

C. *Doing Justice.* The Christian Old Testament is replete with calls for justice and condemnations of injustice directed to the community as a whole (e.g., Isa. 58:6–10; Deut. 24:19–22; Prov. 31:8–9). In the latter passage the text is calling for the community to "speak up for those who cannot speak for themselves, for the rights of all who are destitute," and to "speak up and judge fairly; defend the rights of the poor and needy."

---

16. See Marvin Olasky, *The Tragedy of American Compassion* (Chicago: Regnery, 1992).

17. Jim Wallis, *God's Politics: Why the Right Gets It Wrong and the Left Doesn't Get It* (San Francisco: HarperCollins, 2005).

The author of Proverbs assumes that we already have an intuitive awareness of justice and injustice and, for this reason his words do indeed make sense to us. This is why it was perfectly just for God to punish Cain for murdering Abel, even though there were no criminal statutes on the books at the time (Gen. 4:1–16). So, for the Christian, justice is something prior to the existence of the state to which the state must conform.

D. *Following God's Plan for Society.* The Ten Commandments (Ex. 20:2–17) tells the Christian that there is a rightly ordered social fabric. We are to worship God, honor our mothers and fathers, remain faithful to our spouses, avoid coveting our neighbors' property, maintain integrity in word and deed, and respect the intrinsic dignity of human life. In political terms this can be translated to the government respecting and privileging religious liberty, the right to life, private property, marriage, and integrity in public life.

Consequently, a candidate who embraces these ideals, even if he or she is not a traditional Christian, is a candidate that traditional Christians who share these ideals may support with a clear conscience. Thus, if one does not support a Mormon candidate, it should not be because she is a Mormon. It should be because one has good reason to believe she is not the best candidate for the office.

Not surprisingly, not everyone agrees with this reasoning. Consider, for example, the argument offered by Evangelical Christian journalist, Warren Cole Smith. Smith argues that a vote for an LDS candidate is a vote for an ecclesiastical body, the Mormon Church, which embraces a belief system that is both false and unstable. He writes:

> The Christian worldview teaches that there is a short tether binding beliefs to the values and behaviors that flow from them. If the beliefs are false, then the behavior will eventually—but inevitably—be warped. Mormonism is particularly troubling on this point because Mormons believe in the idea of "continuing revelation." They may believe one thing today, and something else tomorrow. This is why Mormons have changed their views, for example, on marriage and race. Polygamy was once a key distinctive of the religion. Now, of course, it is not. Mormons once forbade blacks from leadership roles. Now they do not. What else will change?[18]

---

18. Warren Cole Smith, "A Vote for Romney is a Vote for the LDS Church,"

Because Warren Smith confuses the question of a religion's ultimate truth with the question of whether any of a religion's teachings are true or plausible, he does not avoid the creedal mistake.

First, the claim that "if beliefs are false, then the behavior will eventually—but inevitably—be warped," depends on the plausibility of the belief in question and not on the overall plausibility of the worldview from which it heralds. For example, suppose that Romney believes that marriage is a one-flesh communion between one man and one woman, and thus he aligns himself with traditional Christians—though he believes this understanding of marriage because he heard it from a Mormon prophet and believes that the prophet speaks infallibly on such matters.

Although, as a Catholic, I do not believe that Mormon prophets are real prophets, this does not mean I believe that Mormon prophets may not utter true beliefs. After all, Mormonism developed out of nineteenth-century American Protestantism, which is, itself, a consequence of the sixteenth-century schism within Catholic Christianity. In addition, because I believe that there is a natural moral law to which all human beings in principle have access, I know that citizens who do not share my religious faith may in fact embrace positions that are derived both from that faith and the deliverances of the natural law. For these reasons, it should not be a surprise to discover that the LDS Church gets a lot of things right about the nature of the moral life and civil society—even though one may have good reason to believe that Mormonism *as a theological tradition* is mistaken. Thus, there is nothing incoherent in saying that one may have good reasons to reject a particular theological tradition, such as Mormonism, Islam, or Zoroastrianism, while at the same time claiming that the tradition embraces beliefs that are nevertheless true.

Second, Smith claims that because LDS theology has changed over time based on the directives of an unaccountable magisterium, Mormon candidates cannot be trusted to continue to hold their beliefs that they currently share with traditional Christians. This is reminiscent of the old anti-Catholic canard that one ought not to vote for Senator Kennedy because he will take orders from the pope. So, just as a Catholic candidate must unthinkingly listen to the Supreme Pontiff (as it was

---

Patheos, May 24, 2011, http://www.patheos.com/Resources/Additional-Resources/Vote-for-Romney-Is-a-Vote-for-the-LDS-Church-Warren-Cole-Smith-05-24-2011.html (accessed April 23, 2012).

often depicted during the 1960 election), an LDS candidate must obey his capricious and authoritarian leadership as well.

But in both cases the critic holds a one-dimensional and superficial understanding of doctrinal development. Take, for example, the two LDS cases cited by Smith: polygamy and the priesthood. In both cases the LDS Church moved in the direction of Catholicism, Orthodoxy, and the Reformers, all of which have rejected polygamy as well as racial tests for clerical office. So, far from being a sign that portends to a theologically arbitrary LDS future, these shifts are positive and reasonable developments in Mormon doctrine that traditional Christians should applaud and support. That is, one may view these shifts as evidence that Mormonism is moving closer to the moral and doctrinal commitments of the Christian communities from which it sprang in the nineteenth century.

Third, it seems that the changes within Mormonism are far more modest than the sort one finds within Smith's own Evangelical Protestantism. For example, on the matters of women's ordination,[19] abortion,[20] divorce,[21] eternal punishment,[22] the doctrine of creation,[23] infant baptism,[24] ecclesiology,[25] the Lord's Supper,[26] the nature of God,[27]

---

19. Bonnidell Clouse and Robert G. Clouse, eds., *Women in Ministry: Four Views* (Downers Grove, Ill.: InterVarsity Press, 1989).

20. See, Walter R. Martin, *Abortion: Is It Always Murder?* (Santa Ana, Calif.: Vision House, 1977); Robert Wennberg, *Life in the Balance: Exploring the Abortion Controversy* (Grand Rapids, Mich.: Eerdmans, 1985); and Scott Klusendorf, *The Case for Life: Equipping Christians to Engage the Culture* (Wheaton, Ill.: Crossway Books, 2009).

21. H. Wayne House, ed., *Divorce and Remarriage: Four Christian Views* (Downers Grove, Ill.: InterVarsity Press, 1990).

22. Stanley N. Gundry, ed., *Four Views on Hell* (Grand Rapids, Mich.: Zondervan, 1997).

23. J. P. Moreland and John Mark Reynolds, eds., *Three Views on Creation and Evolution* (Downers Grove, Ill.: InterVarsity Press, 1999). See also Bernard Ramm, *The Christian View of Science and Scripture* (Grand Rapids, Mich.: Eerdmans, 1954).

24. Paul E. Engle, ed., *Understanding Four Views on Baptism* (Grand Rapids, Mich.: Zondervan, 2007).

25. Stanley N. Gundry, ed., *Who Runs the Church?: Four Views on Church Government* (Grand Rapids, Mich.: Zondervan, 2004).

26. Gordon T. Smith, ed., *The Lord's Supper: Five Views* (Downers Grove, Ill.: InterVarsity Press, 2008).

27. Stanley N. Gundry, ed., *Four Views on Divine Providence* (Grand Rapids, Mich.: Zondervan, 2011).

sanctification,[28] and justification,[29] Evangelicals have held a wide variety of views over the past fifty years, all of which are considered by many Evangelical scholars as being well within the bounds of orthodoxy. However, unlike Mormonism—or even Catholicism or Eastern Orthodoxy—there is no magisterium within Evangelicalism that is constrained by the doctrinal pronouncements of its predecessors, such as in church councils or in official catechisms. Pastor Rick Warren of Saddleback Church has far more latitude for changing his church's doctrine than do Pope Benedict XVI and LDS President Thomas S. Monson in tinkering with their own.

The lesson to be learned here is that one should examine another's theological tradition with at least as much charity and rigor as one expects others to assess one's own. (I know that this last sentence will likely come back to haunt me, as it should.)

---

28. Stanley N. Gundry, ed., *Four Views on Sanctification* (Grand Rapids, Mich.: Zondervan, 1996).

29. James K. Beilby and Paul Rhodes Eddy, eds., *Justification: Five Views* (Downers Grove, Ill.: InterVarsity Press, 2011).

6

The Enigma of Mormonism: Ruminations of an Anglican Friend and Critic

Paul Owen, *Montreat College*

Though it is hard to believe, I have had the privilege of knowing David Paulsen for more than a decade now. I first made his acquaintance as an inquisitive graduate student in the mid 1990s, as I began to familiarize myself with his doctoral dissertation and subsequent writings in the field of Mormon studies.[1] Eventually, through contacts at BYU, I came to know him on a more personal level. From the beginning I have been impressed with his humility, his gracious character, his intellectual curiosity, his wide range of inquiry, and his commitment to his church. I gladly offer this essay in honor of his fruitful career as a teacher, philosopher, and theologian in the service of his faith. Here I would like to focus on the topics of the Book of Mormon and the doctrine of the Trinity as points of dialogue, as well as present-day barriers to communion between Latter-day Saints and catholic Christians.[2]

---

1. See David L. Paulsen, "Comparative Coherency of Mormon (Finitistic) and Classical theism" (Ph.D. diss., University of Michigan, 1975); "Early Christian Belief in a Corporeal Deity: Origen and Augustine as Reluctant Witnesses," *Harvard Theological Review* 83, no. 2 (1990): 105–16; "The Doctrine of Divine Embodiment: Restoration, Judeo-Christian, and Philosophical Perspectives," *BYU Studies* 35, no. 4 (1995–96): 6–94; Ari Bruening, "The Development of the Mormon Understanding of God: Early Mormon Modalism and Other Myths," *FARMS Review of Books* 13, no. 2 (2001): 109–69; "Joseph Smith Challenges the Theological World," *BYU Studies* 44, no. 4 (2005): 175–212; with Brett McDonald, "Joseph Smith and the Trinity: An Analysis and Defense of the Social Model of the Godhead," *Faith and Philosophy* 25, no. 1 (January 2008): 47–74.

2. By catholic Christians I do not specify members of the Roman Catholic Church, but rather adherents of all churches which have historical links to the ancient church through common sacraments, Episcopal ministry, Scripture and Creeds. This would include, in addition to the Roman communion, those bodies within Eastern

In the last fifteen years or so (since I first began to familiarize myself with LDS scholarship and apologetics), my opinion of the Mormon church has not remained static; I have continued to listen, to learn, and, like Joseph Smith, to pray for divine guidance. My own theological pilgrimage during that time has taken me from the Charismatic/Evangelical community of my teen and college years, through a period of time among Reformed/Presbyterian churches in Scotland and finally, here at home, to the safe haven of traditional Anglo-Catholicism (since 2005). This journey has necessarily affected my own perspective on a range of issues related to dialogue with Mormons. In the meanwhile, my interface with the faith and witness of the Latter-day Saints, through the media of both writing and personal conversation, has forced me to think hard about the issues that seem to divide us.[3] Not only is it impossible to enclose, or precisely capture, the mystery of personal faith in a list of doctrinal commitments, but the reasons *why* those commitments are expressed in the forms they take is itself a matter of considerable complexity.[4]

Orthodoxy and Anglicanism which have maintained valid ministerial orders, and also, in a secondary sense, other bodies stemming from the Reformation (namely the Lutheran and Reformed churches). See Michael Ramsey, *The Gospel and the Catholic Church* (Cambridge, Mass.: Cowley Publications, 1990).

3. For helpful models of the sort of dialogue that must continue, see Robert L. Millet and Gerald R. McDermott, *Claiming Christ: A Mormon-Evangelical Debate* (Grand Rapids, Mich.: Baker, 2007); and Craig L. Blomberg and Stephen E. Robinson, *How Wide the Divide? A Mormon and an Evangelical in Conversation* (Downers Grove, Ill.: InterVarsity Press, 1997).

4. There is more to this point than can be explored here. Suffice it to say that the beliefs we cherish in our hearts are at times articulated in terms that owe more to historical precedent and community pressure than personal conviction. Furthermore, a comparison between doctrinal statements and theology in prayer, liturgy, and hymns sometimes reveals the inadequacy of propositional assertions to articulate the secrets of a community's deepest convictions. Who can possibly read through the LDS hymnbook, or listen to the Eucharistic prayers of the church (Moroni 4–5), and fail to pause at the evident expression of sincere faithful piety? Hymns such as The Morning Breaks (#1), Israel, Israel, God is Calling (#7), 'Twas Witnessed in the Morning Sky (#12), An Angel from on High (#13), The Happy Day at Last Has Come (#32), Come, All Ye Saints of Zion (#38), Arise, O Glorious Zion (#40), and Let Zion in Her Beauty Rise (#41) give beautiful and moving expression to the Restorationist vision of the Latter-day Saints. See *Hymns of the Church of Jesus Christ of Latter-day Saints* (Salt Lake City: The Church of Jesus Christ of Latter-day Saints, 1985).

The Book of Mormon: Scripture, Heresy, or Witness of Christ?

The Book of Mormon continues to impress me. Its range of genres and literary styles, its fascinating appropriation of biblical texts, the variety of plots and characters, the stirring testimony to the Godhead, the deity of Christ, and salvation by grace, should all serve to make a positive impression upon the Christian reader. Certain lines of evidence compel me to believe that the book came at least in part from the hand of Joseph Smith himself, and to a large degree reflects his religious genius and experience.[5] Yet, the complexity of his literary masterpiece and the story of its revelation leave me with questions that lack airtight resolutions and entirely satisfactory answers. I wonder, for instance, why the Book of Mormon witnesses remained so faithful to their testimonies, even after their rejection of Smith's prophetic calling.[6] Some of the incidental textual features of the Book of Mormon also raise legitimate questions about its origins, which should give any critic pause. Why does the book have so many points of contact with the religious texts of antiquity?[7] The issue is not so much whether sources of information about the ancient world *could have* been accessed by Smith

---

5. See Thomas J. Finley, "Does the Book of Mormon Reflect an Ancient Near Eastern Background?" in *The New Mormon Challenge: Responding to the Latest Defenses of a Fast-Growing Movement*, eds. Francis J. Beckwith, Carl Mosser, and Paul Owen (Grand Rapids, Mich.: Zondervan, 2002), 337–66; David J. Shepherd, "Rendering Fiction: Translation, Pseudotranslation and the Book of Mormon," in *The New Mormon Challenge: Responding to the Latest Defenses of a Fast-Growing Movement*, 367–95; and David P. Wright, "Isaiah in the Book of Mormon: Or Joseph Smith in Isaiah," in *American Apocrypha: Essays on the Book of Mormon*, ed. Dan Vogel and Brent Lee Metcalfe (Salt Lake City: Signature, 2002), 157–234.

6. See the discussion of Terryl L. Givens, *By the Hand of Mormon: The American Scripture that Launched a New World Religion* (Oxford: Oxford University Press, 2002), 37–42; and Richard L. Anderson, *Investigating the Book of Mormon Witnesses* (Salt Lake City: Deseret Book Co., 1981).

7. See Noel B. Reynolds, ed., *Book of Mormon Authorship: New Light on Ancient Origins* (Provo, Utah: BYU Religious Studies Center, 1982); *Book of Mormon Authorship Revisited: The Evidence for Ancient Origins* (Provo, Utah: FARMS, 1997); John W. Welch, ed., *Reexploring the Book of Mormon: A Decade of New Research* (Provo, Utah: FARMS, 1992); John L. Sorenson and Melvin J. Thorne, eds., *Rediscovering the Book of Mormon* (Provo: FARMS, 1991); Givens, *By the Hand of Mormon*, 117–54; and Donald W. Parry, Daniel C. Peterson, and John W. Welch, eds., *Echoes and Evidences of the Book of Mormon* (Provo: FARMS, 2002).

from his cultural environment as he worked on his new scripture,[8] but rather how might we imagine so many linguistic, cultural, and historical details being inserted into the text or being placed there by coincidence in such a casual and natural manner by an unsophisticated and uneducated young man? And how can I reconcile the evident piety and richly textured theological vision of the mind behind the Book of Mormon with the hypothesis of a literary fraud?

As a friendly critic of the LDS church—and winsome skeptic of some of Smith's claims about his divine calling and experiences—I fully recognize that the answers to such questions can vary among equally sincere people after studying the evidence. For my own part, while I do not view the Book of Mormon as a *literal* historical record, nor do I accept its *canonical* authority, I do view Smith's ministry as having a sort of prophetic character—a valid testimony from heaven to the people of God, albeit one outside the boundaries of the catholic Church.[9] In this respect, he is not without biblical parallels. I think especially of Balaam (Num. 22–24), the Rechabites (Jer. 35), and the parabolic Good Samaritan (Luke 10:25–37).

Personally, I do not doubt that Joseph was the recipient of some form of heavenly visitation.[10] The angel Moroni, in my view, is better

---

8. As demonstrated time and again by, among others, D. Michael Quinn, in his important work, *Early Mormonism and the Magic Worldview* (Salt Lake City: Signature Books, 1998).

9. I do not discount the possibility that a small population of Old World immigrants settled in an isolated geographical locale in the Americas, persisted for a time, and was visited by Jesus after his resurrection. I view the narrative of the Book of Mormon as imaginative historical fiction, whether authored by Joseph Smith or not (an ancient text can still be fictional narrative). Whatever the historical status of the records alluded to within the book, in its present form it is clearly affected by the influence of Christian hands subsequent to the life of Christ. See Kent P. Jackson, "Joseph Smith and the Historicity of the Book of Mormon," in *Historicity and the Latter-day Saint Scriptures*, ed. Paul Y. Hoskisson (Provo, Utah: BYU Religious Studies Center, 2001), 123–40. Jackson argues that the frequent reference to records within the story precludes a fictional element (pp. 125–27), despite the fact that the fictional pseudepigrapha of antiquity do the same thing (see *2 Esdras* 12:37–38; 14:25–26, 42–46; 15:1–2).

10. Jackson, "Joseph Smith," 132–33, gives four options, and I would maintain either #2 (Smith believed he was visited by an angel), or more likely #3 (Smith was visited by an angel but there were no ancient plates, and the book is not historical). I view his option #4 (angelic visitation with real plates, but not a historical record),

understood along the lines of a spirit, sent by God to confuse and rebuke the councils of a worldly and erring church (see 1 Kgs. 22:19–23), than some sort of emissary of Satan masquerading as an angel of light. Joseph's divine calling has historic precedents in the experiences and callings of the founders of other movements on the fringes of mainstream Judaism and Christianity. One thinks of the Teacher of Righteousness and the Essenes at Qumran, Montanus and Montanism, Mani and Manichaeism, and numerous Anabaptist groups like those of Thomas Müntzer and the Zwickau Prophets, and Melchior Hoffmann and the Melchiorites.

I see the Book of Mormon, and the Mormon faith, as arising out of a religious need. I do not see it in negative terms, but rather as a witness to Jesus Christ and the inadequacy of Protestant revivalism and its religious methods. What was manifestly lacking in the region of Palmyra, New York where Joseph lived, in the experience of the Second Great Awakening, was the influential presence of a powerful *catholic witness* for the Christian faith in its sacramental fullness.[11] What was clearly dominant in the perception of young Joseph was a Christianity chiefly characterized by a deeply divided and sectarian Protestant revivalism.[12] Far from bringing unity to the Church, the evangelistic methods of the time were creating bitter divisions among the churches (JS–H 1:5–12). When young Joseph sought guidance from God, he was granted an unusual divine visitation. Like the later experiences of the plates of gold, I do not understand this visitation in crassly physical terms, but in the context of ecstatic vision, something along the lines of

---

as a remote possibility.

11. It is ironic that at the end of Joseph Smith's last public discourse he stated, "The old Catholic church traditions are worth more than all you [the sectarian world] have said.... If the Catholic religion is a false religion, how can any true religion come out of it? If the Catholic church is bad, how can any good thing come out of it? The character of the old churches have always been slandered by all apostates since the world began." See Joseph Fielding Smith, comp., *Scriptural Teachings of the Prophet Joseph Smith* (Salt Lake City: Deseret Book Company, 1993), 423–24.

12. On the pitfalls of revivalism, and its subsequent effects on evangelicalism, see Iain H. Murray, *Revival and Revivalism: The Making and Marring of American Evangelicalism 1750–1858* (Edinburgh: Banner of Truth, 1994).

John's vision of Jesus in the first century (Rev. 1:10–20)—though obviously of a different level of significance and prophetic authority.[13]

Not unlike John on the Isle of Patmos, perhaps Joseph was "in the Spirit" as he prayed in the woods (JS–H 1:14). In his 1832 account he says he was "filled with the spirit of god." He was directly told by Jesus in the vision that his sins were forgiven and that "the world lieth in sin at this time and none doeth good no not one[;] they have turned aside from the gospel and keep not my commandments[;] they draw near to me with their lips while their hearts are far from me[,] and mine anger is kindling against the inhabitants of the earth to visit them according to th[e]ir ungodliness and to bring to pass that which hath been spoken by the mouth of the prophets and Ap[o]stles."[14] Later, Joseph would interpret these words to imply a divine rejection of all the Protestant sects and their creeds (JS–H 1:19).

It would appear that God had directed the praying boy in the woods to Psalm 14:3 and Isaiah 29:13. In context these texts condemn those whose eyes are closed to prophetic words and visions (Isa. 29:10–11), and who no longer seek after God (Ps. 14:2) nor call upon him (14:4)—surely a commentary upon the spiritual condition of the Protestant ministers participating in the revivals. I will not deny the sincerity of Joseph's First Vision—though I do doubt it was a physical visitation, and would call into question some of the later layers of interpretation which he put upon his experience (likely a result of his negative experiences with local preachers). As for the plates themselves, the tangible character of Joseph's descriptions (JS–H 1:51–52) *by no means* puts them beyond the pale of ecstatic vision, any more than John's descriptions of his transport to heaven (Rev. 4:1–2) and his own handling (and eating!) of a heavenly book while there (10:8–10). Perhaps Joseph's vision was something like that of the apostle Paul, recorded in 2 Corinthians 12:1–4. Whether it was "in the body or out of the body" is not always easy to determine in an ecstatic state.

---

13. On the whole I am persuaded by Grant Palmer, *An Insider's View of Mormon Origins* (Salt Lake City: Signature, 2002), 175–213. See also Jackson, "Joseph Smith," 135–37. Again, of Jackson's options, I would strongly suggest #3, though I view the "events" as ecstatic and not physical experiences.

14. As cited by Grant Palmer, *Mormon Origins*, 236–37. See also documentation in Dean C. Jessee, ed., *The Papers of Joseph Smith: Autobiographical and Historical Writings*, 2 vols. (Salt Lake City: Deseret Book Co., 1989), 1:5–7.

But what about the contents of the Book of Mormon? Do they not clearly put the text beyond the pale of charitable Christian tolerance? Are they not an insuperable barrier to future communion between our communities? Let us examine the question more closely. There is, for example, the issue of the "great and abominable church" (1 Ne. 13). Does the Book of Mormon not identify historic Christianity itself (or the Roman Catholic Church at the very least) as the enemy of the Lamb and his *true* church (1 Ne. 14:10)? A number of points must be taken into account here.

First, I believe it would be wrong to take 1 Nephi 13:5 as a reference to literal persecutions, such as would bring to mind accounts like those compiled in *Foxe's Book of Martyrs*: "Behold the formation of a church which is most abominable above all other churches, which slayeth the saints of God, yea, and tortureth them and *blindeth them* down, and yoketh them with a yoke of iron, and bringeth them down into *captivity*" (italics added). Were this true, the Book of Mormon would be identifying the early Protestant martyrs as "saints of God," which itself would have interesting ecclesiological implications. However, I think it more likely that these images should be understood as metaphors for the *spiritual effects* of false teaching, much like the prophet Isaiah's use of the images of Israel's blindness, prison, and poverty (Isa. 42:7 and 61:1). As the chapter continues, "an exceedingly great many do stumble, yea, insomuch that Satan hath great power over them" (13:29), and the Gentiles will be "in *that awful state of blindness* ... because of the plain and most precious parts of the gospel of the Lamb which have been kept back by that abominable church" (13:32, italics added). Further clarity is gained by the language used in 1 Nephi 14. There, *destruction* is defined in terms of the damnation of hell (14:3). *Captivity* is defined as bondage to "the devil" (14:4). *Deliverance* is glossed as redemption from the "hardness ... blindness ... and captivity of the devil" (14:7).

1 Nephi 14:10 clarifies that in reality there are only two churches: "Behold there are save two churches only; the one is the church of the Lamb of God, and the other is the church of the devil; wherefore, whoso belongeth not to the church of the Lamb of God belongeth to that great church, which is the mother of abominations." What is important to recognize is that Nephi is told this in the sixth century B.C. The "church of the Lamb of God" signifies all the true followers of Christ

under both testaments; the church of the devil consists of "the devil and his children," in other words, all who are led "down to hell" (14:3).[15]

Consequently, the division between the churches cannot be defined denominationally. However, there is a specific historical statement about the activity of the false church which requires clarification. 1 Nephi 13:20–29 describes a book, and the fate which befell this book in the hands of the apostate church: "The book that thou beholdest is a record of the Jews, which contains the covenants of the Lord, which he hath made unto the house of Israel; and it also containeth . . . the covenants of the Lord, which he hath made unto the house of Israel; wherefore, they are of great worth unto the Gentiles" (13:23). The following verses fill out the picture. The book is said to have "proceeded forth from *the mouth of a Jew*; and . . . it contained the fulness of the gospel of the Lord" (13:24, italics added). However, due to the activities of the apostate church, we are told that, "they have taken away from the gospel of the Lamb many parts which are plain and most precious; and also many covenants of the Lord have they taken away" (13:26). This will take place, "after they go forth by the hand of the twelve apostles of the Lamb, from the Jews unto the Gentiles" (v. 26).

The meaning of all this is open to some debate, but for my part the following seems most likely. The "book" which the angel asks Nephi about is specifically the Old Testament, an influential text among the Pilgrim and Puritan settlers of America (see 1 Ne. 13:14–20). Though I cannot prove it, I suspect "the mouth of a Jew" that is spoken of in 13:24 alludes to the work of Ezra the scribe (see 2 Esdras 14). The following parallels with 2 Esdras are especially illuminating:

1. From the times of Moses, some revelations were made public to the people of God and others were reserved for the wise (2 Esdras 14:6; 14:46).
2. The course of the world will grow worse and worse in the times leading up to the end (14:16–18).
3. Ezra worries about the future, because of *the loss of scripture* (14:20–21). Ezra laments that, "the world lies in darkness, and its inhabitants are without light. For thy law has been burned,

---

15. See Stephen E. Robinson, "Early Christianity in 1 Nephi 13–14," in *The Book of Mormon: First Nephi, the Doctrinal Foundation*, ed. Monte S. Nyman (Provo, Utah: BYU Religious Studies Center, 1988), 177–91.

and so no one knows the things which have been done or will be done by thee" (vv. 20–21).
4. Ezra prays for divine inspiration so that he can restore God's revelation: "If then I have found favor before thee, send the Holy Spirit into me, and I will write everything that has happened in the world from the beginning, the things which were written in thy law, that men may be able to find the path, and that those who wish to live in the last days may live" (14:22).
5. God tells Ezra to dictate the record to chosen scribes on "tablets" (14:24). Some of the revelations are to be made public, others are to be delivered "in secret to the wise" (14:26).
6. The text places an emphasis on the "mouth" of Ezra as the contents of the restored scriptures are revealed to him: "Ezra, open your mouth . . . Then I opened my mouth . . . and my mouth was opened" (14:38, 39, 41). Nephi is specifically told by the angel that, "the book proceedeth forth from the mouth of a Jew" (1 Ne. 13:24).
7. The scribes mysteriously penned the restored record "in characters which they did not know" (2 Esdras 14:42). Likely a reference to a Hebrew script with square characters, which emerged later than Ezra's time, but possibly anticipating what appears in the Book of Mormon as the Hebrew language in Egyptian script, or "reformed Egyptian" (see 1 Ne. 1:2; Mosiah 1:4; Morm. 9:32).
8. By way of comparison, the secret revelations, which would include apocryphal books like 2 Esdras itself, are to be kept from unworthy readers by being stored away: "Therefore write all these things that you have seen in a book, and put it in a hidden place" (12:37). The similarities with the Book of Mormon are obvious.

This utilization of 2 Esdras provides a great deal of illumination for 1 Nephi 13. When the Old Testament record went forth from "the mouth of a Jew" (Ezra), "it contained the fullness of the gospel of the Lord, of whom the twelve apostles bear record" (1 Ne. 13:24). In other words, the apostles possessed a version of the Old Testament that included all "ninety-four" books (2 Esdras 14:44); that is, the books of the public canon of the Jews *and seventy other esoteric texts*. However, these other texts were "taken away" by the "great and abominable church" (that is, by unbelievers within visible Christendom) sometime shortly after the death of the apostles.

There are several ways this could take place. Some books may have been destroyed, others kept in existence in an altered form, others perhaps left untampered but safely kept out of the canon. Therefore, the early church of the mid-second century and beyond—which continued the spread of the gospel to the Gentiles throughout the Roman Empire—lacked *the same form* of the Old Testament passed on from Ezra to the apostles. These lost texts contained "covenants" and "prophecies" (1 Ne. 13:23), and "many plain and precious things which have been taken out of the book, which were plain unto the understanding of the children of men, according to the plainness which is in the Lamb of God" (v. 29). In other words, they provided an explicitly Christian ("plain and precious") hermeneutical context which the author(s) of the Book of Mormon view as vital to a proper understanding of the gospel of the Lamb contained in the New Testament (vv. 24–26). Without the lost texts, the New Testament cannot be understood, as it is now read against the backdrop of a doctrinally obscure and mysterious, de-Christianized Old Testament, with the "plain and precious" truths removed.

In short, the books that the apostate church of unbelievers took away from the collection of the Old Testament very much resembled the Book of Mormon in character, making plain the clarity of Christian doctrine which was understood by the faithful saints through the dispensations from the beginning of the world. While catholic Christians (like myself) will of course demur from the substance of these claims, they do not present an insuperable barrier between the LDS community and Christian orthodoxy.

Another potential problem for shared charity between our respective traditions is Moroni 8, which seems at first glance to condemn the catholic practice of infant baptism in no uncertain terms: "I know that it is solemn mockery before God, that ye should baptize little children" (v. 9). And even more strongly: "Behold I say unto you, that he that supposeth that little children need baptism is in the gall of bitterness and in the bonds of iniquity; for he hath neither faith, hope, nor charity; wherefore, should he be cut off while in the thought, he must go down to hell" (v. 14). Does this not present an insuperable obstacle to those who might hope to reconcile the Book of Mormon with the catholic tradition? The rejection of infant baptism would seem to create sacramental barrier between Mormons and the catholic tradition that could never be bridged.[16]

It does not, for while the denunciation of *the practice* of baptizing infants is at serious variance with the consensus of the Church, what Mormon writes to Moroni is an epistle clarifying the issue of *the necessity* of baptism for the salvation of young children. Mormon is addressing "disputations" (v. 5) concerning a very specific "error" (v. 6). The error that his polemic is aimed at is not *the practice of infant baptism itself*, but the doctrinal basis which was supporting the practice among some of the Nephites; namely the mistaken belief that the curse of Adam is not removed from infants by the atonement of Christ from the moment of birth (v. 8).[17]

The reason that infant baptism is said to be a "mockery before God" is because it was being carried out under the assumption that the atonement of Christ cannot be applied to little children without the sacrament. That is the error which the chapter is directed against. It is the absolute *necessity* of baptism for the salvation of infants, not its performance *per se*, that is the object of Mormon's polemic (see Moro. 8:11–12, 13–14, 15, 19–20). Now, it is true of course, that Mormon prohibits the continuation of the practice among the Nephites, but his counsel must be understood against the backdrop of the situation he addressed. To allow the practice to continue under those circumstances would be to encourage what the Book of Mormon views as a cruel superstition that promotes salvation by "dead works" (Morm. 8:23), and constitutes a denial of the merciful character of God (vv. 19–20, 23). Since most modern Christians who practice infant baptism deny its absolute necessity for the salvation of infants, this point does not represent an insuperable barrier of reconciliation between us. In fact, there is nothing in theory to prevent the LDS Church from changing their sacramental practice on this point. Baptism could easily be applied to

---

16. Full communion between Mormons and the catholic tradition would certainly require a shared understanding of baptism (as the primary rite of initiation into the one visible church). It would also require the adoption of a shared liturgy, creedal framework and succession of holy orders/priesthood.

17. See Smith, *Scriptural Teachings of the Prophet Joseph Smith*, 224: "The doctrine of baptizing children, or sprinkling them, or they must welter in hell, is a doctrine not true, not supported by Holy Writ, and is not consistent with the character of God."

infants as a sign and seal of the gift of forgiveness already secured by Christ's universal atonement for them.

The Holy Trinity: Council of Gods or Shared Life?

It is universally recognized that the defining doctrinal symbol of the Christian faith, as enshrined in the liturgical role of the Nicene Creed, is the confession of faith in the Trinity.[18] The Christian religion teaches that there is one God, creator of all temporal reality ("all things visible and invisible"). We identify that God as the Father of the Lord Jesus Christ, and profess that the Father is "of one substance" with his divine Son. The Holy Spirit proceeds from the Father (and or through the Son), and is himself the Lord of the Church and the Giver of life. Does the Mormon Church share that faith? Evidence can be marshaled in support of divergent answers to that question.

On the one hand, we find Joseph Smith saying (or at least being reported to say) in 1844: "Many men say there is one God; the Father, the Son and the Holy Ghost are only one God! I say that is a strange God anyhow—three in one, and one in three! It is a curious organization.... All are to be crammed into one God, according to sectarianism."[19] While such statements are purely commentary, and not canonized doctrine, they do reflect notions that are popular among some Latter-day Saints. The Prophet also apparently said that God the Father was himself fathered by another Father, who was himself the Son of yet another Father.[20] He maintained (anticipating Orson Pratt

---

18. See the useful collection of essays in Christopher Seitz, ed., *Nicene Christianity: The Future for a New Ecumenism* (Grand Rapids, Mich.: Baker, 2001).

19. As cited in Smith, *Scriptural Teachings of the Prophet Joseph Smith*, 420. Perhaps Joseph is only rejecting a modalistic Godhead in his intentions here? Elsewhere he said: "The teachers of the day say that the Father is God, the Son is God, and the Holy Ghost is God, and they are all *in one body* and one God" (p. 349). The reference to "one body" would point to a modalistic Godhead, since in classical Trinitarianism, only God the Son became incarnate in the human life of Jesus.

20. Ibid., 421. Alternatively, Blake Ostler has argued that Joseph Smith was speaking of fatherhood in terms of earthly incarnate conception of God the Father in a previous world, in which another member of the Godhead was the Father of our God the Father. See Blake T. Ostler, *Exploring Mormon Thought: The Problems of Theism and the Love of God* (Salt Lake City: Greg Kofford Books, 2006), 444–46. While ingenious, it does not adequately explain the connection between Smith's statements and the "testimony concerning Abraham" and "the

and B. H. Roberts) that these Gods were somehow joined in one nature: "The scriptures say there are Gods many and Lords many, but *to us there is but one living and true God*, and the heaven of heavens could not contain him; for he took the liberty to go into other heavens."[21]

This "one living and true" God is identified as "the head of the Gods" in another place, where 1 Corinthians 8:5–6 is linked with a midrashic reading of Genesis 1:1.[22] The "head of the Gods" is clearly the figure spoken of as the "Eternal God of all other gods" in Doctrine and Covenants 121:32, and the most intelligent of all spirits in Abraham 3:19. So, while far from being stated in orthodox catholic terms, it is evident that, despite later speculation among the LDS, Smith did not envision the progression of an *infinite* number of Gods,[23] but one and only one true eternal God who inhabits the heavens in different bodies (i.e., Gods who beget other sons). All of this later commentary appears to be based on Smith's (unofficial) reflections upon Abraham 3:8, 16–17, 19.[24]

It seems to me that there are three possible ways of handling these ideas:

1. One could simply discard them as uncanonized commentary which Joseph did not have the chance to clarify.[25] Since they are possibly inconsistent with official LDS doctrine and scrip-

---

God of heaven" which immediately precedes (Smith, *Scriptural Teachings of the Prophet Joseph Smith*, 420). He is reasoning about how intelligences "exist one above another" (ibid., 421).

21. Smith, *Scriptural Teachings of the Prophet Joseph Smith*, 348–49; emhasis added.
22. Ibid., 418–19.
23. When Joseph Smith says, "Intelligences exist one above another, *so that there is no end of them*" (ibid., 421), this is surely hyperbole. Abraham 3:19 makes it clear that there is one supreme intelligence above the Gods.
24. In an earlier discourse delivered in 1841, Smith identifies the council of Gods in "Abraham's record" with the "three personages" of the Christian Godhead, and identifies the head as "God the first, the Creator" (ibid., 215). Furthermore, Abraham 3:19 identifies the Lord himself as the most intelligent of all spirits, presumably meaning there is no God above him.
25. Scholars are agreed, at least with the King Follett Discourse, that we possess only fragments of the original sermon. Furthermore, LDS leaders such as George Albert Smith and Charles Penrose have historically been uncomfortable with the theological views expressed therein. See Blake Ostler, "The Idea of Preexistence in Mormon Thought," in *Line Upon Line: Essays on Mormon Doctrine* (Salt Lake City: Signature Books, 1989), 138.

tural teachings, they should not be used as a basis of formal theological reflection.
2. We might presume that they contain the seed of Brigham Young's later Adam-God doctrine, and that the human "God" of which Joseph Smith spoke was in fact Adam.[26] In this case, the LDS Church has (in effect) already set aside the substance of these notions in its official doctrine.
3. It is possible that Joseph did believe that God the Father had a Father of his own, and that this lineage of Gods (vast as the heavens but not literally infinite) emanates from an "eternal God of all other gods" who presides over all. Each God is an earthy tabernacle of the one God, with spatially distinct bodies, and different spheres of jurisdiction throughout the heavens. This speculative notion (non-binding for LDS) might be compatible with some sort of untraditional Christian monotheism.[27]

On the other hand, the Book of Mormon is very clear about the nature of the Godhead, and it does not cohere very naturally with the multi-theistic perspective of Smith's later statements.[28] An angel tells Nephi, "There is one God and one Shepherd over all the earth" (1 Ne. 13:41). 2 Nephi 31:21 says that the Father, the Son and the Holy Ghost "is one God" (using the singular verb). Mosiah 15:1–5 offers its own illuminating commentary on the nature of the Godhead. The incarnation of God involves the coming down of the one who subsequently exists in a two-fold nature, "being the Father and the Son." Abinadi identifies this incarnate God as the Father "because he was conceived by the power of God." This does not refer to his *human* conception by the power of God, for in verse 5 Fatherhood is equivalent to "the Spirit" ("thus the flesh becoming subject to the Spirit, or the Son to the Father"), or in other words, equivalent to *the divine nature of the one who became incarnate as the Son*. So it must be a way of referring to his

---

26. See Smith, *Scriptural Teachings of the Prophet Joseph Smith*, 51–52, 179.
27. If one God can be three persons, why could he not be more than three? And if one of the divine persons could be embodied on earth, why not others?
28. I use the term "multi-theistic" rather than polytheistic to describe this point of view, because the theism of Pratt-Roberts (and possibly Joseph Smith) sees one God dwelling in multiple heavens. There are not many Gods, so much as many bodily tabernacles in which one God resides.

pre-mortal generation by God the Father (the "power of God" speaking of the mystery of divine generation within the Godhead).

Verses 1–2 parallel "God" and "Son of God" in a manner corresponding to the relation between "the Spirit" and "the flesh" in verse 5. What these statements amount to is an assertion that the one who became incarnate was both divine and human, both "Spirit" and flesh, both God and Son of God, both Father and Son. To use later language, Jesus Christ is consubstantial with God the Father in his divine nature, and consubstantial with us in his mortal nature of flesh. He is *what the Father is* in his deity, and he is what we are in his fleshly humanity. And the incarnate Son of flesh is said to be "one God" with the Father (vv. 3–4). Abinadi does not actually deny that the Father and Son are distinct persons, for verses 2 and 5 state that the Son is *subjected* to the will of the Father. Yet the text also identifies the Son as *being* the Father in verses 2–3. How can the Son be the Father in one sense, and yet distinct from the Father in another? The most straightforward explanation is that the Son is linked with the Father because he shares the identical nature of the Father through premortal generation, and he is linked with the flesh because he partook of a fleshly nature through the incarnation and mortal conception of Jesus.

Alma 11:44 speaks of "Christ the Son, and God the Father, and the Holy Spirit, which is one Eternal God." The use of the singular pronoun makes it possible to reverse the order conceptually: "The one Eternal God *is* Christ the Son, and God the Father, and the Holy Spirit." One could ask for no clearer statement of the Holy Trinity. 3 Nephi 11:27 links this oneness of the Godhead with the perichoretic indwelling of the three persons: "the Father, and the Son, and the Holy Ghost are one; and I am in the Father, and the Father in me, and the Father and I are one." This time the plural verb "are" is employed, placing more of an emphasis upon the distinctness of the three persons, who are inseparably linked by their perichoretic bond. Though they are three persons, they are not autonomous identities; their mutual indwelling makes their separation impossible.[29]

---

29. Though some would appeal to John 17:21–23 to show that such language need not rule out autonomous identity, the Johannine language is surely misapplied. Jesus prays that his disciples may have a share in the oneness of the Father and the Son, but there is never any indication that the unity within the Godhead came about through time or process. John 17:22 says that it is through the gift of the

Finally, we must note Mormon 7:7, in which Mormon says that the person who is acquitted at the final judgment will be able "to dwell in the presence of God in his kingdom, to sing ceaseless praises with the choirs above, unto the Father, and unto the Son, and unto the Holy Ghost, which are one God." The language employed is striking, for the one God is identified as a singular being ("his kingdom"), who exists in a plurality as Father, Son, and Holy Ghost.

If we allow this LDS scriptural data to guide us, then the "Gods" of Abraham 4 must be understood as the persons of the Christian Godhead. Moses 2 teaches this explicitly. Doctrine and Covenants 130:22 says that the Father has a tangible body of flesh and bones, distinct from that of the Son. However it is not clear at all that this should preclude the sort of strict monotheism taught in the Book of Mormon. Just as there are properties distinct to each person in the Trinity, and actions proper to their economic roles, so there could be, hypothetically, spatially distinct bodies *possessed* and made use of by each person. After all, the fact that the "whole fullness of deity dwells bodily" in the incarnate Son (Col. 2:9) does not mean that the divine nature of the Word is somehow cut off from the essence of the Father and Holy Spirit.[30] Therefore, were the Father to also possess his own tangible body, by means of which he might make visible appearances to men alongside the Son (D&C 130:3), this need not cause any ontological separation within the substance of God. Neither the Father nor the Son, as divine

---

divine "glory" that this oneness is created, and 17:24 makes it clear that the Son shared in the glory of the Father from "before the foundation of the world." The prayer for the church is that they may be one "as we are one" (not "as we came to be one"). Jesus speaks of the shared glory of the Trinity as the basis for ecclesial unity, but he does not say that we share in that glory in precisely the same manner.

30. The reasoning of Paulsen and McDonald ("Joseph Smith and the Trinity," 59–60) is faulty. It is not in the least bit Nestorian to deny that the divine nature of the Logos somehow became finite and spatially limited at the incarnation. The divine nature of the Son continued with all its inherent properties, though now bound to his human nature in the hypostatic union. Orthodox, Chalcedonian Christology insists that God became Man in such a way that his divine properties were undiminished, whereas he added to himself a human soul and body with all their finite and natural properties. Therefore the incarnation and resurrection does not imply any spatial separation within the Trinity, for the divine substance of the Logos/Son came from the Father and is of the same essence. While God the Father did not personally assume the properties of manhood in the human life of Jesus, the Son *to whom he imparts his same essence in eternal generation*, does.

persons, can be confined to *any* physical space; hence the notion of separation between them is unthinkable regardless of their use of physical bodies for the purpose of visibility.

Furthermore, we must be careful not to read more into this assertion of the distinct bodies of the Father and the Son than is explicitly communicated in the revelation. For instance, the possession of a tangible *body* of "flesh and bones" by the Father does not require the hypothesis of a previous incarnation in another world. The text attributes a tangible *body* to the Father, but it says nothing of the Father having the *mind or soul* of a man (such as orthodox Christian theology attributes to the full human nature of Jesus). Furthermore, it says nothing of *the origin* of the Father's body. Was it derived from an earlier descent into mortality on another earth (as many Mormons have assumed based on reports of some of Joseph's later statements), or was this body simply formed in heaven (like the tangible bodies in which angels make their appearances in the Bible)?

As Latter-day Saints and Catholic Christians attempt to talk together and move toward unity of understanding in the mysteries of the Faith, an important step forward has been taken through a recent article on the topic of the Trinity by David Paulsen and Brett McDonald.[31] Their article addresses modern Trinitarian theorizing, and proposes that Joseph Smith's insights may offer a more satisfactory form of social trinitarianism than other philosophical models within the broader Christian world. Although I consider the article to be a commendable piece of scholarship, and there are limits to the amount of interaction I can provide to do the work justice, I would like to comment on several aspects of their argument as a means of carrying the discussion forward.

First of all, Paulsen and McDonald suggest that the charge of "tritheism" does not properly apply to Mormonism, for unlike the old Arian heresy, Mormons do not assert that the persons of the Trinity are ontologically graded.[32] While it is true that Athanasius accused the Arians of, among other things, reintroducing polytheism,[33] it is not clear that all forms of Mormon thought avoid an ontologically graded Godhead. What is consistent in the orthodox tradition is the assertion

---

31. David Paulsen and Brett McDonald, "Joseph Smith and the Trinity," 47–74.
32. Ibid., 49.
33. See J. N. D. Kelly, *Early Christian Doctrines* (San Francisco: HarperSanFrancisco, 1978), 233.

that the divine Son is co-eternal with God the Father, and this was a key claim of Nicene orthodoxy. As J. N. D. Kelly notes, the key issue at stake at the Nicene Council "was the Son's co-eternity with the Father, which the Arians denied."[34] Many Latter-day Saints believe that while the "intelligence" out of which Jesus' preexistent spirit was formed was eternal, his actual person came into being when he was organized as a spirit out of eternal intelligent matter in the pre-existence.[35] Hence, those Mormons who imagine a time "when the Son was not" a divine person within the Godhead most certainly do fall into something akin to the Arian heresy.[36]

Paulsen and McDonald also suggest that first century Judaism was not universally monotheistic, citing the notion of a council of gods, which is entertained in the Dead Sea Scrolls.[37] Yet, as I have demonstrated elsewhere, the Essenes who wrote and copied the scrolls at Qumran were adherents of strict monotheism, and carefully distinguished between the one God and the created realm (which includes the angelic council).[38]

Another notion which is put forth in their article is the fact that the term *homoousios* originally allowed for a generic as opposed to spe-

---

34. Ibid., 236.

35. There are two competing theories about intelligence in LDS theology. "Some LDS leaders have interpreted this to mean that intelligent beings—called intelligences—existed before and after they were given spirit bodies in the premortal existence. Others have interpreted it to mean that intelligent beings were organized as spirits out of eternal intelligent matter, that they did not exist as individuals before they were organized as spirit beings in the premortal existence." Dennis J. Packard, "Intelligence," in *The Encyclopedia of Mormonism*, ed. Daniel H. Ludlow (New York: Macmillan, 1992), 2:692. From an orthodox Christian point of view, the first view is less problematic for Christology, the second is preferable for a doctrine of humanity.

36. Admittedly, Arius would not have affirmed the eternality of the substance out of which the Son was created by the Father. And Mormons would not speak of God as creating the Son (*ex nihilo*), but rather *conceiving* him before the creation of the world. Nonetheless, those Mormons who deny the eternality of the Son as a divine person (believing instead in the eternality of the "stuff" out of which his spirit was formed) certainly make of the Son a second God whose personal existence was *temporally* caused by the Father. There is no question that this point of view would have been rejected as polytheism by all the Nicene Fathers.

37. Paulsen and MacDonald, "Joseph Smith and the Trinity," 50.

38. Paul Owen, "Monotheism, Mormonism, and the New Testament Witness," in *The New Mormon Challenge*, 298–300.

cifically numerical identity of substance within the Trinity.³⁹ In other words, it only secures the fact that the Father and the Son are of the same kind of nature, as opposed to the Arian notion that the Father was eternal but the Son was created of another substance than God. There is indeed good evidence in support of the claim that originally the term *homoousios* was understood vaguely enough so as to allow for *either* generic or numerical oneness of substance between the Father and the Son. And the LDS surely do affirm an identity of nature among the persons of the Trinity in that generic sense.

However, while it may have been within the boundaries of fourth-century orthodoxy to understand the term *homoousios* generically, that would only be the case for those who at least confess the eternality of both Father and Son as divine persons (as all the Nicene Fathers and their successors most surely did). Therefore, it is disingenuous to make pretensions of creedal orthodoxy on the part of any Mormon theology that would include those views that postulate a premortal *beginning* of the existence of the Son as a divine person (after his intelligence was formed into a spirit in the preexistence). Furthermore, all the Nicene Fathers would have agreed that there was only one Father in the Godhead, *who has always been God both by nature and status*, and that there was no God or Father to be imagined before him. Those versions of Mormon thought that postulate prior Fathers in other heavens, and who imagine that God the Father progressed over time into godhood would quite clearly have been anathematized by *all* the clergy represented at the Council (both Athanasian and Arian) and the entire united voice of subsequent orthodoxy.

In the discussion of Smith's view of the Godhead, Paulsen and McDonald discuss in what sense the LDS believe the persons of the Trinity to be "three Gods."⁴⁰ Among the statements they make in explaining Smith's views are the following: "For Smith, each of these persons is uncreated and self-existent."⁴¹ And: "Each of these persons is independently self-existent and each possesses his own distinct center of consciousness, will and emotion."⁴² It is very difficult to see how three "independently self-existent" persons can be meaningfully incor-

---

39. Paulsen and MacDonald, "Joseph Smith and the Trinity," 50–51.
40. Ibid., 52–53.
41. Ibid., 52.
42. Ibid., 53.

porated within the framework of Christian monotheism. Furthermore, there is a problem of communication here, for many Mormons believe that what is self-existent and eternal in the Son (and the Father) is only the *intelligent matter* out of which his spirit was organized, not his divine personhood. While it is easy on these terms to understand how the three persons can be called "Gods" in the plural, it is not clear how such a view can be reconciled with other claims in the article.

If all that Latter-day Saints meant when using the plural "Gods" to describe the Trinity were a plurality of divine persons, this would only be a quibble about the use of language in theology. However, when Latter-day Saints insist that each person in the Trinity is "independently self-existent," then the unity of the Godhead can only be understood in terms of cooperative choice and action.[43] In fact, they insist, "if one posits divine persons that are free, then it is not compossible to also assert necessary unity between the three."[44] Paulsen and McDonald explicity deny what the entire Christian tradition affirms, that the unity of the Trinity is a *necessary* one, opting instead for a form of Trinitarian "republicanism,"[45] which they call "Elyonic Monotheism."[46] This truly is a coherent model of three Gods in council cooperatively functioning as one divine unit, but it then renders rather incoherent their earlier objection to the label of "Tritheism."[47]

In other words, for these LDS theologians, the unity of the Trinity is a willed unity, that is maintained through time by their free choice of love.[48] This viewpoint has far-reaching implications. It means that God is not a Trinity *by nature*, but by will; which in turn means that the revelation of God in the New Testament is not a revelation of the *true, constant, and necessary* being of God, but is only a vision of the *form* God (as a joint council of three persons) presently *chooses* to take.

For many Mormons, God has not always existed as the Trinity (prior to the organization of the Son and Holy Spirit out of intelligent matter). And it is apparently possible that God *could* choose in the future not to continue in love as the Trinity. So *if* the Trinity is taken as a

---

43. Ibid., 61–62.
44. Ibid., 64.
45. Ibid., 62.
46. Ibid., 63.
47. Ibid., 48–49.
48. Ibid., 62, 64.

faithful disclosure of the identity of God, and that disclosure is limited to the present choice of the three persons, what at all can we really *know* of the *nature* of God (as opposed to the mere choices of God)? In effect, this form of Elyonic monotheism abolishes the ontological Trinity and replaces it with a purely economic Trinity, which leaves us with no faithful and necessarily true knowledge of the being of God at all—assuming of course that what we can know of God is disclosed through the revelation of God as the Holy Trinity.[49]

The doctrine of the Trinity does not require modern reformulation, either through philosophical subtlety or new revelation. There is one life in God, which is shared among the three persons. A life is simply a distinct identity that remains constant. The life of God is possessed by the Father, passed on to the Son through eternal generation, and conveyed to the Holy Spirit in eternal procession. The one life which is common to the three divine persons is simply the divine substance which constitutes the ontological ground of monotheistic principle in the Trinity (Deut. 6:4).

As catholic Christians and Latter-day Saints seek to serve God in the unity which Jesus desires for all his true followers (John 17:20–23), may we work together to grow past our limitations and misunderstandings, "till we all come in the unity of the faith, and of the knowledge of the Son of God, unto a perfect man, unto the measure of the stature of the fullness of Christ" (Eph. 4:13).

---

49. Blake Ostler argues that the Godhead has metaphysically necessary existence by virtue of the fact that it would be "irrational" for the persons of the Trinity to exit their relationship of love. See *Exploring Mormon Thought: The Attributes of God* (Salt Lake City: Greg Kofford Books, 2001), 466. Nonetheless, it is a curious kind of metaphysical necessity in which the Godhead could "logically" fail to exist, since love must be "freely chosen."

7

Pursuing Truth, Justice, and Dialogue: A Primer on Liberation Theology Toward an Intra-Christian Dialogue

Joseph L. Price, *Whittier College*

My privilege in writing and contributing this essay in honor of David Paulsen grows out of the collaboration that we began in the mid-1990s. While he held the Richard L. Evans Chair of Religious Understanding at Brigham Young University, he conceived and initiated a dialogue between theologians from Christian traditions outside the Mormon orbit and distinguished Mormon philosophers, educators, and Church leaders. These Mormon interlocutors' spiritual and intellectual paths had intersected with non-Mormon theologians whose work provided the focus for a sustained series of presentations and exchanges. I personally enjoyed the opportunity to make several presentations on the stimulus package that Paul Tillich's thought might offer to Mormons encountering him for the first time. Indeed, the occasion of meeting David, benefitting from his generosity as a host, and speaking to the students, faculty, and community members at BYU has been one of the highlights of my academic career.

In the process of meeting David, I discovered his graciousness, warmth, humor, while at the same time I was challenged by his probing queries, his searing search for theistic truth, and his courageous desire for ecumenical dialogue—the formidable task of creating a forum for respectful listening and speaking. In so doing he was able to move participants beyond the more frequent quasi-dialogical modes of amiable conversation or ideological confrontation, each of which has traditionally typified the character of written exchanges between non-Mormon thinkers and advocates for Mormonism. His initiative in providing the context and support for non-Mormon Christian theologians to meet directly with Mormon professors and students moved the prospects of dialogue to a more personal, professional, and especially productive level.[1]

Throughout our days of genuinely amicable and quizzical conversation about faith and church polity, I also learned of David's early vocational interest in legal studies—discovering, in fact, that he had received a law degree from our mutual alma mater, the University of Chicago. This was approximately a decade before he completed his doctoral work in philosophy, wherein he focused on matters of truth, especially as it is pursued in theistic thought. Thus, in an attempt to bring together several of these threads—the jurist's commitment to justice, the philosopher's passion for truth, and the devout believer's desire to engage in genuine dialogue—I turn to the way in which justice and truth interweave in one of the theological dialogues that was initiated in the series of lectures at BYU, and which was subsequently featured in David's co-edited volume (with Donald W. Musser), *Mormonism in Dialogue with Contemporary Christian Theologies*.[2] Respecting and building upon Robert McAfee Brown's lucid essay in that volume, "Liberation as a Faith Option," I want to address a fundamental question related to the articulation of liberation theology and then introduce two other large issues embedded in that question. Each of these issues resonates with David's devotion to particular philosophical and theological themes. The first issue focuses on whose theological voice provides the melodic line of, or for, liberation theology.[3] Consistently, the advocates

---

1. As an illustration of this personal level of engagement, allow me to share a few more words of personal contact with and appreciation for David. When we also learned that our interests converged in the ways that sports and faith often seem to intersect, he invited me to return to the BYU campus to lecture on sports and religion, and to deliver the invocation before a BYU-TCU football game (which the Cougars won). Capping each of my visits to Provo, he also provided me with opportunities to experience some of the richness of Mormon spirituality by making it possible for me to sing a rehearsal with the Mormon Tabernacle Choir (a dream that I had held since childhood, when I would weekly hear their glorious music on radio broadcast), and also by taking me to an LDS worship service in his stake. These experiences expanded the depth of the dialogue that we had begun in light of my lectures on Tillich.

2. Donald W. Musser and David L. Paulsen, eds., *Mormonism in Dialogue with Contemporary Christian Theologies* (Macon, Ga.: Mercer University Press, 2007).

3. The choice of the melodic metaphor is intentional as a tribute to Brown, one of the initial North American advocates for Latin American liberation theology. He used musical metaphors as the organizing feature of his first work on

for and critics of liberation theology have shared a common characteristic: among the various liberation theologies—Latin American, black, feminist, womanist, gay, *mujerista*, Asian, indigenous, *mestizo*, etc.—the common starting point is that they claim to emerge from the underside of history. Liberation theology identifies itself as the voice of the voiceless; it is an expression from marginalized believers.

My first (and most extensive) inquiry, then, probes the creation of liberation theology in two distinct ways: one deals with its emergence in history, and the other considers whose voice is actually heard in the creation and articulation of liberation theology. While the former involves historical movements, actions, and documents, the latter explores epistemological issues: how do we know that the voice claiming to be that of the voiceless is indeed spoken by those who are oppressed? How can we know if the voiceless are indeed both the subjects and objects of liberation theology?

The second inquiry grows out of the recognition that liberation theology starts with a new way of doing theology. In this regard, the question deals with the possibility that the new method of doing liberation theology also generates new "content"—a "new"[4] theology entirely.

The third inquiry is interwoven with the first two. If the lens of liberation theology—this new way of doing theology—also locates and surveys distinctly different fields of vision, we must also consider whether the reflections, proposals, and queries generated by this theological method actually constitute "theology" itself or a form or forum of practical ethics. Growing out of the consideration or introduction of each of these issues, I suggest how the shifts in liberation theology might stimulate further dialogue between Mormons and other Christians.

Although the conditions for generating liberation theology had long been simmering in the conflicting colonial structures and class disequilibrium in Latin America, the charter document for the foundation of liberation theology was a paper presented by Gustavo Gutierrez in Chimbote, Peru. A few weeks before the convening of the Council of Latin American Bishops at Medellín, Colombia, in late summer

---

liberation theology. See Robert McAfee Brown, *Theology in a New Key: Responding to Liberation Themes* (Philadelphia: Westminster Press, 1978).

4. I say "new" theology though liberation theology technically began as a movement in the Roman Catholic Church in Latin America in the 1950s and 1960s. However, in many ways liberation theology remains a "new" theology in the sense that it remains an unconventional way of interpreting theological concepts and religious events.

1968, Gutierrez fanned the flames that had begun to flicker within the Roman Catholic Church following Vatican II. Several of the changes introduced by Vatican II had provided a conceptual seedbed for the movement that would become known as liberation theology.

The paper that Gutierrez prepared and presented prior to the Medellín Conference used the phrase "liberation theology" in its title, and it proved to be both a précis and a prompt for the subsequent development of liberation theology proper. Most immediately, the paper stimulated and focused the deliberations of the bishops, consultants, and observers who were directing and participating in Medellín. Gutierrez's work served as the anticipatory summary of his own magnum opus, *Teología de la liberación—Perspectivas*, which was published three years later.[5]

Meanwhile, as the conference convened at Medellín, the bishops deliberated about how to apply the advances of Vatican II to the Latin American situation. Certainly several of the liturgical changes authorized by Vatican II had already become spiritual stimuli for the people. Having approved the shift of the language of the mass from Latin to the vernacular, Vatican II had ushered in the prospect for worship to become increasingly relevant to the daily lives of the people. By using the ordinary language of the people, the services became more comprehensible; and by emphasizing the role of preaching, priests were able to comment more publically, frequently, and authoritatively on the social conditions affecting the people—especially on the plight of the impoverished.

A second significant change initiated by Vatican II expanded the roles that laypersons could play in the ministerial efforts of the Church. Within the liturgy of the mass itself, laypersons were able to assume roles formerly restricted to priests: reading lectionary texts and assisting in the distribution of the priestly consecrated elements of the host. This expansion of the roles of laypersons had already begun to impact the lives of many of the *campesinos* and barrio dwellers, for they had begun to form Basic Christian Communities—a kind of revival of the biblical model of "house churches"—to read scripture and share their experiences with each other. Most often led by laypersons in the absence of priests or religious authorities, the Bible studies and prayers in these base communities repeatedly turned to their experiences of oppression and deprivation that characterized their condition of poverty.

---

5. See Gustavo Gutierrez, *A Theology of Liberation: History, Politics, and Salvation*, trans. Caridad Inda and John Eagleson (Maryknoll, N.Y.: Orbis Books, 1973), x.

At times, however, priests were present, and they often utilized the opportunities not for exercising traditional priestly roles but for listening to the people. For example, shortly after the Medellín bishops had concluded their deliberations, Fr. Ernesto Cardenal introduced a popular form of biblical exposition and discussion to the *campesinos* in Solentiname. He began to meet with the people in select houses, and he would give to those who could read—usually the children—the text of the Gospel lesson for the day. Then, rather than deliver a homily, Cardenal would stimulate a discussion—a communal commentary— on the text that the child would read from the Protestant translation of *Dios llega al hombre*. So powerful were their spiritual insights—embedded in political protest and economic agony—that Cardenal began to reconstruct from memory the conversations that had developed. He regarded their commentary as having "greater profundity than that of many theologians" and as exemplifying "a simplicity like that of the Gospel itself," which, he concluded, was consistent with the purpose of the Gospel. For "the *Gospel*, or 'Good News' (to the poor) was written for them, and by people like them."[6]

During the decade preceding the council at Medellín, a growing number of parish priests had become dissatisfied with their opportunities to serve in secure and privileged parishes where their ministries had often been called upon to reinforce the status quo by quelling initiatives for change. For some of these priests, as Brown notes in another of his works on liberation theology, their dissatisfaction had prompted

a literal "conversion"—that is, being "turned around" no longer to identify with the rich but with the poor. As they read their Bibles alongside the poor (new experiences for many of them), they concluded that it was by and for just such people that the Bible had originally been written. Read from that perspective, the clear biblical message was "good news *to the poor*," as Jesus had said in the first public setting out of his agenda in a synagogue in Nazareth.[7]

This dissatisfaction was not merely confined to the committed parish priests who began to identify with the poor. As the Medellín document attests, others had complained openly and directly "that the

---

6. Ernesto Cardenal, *The Gospel in Solentiname*, vol. 1, trans. Donald D. Walsh (Maryknoll, N.Y.: Orbis Books, 1976), vii.

7. In Robert McAfee Brown, *Gustavo Gutierrez: An Introduction to Liberation Theology* (Maryknoll, N.Y.: Orbis Books, 1990), 6.

hierarchy [of the Church], the clergy, the religious, are rich and allied with the rich." And without fully embracing these complaints, the bishops noted that multiple factors contributed to the perception that the Church was an institution of the rich. Specifically, they identified as possible contributors to this perception "the great buildings, the rectories and religious houses that are better than those of their neighbors, the often luxurious vehicles, [and] the attire."[8]

In contrast to the documents issued by previous councils of the church, which often focused on ecclesiastical history or doctrinal conundrums, the documents issued by the council at Medellín begin with an analysis of the reality of the situation in Latin America by featuring its social, political, and economic dimensions and challenges. This analytical section is followed by a consideration of doctrinal traditions, challenges, and proposals. The concluding portion of each document provides guidelines for pastoral implementation. The first of the four documents focuses on justice, a topic to which we will return in a subsequent section of this essay; and the final document considers the theme of the "Poverty of the Church." One of the documents' "pastoral orientations," or recommendations for implementation, indicates that the bishops themselves needed to make a commitment to identify with the poor:

> We, the bishops, wish to come closer to the poor in sincerity and brotherhood, making ourselves accessible to them. We ought to sharpen the awareness of our duty of solidarity with the poor, to which charity leads us. This solidarity means that we make ours their problems and their struggles; that we know how to speak with them.[9]

Indeed, the method of priests and bishops establishing solidarity with the poor is one possible way for assuring that the voice of the poor might be heard—though, importantly, even the fact of establishing solidarity with the poor is not experiencing the destitution of poverty itself.

The effort to understand another social class by establishing solidarity with that class is certainly an admirable and informative exercise. This is especially the case for members of a social class who might distrust people, voices, and visions of the marginalized and oppressed. In North America two significant literary accounts have been published by concerned journalists who temporarily identified with an oppressed class

---

8. Joseph Gremillion, comp., *The Gospel of Peace and Justice: Catholic Social Teaching since Pope John* (Maryknoll, N.Y.: Orbis, 1976), 471.
9. Ibid., 474.

in order to tell a potentially wary audience stories from the perspective of the oppressed. During the early years of the Civil Rights Movement, John Howard Griffin darkened his skin and trekked through the southern United States in an attempt to experience and understand what life was like for a person of African descent. Indeed, he experienced the racial hatred and oppression that were typical in the South at that time, typified by his difficulty in finding places to eat, sleep, sit down, and go to the restroom—all human functions regardless of social class. In addition, he consistently suffered threats of violence and acts of humiliation. As he recorded in his diary, these persistently demeaning experiences caused him to battle prolonged depression. Yet for all of his experience within the African American culture, he was of course able to escape by resuming his white identity following his nine-month exploration.[10]

More recently, Barbara Ehrenreich, a successful journalist with a doctoral degree, made a similar attempt to identify with the oppressed by trying to live as a single person on minimum wages. In her perceptive and provocative book *Nickel and Dimed*, she narrates and evaluates her work experiences as a waitress, a hotel housekeeper, a nursing home attendant, and a Walmart clerk. As she began her experiment she decided, unlike Griffin, that she would not put her personal safety at risk—even though the dilapidated and dirty motel where she lived in Minneapolis lacked protective locks on the door. She kept her laptop computer with her for the purpose of keeping her notes and journal for the book, and she recognized that her possession of a computer for recording her daily notes separated her from the genuinely poor. While she found that she had difficulty in making ends meet, she knew that in a dire emergency she could resort to the credit card that she carried with her. And while she established an understanding of and sympathy for the poor who are locked into a subsistent life, she herself was neither destitute nor hopeless since she knew that her experience was temporary and, at a deeper level, that she would be making money on the book that she was contracted to write.[11]

In both of these North American situations, persons who sought to establish solidarity with the poor and oppressed *narrated* the plight of the poor and the oppressed. In both cases the authors sought ways

---

10. John Howard Griffin, *Black Like Me* (New York: Signet Books, 1964).
11. Barbara Ehrenreich, *Nickel and Dimed: On (Not) Getting by in America* (New York: Metropolitan Books, 2001).

to increase understanding among the oppressors and to inspire them to social action. Yet in neither case did we actually hear the anguished wails nor see the infested conditions of those who are poor and oppressed. Similarly, the bishops at Medellín were self-conscious about a fundamental disparity between their attempts to establish solidarity with the oppressed and actually experiencing the acute forces of oppression. In the final portion of their analysis of the condition of poverty in Latin America, they acknowledged that:

> Within the context of the poverty and even of the wretchedness in which the great majority of the Latin American people live, we, bishops, priests and religious, have the necessities of life and a certain security, while the poor lack that which is indispensible and struggle between *anguish* and *uncertainty*.[12]

If these bishops and priests' compassionate efforts to establish solidarity with the poor could not fully experience nor understand the abject depths of poverty, how might we truly know the experience of the poor? How might we be certain that the voice that we hear is the previously imperceptible voice of the voiceless?

If the poor, as Brown suggests, are indeed these "true creators" of liberation theology in Latin America, then how do they come to reflect on God's ways in the world and God's purposive hope for them? If most of the marginalized people in Latin America are illiterate or perhaps, at best, functionally literate, then the articulate arguments in liberation theology would hardly seem to be those *of* the marginalized people themselves. The epistemological problem is essentially this: How can we know what a theology of the poor themselves might be if indeed the poor often lack the skills of literacy traditionally associated with doing theology? Such is certainly the case in several Latin American regions where during the heyday of liberation theology in the 1970s and 1980s illiteracy was quite common, especially among the poor and dispossessed. During those decades in Brazil and El Salvador (two of the archdiocese that germinated much liberation theology), illiteracy rates in the country as a whole approached 33%, while in more rural areas of Central America (specifically, in Honduras and Guatemala) the rates of illiteracy often exceeded 50%.[13] Throughout the years and

---

12. Gremillion, *The Gospel of Peace and Justice*, 472.

13. The CIA Factbook with information about each nation is available online at CIA–The World Factbook, https://www.cia.gov/library/publications/the-world-

across the various regions, the rates of illiteracy among barrio dwellers and *campesinos* were markedly higher than the national averages.

Without having the reading and writing skills necessary for studying scriptures and examining church dogmas, is it fair to ask that, even if we can hear the voices of believers who identify themselves as marginalized, is their exposition and application of scripture, for instance, truly theology, or is it really an expression of social frustration and political hope? In the terms often used in association with liberation theology, does theology as a "second order" require cognitive skills associated with literacy? Although philosophical forms of reasoning had characterized the classical "second order" theological treatises that Gutierrez had studied in Europe, he insisted that the experiences of the people served as the first order groundwork for their spiritual expressions, which could be understood as theological statements and propositions. In addition, like the first Christians who were poor, oppressed, and illiterate, the peasants in Latin America are able to experience and express their faith in ways that can also be constructed as theological formulations.

If solidarity itself proves insufficient for the bishops and pastors to claim the full experience of oppression as poor, then is it perhaps possible that the prospect of one who has emerged out of the oppressive structures of poverty and who has directed his or her own thinking toward the matters of God's working in the world might be able to voice the genuine and full anguish of oppression?

Gustavo Gutierrez himself closely identifies with the poor in Latin America. Born as a *mestizo* in an impoverished area of Lima in 1928, Gutierrez contracted a crippling case of osteomyelitis—a bacterial bone marrow infection—when he was beginning adolescence, and throughout his teenage years he spent much of his time bedridden or confined to a wheelchair. Initially, he had hoped to become a physician, but while attending university, he committed his life and his studies to prepare for the priesthood. Because of his excellent academic record in the university and seminary, he was selected to continue his theological and pastoral training in some of the best European institutions at Louvain and Lyons, followed by Rome. After completing his classical theological studies there, he returned to Peru in the early 1950s to work with the poor. As he began to recognize their needs, he realized

---

factbook/geos/us.html (accessed May 8, 2012). The Factbook provides ongoing data about literacy rates.

the inadequacy of his privileged theological studies, and he resumed his identification with the poor, living among them in the *barrio* and re-learning the faith, as he often put it, from "the underside of history." Even following his international acclaim for the significant theological contribution and compassionate work among the poor, Gutierrez spent at least half of each year serving as a parish priest in Lima, restricting his academic work and invited lectures to a confined period.

Despite his emergence *from* the poor and his ministerial solidarity *with* the poor, Gutierrez recognized that following his education, ordination, and occupation, he was "no longer really one of 'the poor.'"[14] His education had provided illumination for his understanding and his expression; his ordination had secured a foundation for his hopefulness and his helpfulness; and his occupation had enriched his reputation in moving beyond the nameless to the named, from the masses to a leader. In each of these distinct ways, he had been separated from the sense of helplessness and hopelessness that characterize the systemically and abjectly poor. Indeed, in each of these dimensions of life—intellectual, spiritual, and vocational—he had experienced liberation.

Gutierrez is not alone in this transformational shift. More recently, his rise from *barrio* poverty to the university professoriate has been replicated by the Argentinian feminist liberation theologian Marcella Althaus-Reid, late professor of theology at the University of Edinburgh. Like Gutierrez, Althaus-Reid flourished in her academic pursuits, traveling, like Gutierrez, from South America to Europe for her doctoral studies. After completing her undergraduate studies in theology, she undertook her graduate studies at the University of St. Andrews in Scotland. But unlike Gutierrez, she assumed a permanent academic appointment in Europe. While her theological interests to a certain extent shifted from a focus on economic oppression in a Latin American context to issues and identities related to gender, she nonetheless maintained and affirmed her earlier identification with the poor. Specifically, she cited her own experience some years earlier as having been a lemon peddler on the streets in Argentina before pursuing her intellectual development and theological training. But while she became more educated and accomplished than her former compatriot street merchants, she continued to articulate their plight even while she did

---

14. Robert McAfee Brown, "Liberation as a Faith Option," in *Mormonism in Dialogue*, 221.

not experience their ongoing destitution. Among her most trenchant and lasting theological contributions is a provocative essay entitled, "From Liberation Theology to Indecent Theology: The Trouble with Normality in Theology," which is included in the stimulating collection *Latin American Liberation Theology: The Next Generation*.[15]

These two examples of Gutierrez and Althaus-Reid suggest that, to a certain extent, the process of becoming an academic theologian separates the theologian from the very people whose poor and illiterate voice he or she wants to channel. This recognition was even apparently articulated by Gutierrez himself: recalling a clarification offered by Gutierrez some years after his initial publication *A Theology of Liberation*, womanist theologian Delores Williams indicated that Gutierrez had specified that "liberation theology [is] *not* the voice of the poor. It is a bridge *to* the poor."[16]

The recognition, then, that Latin American liberation theology might not be the actual voice *of* the poor, but an advocacy *for* the poor in light of one's establishing solidarity with them, does not necessarily invalidate the positions and priorities of liberation theology. Rather, it invites questions about the origin and purpose of liberation theology. It calls into question its real audience and subject. For regardless of the good intentions underlying much of liberation theology, it is still a theology articulated (and published) by educated believers (often seminary trained) on behalf of those to whom they have ministered and with whom they have established solidarity. And its primary audience thus does not seem to be the marginalized people themselves, who would not have access to the theological tomes nor the skills to pore through them; instead, the major audience for published liberation theology seems to be the privileged oppressors whose potential acceptance, support, and transformative work are solicited by the theological expressions and arguments. The prospect of establishing solidarity with the poor, as Brown attests, "means that in encountering the poor, they are somehow encountering God, learning that whoever else God is, God is 'the God of the poor. . . .' This is what 'a preferential option for the

---

15. Marcella Althaus-Reid, "From Liberation Theology to Indecent Theology: The Trouble with Normality in Theology," in *Latin American Liberation Theology: The Next Generation*, ed. Ivan Petrella (Maryknoll, N.Y.: Orbis Books, 2005), 20–38.

16. Delores S. Williams, "Liberation: Summing up the Negatives," *Christianity and Crisis* 49, no. 9 (June 12, 1989): 183.

poor' is all about."[17] In this sense, then, the poor become not merely the creators or subjects of liberation theology but also, to a certain extent, the "objects" of their theology.[18]

Even while we wrestle with questions about the authenticity of the voices of liberation theology, the origin of their theological reflections, and their intended audiences, we also must pose self-critical questions about both our motivation for posing such questions or our orientation to them in the first place. We must consider whether the new method of liberation theology indeed actually reflects a new process of doing theology, or whether it indicates a new theology per se—if it is theology (rather than ethics, for instance) at all. Raising this question is important even in assuming that the published theological works might be for the privileged or the hierarchy within the church.

At the outset of his essay on Latin American liberation theology in the *Mormonism in Dialogue* volume, Robert McAfee Brown avers that liberation theology in the Latin American context does not focus on new content but on a new way of undertaking and prosecuting the theological task. Part of the new way of doing theology is its method of praxis. With this caveat, he shifts the focus of "initiating theology" from the pastoral or academic official to the poor, whom he calls "the true creators of liberation theology."[19] Certainly, the creators of liberation theology are the poor, whether their voices are precisely recorded or are transmitted through priests and others who have tried to establish solidarity with them. As Brown notes, the first level of spiritual experience by the poor and oppressed often elicits a response of commitment. That is the first step identified with the theological process of praxis, which is the ongoing interplay of experience informed by theory, which then enlightens action that germinates new reflections that influence subsequent action, etcetera. For praxis is the ongoing crescendo of work and thought, or action and reflection. As Gutierrez himself points out, because liberation theology's praxis "starts out from an authentic solidarity with the poor and oppressed, [it] is ultimately a praxis of love— real love, effective and concrete, for real, concrete human beings. It is

---

17. Robert McAfee Brown, *Liberation Theology: An Introductory Guide* (Louisville, Ky.: Westminster John Knox Press, 1993), 56.

18. See Michael R. Candelaria, *Popular Religion and Liberation: The Dilemma of Liberation Theology* (Albany, N.Y.: SUNY Press, 1990), 38.

19. Ibid., 211.

a praxis of love of neighbor, and of love for Christ in the neighbor, for Christ identifies himself with the least of these human beings, our brothers and sisters."[20]

Yet theology is not merely the first act of commitment that grows out of an experience of alterity. Instead, liberation theologians associate theology with the second order of reflection that grows out of a transformative spiritual experience understood in light of the Word of God. As Gutierrez affirms, "All theology is rooted in the act of faith. But the act of faith is not a simple intellectual adherence to a message." Instead, as he reflects, "the life of faith . . . is not just a point of departure for theology. It is also its point of arrival. Belief and understanding have an annular relationship."[21] Specifically connecting the process of theology to the first and second order acts, Brown indicates, "those who are living in the midst of such a situation *do* engage in 'the second act,' the attempt to think through, in the light of faith, what this all means for them and what it demands of them."[22]

While liberation theology certainly takes a new tack in identifying theology itself with the interplay between a spiritual experience and reflection on that sensation in light of the Word of God, it also focuses on a different goal than that which had been the locus of classical theology. Rather than identifying doctrinal truths as being the goal of theology, liberation theologians shift the focus to justice. Drawing particularly on the insights of the Hebrew prophet Jeremiah—that to know God is to do justice (Jer. 22: 13–16)—Gustavo Gutierrez notes that God "liberates by establishing justice and right in favor of the poor."[23] Theology is not primarily about doctrinal affirmations. Instead, it is about the pursuit of justice. As Brown puts it, "To know God is not to engage in private piety or subscribe to orthodox statements or worship correctly on the Sabbath. *To know God is to do justice.*"[24] And he goes on to affirm, "If the biblical message is that 'to know God is to do justice,' then the doing of justice must be the 'engagement' by which contemporary readers of the Bible come to know God."[25]

---

20. Gustavo Gutierrez, *The Power of the Poor in History: Selected Writings*, trans. Robert R. Barr (Maryknoll, N.Y.: Orbis Books, 1983), 50.
21. Ibid., 55, 56.
22. Brown, *Liberation Theology*, 56.
23. Gutierrez, *Power of the Poor in History*, 17.
24. Brown, *Theology in a New Key*, 91.
25. Ibid., 98.

Since the way of undertaking liberation theology is distinctly different from the traditional mode of applying reason to matters of scripture and dogma, a final question needs to be posed about whether the project of liberation theology merely constitutes a new way of doing theology, or whether it is, in fact, so radically different that it is not theology *per se*, but a project in theoretical and applied ethics. To answer this question, it is instructive to consider the etymology of "theology." Derived from the Greek words *theos*—or God—and *logos* (which in the Gospel of John, of course, is rendered as *word*), "theology" in its simplest formulation means "God talk." Consequently, all who talk about God, and especially their experience of Otherness, engage in "God talk" and "do" theology.

Traditionally, however, theology has been defined as discourse about God or divine matters and purposes; and classically, as Gutierrez himself points out in the opening pages of *A Theology of Liberation*, theological discourse has been identified with wisdom and rational knowledge. Wisdom could be pursued through meditation on biblical texts, and rational knowledge could be acquired by disciplined application of reason to biblical texts and dogmas. The inherited tradition that provided the context and method of Gutierrez's initial exploration into doing theology derived from Catholic theologian and Doctor of the Church Thomas Aquinas, who, in Gutierrez's words, considered theology "an intellectual discipline, born of the meeting of faith and reason."[26] Yet for all of its grounding in biblical testimony, ecclesial documents, and the works of intellectual giants like the patristic theologians and medieval priests, theology is not sentimentally tethered in uncritical ways to classical propositions. Instead, recognizing that theology must speak to its present audience, Vatican II embarked on the project of *aggiornamento*, or updating, in ways consistent with Henri Bouillard's dictum that "a theology that is not up-to-date is a false theology."[27]

Echoing Bouillard's principle, philosophical theologian Paul Tillich preached a sermon on "Doing the Truth" in which he connected truth with action. "In Christianity truth is found if it is done, and done if it is found," Tillich proclaimed. And he concluded, "no statement is theological which does not contain, directly and indirectly, saving truth," which means "truth that is done," because "saving truth is in 'him that does

---

26. Gutierrez, *Theology of Liberation*, 5.
27. Quoted in Gutierrez, *Theology of Liberation*, 13.

the truth.'"[28] Liberation theology builds upon this active and participatory understanding of truth. By focusing on justice as the expression of truth and the means for knowing God, liberation theology maintains its continuity with the content of classical theologies, while it also manifests current Christian concerns about the relevance of theology in the present day. In this way, liberation theology also provides a new stimulus and point of reference or departure for ecumenical dialogue.

Having considered the origins of liberation theology in the experience and voices of the poor, and having recognized that liberation theology's new way of doing theology in fact represents a shift from theology's focus on matters of truth to the pursuit of justice, we now can project a new foundation or focus for theological dialogue between Mormons and Christians outside the LDS purview. Fundamental differences in beliefs about the *finality* of revelation need not stifle dialogue between Mormons and other Christians.

Indeed, one of the great possibilities afforded by a shift from a theological focus on propositions of truth to a recognition that justice lies at the heart of knowing God is that the freshness of such a perspective might provide a more engaging and productive forum for dialogue. Even so, as we consider the prospect for a shift of focus from truth to justice, we will need to recognize that considerable challenges are likely to persist about the pursuit and exercise of justice itself. For some, contrast and conceptual conflict are likely to continue among and between communities of faith about flash-point issues of justice regarding life and death. For instance, profound differences might be perceived and expressed about the question of when, if ever, can justice be served by the termination of life: in abortion, euthanasia, or capital punishment? Despite such potentially volatile issues perhaps dividing various Mormons and some other Christians, the prospect for focusing dialogue in matters of justice rather than doctrine might provide a common ground to affirm, in concert with liberation theologian Jon Sobrino, that there is "no salvation outside the poor."[29] Then, perhaps, discussions between Mormons and other Christians about the character of the divine, the prospects of life after death, and the design of the Kingdom of God might be more embracing and productive.

---

28. Paul Tillich, *The Shaking of the Foundations* (New York: Charles Scribner's Sons, 1948), 117.

29. Jon Sobrino, *No Salvation Outside the Poor: Prophetic-Utopian Essays*, trans. Margaret Wilde (Maryknoll, N.Y: Orbis Books, 2008).

8

The Messiah and Prophet Puzzle: Explaining Jesus Christ and Joseph Smith

Lyndsey Nay and John W. Welch, *Brigham Young University*

David Paulsen, a superb scholar, teacher, and colleague, has been instrumental in building bridges between the philosophical and theological foundations of traditional Christians and Latter-day Saints. He has demonstrated a particular interest in comparative studies, a lens through which he has considered such topics as similarities between Joseph Smith and Søren Kierkegaard, William James and finitistic theologies, and Mormonism and Christian theology[1] to name a few. In addition, he has been a tremendous mentor, working tirelessly and very effectively with his students as research assistants, co-authors, and eventually colleagues.

As an expression of gratitude for his wisdom in promoting our understanding of similarities in the midst of difference, and echoing his marvelous role as a model mentor, the two of us have worked together as student and teacher, utilizing David's comparative paradigm in identifying the parallel efforts that various scholars have made to account for or to explain the character and contributions of both Jesus Christ and Joseph Smith.[2] Although one must always acknowledge that no such comparisons are ever completely symmetrical, and recognizing that fundamental differences for the Mormon faithful must always distinguish the singular mission and divine person of the Savior from

---

1. David L. Paulsen, "What Does It Mean to Be a Christian? The Views of Joseph Smith and Søren Kierkegaard," *BYU Studies* 47, no. 4 (2008): 55–91; "The God of Abraham, Isaac, and William James," *The Journal of Speculative Philosophy* 13, no. 2 (1999); Donald W. Musser and David L. Paulsen, eds., *Mormonism in Dialogue with Contemporary Christian Theologies* (Macon, Ga.: Mercer University Press, 2007).

2. This paper was originally presented at the 34th Annual Sydney B. Sperry Symposium, *Joseph Smith and the Doctrinal Restoration*, October 28–29, 2005, under the title "Theoretical Explanations of Jesus Christ and Joseph Smith."

that of the Mormon Prophet, we propose that interesting observations emerge from the fact that their lives have often drawn comparable reactions from their would-be detractors.[3]

As is well known, Joseph Smith's life has been a persistent topic of scholarly debate. As a young man, he said he was told that "both good and evil" would be "spoken of [him] among all people" (JS–H 1:33). This statement seems to have proven accurate; Joseph's supporters have described him as wise and thoughtful, while detractors have suspected and defamed his character. Although many biographers have advanced various propositions that, in their minds, explain his troubles or accomplishments, such ideas are often heavily based on preconceived opinions.[4] Since scholarly works always begin with the premise that spiritual forces cannot explain human experiences, alternative means are utilized to explain extraordinary or exceptional people such as Jesus or Joseph Smith.[5]

Similarly, some commentators have depicted Jesus of Nazareth as having been both meek and humble, while others see him as having been bold and powerful. His ministry was clearly polarizing. Although he left indelible impressions of loyalty and devotion on those who embraced his teachings and became his disciples, other people challenged his words and plotted against his life. Over the years, believers, opponents, curious bystanders, and scholars have felt irresistibly compelled to give their answers to the question that Jesus himself asked: "Whom do men say that I the Son of man am?" (Matt. 16:13). This inquiry has often resulted in a cacophony of responses generated from various assumptions, theoretical notions, and biases.[6]

---

3. The authors acknowledge that this essay does not plow this field exhaustively, but rather provides a basic foundation from which further studies can be pursued.

4. See, for example, Davis Bitton, *Knowing Brother Joseph Again: Perceptions and Perspectives* (Salt Lake City: Greg Kofford Books, 2011). Bitton's book does an excellent job of surveying the opinions people have had of Joseph Smith and how those opinions have been expressed through various media, including art. Very helpful, also, is Dean C. Jessee, "Sources for the Study of Joseph Smith," in *Mormon Americana: A Guide to Sources and Collections in the United States*, ed. David J. Whittaker (Provo, Utah: BYU Studies, 1995).

5. See, for example, Luke Timothy Johnson, *The Real Jesus: The Misguided Quest for the Historical Jesus and the Truth of the Traditional Gospels* (San Francisco: HarperCollins, 1996).

6. Three recent attempts to look at the array of views on Jesus include Clinton Bennett, *In Search of Jesus* (London: Continuum, 2001); C. Stephen Evans, *The Historical Christ and the Jesus of Faith: The Incarnational Narrative as History* (New

Indeed, a large body of literature has been advanced to explain how Jesus did what he did, or to argue that he actually did not do what he is recorded to have done. Rather than seeing Christ as the divine Son of God, many scholars have variously dismissed him as a mental psychotic, a political revolutionary, or the invention of misguided followers. Even among faithful Christians one finds a wide range of interpretations. Indeed, all Christs are not created equal. Identifying this problem, John Meier explains: "From the violent revolutionary to Jesus the gay magician, from Jesus the apocalyptic fanatic to Jesus the wisdom teacher or Cynic philosopher unconcerned with eschatology, every conceivable scenario, every extreme theory imaginable, has long since been proposed, with opposite reactions canceling each other out and eager new writers repeating the mistakes of the past."[7] Because of the controversial and contradictory theories that the academic community has generated, a plethora of diverse books on the subject are available.

Noting the diversity of opinion and lack of consensus about Christ, Clinton Bennett, author of *In Search of Jesus*, argues, "When Christians peruse the Gospels, they see Jesus through the lens of what they already believe to be true about him."[8] This observation applies to non-Christians as well. Due to limited primary sources, none of which are indisputably authentic, and because he personally left no writing, Jesus has been viewed through multiple lenses, some of which enlarge certain details while simultaneously blinding the viewer to others.[9] A list of common classifications would include such categories as: peasant, teacher, prophet, messianic figure, redeemer, reformer, Jewish apostate, revolutionary, magician, criminal, and mythical construct.

York: Oxford University Press, 1996); Gerd Theissen and Dagmar Winter, *The Quest for the Plausible Jesus*, trans. M. Eugene Boring (Louisville, Ky.: Westminster John Knox, 2002). No study, as far as we know, has tried to list, as we do here, all of the main theories that have been employed to explain how Jesus did what he did.

7. John P. Meier, *A Marginal Jew: Rethinking the Historical Jesus: The Roots of the Problem and the Person* (New York: Doubleday, 1991), 3, quoted in Bennett, *In Search of Jesus*, 9.

8. Bennett, *In Search of Jesus*, 69.

9. Stephen R. Prothero, *American Jesus: How the Son of God Became a National Icon* (New York: Farrar, Straus, and Giroux, 2003); Richard Wightman Fox, *Jesus in America: Personal Savior, Cultural Hero, National Obsession* (San Francisco: Harper San Francisco, 2004).

Many of the ways in which scholars have explained Christ have also been applied to other creative geniuses and religious leaders, Joseph Smith being a prime example. In his case, volumes of records are available that contain primary accounts of his actions, teachings, and contributions as described by family members, friends, associates, enemies, and the Prophet himself. Due to this abundance of information, theorists on all sides who study his life tend to ignore certain details, whereas the lack of information about Jesus encourages theorists to add or assume them.

A number of historians who have studied Joseph Smith have been determined to solve the mystery that Jan Shipps once identified as "the Prophet Puzzle." Shipps suggests that in order to grasp the significance of Mormonism, one must first understand its founder, "the enigma at its core"—a complex person by all accounts.[10] The same is true for those who study the life of Jesus Christ. In order to contextualize the faith of his followers, one must first understand the great "mystery of godliness," as Paul calls it, that "God was manifest in the flesh, justified in the Spirit, seen of angels, preached unto the Gentiles, believed on in the world, received up into glory" (1 Tim. 3:16). Indeed, for two thousand years, scholars and others have been repeatedly at work on what one may rightly call "the Messiah Puzzle."

Despite their differences, similarities in their lives also abound: both Jesus and Joseph were believed by their followers to have received supernatural manifestations from God the Father, Moses, Elijah, and others; both of them emerged from relatively humble backgrounds; had parents who were influenced by dreams; were precocious youths; spoke out sharply against the societies around them; restored ancient orders; performed miracles; gave and fulfilled prophecies; focused on temples; endured steady harassment; suffered persecution; and were martyred by their enemies.[11] Thus, many dramatic factors in the lives of Jesus and Joseph call for explanation. How could they do the things that they

---

10. Jan Shipps, "The Prophet Puzzle: Suggestions Leading toward a More Comprehensive Interpretation of Joseph Smith," in *The Prophet Puzzle: Interpretive Essays on Joseph Smith*, ed. Bryan Waterman (Salt Lake City: Signature Books, 1999), 28.

11. Jesus as a restorer is discussed in Carey C. Newman, *Jesus and the Restoration of Israel* (Downers Grove, Ill.: InterVarsity Press, 1999); Margaret Barker, *The Risen Lord* (Valley Forge, Penn.: Trinity Press International, 1997). Jan Shipps discusses Joseph's role as a reformer in *Mormonism: The Story of a New Religious Tradition* (Urbana, Ill.: University of Illinois Press, 1985).

did? How did they obtain their spiritual powers? What made them so popular with their followers? What did they intend to accomplish? Were they sincere and not deluded about their claims and motives? When and how did they come to understand their own missions? Who were they, really?

In comparing scholarship on Jesus and Joseph, we have identified and will explore seventeen "theoretical notions" that some academicians have used to explain Jesus, and that have also been used by others to explain Joseph. It is not our intent here to refute or substantively challenge these claims; such work must be reserved for a separate inquiry. Instead, we merely wish to explore the ways in which interpretative methods for explaining the life, character, and work of Joseph Smith Jr. have been remarkably similar to those utilized to explain the life, character, and work of Jesus Christ.

1. Rejecting or Discounting Autobiographical (or Quasi-Autobiographical) Declarations

First, it is striking that although primary or early sources exist in which Jesus and Joseph reportedly provide explanations of their own experiences, critics rarely accept such statements as reliable. In contrast, believers accept these as autobiographical declarations and consider them to be powerful explanations of the exemplary lives of the Savior and the Prophet of the Restoration.

When asked by the High Priest if he was the Son of God, Jesus answered, "I am" (Mark 14:62). In other gospel accounts, the declarations of Jesus are less direct but still implicitly powerful (see Matt. 26:64, Luke 22:67, and John 18:20, 34). At the Last Supper, he reportedly spoke plainly to his disciples: "I came forth from the Father, and am come into the world: again, I leave the world, and go to the Father" (John 16:28). Since this account was apparently written as many as sixty years or more following the event, many question its historicity. Similarly, on the road to Damascus, the resurrected Jesus said to Paul, "Saul, Saul, why persecutest thou me.... I am Jesus whom thou persecutest" (Acts 9:4–5). Those who consider Paul to be a religious inventor or a Jewish traitor likewise view this story with skepticism.

The traditional view of Jesus is summarized by Ian Howard Marshall, who writes, "I believe in the historical Jesus. I believe that historical study confirms that he lived and ministered and taught in a way that is substantially reproduced in the gospels. I believe that this Jesus gave his life as a ransom for sinful mankind, and that he rose from the dead and is the living Lord."[12] Beyond the explanation found in Matthew, "with men this is impossible; but with God all things are possible" (Matt. 19:26), no further rationalization is ultimately necessary. Certainly, within this approach, points of theology are debated, such as when Jesus became conscious of his messiahship. But even despite such discussion, those who accept this faithful view of Jesus see him as more than a man.

In a similar vein, Joseph Smith made direct and open declarations of his mission and calling.[13] In his own words, he recounted on several occasions his experience known as the First Vision as well as other divine manifestations. The primary accounts of these experiences are compiled in an extensive and impressive collection from BYU Studies, *Opening the Heavens*.[14] The purpose of that book is to allow, as much as possible, the people who were closest to the events to speak for themselves. Joseph testified: "I have actually seen a vision" (JS–H 1:25). He further declared: "One of them spake unto me, calling me by name and said, pointing to the other—This is My Beloved Son. Hear Him!" (v. 17). As in the case of the New Testament accounts, people have discounted this version of the First Vision on the grounds that it was written in 1838, eighteen years following Joseph's theophany. But Joseph spoke of the First Vision on other occasions, both before and after 1838. Regarding another great vision, jointly experienced with Sidney Rigdon in 1832, they testified in the very moment, "We beheld the glory of the Son, on the right hand of the Father, and received of his fullness" (D&C 76:20). Likewise, when asked how he translated the Book of Mormon, Joseph repeatedly and consistently explained, "By the gift and power of God." As has also been the case with Jesus, simply rejecting these autobiographical explanations falls short of answering a

---

12. Ian H. Marshall, *I Believe in the Historical Jesus* (Grand Rapids, Mich.: Eerdmans, 1977), 246; quoted in Bennett, *In Search of Jesus*, 137.

13. See examples throughout Joseph Smith Jr., *The Personal Writings of Joseph Smith*, ed. Dean C. Jessee (Salt Lake City: Deseret Book, 1984); and Joseph Smith Jr., et al, *History of the Church of Jesus Christ of Latter-day Saints* (Salt Lake City: Deseret Book, 1980).

14. See especially chapters 1 and 2 on the First Vision, by Dean Jessee, James B. Allen, and John W. Welch, in *Opening the Heavens* (Salt Lake City: BYU Press and Deseret Book, 2006).

host of questions, such as how the Book of Mormon came to be or how Joseph Smith accomplished so much in his relatively short life.

2. Religious Reformer Explanation

Throughout history, dissatisfied individuals have sought to transform the existing religious establishment. John Huss, Martin Luther, John Calvin, John Wesley and other Protestant reformers come readily to mind. Socrates lost his life because he challenged the traditional religious orthodoxy in Athens, while Anne Hutchinson was banished to Rhode Island for promoting antinomianism.[15] Likewise, Jesus of Nazareth and Joseph Smith stood up against the excesses or unseemly behavior of the purportedly religious leaders of their days, and consequently some have seen this characterization as sufficiently explaining all their intentions and motives.

Jesus sought to bring about a restoration of Israel by reforming the Sadducean temple order in Jerusalem and by mitigating the grip of Pharisaical legalism in the Jewish countryside. Contemporary Jews commonly hold the popular opinion that he was simply "Jesus the Jew," who set out to reform Judaism.[16] By way of explanation, they argue that Jewish reformers were common to the time and place in which Jesus lived. Geza Vermes indicates that Jesus may have been one of many Galilean holy men called "Hasidim." His Jesus, according to fellow theorist Brandon Bernard Scott, is a product of the common village Judaism as distinguished from the rabbinic Judaism.[17] Vermes depicted Jesus as one of many common Jewish, back-woodsy, charismatic wonder-workers who emphasized religiosity.

Likewise, since Joseph was exposed to "an unusual excitement on the subject of religion" during a period of intense revivalism in an area

---

15. Antinomianism is the theological concept that Christians are released by grace from the obligation of observing the moral law.

16. See the works of several Jewish scholars. For example, Geza Vermes, *Jesus in his Jewish Context* (Minneapolis: Fortress Press, 2003), an earlier edition published under the title *Jesus and the World of Judaism* (Philadelphia: Fortress Press, 1983). Also see Claudia Setzer, "The Historical Jesus," *Tikkun Magazine, A Bi-monthly Jewish Critique of Politics, Culture, and Society* 4, no. 10 (July 17, 1995): 73.

17. Bernard Brandon Scott, "New Options in an Old Quest," in *The Historical Jesus Through Catholic and Jewish Eyes*, eds. Bryan F Le Beau, Leonard Greenspoon, and Dennis Hamm (Harrisburg, Penn.: Trinity Press International, 2000).

of upstate New York that came to be known as the Burned-over District, many historians have simply equated him with other reformers in this area (JS–H 1:5).[18] While the culture of Joseph's society and some elements of his religious reform were typical for this setting, many of his theological and organizational contributions were unique.[19]

3. Characterization as a Social Activist

Defining Jesus as a typical social reformer rather than a religious reformer accommodates the perspectives of many Jews, Christians, and social activists. Thus, thousands of people have attempted to emulate Jesus by embracing a social gospel. In addition to aiding the poor, the removal of gender and racial barriers has also been connected to Christ's ministry. Because Jesus's teachings are subject to interpretation, one is ultimately left with a figure that serves as a spokesman for everyone's favorite cause. Consequently, such interpretations reflect the ideas of the people who instigated these specific causes rather than providing insight into the historical Jesus. For example, Thomas Jefferson believed Jesus to have been a philosopher. Jon Sobrino, who worked with the poor in Latin America, found Jesus among the poor. Walter Rauschenbusch, a social activist who campaigned against racism and supported disarmament and wealth redistribution, believed Jesus would have done the same.[20] Thus, under this theoretical approach, Jesus's versatility is

---

18. Milton V. Backman Jr., "Awakenings in the Burned-over District: New Light on the Historical Setting of the First Vision," *BYU Studies* 9 (Spring 1969): 301–20; Michael Barkun, *Crucible of the Millennium: the Burned-over District of New York in the 1840s* (Syracuse, N.Y.: Syracuse University Press, 1986); Paul E. Johnson, *A Shopkeeper's Millennium: Society and Revivals in Rochester, New York, 1815–1837* (New York: Hill and Wang, 1978); Whitney R. Cross, *The Burned-over District: the Social and Intellectual History of Enthusiastic Religion in Western New York, 1800–1850* (Ithaca, N.Y.: Cornell University Press, 1950).

19. See Richard L. Bushman, *Joseph Smith and the Beginnings of Mormonism* (Urbana: University of Illinois Press, 1984); Jan Shipps, *Mormonism: The Story of a New Religious Tradition* (Urbana: University of Illinois Press, 1985); Robert V. Remini, *Joseph Smith* (New York: Viking, 2002). Critiques and reviews include Louis Midgley, "The Shipps Odyssey in Retrospect," *FARMS Review of Books* 7, no. 2 (1995): 219–52; Jan Shipps, "A Bird's-eye View of the Mormon Prophet," *FARMS Review of Books* 15, no. 2 (2003): 443–52.

20. Bennett, *In Search of Jesus*, 93, 120, 116. See also the work on the social contributions of Jesus in John Dominic Crossan, *The Historical Jesus: The Life of a*

perceived both as his greatest strength and his greatest weakness. Although he appears capable of championing any cause, his adaptability leaves some people behind, unwilling or unable to follow a leader who simply reflects evolving trends.

In many ways, Joseph has been viewed through a similar lens because he espoused political, economic, and social reforms similar to those Jesus advocated. Many of these reforms were common in antebellum America. Newell G. Bringhurst, for example, discusses Joseph's focus on the idea of the community rather than on the individual—a prevalent approach during the Jacksonian era. Characteristic of the reforms in Joseph's time were such things as temperance, health, female "benevolent reform societies," anti-slavery, and economic equality, all of which he attempted to integrate into his religious movement. Bringhurst claims that, "Joseph Smith and the Latter-day Saint movement that he founded can be better understood within the context of the broader movement to bring about significant social, political, and economic reform within American society during the first half of the nineteenth century."[21] To Bringhurst it is clear that the nature of Joseph Smith's social reform was influenced largely by time, location, and circumstances in which he lived; he suggests that this completely explains who the prophet was and what he did.

Jesus and Joseph certainly fit the mold of underprivileged activists, since they came from lower-middle class backgrounds and were unremarkable in regard to family and circumstances. As a result, people have simply defined both men as social reformers and nothing more. Although accurate in some ways, this explanation also leaves much unaccounted for.

4. Anti-Social Violent Reformer Classification

S. G. F. Brandon is known for his theory that Jesus, although concerned with religion, was really something of a revolutionary.[22] He contends that the temple cleansing event was very violent and that Jesus

---

Mediterranean Jewish Peasant (San Francisco: HarperSanFrancisco, 1991).

21. Newell G. Bringhurst, "Joseph Smith, the Mormons, and Antebellum Reform—A Closer Look," in *The Prophet Puzzle: Interpretive Essays on Joseph Smith*, ed. Bryan Waterman (Salt Lake City: Signature Books, 1999), 115.

22. Bennett, *In Search of Jesus*, 27, 140.

was prepared to use similar tactics to further his mission. Jesus's political goals, Brandon suggests, were later obscured by the apostles. Those who have embraced this theory also underscore Jesus's associations with revolutionary zealots and his designation as King of the Jews. They even note that Peter carried a sword in the Garden of Gethsemane. Hermann Samuel Reimarus, for example, removes religious and social dimensions from his explanation of Jesus. He believes that Jesus intended to liberate Israel from Roman rule and failed.[23] He thus argues that he was an anti-establishment zealot, who used grandiose but naïve delusions to overthrow the entire political world. Reimarus further claims that the gospel writers added Jesus's religious and social agendas.

Similar to the work of Brandon and Reimarus, Gary James Bergera argues for a psychological diagnosis of Joseph's megalomania, using political pursuits and failures as substantiation of his symptoms. Bergera's twelve examples include ten that are essentially politically based: "His use of military imagery, his defiance of state laws, his manipulation of the political process, his control of the financial affairs of the church and its members, the creation of the Council of Fifty, his ordination as king, his campaign for the presidency of the United States, . . . his abrogation of established church judicial procedures, his failure to specify an apparent successor, . . . and the destruction of the *Nauvoo Expositor*."[24] Taking Michael Quinn's power theories one step further, Bergera's Joseph seems preoccupied with violence and military command. As with those who apply violent reform to Jesus's life, some theorists suggest that religion may have been secondary to Joseph's goal of building a kingdom for himself.

5. Genius Theory

Because Jesus and Joseph were admittedly uneducated by worldly standards, scholars have sought an explanation for their perspicacity. While faithful followers attribute their insights to a divine nature (in the case of Jesus) or self-attested heavenly revelations (in the case of

---

23. Ibid., 95–98.
24. Gary James Bergera, "Joseph Smith and the Hazards of Charismatic Leadership," in *The Prophet Puzzle: Interpretive Essays on Joseph Smith*, ed. Bryan Waterman (Salt Lake City: Signature Books, 1999), 242.

both Joseph and Jesus), others have suggested that their uncanny acumen and enduring wisdom were the result of natural genius.

Drawing upon the genius theory, several scholars have argued that the movement Jesus founded was successful because of his superb intellect. As evidence, they refer to the rabbis in the temple asking questions of a twelve-year-old boy at his bar mitzvah (Luke 2:46–47). Gerd Theissen and Dagmar Winter in their book *The Quest for the Plausible Jesus* discuss the idea of Jesus as genius. They state that the term genius is a special name given to a person who is naturally creative and inventive and who is unable to be bound by rules.[25] In many ways, the gospel accounts imply that Jesus fit the criterion of genius quite well. Likewise, Jan Shipps, Lawrence Foster, and Harold Bloom, amongst others, have used the term genius to describe Joseph Smith.[26] He, too, was a precocious youth, who, from the age of fourteen, affirmed his First Vision to curious ministers (JS–H 1:21–25).

6. Great Teacher or Philosopher Proposal

Similar to the genius theory, scholars have also proposed that Jesus and Joseph should be seen and explained primarily as great teachers or philosophers. Under this approach, they claim that, although they may not have been brilliant, the two men exhibited an extraordinary influence as teachers.

Although some scholars omit miracles from Jesus's ministry, and even undermine his role as Savior, they do not discredit the philosophical and theological contributions he made. They suggest that the goal to understand and to follow his teachings is appropriate, but the wor-

---

25. Theissen and Winter, *The Quest for the Plausible Jesus*, 46–48, discussing mainly an article entitled "Genie" by J. and W. Grimm, *Deutsches Woerterbuch*, cols. 3396–450.

26. Jan Shipps, "The Prophet Puzzle"; Lawrence Foster, "The Psychology of Religious Genius: Joseph Smith and the Origin of New Religious Movements," in *The Prophet Puzzle: Interpretive Essays on Joseph Smith*, ed. Bryan Waterman (Salt Lake City: Signature Books, 1999), 183–208; Harold Bloom, *The American Religion: The Emergence of the Post-Christian Nation* (New York: Simon & Schuster, 1992). See the section on genius in Bitton, *Knowing Brother Joseph Again*, 129–30. A critique of Harold Bloom is found in Eugene England, Truman G. Madsen, Charles Randall Paul, and Richard F. Haglund Jr., "Four LDS Views on Harold Bloom: A Roundtable," *BYU Studies* 35, no. 1 (1995): 173.

ship of him—a mortal man—is not. Prominent proponents of this view include philosophers or rationalists, such as Jefferson, Kant, Hegel, and others. They describe Jesus as a teacher of truth, an ethical exemplar, and an extraordinary advocate of the philosophy of love.[27]

One can see the same tendency—that of disregarding the prophetic calling and the visitations of heavenly beings—in the conclusions of many scholars and laypeople who have explored the life of Joseph Smith. For such individuals, Joseph is most generously described as a philosopher. Accepting this conclusion, without discrediting the religious dimensions of Joseph's prophetic calling, some LDS writers have greatly emphasized the value of Joseph's teachings. Elder B. H. Roberts extolled Joseph as a philosopher-teacher.[28] And, Eugene England was impressed that he resolved "the great dilemmas that that age-old polarity has posed: law versus freedom, reason versus emotion (or head versus heart), community versus the individual, the necessity but limitations of language." Indeed, a crucial test of a genuine and great religious figure—one that Joseph Smith meets extremely well (better than his critics and even many of his friends have recognized)—is that his work embodies both "Romantic and Classical tendencies in creative tension."[29]

7. Extraordinary Environmental Sponge Theory

Other analysts, who are not particularly impressed with the perceived inherent brilliance of Jesus or Joseph, contend that they absorbed their ideas from the culture and literature of their day. Consequently, such scholars do not see their ministries as innovative and original, nor do they recognize themes of restoration. Rather, they describe duplication and reiteration of the genius of others.

Many scholars attribute Jesus's teachings and works to groups with whom he may have associated, attempting to explain his contributions by examining the cultures with which he came in contact. Allegro, Bahrdt, and Paulus ascribe his teachings to the Essenes who were known

---

27. Discussion on several philosophers' Christs is found in Clinton Bennett's, *In Search of Jesus*, 91–101.

28. B. H. Roberts, *Joseph Smith, The Prophet-Teacher*, 2nd ed. (Salt Lake City: Deseret Book, 1927).

29. Eugene England, "How Joseph Resolved the Dilemmas of American Romanticism," in *The Prophet Puzzle: Interpretive Essays on Joseph Smith*, ed. Bryan Waterman (Salt Lake City: Signature Books, 1999), 174.

for their knowledge of potions and their ability to heal.[30] This provides these theorists with an explanation for many of Jesus's ideas as well as for some of his miracles. Vivekananda suggests that because Buddha had influenced the Essenes, elements of his teachings are apparent in Christ's doctrine.[31] Others have proposed that Jesus was exposed to the teachings of Buddha by some direct contact, even suggesting that he had visited India. Theorists speculate that the eighteen years that are unaccounted for in Jesus's life were filled with extensive travel and learning, preparatory to his ministry. In essence, scholars have contended that Jesus absorbed his surroundings as he traveled.

Joseph Smith, on the other hand, does not have eighteen missing years in his life, nor was he very well traveled; but due to the religious diversity in upstate New York, he could have come into contact with a number of influential ideas. In addition, while in Ohio, Joseph had a Hebrew teacher named Alexander Neibaur from whom, scholars have suggested, he may have obtained a copy of the Zohar, the Kabala holy text. He also purchased pieces of papyrus with Egyptian hieroglyphics and was well acquainted with several prominent Masons (not becoming a Mason, however, until he lived in Nauvoo). Certainly, these situations and many other ideas extant in his world influenced Joseph's teachings, but to what extent remain highly debatable in most cases. As with the case of Jesus, environmental factors played a role in the life of Joseph, but in neither case can they wholly explain their extraordinary claims and successes. More than the ordinary can plausibly be said to be a contributing factor in the lives of both Jesus and Joseph.

8. Prophetic Deceiver Pigeonhole

Jesus and Joseph both gained influence and momentum by claiming that they were fulfilling prophecy. Under the prophetic deceiver theory, some scholars have proposed that both of them consciously orchestrated or took advantage of certain developments so their followers would believe they had been divinely commissioned to perform their duties.

As is particularly evident in the Gospel of Matthew, many Jews claimed that Jesus was the fulfillment of Hebrew prophecies. Those who did not believe his claims, however, considered him a deceiver who

---

30. Bennett, *In Search of Jesus*, 102, 214, 219.
31. Ibid., 320.

could take advantage of his knowledge of the Jewish traditions and messianic expectations to prove his case. In Hugh Schonfield's opinion, Jesus used the scriptures to define worthy goals, but he was not what his contemporaries or current Christians believed him to be.[32]

Joseph has also been accused of using the scriptures to map his career and shape his church. Some even suggest he composed certain scriptures so he could claim to be fulfilling prophecy. Several critics, however, acknowledge that although Joseph was deceptive, he was, as Dan Vogel noted, a "pious deceiver"[33]—someone sincerely religious who justified his deception by his desire to bring people closer to God: "Applied to Smith's pious deception, his reasoning perhaps went something like the following: those who believe the Book of Mormon and repent, regardless of the book's true origin, will be saved.... For this act, Smith—like Jesus—would suffer in a temporary hell and become a savior to his followers."[34] Bitton points out that this view is becoming more common as writers attempt to "understand Joseph Smith by putting him into a recognized category but one that avoids the uncomfortable alternatives of true prophet or fraud."[35]

9. Multiple Personalities Theory

Despite the difficulty of psychoanalyzing people no longer living—and thus unable to be interviewed or to speak for themselves—ambitious authors have written psychobiographies in an attempt to analyze the minds of prominent figures from the past. When exploring the lives of unique individuals such as Jesus and Joseph, this approach allows an author to ascribe their innovations to an abnormal mind.

In his study of the life of Jesus, Thomas Morris introduces what he calls the "two minds" theory of incarnation. According to his perspective, Jesus was "fully human." Everyone else is "merely human," meaning they are limited in knowledge and power. Although Jesus's human mind learned from sensory experience, made new discoveries, and re-

---

32. Ibid., 263–64.
33. Dan Vogel, "'The Prophet Puzzle' Revisited", in *The Prophet Puzzle: Interpretive Essays on Joseph Smith*, ed. Bryan Waterman (Salt Lake City: Signature Books, 1999), 55.
34. Ibid., 62.
35. Bitton, *Knowing Brother Joseph Again*, 158.

flected upon a plethora of arguments, his divine mind was fully omniscient. Morris claims that those who suffer from multiple personality disorders usually have an executive personality that is fully aware but that remains unknown to other parts of the person. These personalities can, on some occasions, become unified and develop coordinated purposes. Such was the case with Jesus, Morris claims; only his condition was not a disorder because it was not involuntary, nor did it cause him to be dysfunctional. Morris goes on to observe that even ordinary people are not fully unified because they are able to "dissociate" parts of the mind. The difference between merely human minds and the two minds of Christ is one of degree, not kind.[36]

Independent of the Jesus analysts, Joseph's examiners have similarly theorized that he had the ability to dissociate different parts of his mind from one another. As noted earlier, Gary Bergera has diagnosed him as a megalomaniac; he believes Joseph's increasing sense of omnipotence is evidenced by his growing tendency to confuse reality with fantasy.[37] Because Joseph claimed his power came from God and angels, Bergera concludes that the young prophet considered himself above the law; his ego was fed by the support of believers, which increased his confidence and resulted in bolder actions. "Joseph's followers not only reinforced his claims to leadership, they accorded him even greater power by their deference to his leadership."[38] His success is thus explained by his ability to detach himself from reality—the devotion of his supporters only widened the gap between reality and fantasy. One may well wonder, however, how many of these symptoms are based on data and how many are driven by the overlay of the theory that this is how megalomaniacs behave.

10. Charismatic Phenomenon Approach

This sociological approach, provided by Max Weber, argues that both Jesus and Joseph (and many other influential individuals) had a large number of followers because of their charisma.[39] Explanations of

---

36. Thomas V. Morris, *The Logic of God Incarnate* (Ithaca, N.Y.: Cornell University Press, 1986), summarized in Evans, *The Historical Christ and the Jesus of Faith*, 128–32.

37. Bergera, "Joseph Smith and the Hazards of Charismatic Leadership," 239–57.

38. Ibid., 240–41.

39. Max Weber, *The Sociology of Religion*, trans. Ephraim Fischoff (London: Methuen, 1963).

Jesus are often couched in terms of his charismatic ability to capture people's attention, to enthrall their spirits, and to galvanize their loyalty. Jesus's attraction and success are considered the results of his charisma.

Similarly, many people describe Joseph as a charismatic in an effort to explain his popularity. Jan Shipps recognizes that although there was "undoubtedly a charismatic quality to [Joseph's] leadership," this may have had more to do with the preconceived notions of the people who were responding to his claims. She states, "when his pronouncements and actions led certain Saints to conclude that Smith was a fallen prophet, his charisma, for them, evaporated."[40] It is important to note that charisma, personality, and appeal are terms that describe genuine love as well as flattery and deceit. This dynamic is portrayed in a pair of insightful chapters in Davis Bitton's book, *Knowing Brother Joseph Again*, which contrasts the differing eyewitness descriptions and artistic depictions of Joseph Smith's physical appearance and social graces. It clearly delineates between those who had positive and those who had negative responses to the prophet.[41]

11. Magician Theory

Magician theorists claim that religious figures such as Jesus and Joseph were able to conjure up magical forces or produce supernatural illusions. The issue debated is whether they employed their powers or illusions in a conscious effort to deceive or with a sincere belief that their occult activities were salutary.

Morton Smith is the leading modern proponent of the idea that Jesus was a magician.[42] In antiquity, Trypho and Celsus were advocates of this explanation of Jesus. After all, early sources indicate that Jesus was accused of being a trickster, a sorcerer, a wonder worker, a *kakopoios* (a magician), and an exorcist. Morton Smith actually suggests that Je-

---

40. Shipps, "The Prophet Puzzle," 38–39.
41. Bitton, *Knowing Brother Joseph Again*, 41–72.
42. Morton Smith, *Jesus the Magician* (New York: Harper and Row, 1978). Graham H. Twelftree refutes most of the claims that Jesus operated through magic, but he does assert that Jesus was indeed an exorcist. See Graham H. Twelftree, *Jesus the Exorcist: A Contribution to the Study of the Historical Jesus* (Tübingen, Germany: Mohr, 1993). Discussed further in John W. Welch, "Miracles, *Maleficium*, and *Maiestas* in the Trial of Jesus," in *Jesus and Archaeology*, ed. James H. Charlesworth (Grand Rapids, Mich.: Eerdmans, 2006), 349–83, esp. 365–79.

sus learned magic while in Egypt.⁴³ As a magician, he was able to carry out supernatural feats, read minds, and perform hypnosis in order to deceive uneducated Jews and to appear to survive his crucifixion.

Joseph, too, has been labeled as a magician of sorts, whose talents included hypnosis and money-digging, and the use of "witching sticks."⁴⁴ Consequently, some scholars underscore his work as a treasure-seeker, immersed in a superstitious culture.⁴⁵ Not unlike Morton Smith's approach to Jesus, Michael Quinn,⁴⁶ and Lance Owens are among those who believe that investigating the life of Joseph Smith through the lens of magic brings elements "to the surface" that have been overlooked, misunderstood, suppressed, or ignored—"substantiating that Smith and his early followers had multiple involvements with magic, irregular Freemasonry, and traditions generally termed 'occult.'"⁴⁷

12. Satanic Agent Dismissal

Some who reject the divinely appointed missions of Jesus and Joseph, and yet acknowledge that supernatural forces were at work in their lives, have propounded the Satanic agency theory. According to

---

43. Bennett, *In Search of Jesus*, 198–99.

44. I. Woodbridge Riley, *The Founder of Mormonism: A Psychological Study of Joseph Smith Jr.* (London: William Heinemann, 1903).

45. Alan Taylor, "Rediscovering the Context of Joseph Smith's Treasure Seeking," in *The Prophet Puzzle: Interpretive Essays on Joseph Smith*, ed. Bryan Waterman (Salt Lake City: Signature Books, 1999), 141–53; quote on page 151. See the entire issue of *BYU Studies* 24:4 (1984) for Mormon scholarship on the suspected folk magic and money digging in New York.

46. D. Michael Quinn's work in the late 1980s focused on theories of magic. In the 1990s, he concentrated on theories relating to the use and abuse of power. See D. Michael Quinn, *Early Mormonism and the Magic World View*, rev. ed. (Salt Lake City: Signature Books, 1998); D. Michael Quinn, *The Mormon Hierarchy: Extensions of Power* (Salt Lake City: Signature Books, 1997). For a critique of Quinn's books see William J. Hamblin, "That Old Black Magic," *FARMS Review of Books* 12, no. 2 (2000): 225–394; Duane Boyce, "A Betrayal of Trust," *FARMS Review of Books* 9, no. 2 (1997): 147–63; Stephen E. Robinson, "Review of D. Michael Quinn," *BYU Studies* 27 (Fall 1987): 88–95.

47. Lance S. Owens, "Joseph Smith: America's Hermetic Prophet," in *The Prophet Puzzle: Interpretive Essays on Joseph Smith*, ed. Bryan Waterman (Salt Lake City: Signature Books, 1999), 162. For a critique of Owens' work, see William J. Hamblin, "Joseph Smith and the Kabbalah: The Occult Connection," *FARMS Review of Books* 8, no. 2 (1996): 251–325.

this proposition, Jesus and Joseph were involved with apparitions concocted by the devil. Those who embrace this theory do not see Jesus and Joseph as agents who followed God's will, but rather propose that their potency came from evil sources.

Indeed, Jesus and Joseph were both widely known as miracle workers. In addition to healing the sick, they performed exorcisms. This further perpetuated the idea that they consorted with evil spirits. For example, the New Testament includes at least thirty-eight of Jesus's miracles. Likewise, Joseph's followers recorded dozens of miracles they had witnessed. Certain Scribes who had come all the way from Jerusalem to Galilee opined of Jesus that "He hath Beelzebub [a devil], and by the prince of the devils casteth he out devils" (Mark 3:22). Despite its convenience, this theory fails to answer Jesus's own response, "How can Satan cast out Satan? And if a kingdom be divided against itself, that kingdom cannot stand" (Mark 3:23–24).

13. Epilepsy Diagnosis

An explanation that has not been well accepted, but is worth mentioning, is the idea that Jesus suffered from epilepsy. Walter E. Bundy proposed this popular diagnosis, in conjunction with a diagnosis of paranoia, in 1922.[48] A few years before Bundy drew his conclusions, Isaac Woodbridge Riley had proposed a similar diagnosis of Joseph Smith, which included the ailments of vertigo, depression, and migraines. Thin evidence has made such theses extremely suspect. Today, the epilepsy theory is rare in literature about Joseph. Still, Riley was convinced: "The psychiatric definition of the epileptic fits the prophet to a dot."[49] His conviction may be partly understood by recognizing that the psychiatric definition of the epileptic has changed in the last century.

Although epilepsy seemed a viable diagnosis for Jesus and Joseph in the early twentieth century, the theory has not remained credible in either case over the ensuing years. As a result, Bundy and Riley's theories contribute very little to the literature that seeks to explain Jesus and Joseph. It is significant, however, because it shows that scholarship is constantly evolving, and suggests that the theoretical models that are constructed may be inherently limited in scope.

---

48. Walter E. Bundy, *The Psychic Health of Jesus* (New York: Macmillan, 1922).
49. Riley, *The Founder of Mormonism*, 74.

14. Manic Phenomena

In another passing psychological attempt, Lawrence Foster equates events in Joseph's life with manic depression, focusing on mania-induced periods of extraordinary energy and creativity. He uses Joseph's psychotic sons and relatives (six mentioned in total) as further evidence of his condition, which, Foster suggests, could be bipolar disorder.

After diagnosing Joseph, Foster applies his diagnosis to other geniuses, especially religious ones, including Jesus Christ. He concludes,

> [F]inally, I ask whether the hypothesis about Joseph Smith's psychological characteristics may help us in understanding the psychological dynamics of other great prophets and foundational religious figures throughout history.... [O]ne cannot help speculating that the most influential of all religious founding figures, Jesus of Nazareth, called the Christ by his followers, may have been subject to manic-depressive tendencies. Of course, the primary records are so limited and the accretions of interpretation so great that almost nothing can be stated with historical certainty about Jesus except that he lived and had a profound impact on those who knew him best. Nevertheless, if one could look freshly at the reported events of Passion Week, for example, one might at least wonder whether such activities may not suggest manic-depressive behavior.[50]

While one could easily understand if both Jesus and Joseph were at times disappointed and exhausted, explanations for any extreme highs and lows in their tumultuous lives should not be limited to manifestations of some manic pathology.[51]

---

50. Lawrence Foster, "The Psychology of Religious Genius," in *The Prophet Puzzle: Interpretive Essays on Joseph Smith*, ed. Bryan Waterman (Salt Lake City: Signature Books, 1999), 184, 198.

51. Robert D. Anderson, "Toward an Introduction to a Psychobiography of Joseph Smith," in *The Prophet Puzzle: Interpretive Essays on Joseph Smith*, ed. Bryan Waterman (Salt Lake City: Signature Books, 1999), 229. Anderson refutes both the notion that Joseph Smith suffered from a manic-depressive illness and the diagnosis of Bipolar Affective Disorder. To Anderson it sounds like Joseph Smith had a steady chronic condition (not an episodic one) that could have been caused by his environment. "It seems to me that proponents of a clinical manic-depressive diagnosis for Joseph Smith must demonstrate repeated episodes of illness in Smith that reversed his usual temperament, and were minimally or not at all precipitated by external factors"(p. 229).

15. Childhood Post-Traumatic Stress Disorder Theory

Psychologists have generated other theories explaining Jesus and Joseph: one theory places their experiences within the context of childhood post-traumatic stress disorder. According to this theory, Jesus and Joseph's psychological problems not only began at an early age, but were caused by traumatic events that occurred during their youth.

When relying upon this view, one must assume Jesus suffered serious stress and trauma as a boy and young man. Andries van Aarde has developed this theory by asserting that he was a "nobody" from the lower class who may even have been abandoned by his stepfather, Joseph. Because his situation was painful and shameful, van Aarde suggests, he came to regard God as his father. Rocky relationships with his immediate and extended family caused him to develop an interest in the fatherless, the widowed, and the downtrodden. These early stresses explain his ministry to the vulnerable and marginalized of society: the women, the children, the poor, and the sick.[52]

Several psychiatrists have likewise used childhood stress as a formative factor in explaining Joseph's religious ideas. According to Robert Anderson, his stresses began at an early age due to frequent relocation, starvation, and exposure to alcoholics.[53] Jess Groesbeck and Woodbridge Riley both emphasize young Joseph's difficult upbringing, which they describe as a somewhat unhappy family life; they suggest that such details are critical for one seeking to understand the man Joseph became.[54] William Morain focuses on Joseph's childhood surgery as a key cause and explanation of his later psychological problems.[55] This trau-

---

52. Andries G. van Aarde, *Fatherless in Galilee: Jesus as a Child of God* (Harrisburg, Penn.: Trinity, 2001).

53. Robert D. Anderson, "Toward an Introduction to a Psychobiography of Joseph Smith," in *The Prophet Puzzle: Interpretive Essays on Joseph Smith*, ed. Bryan Waterman (Salt Lake City: Signature Books, 1999), 209–37. For a critique of Anderson's views, see Michael D. Jibson, "Korihor Speaks, or the Misinterpretation of Dreams," in *FARMS Review of Books* 14, no. 1 (2002): 223–60.

54. C. Jess Groesbeck, "The Smiths and Their Dreams and Visions," *Sunstone*, 12 no. 2 (1988): 22–29, 64.

55. William D. Morain, *The Sword of Laban, Joseph Smith Jr. and the Dissociated Mind* (Washington, D.C.: American Psychiatric Press, 1998). For a critique of Morain's book, see Richard N. Williams, "The Spirit of Prophecy and the Spirit of Psychiatry: Restoration or Dissociation?" *FARMS Review of Books* 12, no. 1 (2000): 435–44.

matic event, he claims, had several effects on Joseph, which included his fascination with violence and led to his subsequent creation of the Book of Mormon and its focus on war stories.

16. Heroic Monomyth Configuration

Some folklorists have used the heroic monomyth to explain Jesus and Joseph. Stories of virgin births and gods rising from the grave are not limited to a specific religion or culture, and thus Christian variations on these stories are often viewed by anthropologists as adaptations of pagan myths. Consequently, Jesus is believed by many to be just another version of common savior stories that seem to arise from a universal library. These stories, or "archetypes" as Jung and Campbell refer to them, are simply part of the human condition. The fairytale-like elements of Jesus's life add to the conviction of those who subscribe to this theory.[56]

A common misconception among non-Mormons is that Joseph is the Jesus of the Mormons. For many critics Joseph Smith seems to fit nicely into this archetypical savior role as certain parallels between the lives and deaths of Jesus and Joseph would suggest. While casting Joseph Smith as the hero of the Mormon version of the great "monomyth" is a part of the myth theories, it is important to note that it differs from the final theory of "nonexistence or pious exaggeration."

17. Pious Exaggeration Theory

Several analysts have suggested that Jesus was made into a larger-than-life savior by his followers. In many cases, he is believed to have been an ordinary man, perhaps one who did a few noteworthy things, but then became famous after his death because of the exaggerated stories told about him that grew to mythical proportions as they were told and retold. Because the movement of Christianity is believed by many to be Paul's creation, some have suggested that this apostle may have marketed the fictional gospels as fact. And, finally, the deceiver is often defined as "the church" itself which, though it knows the mythical truth of its savior, continues to attest that he was a reality.[57] In many

---

56. See various works of Joseph Campbell, particularly exemplary in *The Power of Myth* (New York: Anchor Books, 1991); also Bennett, *In Search of Jesus*, 202–8.

57. Bennett, *In Search of Jesus*, 202–13.

cases, this theory expands into the claim that the Jesus of the Gospels himself never existed.[58]

Similar claims are made with respect to Joseph: many note that he became larger than life in the minds of his supporters. Exaggerations of some details undoubtedly occurred, but just because theory tells us that the reports of some pious people tend to be overstated, that should not be interpreted to say that all such reports should be viewed as myths. And fortunately—at least so far—no one has suggested that Joseph Smith was a fiction of Brigham Young or Parley P. Pratt.

Concluding Observations

In conclusion, this brief survey of some of the various explanations that have been given to account for theory-based explanations often to serve as interpretive lenses through which data about Jesus Christ and Joseph Smith have been sorted and understood and in which missing information can be provided and inferred. However, if not handled with care theories may be hazardous to one's academic and spiritual health. By their nature, they isolate and elevate certain factors. As abstractions, they necessarily oversimplify. In their efforts to explain, they reduce the complex to the simple. In creating order, they reduce the extraordinary to the ordinary. These moves are not, however, always in the service of truth. The sheer number of explanations which have been developed indicate that none of them is entirely compelling. Of course, the Jesus or Joseph of faith must be seen, ultimately, through the lens of faith or predilection. But then so must any theory.

In the end, our purpose in reviewing these theories has not been to critique in any depth their various strengths and weaknesses. Furthermore, we have not attempted to explain the inexplicable. Nor is our concern based upon whether these theories are right or wrong, or if they are correctly or incorrectly applied. Those tasks are left for another investigative inquiry. Instead, what we have found most intriguing is the high degree of congruence between the set of explanations that are used to describe Jesus and the set of theories mainly used to account for Joseph Smith. What one should make of this congruence, we leave for readers and philosophers like David Paulsen to ponder. Perhaps this phenomenon will reveal something about the finite number of possible

---

58. Ibid., 209–13.

explanations open to one who rejects the autobiographical declarations attributed to Jesus or made by Joseph and his contemporaries. Does it say something about the natural human reactions to supernatural interruptions into ordinary life? Might these similar reactions suggest something about the shared means and methods of their respective missions or about a possible common source of their light and power? Is it possible that this pattern of comparable explanations offers a key that can simultaneously solve both the foundational "Prophet puzzle" as well as the all-important "Messiah puzzle"?

9

Is Evangelical Mormonism a Viable Concept for the Near Future?

Craig L. Blomberg, *Denver Seminary*

In 1991, Richard Mouw authored a small sidebar to an article on new developments in the Church of Jesus Christ of Latter-day Saints entitled "Evangelical Mormonism?"[1] Intrigued by recent publications of Mormon authors that seemed to reflect views noticeably closer to Protestant orthodoxy than he was accustomed to seeing, Mouw wondered whether the time would soon arrive when there would be an identifiable minority within Latter-day Saints that could be accepted by other Evangelicals as theologically kindred spirits. Today it would appear that such individuals, to varying degrees, do exist, so that the more important question has become whether an Evangelical *wing* or *movement* within Mormonism might be emerging.

Prior to Vatican II in the mid-1960s, it was virtually unheard of to call someone an Evangelical Catholic; after that council and the charismatic renewal *movement* within Catholicism, it became not at all uncommon to hear Protestants and Catholics alike using the term as a label for individuals. It is possible to speak of entire parishes, seminaries, or publishing houses within Catholic circles as more or less Evangelical.[2] Might these developments represent a helpful analogy for what we have in mind?

Early in his ministry, Walter Martin considered Seventh-day Adventists (SDA) a cult—in the sense of being a heterodox, sectarian off-

---

1. Richard Mouw, "Evangelical Mormonism?" *Christianity Today* 35 (November 1991): 30.
2. Perhaps the most famous outgrowth of these developments is the document entitled "Evangelicals and Catholics Together," *First Things* 43 (May 1994): 15–22. For detailed reflection on the document, see Charles Colson and Richard J. Neuhaus, *Evangelicals and Catholics Together: Toward a Common Mission* (Nashville, Tenn.: Nelson, 1995).

shoot of a major religion, in this case Protestant Christianity. By the time he wrote *The Kingdom of the Cults*, however, he devoted a lengthy appendix to explaining why he had disavowed this categorization.[3] Evangelicalism was by then one of three full-fledged *wings* or *branches* of SDA life, along with traditional and liberal segments. More recently, the Worldwide Church of God, once acknowledged by insiders and outsiders alike as heterodox, made a dramatic change in its doctrinal statement and was welcomed into the National Association of Evangelicals.[4] Could either of these developments be useful analogies for what could unfold in the LDS world?

If not something akin to the developments that occurred in each of these three religious groups, might *other* processes unfold leading to an Evangelical Mormonism? Or might an Evangelical understanding of the meaning of LDS doctrinal affirmations, and the breadth of interpretation of them allowed, permit at least some identifiable group of Mormons to be fairly categorized as Evangelical? Or, finally, could some combination of both kinds of shifts occur? Senator Orrin Hatch of Utah, speaking to a gathering of Christian broadcasters in Washington, D. C., in 2000 during his bid for the Republican presidential nomination, publicly identified himself as an Evangelical Mormon. But he did not clarify in any detail what he meant by the label.[5] Over the past fifteen years, various Evangelical and LDS scholars and church leaders have sat down together for theological dialogues, seeking to clarify just what it is that each person or group believes concerning the major theological issues of their faiths, along with the currently acceptable diversity of perspectives in their traditions on any given doctrine. More often than not, the two "sides" have discovered that they were closer to each other than they had previously thought.[6] Is all this lead-

---

3. Walter R. Martin, *The Kingdom of the Cults* rev. ed. (Minneapolis: Bethany, 1977), 360–423.

4. For the story, see J. Michael Feazell, *The Liberation of the Worldwide Church of God* (Grand Rapids, Mich.: Zondervan, 2003); Larry A. Nichols and George Mather, *Discovering the Plain Truth: How the Worldwide Church of God Encountered the Gospel of Grace* (Downers Grove, Ill.: IVP, 1998).

5. This story was shared with me by Robert P. Dugan Jr., then Director of the Office of Public Affairs of the National Association of Evangelicals in Washington, DC, who was in attendance.

6. The three such dialogues published in book-length form are Craig L. Blomberg and Stephen E. Robinson, *How Wide the Divide? A Mormon and an*

ing anywhere? Because of Dr. David L. Paulsen's continuous interest in and participation in these kinds of conversations,[7] I would like to pursue this question further in this collection of essays honoring his illustrious career.

Clarifying Contexts

Mormonism has historically been ambivalent about its relationship with the rest of what it calls "Christendom." On the one hand, its whole *raison d'etre* centers around the conviction that Joseph Smith Jr., was a prophet of God, appointed to restore true Christianity to earth, after the Great Apostasy that began in the second century A.D. quickly corrupted the true apostolic faith and led to the loss of many "plain and precious parts" of the Gospel.[8] Early nineteenth-century Protestants, Catholics, and Eastern Orthodox alike all shared the term "Christian" and assumed that the entirety of the Christian world fell into one of these three subdivisions. As Latter-day Saints emerged they understandably tried to distance themselves to avoid being viewed as just one more form of Christianity—at best no better than, and at worst considerably inferior to, the rest (if not outside the pale altogether).[9]

Evangelical in Conversation (Downers Grove, Ill.: IVP, 1997); Robert L. Millet and Gerald R. McDermott, *Claiming Christ: A Mormon-Evangelical Debate* (Grand Rapids, Mich.: Brazos, 2007); and Robert L. Millet and Gregory C. V. Johnson, *Bridging the Divide: The Continuing Conversation between a Mormon and an Evangelical* (Rhinebeck, N.Y.: Monkfish, 2007).

7. Early in his academic career, David Paulsen studied for his doctorate in philosophy with evangelical scholar, George I. Mavrodes, at the University of Michigan. Since 1999, with a handful of exceptions, semi-annual gatherings of Evangelical and Mormon scholars have alternated meeting at either Fuller Seminary or Brigham Young University and the Society of Biblical Literature/American Academy of Religion meetings. Paulsen has been a regular, active and engaging participant. He was also instrumental in initiating and publishing the results of dialogues with non-evangelical Christians; see Donald W. Musser and David L. Paulsen, eds., *Mormons in Dialogue with Contemporary Christian Theologies* (Macon, Ga.: Mercer, 2007).

8. See Kent P. Jackson, *From Apostasy to Restoration* (Salt Lake City: Deseret, 1996). The language in quotation marks appears in 1 Nephi 13:34–35.

9. At the same time, nineteenth-century Christians do not seem to share the general assumption that all Mormons were non-Christian, as Christians frequently have been assuming in the last half century or so.

After all, they believed themselves to be the *one*, true, restored Church. On the other hand, for that very same reason, it made no sense to them when others called them non-Christian. They insisted that they served the Jesus of the New Testament. They were certainly not a kind of Jew, Muslim, Buddhist, Hindu, nor a devotée of any other world religion. What else could they be but Christian?[10]

Evangelicals, on the other hand, while understanding the broader use of the term Christian as a descriptor of anyone who professes some kind of allegiance to Jesus or is a member of a "Christian" church, have typically used the word as a synonym for someone who is "saved"—that is to say, who has trusted in Jesus as his or her Lord and Savior and thus had a conversion experience, however instantaneous or gradual it may have been. Among *scholars* worldwide, the four-part definition of British historian, David Bebbington, is probably the most commonly cited: Evangelicals are those who have a generally high view of the inspiration and authority of the Bible, who have had a conversion experience, who seek to live a cruciform lifestyle; and who are evangelistic in their mission, seeking to win others to the faith.[11]

Definitions like these, whether popular or scholarly, make good sense when distinguishing between conservative and liberal members of historic Christian churches. Since the Enlightenment, liberal Christianity has been characterized by a lower view of Scripture, which at best adopts a *de facto* canon within the canon, while rejecting as inspired and authoritative those parts of the Bible they deem theologically or morally unacceptable. Liberals have typically not taught the need for a conversion experience, have not sought to evangelize others, nor have they stressed salvation by grace through faith apart from works. Indeed, they have often outperformed Evangelicals in venues of social action, which Evangelicals until recently unnecessarily shunned, fearing that their emphasis on Christ and his substitutionary atonement would be transformed into a works-based message of self-help.[12]

---

10. Among contemporary Latter-day Saints, see especially Stephen E. Robinson, *Are Mormons Christians?* (Salt Lake City: Bookcraft, 1991).

11. David W. Bebbington, *Evangelicalism in Modern Britain: A History from the 1730s to the 1980s* (London: Unwin Hyman, 1989), 2–3.

12. Richard J. Mouw, *The Smell of Sawdust: What Evangelicals Can Learn from Their Fundamentalist Heritage?* (Grand Rapids, Mich.: Zondervan, 2000), 71–76, likewise emphasizes the role of liberal denials of various historic Christian doctrines as the key motivation for their central function in Evangelicalism.

It is not clear that Bebbington's definition is as useful in the twenty-first century, however, when self-identified Evangelicals have often outdone self-identified liberals in social action, are overall richer and more materialistic (at least in the U.S.), and, as a result, far less cruciform than they were even just a generation ago. Evangelicals' strong emphasis on evangelism and conversion, moreover, is somewhat more muted today than in generations past. Of course, one could reply that this simply shows that those who self-identify as Evangelical are watering down the term through the breadth of their practices and beliefs, and that those who do not conform to Bebbington's definition should be called something else. But it is perhaps better to observe that, at least in the last hundred years, Evangelicals have typically placed theological or doctrinal confessions above all other indicators of the faith, so that people who still affirm in good conscience the so-called fundamentals of the faith should continue to merit the label, even if their praxis is becoming more varied.[13]

The problem with applying any one of these approaches to defining "Evangelical" to the question of an Evangelical Mormonism is that many Mormons appear quickly to qualify for the label! They regularly profess Jesus Christ as Lord and Savior, with approximately one-quarter of them acknowledging a distinct conversion experience,[14] while many more, if more conversant with Evangelical terminology, would at the very least admit that the date of their baptism and confirmation could be considered the time at which they were "born again." Their evangelistic fervor may be unparalleled among the religions and denominations of the world. They believe the Bible is God's inspired word. Perhaps their life and thought is not as Cross-centered as many Evangelicals could wish, but it is hard to argue that either group demonstrates huge amounts of self-denial these days, despite the considerable histories of both that have been so characterized. Evangelicals and Mormons, nevertheless, still sense that important issues separate them, preventing facile application of either term to the other group.[15]

---

13. Cf. Robert K. Johnston, "American Evangelicalism: An Extended Family," in *The Variety of American Evangelicalism*, eds. Donald W. Dayton and Robert K. Johnston (Knoxville: University of Tennessee Press, 1991), 254.

14. See Craig L. Blomberg, "Is Mormonism Christian?" in *The New Mormon Challenge: Responding to the Latest Defenses of a Fast-Growing Movement*, eds. Francis J. Beckwith, Carl Mosser, Paul Owen (Grand Rapids, Mich.: Zondervan, 2002), 330, 488 n. 66.

15. See briefly Matthew R. Connelly and BYU Studies Staff, "Sizing up the

What then stands in the way of the identification of Mormonism, or a subset thereof, as viably (i.e., meaningfully) Evangelical? It is doubtless the sum total of the distinctive LDS creedal affirmations and the larger culture that they and the shared histories of the membership have created.[16] Although Mormons have historically been opposed to creeds and creedalism, Joseph Smith's Articles of Faith nevertheless appear in form, and function in practice, remarkably like the Apostles' or Nicene Creeds do for many Christians, or like the Westminster Confession does for Calvinist Christianity, or like modern denominational and parachurch statements of faith do for the churches or organizations that subscribe to them. At the same time, most creeds contain some affirmations that are deemed more peripheral or less central than others, such that subscribers can disagree with them and yet still be "in the fold." For example, the "descent into hell" clause was not officially adopted into the Apostles' Creed for a full half-millennium (eighth century) after the development of the creed's earliest forms (third century) and has been changed to "he descended to the dead" or some equivalent in various modern formulations.[17] Ordinands for certain Presbyterian denominations are allowed to disagree with certain clauses of the Westminster Confession with impunity.[18] Evangelical colleges and seminaries may have a detailed statement of faith to which full-time faculty must subscribe "with hearty and unfeigned acceptance" while allowing students, staff and adjunct faculty the leeway to affirm their agreement merely with the much briefer and more generic statement of faith of a group like the National Association of Evangelicals (NAE).[19] So perhaps there is, or could be, recognition of more and less central parts of LDS doctrinal statements, too.

Divide: Reviews and Replies," *BYU Studies* 38 (1999): 163–72. For extensive documentation, see the various reviews of Blomberg and Robinson, *How Wide the Divide?* in *FARMS Review of Books* 11.2 (1999): 1–209.

16. See esp. David L. Rowe, *I ♥ Mormons: A New Way to Share Christ with Latter-day Saints* (Grand Rapids, Mich.: Baker, 2005). Cf. Ross Anderson, *Understanding Your Mormon Neighbor* (Grand Rapids, Mich.: Zondervan, 2011).

17. See "The Apostles' Creed," Evangelical Lutheran Church of America, http://www.elca.org/What-We-Believe/Statements-of-Belief/The-Apostles-Creed.aspx (accessed April 24, 2012).

18. For example, in the Evangelical Presbyterian Church. Disagreements are presented to local presbyteries, who then vote on whether or not to accept the ordinand, in view of the specific issues involved.

19. This is, for example, the exact policy of Denver Seminary, where I teach.

Comparing Latter-day Saints and the National Association of Evangelicals

Presumably, a good way to address the question of a viable Evangelical Mormonism would be to see if Latter-day Sainsts could remain in good standing with their Church and simultaneously affirm in good conscience the NAE statement of faith. That statement reads:

> We believe the Bible to be the inspired, the only infallible, authoritative Word of God. We believe that there is one God, eternally existent in three persons: Father, Son and Holy Spirit. We believe in the deity of our Lord Jesus Christ, in His virgin birth, in His sinless life, in His miracles, in His vicarious and atoning death through His shed blood, in His bodily resurrection, in His ascension to the right hand of the Father, and in His personal return in power and glory. We believe that for the salvation of lost and sinful people, regeneration by the Holy Spirit is absolutely essential. We believe in the present ministry of the Holy Spirit by whose indwelling the Christian is enabled to live a godly life. We believe in the resurrection of both the saved and the lost; they that are saved unto the resurrection of life and they that are lost unto the resurrection of damnation. We believe in the spiritual unity of believers in our Lord Jesus Christ.[20]

Let us look at each of these seven sentences, in turn, in light of recent LDS doctrinal discussions.

Latter-day Saints affirm five works of inspired scripture as uniquely authoritative for belief and practice: the Old Testament, New Testament, Book of Mormon, Doctrine and Covenants, and Pearl of Great Price. Although the Joseph Smith Translation of the Bible is used (in widely varying degrees) by various Mormons—often more as an interpretation than as a competing translation—it is the King James Version of the Bible that is the officially endorsed version to which Mormon bibliology applies.[21] Evangelical bibliological affirmations typically apply to the original Hebrew/Aramaic and Greek manuscripts of the Bible. It would be only in a few Fundamentalist circles where inspiration would be ascribed to the KJV, but almost no one would disqualify a per-

---

20. "Statement of Faith," National Association of Evangelicals, http://www.nae.net/about-us/statement-of-faith (accessed April 24, 2012).

21. See in particular Robert J. Matthews, *"A Plainer Translation": Joseph Smith's Translation of the Bible –A History and Commentary* (Provo, Utah: Brigham Young University Press, 1975).

son as not being an Evangelical solely on the basis of this conviction. To be sure, the re-emergence of the term Evangelical in the United States after World War II set one group of conservative Christians off from the even more conservative Fundamentalists,[22] but in the decades since, as noted above, "Evangelical" has become used primarily as an antonym for a theological liberal. Taking what most Evangelicals would consider an *overly* conservative view of the Bible simply moves a person in an even *more* Evangelical direction in this latter, more dominant sense of the term. That leaves just the adverb "only" in the first sentence of the NAE statement of faith as a barrier to Latter-day Saints affirming it, at least as long as they treat their other three books of scripture as on an exact par with the Old and New Testaments in divine origin and authority in the believer's life.

Turning to theology proper (the doctrine of God), Mormons unequivocally believe in Father, Son, and Holy Spirit but would often demur at the wording "one God, eternally existent in three persons," especially when it is used to express the historic Christian doctrine of the Trinity. Two issues call for attention here. First is the relation between the oneness and the "threeness" of God. In large part due to Joseph Smith's "First Vision" of Father and Son as separate embodied persons, Latter-day Saints prefer to speak of one Godhead, a community of divine persons united in mind, will and purpose, but not ontologically or essentially one Being.[23] On the other hand, David Paulsen and Brett McDonald have committed themselves in print to a kind of social Trinitariansim closely akin to that espoused by Evangelical Cornelius Plantinga. In an essay now twenty years old but still not as well-known as it should be, Plantinga argues that a biblical doctrine of the Trinity must recognize each of the three persons "as distinct centers of knowledge, will, love, and action," and thus "of consciousness." Descriptions of God's unity must cohere with this definition of distinct persons even while the three must be sufficiently united to "constitute a particular social unit."[24]

---

22. Sparked particularly by Carl F. H. Henry, *The Uneasy Conscience of Modern Fundamentalism* (Grand Rapids: Eerdmans, 1947).

23. Robinson, *How Wide the Divide?* 127–41.

24. Cornelius Plantinga, "Social Trinitarianism and Tritheism," in *Trinity, Incarnation and Atonement*, eds. Ronald J. Feenstra and Cornelius Plantinga (Notre Dame, Ind.: University of Notre Dame Press, 1989), 21–47, quotations on p. 34.

Paulsen and McDonald concur thus far. They proceed to defend, with classic LDS thought, a hierarchical rather than a fully egalitarian model of the relationship of the three persons, consistent with what at least some Evangelicals likewise affirm.[25] Also differing from Plantinga is Paulsen's adoption of a libertarian approach to free will, so that the unity maintained among the persons of the Godhead "*cannot* be one of coercion of any type, nor can it be simply a matter of necessity. Instead any and all unity within the Godhead must principally arise and be maintained through freely given and freely reciprocated love."[26] Many Evangelicals may demur, but again the debate between compatibilist and libertarian free will is an *intra-evangelical* one. Many Latter-day Saints, hearing popular formulations of the doctrine of the Trinity, think that *Evangelicals* have fallen into heresy, specifically the heresy of modalism, but the language of "distinct centers of personal consciousness" is standard in scholarly circles.[27]

The second issue related to the doctrine of the Trinity involves the words, "eternally existent in." Mormons believe that Jesus is the literal Son of God, so that by some process unspecified in their canonical scriptures, Jesus shares, as we might phrase it today, the actual DNA of both God the Father and Mary.[28] Evangelicals, like most (but not all) Christians throughout history, do not believe God the Father has ever been *essentially* embodied, but they agree with Mormons that God the Son became incarnate for the first time in Jesus of Nazareth.[29] Because Jesus,

---

25. See Robert Letham, *The Holy Trinity: In Scripture, History, Theology and Worship* (Phillipsburg, N.J.: Presbyterian & Reformed, 2004).

26. David Paulsen and Brett McDonald, "Joseph Smith and the Trinity: An Analysis and Defense of the Social Model of the Godhead," *Faith and Philosophy* 25 (2008): 63–64, italics in original. The significance of this article is seen in that it is the first Mormon offering ever accepted for publication in this historically Christian journal.

27. Gordon R. Lewis and Bruce A. Demarest, *Integrative Theology*, vol. 2 (Grand Rapids, Mich.: Zondervan, 1990), 258, 271.

28. Robinson in *How Wide the Divide?* 135–36, and in personal conversation.

29. Distinctive, however, is the equation of Jesus with Jehovah of the Old Testament, understood by everyone else as God the *Father*, rather than God the Son. As Roger R. Keller phrases it: "The unique Christian surprise is not that Jehovah has a son who is Jesus but rather that Jesus who is Jehovah has a Father." Roger R. Keller, "Jesus is Jehovah (YHWH): A Study in the Gospels," in *Jesus Christ: Son of God, Savior*, eds. Paul H. Peterson, Gary L. Hatch, and Laura D. Card (Provo, Utah: Religious Studies Center, Brigham Young University, 2002), 121.

in LDS thought, like all other people (and even angels), pre-existed as a spirit being, there is no difficulty saying that Jesus eternally existed. The question is whether he eternally existed *in* his role as fully God. Traditionally, Mormons have not expressed themselves in this fashion, but it would not seem that there is anything in their canonical scriptures to preclude it. The Lorenzo Snow couplet, "As man now is, God once was; as God now is, man may be,"[30] of course, contradicts even the eternal deity of God the *Father*. Granted this affirmation has functioned, like Joseph Smith's subsequent King Follett discourse, with its apparent affirmation of God as once *merely* human, as quasi-canonical;[31] some recent LDS writers have stressed that Mormons are not bound by these assertions, that they actually know little of what Smith (or Snow) meant in any detail, and that musings related to the idea that God or Jesus was once only a man are less influential today than ever and should not stand as barriers to interfaith doctrinal agreement.[32]

The third sentence of the NAE statement, on the person and work of Jesus, would appear to be wholly amenable to Latter-day Saints. Whatever the outcome of the debate over Christ's deity in eternity past is, "the deity of our Lord Jesus Christ" from a time at least long before the creation of the universe, his "virgin birth," "sinless life," "miracles," "vicarious and atoning death through his shed blood," "bodily resurrection," "ascension to the right hand of the Father," and "personal return in power and glory" are all important tenets of Mormon Christology.[33] To be sure, the cross has not always been as central as Evangelicals could have wished it were, but recent writers are starting to correct this imbalance of emphasis as well.[34] Of course, one of the distinctive elements of

---

30. First shared with Joseph Smith in 1843. The King Follett funeral sermon in 1844 would elaborate this concept.

31. As stressed by Ronald V. Huggins, "Lorenzo Snow's Couplet: 'As Man Now Is, God Once Was; As God Now Is, Man May Be:' No Functioning Place In Present-Day Mormon Doctrine?" A Response to Richard Mouw," *Journal of the Evangelical Theological Society* 49 (2006): 549–68.

32. Robert L. Millet, *The Vision of Mormonism: Pressing the Boundaries of Christianity* (St. Paul, Minn.: Paragon House, 2007), 275–76. Cf. Robinson, *How Wide the Divide?* 84–88.

33. See Craig J. Ostler, "The Divine Nature of Jesus Christ During Mortality," in *Jesus Christ, Son of God, Savior*, eds. Peterson, Hatch and Card, 207–24; Robert L. Millet, *A Different Jesus? The Christ of the Latter-day Saints* (Grand Rapids and Cambridge, Mich.: Eerdmans, 2005), 66–69.

34. Andrew C. Skinner, *Golgotha* (Salt Lake City: Deseret, 2004); Robert L.

the LDS theology of the atonement is that it began in the garden of Gethsemane, and sometimes Gethsemane has been emphasized above Golgotha. But Mormon doctrine is clear that Gethsemane without Golgotha could never have atoned for the sins of the world. It is not spilled blood alone but blood spilled *in death* that satisfies God's demand for "a life for a life."[35] Paradoxically, Joseph Smith's lack of access to any ancient Greek manuscripts of the New Testament meant that he relied on the KJV's inclusion of Luke 22:44, with its insistence that Christ's sweat in the garden "was as it were great drops of blood falling down to the ground," without being aware of the strong likelihood that this verse and its predecessor did not form part of Luke's original text.[36] He also appears to have misinterpreted (or deliberately changed) the simile so that Jesus actually sweat blood (Mosiah 3:7; D&C 19:16–19).[37] But this simply meant that there was even more blood for Latter-day Saints to point to as involved in Christ's atonement—hardly a concept to which Evangelicals should object, at least in principle.

One of the astonishing omissions in the NAE statement is any sentence or clause about the need for human faith in Christ and his Cross-work, any affirmation of salvation by grace through faith alone (*sola gratia* or *sola fide*), or any denial of synergism or works-righteousness. Presumably, the statement's framers believed that "regeneration by the Holy Spirit" adequately communicated these truths and guarded against any heterodox views, while allowing for the full range of Calvinist through Arminian soteriologies. Again, while historically it has often appeared clear to non-Mormons that Mormon doctrine has taught salvation by faith plus works,[38] recent writings have clarified the theological language in ways that suggest agreement could be reached with Evangelicals that works are the essential outgrowth of saving faith but not what saves *per se*.[39]

Millet, *What Happened to the Cross? Distinctive LDS Teachings* (Salt Lake City: Deseret, 2007).

35. Andrew C. Skinner, *Gethsemane* (Salt Lake City: Deseret, 2002), 16.

36. Bruce M. Metzger, ed., *A Textual Commentary on the Greek New Testament*, rev. ed. (Stuttgart and New York: United Bible Societies, 1994), 151.

37. Mormons, of course, would attribute Smith's convictions to divine revelation.

38. Seemingly as recently as Stephen E. Robinson, *Believing Christ: The Parable of the Bicycle and Other Good News* (Salt Lake City: Deseret, 1992), 30–34.

39. See the changed phraseology in Stephen E. Robinson, *Following Christ: The Parable of the Divers and More Good News* (Salt Lake City: Deseret, 1995), 78–90.

Latter-day Saints have numerous scriptures that clearly support justification entirely by God's grace through faith in Christ's completed Cross-work (e.g., 2 Ne. 2:4–8, 10:24, 31:19; Mosiah 3:12; Alma 2:14–16). But it is their insistence on the necessity of ordinances, especially baptism, for salvation that seems most clearly to call this other strand of teaching into question. Spencer Fluhman, however, highlights the language of D&C 84:35–38 in which the priesthood, like "all that my father hath" is given freely to humans, dependent solely on their reception of it. Fluhman elaborates:

> For me, that word *receive* is the grand key. Every ritual act in the Church is in fact an act of reception or acceptance. In my mind, participation in the ordinances of the Church does not *earn* salvation for the Saints. I am not convinced that ordinances can *qualify* us for exaltation, either. No decision, no earthly work, no human striving could possibly *merit* "all that my Father hath." Does any Latter-day Saint think that the accumulated righteousness of a lifetime could deserve *that*? No. Latter-day Saints stand with the rest of Christendom, "all amazed . . . [and] confused at the grace that so fully he proffers" us. . . . His unmatched gifts are just that: gifts. And no one earns gifts.[40]

Much Mormon theologizing that seems to stand in tension with this way of phrasing things has been an understandable reaction to the old dispensationalist view that one can be saved by Jesus without accepting him as Lord, however desirable such a second step is, and therefore that good works are optional for the believer.[41] Evangelicals would do well, not merely in interfaith conversations but for the good of their own flock, to repudiate this potentially damning heresy once and for all.[42] While it is true that believers coming to Christ can never know in advance everything he might ask them to do throughout their lives,

---

Cf. Robert L. Millet, *After All We Can Do. . . Grace Works* (Salt Lake City: Deseret, 2003), 115–45.

40. J. Spencer Fluhman, "1835: Authority, Power, and the 'Government of the Church of Christ,'" in *Joseph Smith: The Prophet and Seer*, eds. Richard N. Holzapfel and Kent P. Jackson (Provo, Utah: BYU Religious Studies Center, 2010), 226.

41. Richard R. Hopkins, *Biblical Mormonism: Responding to Evangelical Criticism of LDS Theology* (Bountiful, Utah: Horizon, 1994), 130–36.

42. Damning if people die without trusting in Christ as Lord. Cf. further John F. MacArthur, Jr., *The Gospel according to Jesus*, rev. ed. (Grand Rapids, Mich.: Zondervan, 1994); John F. MacArthur Jr., *The Gospel according to the Apostles* (Nashville, Tenn.: Word, 2000).

and that it is impossible to establish any criterion of a certain quality or quantity of obedience to which all believers must attain, given their vastly different life spans and circumstances after their conversions, any formulation of the Gospel that pretends that people can be truly saved while consciously refusing to let Jesus be master over their lives is such a distortion of biblical teaching that it in fact saves no one.[43] But the NAE's lack of any statement at all with respect to this debate certainly allows Latter-day Saints to agree with the one sentence about the essential need for regeneration by the Holy Spirit.[44]

The next sentence of the NAE statement treats the indwelling Holy Spirit in the life of believers "enabling" them to live godly lives. Intriguingly, while omitting any explicit affirmation of salvation by grace through faith, there is express mention of the doctrine of sanctification—living godly lives. Again, doubtless because of the range of Evangelical convictions concerning how much sanctification a believer can attain in this life, no further refinement of the doctrine appears. But Latter-day Saints desire for Christian perfection, more akin to Wesleyan than Calvinist or Lutheran thought,[45] certainly falls within the range of options here. Interestingly, the adjective chosen ("godly") is merely one of several that could have communicated roughly the same central Evangelical conviction. "Holy," "sanctified," "set apart," or "righteous" may well have been considered in the process of formulating this sentence. But by choosing "godly," the framers of the NAE confession have chosen the term etymologically and conceptually closest to "godlike," the very concept in Mormonism that often casts a pall of suspicion over their doctrine of sanctification in the minds of outsiders.

Historically, there have been times and places in which Mormons, including their highest leaders and Church authorities, have indeed

---

43. See further, Darrell L. Bock, "Jesus as Lord in Acts and the Gospel Message," *Bibliotheca Sacra* 143 (1986): 146–54; and Darrell L. Bock, "A Review of *The Gospel According to Jesus*, by J. F. MacArthur, Jr., 1988," *Bibliotheca Sacra* 146 (1989): 21–40.

44. Andrew C. Skinner, "Rebirth in Christ: A Latter-day Saint Perspective," in *Salvation in Christ: Comparative Christian Views*, eds. Roger R. Keller and Robert L. Millet (Provo, Utah: Religious Studies Center, Brigham Young University, 2005), 7–27.

45. As is Mormonism's rejection of the Calvinist "TULIP" (total depravity, unconditional election, limited atonement, irresistible grace, and perseverance of the saints), its emphasis on subjective personal feelings and experience; its overt conversionism; its manner of local organization; and its empowerment of the laity.

spoken of attaining to godhood, while their distinctive canonical scriptures use the language of humans becoming "gods."[46] But if it remains acceptable, as it is currently, to define such terminology in the same way that C. S. Lewis did,[47] so that exalted humans always remain subordinate to God and Jesus, contingent beings dependent on Father and Son, and never appropriate objects of worship by others,[48] even this initially jarring use of theological language does not create any necessary contradiction of meaning between its Mormon proponents and classic Evangelical theology.

The penultimate sentence of the NAE confession affirms the resurrection of all people, some to everlasting life and some to everlasting death—that is, to heaven or hell. Mormonism goes considerably beyond classic Christian thought in affirming three kingdoms for those resurrected to life—the celestial, terrestrial and, using a word Joseph Smith apparently coined, the telestial (D&C 76). Different categories of people wind up in each of these three kingdoms, with the celestial kingdom being the most desirable, where both God and Jesus are present and believers can be continuously and increasingly exalted via the concept of eternal progression. We need not detain ourselves here with either the explicit teaching or the subsequent theological inferences about who attains to each kingdom and what exactly each sphere of existence is like, other than to observe, as Stephen Robinson points out, that the middle or terrestrial kingdom approximates the traditional Christian concept of heaven.[49] Latter-day Saints, however, affirm that its residents get to be only with Jesus, but also with God the Father. The telestial kingdom is noticeably less attractive than traditional "heaven," but it apparently is still more desirable than undesirable, and far better than hell. From an Evangelical perspective, the only potentially objectionable parts of the doctrine of the celestial kingdom would be the additional, non-canonical assumptions that sometimes accrue to it, especially that its residents—those who accept the restored gospel as Latter-day Saints understand it,

---

46. See esp. D&C 76:58; 132:20.

47. Such as beings whose glorified states, if we could see them today, would tempt us to worship them. See his *The Weight of Glory and Other Addresses*, rev. ed. (New York: Macmillan, 2001), 18.

48. Robinson, *Are Mormons Christian?* 63–65. Cf. Skinner, *Gethsemane*, 99.

49. Robinson, *How Wide the Divide?* 152.

whether in this life or the next—attain to it by works apart from grace, which issue we have already dealt with above.

It is often said that if one combines Mormon soteriology and eschatology, the result is "salvation by grace but exaltation by works." That is to say, salvation is equated with mere resurrection to new life, whereas the kingdom in which one finds one's self is entirely dependent on one's performance as a believer in this life.[50] Whether this is an accurate portrayal of various Latter-day Saints' beliefs (and Fluhman clearly rejects it above), what is intriguing is its close correspondence to the Calvinist and Wesleyan carry-over from the Roman Catholic doctrine of purgatory,[51] namely, that Christians attain to heaven by grace through faith alone but then are assigned degrees of glory or eternal rewards based on their works in this life. Yet instead of three kingdoms, there is the potential for as many degrees of blessing or gradations of reward as there are inhabitants of heaven itself! Martin Luther strenuously objected to this notion, however,[52] and, while most popular Evangelical thought asserts some kind of degrees of reward in heaven, the more one studies the LDS mutation of this doctrine, the more one may well appreciate Luther's wisdom in steering clear of it altogether. Of course, many who claim to believe in it subsequently eviscerate it of all its motivating power by arguing that we are unaware of these rewards, that we all enjoy heaven equally even if we have different capacities with which to enjoy it, or that we cast our "crowns" back at Jesus' feet.[53] Such caveats reflect a correct, intuitive dissatisfaction with the doctrine by those who nevertheless think the Bible teaches it, when in fact a good case can be made for insisting that it does not teach it at all.[54] But for our purposes,

---

50. Jerald and Sandra Tanner, "Terminology," in *The Counterfeit Gospel of Mormonism*, ed. Norman L. Geisler (Eugene, Ore.: Harvest House, 1998), 205–6, citing Bruce R. McConkie.

51. Emma Disley, "Degrees of Glory: Protestant Doctrine and the Concept of Rewards Hereafter," *Journal of Theological Studies* 42 (1991): 77–105. Bruce Wilkinson, *A Life God Rewards: Why Everything You Do Today Matters* (Sisters, Ore.: Multnomah, 2002) epitomizes the contemporary, popular version of this notion, citing luminaries from Wesley to Edwards in support.

52. See his "The Sum of the Christian Life," preached in Wörlitz on Nov. 24, 1532, in *Luther's Works*, 55 Vols. (Philadelphia: Muhlenberg, 1959), 51:282–83.

53. See, e.g., Millard J. Erickson, *Christian Theology* rev. ed. (Grand Rapids, Mich.: Baker, 1998), 1241–42.

54. See further Craig L. Blomberg, "Degrees of Reward in the Kingdom of Heaven?" *Journal of the Evangelical Theological Society* 35 (1992): 159–72.

the bottom line once again is that there need be no contradiction between Mormon eschatology and the NAE statement.

The final sentence of the statement asserts the spiritual unity of believers in Christ. The term "spiritual" clearly contrasts with "institutional" inasmuch as the NAE is a parachurch organization designed to promote voluntary, co-operative endeavors among Evangelicals from numerous churches and denominations. There would be many individual supporters and member churches of the NAE that could not affirm key items of the doctrinal statements of various other participating churches and organizations. There would be ordained clergy who would not be allowed to administer the sacraments (or ordinances) of baptism and the Lord's Supper in other participating congregations because they were not ordained in their particular denominations. Others could not administer them because they were not ordained at all, whereas some member churches would not ordain *anyone*. So this final sentence in the NAE statement can scarcely be suggesting that participating churches acknowledge each other's sacraments or ordinances as fully valid and sufficient according to their understanding of biblical teaching.

Nor does this final sentence of the NAE statement suggest that all who subscribe to it find each participating church or denomination an equally biblical expression of Christianity. Many Baptists would see paedobaptism as not satisfying the New Testament's command for what they are convinced is believer's baptism by immersion. Many Presbyterian and Reformed churches would find a dispensational approach to the biblical covenants seriously misguided. Wesleyan congregations would often reject the entire Calvinist TULIP (total depravity, unconditional election, limited atonement, irresistible grace, and perseverance of the saints). Examples could be multiplied. But unlike some wings or individual churches in those same Protestant traditions, participants in the NAE would all affirm that other member churches and denominations were *adequate* expressions of Christianity—adequate for salvation, adequate for living a mature Christian life, and adequate for being a strand of Christianity with whom believers ought to co-operate for joint fellowship, witness, and service to the world in a variety of contexts.[55]

---

55. The NAE mission statement thus reads: "The mission of the National Association of Evangelicals is to honor God by connecting and representing evangelical Christians . . . We work to make denominations strong and effective and to support churches and ministries. Our breadth and diversity of partners

Could Latter-day Saints and current NAE members share this kind of spiritual unity? A variety of Latter-day Saints over the years have acknowledged that there are many true Christians outside the LDS Church.[56] Increasingly, at least some Evangelicals are open to the concept that individual Latter-day Saints here and there might really know the Lord.[57] It is arguable that this alone suffices to constitute spiritual unity. More likely, however, the intention of the NAE is more along the lines of the last sentence in the previous paragraph, inasmuch as Evangelicals have typically acknowledged born-again believers in non-evangelical or liberal churches or denominations (even at times in the majority),[58] without thereby labeling those churches as Evangelical or admitting them into the NAE.

The difference involves the official documents and theological affirmations of those churches. I may (and do) disagree with certain details of the doctrinal statements of NAE participants, but by acknowledging them as Evangelical I am affirming that I understand how they derive those doctrines in good faith from the Bible, even though I may not be convinced by their interpretations. My liberal friends distinguish themselves from Evangelicals with whom I disagree not merely by having different interpretations of the Bible in places but by going one step further and, in one or more key instances, acknowledging that the Bible intends for me to believe or act in a certain way but that they simply cannot accept those beliefs or commands.

Thus, for there to be not merely individual Evangelical Mormons, but at least one branch, or informal grouping, of Latter-day Saints that could be called Evangelical Mormon*ism* (the question posed by the title

---

allow us to organize gatherings, conversations and movements that are unrivaled." "Mission and Work," National Association of Evangelicals, http://www.nae.net/about-us/mission-statement (accessed April 24, 2012).

56. Robinson, *How Wide the Divide?* 153. Robert L. Millet, *Getting at the Truth: Responding to Difficult Questions about LDS Beliefs* (Salt Lake City: Deseret, 2004), 16, cites Ezra Taft Benson citing Orson F. Whitney.

57. Blomberg, "Is Mormonism Christian?" 328–31.

58. The Conservative Baptist Association of America was formed, after World War II, as a breakaway movement from the old Northern Baptist Convention (now called the American Baptist Convention) after more than two decades of working for reform, yet stymied by a liberal oligarchy that did not reflect the desires of the conservative majority. See Bruce L. Shelley, *A History of Conservative Baptists* (Wheaton, Ill.: Conservative Baptist Press, 1983).

of this essay), either the wording or the tacit practice of official LDS ecclesiology would have to allow for the one true Church of Jesus Christ in these latter days to be bigger than merely the LDS Church. For all the rhetoric from many Evangelicals as to why Mormonism cannot yet be considered genuinely Christian, which is admittedly often too strident and uncharitable and at times significantly inaccurate, Latter-day Saints must accept a certain portion of the blame as well for poor interfaith relationships. The LDS Church, if it wants to be taken seriously as a genuine expression of Christianity, must revise its own ecclesiological language and claims in order to allow for other Churches to be expressions of the one true Church of Jesus Christ as well. It must abandon its metaphors (like those of the various wattages of light bulbs) and acknowledge that it is fully possible to be an obedient Christian eligible for whatever the optimal heavenly experience turns out to be, whether or not a person ever converts to the LDS Church, and irrespective of whether there are any post-mortem opportunities for changing one's eternal status. Fortunately, it would appear Latter-day Saints have the theological resources to make these changes from no less than Joseph Smith himself in Doctrine and Covenants 10:53–54, in which the Lord identifies his church as existing in 1828, two years before the official beginning of the Restoration![59] If it existed apart from the Restoration then, it can do so today also.

Reflecting on the Results

Readers steeped solely in traditional "countercult" literature may well be surprised at how much agreement between at least some LDS and Evangelical thought is represented here. When *How Wide the Divide?* first appeared, it received two very different kinds of responses with hardly any middle ground. Most were appreciative, but a vocal minority, comprised largely of counter-cult leaders and ex-Mormons, was quite critical, often in a spirit flagrantly contrary to Galatians 6:1. Accustomed to emphasizing almost exclusively the differences between the two faiths and often hurt by the worst possible LDS reactions to their viewpoints and/or exodus from the Church, these critics were precisely the people one would most expect to remain hostile, not always up-to-date on encouraging developments within the Church, and least

---

59. As highlighted in Millet, *Getting at the Truth*, 21–22.

willing to countenance the possibility that new developments not initiated by Church authorities might in fact be welcomed by them.[60]

Much by way of encouragement has indeed occurred over the past fifteen years in Mormon-Evangelical dialogue, but describing the details would require a separate essay. What is fascinating here is that *potentially* the only barriers between Latter-day Saints' acceptance of the NAE statement of faith emerge in its first and last sentences—with the doctrines of bibliology and ecclesiology. Of course, in other areas, as with the nature of Christ's pre-existence or the adoption of a social Trinitarianism, Mormons (in the first instance) and Evangelicals (in the second) would have to become familiar with legitimate options within their traditions to a considerably greater degree than they currently are, lest further differences appear irresolvable. But in a century of unprecedented interaction (and the media that enable easy interaction) between almost any two groups of people on the planet, and certainly in the West, such education is hardly inconceivable.

What, then, about the three additional canonical scriptures that Mormons accept? Curiously, theological cessationism (the view that the charismatic gifts of the Spirit, especially prophecy, have ceased) dominated the Christian world into which Mormonism was birthed. Had that not been the case, perhaps Joseph Smith would have been content to put forward his revelations in the Pauline category of the results of the spiritual gift of prophecy—true words from the living God but not to be elevated to the level of the Bible in accuracy or authority.[61] Had the Azusa Street revival and the subsequent founding of Pentecostal congregations occurred a century earlier, perhaps one of Smith's biggest felt needs for breaking with the Christian world that surrounded him would have remained absent. One can only speculate.

But perhaps our initial analogy of Catholicism may prove instructive here. Vatican II, the charismatic renewal movement in Catholic circles and Bible-reading initiatives by and for the laity in numerous parts of the world, have all led to a treatment of the Apocrypha as "deutero-canonical" by many Catholics. Official magisterial proclamations have not always changed, but one senses among various scholarly

---

60. See my (and Robinson's) replies to "Sizing up the Divide," *BYU Studies* 38 (1999): 172–83.

61. On prophecy as a spiritual gift, see esp. David Hill, *New Testament Prophecy* (Atlanta: John Knox, 1979).

and grass-roots Catholics that the Apocrypha are *de facto* treated not quite as central or crucial for dictating Catholic belief and practice as the Old and New Testament books on which Catholics and Protestants otherwise agree. A trend among Latter-day Saints to treat the Book of Mormon, Pearl of Great Price, and Doctrine and Covenants as important, supplemental religious literature (even the *most important* supplemental religious literature) to the Bible, but allowing the Bible to interpret these other documents rather than vice-versa could be an outstanding analogous step. The oft-cited call by President Ezra Taft Benson in the mid-1980s for the faithful to focus much more on the Book of Mormon than on the Doctrine and Covenants and Pearl of Great Price can be viewed as precedent for this kind of move. It need not be a big next step, internally, to encourage Latter-day Saints to focus on the Bible as even more central than the Book of Mormon, inasmuch as the theology of the latter is already extremely close to the former, arguably much closer to the Bible than to Joseph Smith's later works.[62] But for outside observers of Mormonism, such a step would appear huge.

Recent Catholic history may help with respect to ecclesiology as well. It is not at all uncommon to hear Catholic scholars and leaders affirming that various Protestant churches are quite valid expressions of the Christian faith and to seek spiritual unity with their members. Yet, at the same time, more exclusivist language remains "on the books" of official Vatican doctrine. Indeed, Pope Benedict XVI has, unfortunately, re-emphasized the Catholic version of the "we are the one, true Church" that so damages the potential for spiritual unity in ways that John Paul II before him did not.[63] But the Catholic magisterium has not rescinded the fair amount of freedom that it permits its members with respect to interpretation and implementation of official Catholic doctrine, while the diverse, international expressions of Catholicism are unlikely to allow so traditional a viewpoint to remain a controlling force in the decades to come. From an outside observer's perspective, enough of the identical mainstreaming, internationalizing, and interfaith forces

---

62. The classic demonstration remains that of George B. Arbaugh, *Revelation in Mormonism: Its Character and Changing Forms* (Chicago: University of Chicago Press, 1932).

63. See John Kreiser, "Pope: Only 'One' True Church," CBS News, http://www.cbsnews.com/stories/2007/07/10/world/ main3037922.shtml?source=RSSattr=HOME_3037922 (accessed April 24, 2012).

are at work in the LDS world as well, so that only intentional ideological reversion to procedures of past eras can prevent analogous developments in Mormonism, a move which would be highly discouraging in the short-run and probably counterproductive even to LDS objectives in the long run. However, the address given by Elder Jeffrey Holland, of the Quorum of the Twelve, to the historic first-ever meetings of the NAE board in Utah in March 2011, represent very encouraging theological clarifications indeed.

The question has been raised, though, as to what purposes there would be for Latter-day Saints to remain a separate Christian entity in any sense, if the most distinctive (and, therefore, often most offensive) claims of the Restoration's *superiority* to purely biblical Christianity (in LDS bibliology) and of its *exclusivity* (in LDS ecclesiology) were eliminated or even just toned down. I addressed that question in print once before, but I think my comments may bear repeating:

> Shorn of its unorthodox theology, Mormonism would still have enormous religious contributions to make to the contemporary religious world: a strong commitment to win people to Christ; a biblical emphasis on numerous fundamental moral values, including putting family relationships as a central priority in life; generous financial giving; a good blend of self-reliance and helping others who genuinely cannot care for themselves; all the strengths of classic Arminianism with its emphasis on human free will and responsibility; mechanisms for spiritual growth and accountability for every church member; educational institutions for all ages of people; elaborate church organization, accompanied by genuine community and warm interpersonal relationships; a desire to restore original Christianity and remove corrupting influences from it; social and political agendas often similar to evangelical counterparts; and so on.[64]

Surely, that is more than adequate justification for the continuance of any church!

Intriguingly, as I was growing up as a grade-school aged child, David Paulsen was embarking on his missionary work as a young man in my same community in Rock Island, Illinois. To my knowledge, our paths never crossed in those years, though it is not impossible that he came to our house and talked to one of my parents as part of his door-

---

64. Blomberg, "Is Mormonism Christian?" 327.

to-door work.[65] The first Mormon I remember actually getting to know was our family's chiropractor, Roger K. Waddell, who I first started seeing for periodic adjustments in junior high school. In high school, after my conversion to Evangelical Christianity, Dr. Waddell and I had occasional conversations about religious things, and he gave me a Book of Mormon and invited me to read it, which I did. Obviously, I wasn't as impressed with it as he had been! Little could I have imagined in those years that I would one day become a biblical scholar, much less one who would be part of extended dialogues with Latter-day Saint counterparts. I am sure Dr. Paulsen never imagined many of the developments in his own career or in the broader worlds of religion that have unfolded in the decades since his youth.

Perhaps dreaming of the day when there could be a viable Evangelical Mormonism (or a Mormon Evangelicalism) sounds naïve. But how many people envisioned the collapse of worldwide Communism to the extent that it has occurred, or the rise of contemporary Islamic fanaticism and terrorism, or the majority of Evangelicals (and Mormons!) no longer being found in North America or Western Europe but in the Two-Thirds World? Examples could be multiplied. Perhaps such a day will not occur in David's lifetime or in mine, but in those of our children. Perhaps it will come even later or maybe not at all. Not everything that is dreamed is accomplished. But few things occur that are not first dreamed. In the more poetic words of Alfred Lord Tennyson, "Maybe wildest dreams are but the needful preludes of the truth."[66]

Or, perhaps most profoundly of all, in the language that both Mormons and Evangelicals declare inspired, "with God all things are possible" (Matt. 19:26).

---

65. When I told him where I lived, he thought he might have worked in that neighborhood at one point but after all these years was understandably uncertain.

66. Lord Alfred Tennyson, "The Princess," The Literature Network, http://www.online-literature.com/tennyson/4100/ (accessed April 24, 2012).

10

Conceptual Metaphor Theory and the Mormon Understanding of God

John E. Sanders, *Hendrix College*

It is with pleasure that I write this contribution for David Paulsen's *festschrift*. David is a good philosopher and a devout Mormon. He has been at the forefront of Mormon intellectuals' attempts to bring some key classical Christian concepts, such as the Trinity, into harmony with Mormon teachings. Paulsen and others have asked Christian theologians to revise traditional theological formulations. These Mormon intellectuals have not, so far as I am aware, asked their fellow Mormons to revise their own theology. That may be too dangerous an enterprise given LDS authority structures. Nonetheless, I will invite Mormons to do just that. My chapter explores a prominent new way of thinking about metaphor and language that would require Mormons to seriously rethink their understanding of God. Since this rethinking involves some of their most distinctive beliefs, I doubt it is possible for them to agree with my approach. Nevertheless, I offer this essay in the spirit of honest, good-natured dialogue.

Reading the Bible Literally

In 2001 the annual meeting of the Evangelical Theological Society debated an article on a theology known as "dynamic omniscience," which is a theological position held by open theists. Dynamic omniscience claims that God does not know with absolute certainty what creatures with libertarian freedom will do in the future. The Society passed the following resolution: "We believe the Bible clearly teaches that God has complete, accurate, and infallible knowledge of the past, present, and future, including all future decisions and actions of free moral agents." Evangelical Calvinists have taken the lead in arguing that the Bible "clearly teaches" God's exhaustive definite foreknowledge of all future contingent events.

Steven Roy, for example, claims that there are 4,017 biblical texts that "clearly and explicitly" teach exhaustive foreknowledge.[1] He cites familiar texts such as Psalm 139:4, 16 where God is said to know what we will say before we utter it and knows all of our days before they existed. For Roy it seems clear that the Bible teaches exhaustive foreknowledge, and that those who reject this claim (such as open theists) are reading their position into the Bible rather than from it.

There are many responses I could offer to this criticism, but here I shall focus on the issue of reading the Bible literally. In part, the disagreement concerning what the Bible teaches about divine foreknowledge arises out of a debate about which texts of scripture are literal and which are metaphorical. Open theists have sometimes claimed that they read the Bible literally, or in a straightforward fashion.[2] Calvinist critics have claimed that open theists are inconsistent when they interpret the "God changed his mind" texts literally but do not take the texts about God's body parts literally.

Millard Erickson and Bruce Ware established the following hermeneutical criterion for biblical interpretation: we should take all the biblical texts literally unless there are compelling reasons that show that the biblical author did not intend the text to be taken literally.[3] Ware concedes that the texts used by open theists, "*when interpreted in a straightforward manner*, yield the conclusion that God lacks exhaustive knowledge of the future." But, he adds, "The issue is whether the authorial intended meaning is the straightforward meaning."[4] For Evangelical Calvinist critics of open theism, the biblical authors did not intend the meanings that open theist interpretations ascribe to them for the simple reason that such a reading would contradict the literal passages of scripture that clearly teach God's exhaustive foreknowledge.

---

1. Steven Roy, *How Much Does God Foreknow? A Comprehensive Biblical Study* (Downers Grove, Ill.: InterVarsity Press, 2006), 312. See also Millard Erickson, *What Does God Know and When Does He Know It?* (Grand Rapids, Mich.: Zondervan, 2004), 39–57. Roy claims that a "straightforward reading of the omniscience texts" requires exhaustive definite foreknowledge, whereas the openness type texts do not require a rejection of foreknowledge (220–21).

2. See, for example, Gregory Boyd, *God of the Possible: A Biblical Introduction to the Open View of God* (Grand Rapids, Mich.: Baker, 2000), 14, 118.

3. Bruce Ware, *God's Lesser Glory: The Diminished God of Open Theism* (Wheaton, Ill.: Crossway, 2000), 67, 85.

4. Ibid., 85; emphasis his.

Several years ago I gave a lecture on open theism at Brigham Young University. In the questions that followed I was asked why I took the "God has emotions" texts literally but not the "God has a body" texts. Are not, the speaker asked, Mormons more consistent in their reading of the Bible than open theists? Here, I was being confronted by the same criticism—albeit for different reasons—from Evangelical Calvinists and Mormons. My response to the questioner was that I did not take either of these texts literally. The audience was quite surprised because they were sure I was interpreting the biblical texts literally. Subsequently, I realized that I needed to explain my view of language more fully.

This is a partial response to the criticism that I am inconsistent about which texts of scripture I take literally. The main section will explore some relevant material in the field of cognitive linguistics. This material will then be applied first to biblical depictions of God and then to Mormon teachings on God.

Conceptual Metaphor Theory

In general, my approach is shaped by some of the recent work in the field of cognitive linguistics, which seeks to understand how humans reason about various aspects of life. More particularly, I draw upon the insights of what is called "conceptual metaphor theory," which attempts to document how different cultural and language groups conceptualize human experiences.

The first insight of cognitive linguistics that I will mention here is that the human mind is inherently embodied. We conceptualize our world in terms of that which we know best: our experiences as embodied creatures. We use our embodied experience to understand what is important to us. Consider the following expressions: "the heart of the problem"; "to shoulder a responsibility"; "the head of a department"; "a healthy economy"; "my feelings are hurt"; "exports flourished last year"; "his finances are ruined"; "she received a warm welcome"; and "spend your time wisely."[5] Each of these statements utilizes different facets of our embodied experience in order to understand various aspects of human life.

---

5. See Zoltan Kövecses, *Metaphor: a Practical Introduction* (New York: Oxford University Press, 2002), 16–24. Kövecses does not, however, claim that all thought is directly related to physical experience.

Humans have particular kinds of bodies that allow us to do some things and not other things. Our visual system allows us to use spatial relations in order to understand the separable elements of our experience. We have the ability to move, and motion plays a significant role in our ability to understand the world. For example, the force utilized by our arms and legs gives rise to causal concepts. It is important to understand our visual system, motor system, and the general mechanisms of neural binding because the same neural and cognitive mechanisms that allow us to perceive and move around are also the basis of our conceptual systems and modes of reason.

That embodiment is fundamental for human thought is seen in the research on how infants learn. Infants with normal vision attend to movement more than anything else.[6] Repeated motions form neural pathways which are the neurological basis for our abstract conceptualizations. Infants are also highly attuned to other human faces. The face of the primary caregiver provides security and peace. Moreover, being held by the caregiver provides literal warmth and protection. These initial experiences eventually give rise to several of our basic cognitive image schemas. That is, we use our experiences of warmth, security, and movement to form basic understandings of the world.

"Basic-level image schemas" is the term cognitive linguists apply to notions such as "up-down," "part-whole," and "near-far." They are spatial structures that are mapped or applied to conceptual structures.[7] According to Jean Mandler, "Even though image-schemas are derived from perceptual and . . . motor processes, they are not themselves sen-

---

6. See Shaun Gallagher, *How the Body Shapes the Mind* (New York: Oxford University Press, 2005), 247. See also Raymond Gibbs, *Embodiment and Cognitive Science* (New York: Cambridge University Press, 2005) and Mark Johnson, *The Body in the Mind: the Bodily Basis of Meaning, Imagination and Reason* (Chicago: University of Chicago Press, 1990).

7. See Jean Mandler, "How to Build a Baby II: Conceptual Primitives," *Psychological Review* 99 no. 4 (1992): 591–92. See also George Lakoff, *Women, Fire, and Dangerous Things: What Categories Reveal About the Mind* (Chicago: University of Chicago Press, 1987), 416–61; and George Lakoff and Mark Johnson, *Philosophy in the Flesh: the Embodied Mind and Its Challenge to Western Thought* (New York: Basic Books, 1999), 31–35. For an excellent overview of conceptual metaphor theory and the key literature see Bonnie Howe, *Because You Bear This Name: Conceptual Metaphor and the Moral Meaning of 1 Peter* (Atlanta: Society of Biblical Literature, 2008), Chap. 2.

sorimotor processes."[8] Our perceptual information leads us to form a small number of image schemas, and the image schemas become the main generator of the conceptual system. For example, because we have eyes on one side of our head we form the image schema "front-back." The concepts "in front of" and "in back of" are based on the type of bodies we have. Similarly, we have bodies that take in and expel things—which gives rise to the "inside-outside" image schema. Some of the other image schemas are: "whole-part orientation" (our bodies consist of parts); "center-periphery" (we sense that our head and torso are central and that our limbs are peripheral since life goes on without a finger but not without a head); "up-down" (our erect posture and lying down); and "source-path-goal" (to reach an object or place requires movement from our present location to the location of the object). If we had different types of bodies then we would form different image schemas. For instance, if we had bodies similar to those of jellyfish then we would not have the "front-back" schema, since there is no front or back for jellyfish. Our basic image schemas are derived from our embodied experience and imprinted in our neural network.

Image schemas form the conceptual building blocks for the most basic levels of concepts. Examples of basic-level concepts are: "time," "quantity," "state," "change," "action," "cause," "purpose," and "category." For example, the image schema "in-out" is developed into the concept of "category." The very notion of category presumes a container into which items may be placed. To categorize something is to place it "into" a cognitive container. In other words, the concrete properties of containers are mapped onto, or used to understand, the abstract notion of categories.

Since image schemas have very little content we use them to form metaphorical extensions. The chart below contains some examples.[9]

Image Schema	*Metaphorical Extension*
In-out	I'm out of clothes.
Head	She's at the head of her class.
Up-down	I'm feeling low.
Motion	She went crazy.

---

8. Mandler, "How to Build a Baby," 591.
9. These examples are drawn from Kovecses, *Metaphor: A Practical Introduction*, 37.

Conceptual metaphor theorists identify several types of metaphor, but I will discuss only some of these here.[10] The most fundamental ones are called *primary metaphors* and are based on our embodied experiences. For example, we know what it is to have experiences such as having fluid inside the body, feeling pressure, and being hot or cold in parts of our bodies. We apply such experiences to more abstract experiences in order to understand them. For instance, physically grasping an object is used for understanding concepts ("he could not *grasp* the topic"); sight is used for knowledge ("I *see* your point"); hearing is used for internal receptivity ("my parents just don't *hear* me"); touch/feeling are used for emotions ("I *feel* great today"); and taste is used for personal preference ("the room was *tastefully* decorated").

When we say to children, "let's see what is in the box," we are using the verbs for vision in such a way that knowing what is in the box depends upon vision. Eventually, we metaphorically extend the meaning of the verb "to see" when we say, for example, "Let's see if I can fix your toy." At first, young children do not understand the second usage of "see" because they conflate the actual use of vision with the metaphor of seeing. It is confusing when adults use "seeing" to mean something that is not visually seen at all in a statement such as, "I see what you mean." In time, children are able to separate literal seeing from the conceptual metaphor.[11]

Some other key primary metaphors are: *affection is warmth*[12] ("give grandma a *warm* welcome"); *happy is up* ("I'm feeling *up* today"); *intimacy is physical proximity* ("they are *close* friends"); *difficulties are burdens* ("he's *weighed down* with responsibilities"); *more is up* ("the price of the toy is too *high*"); *categories are containers* ("lions are *in* the feline family)," *time is motion* ("the day just *flew* by"); and *purposes are destinations* ("she is well on her *way* to being a success").

The other main type of conceptual metaphor is the *complex metaphor*, which utilizes primary metaphors. This can be illustrated by looking at two complex metaphors. In the culture of North America we use the *love is a journey* metaphor when we say things like, "we've come a

---

10. Ibid.

11. Lakoff and Johnson, *Philosophy in the Flesh*, 48–56.

12. Conceptual metaphor theorists typically identify the metaphor of which they are speaking in one of several ways: by capitalizing the first letter of each word, by placing it in quotation marks, or by putting all the letters in caps. Here they are italicized.

long way in our marriage," or, "our relationship is *at* a crossroads," or, "our romance is *moving* right along." In this metaphor, the lovers are travelers, their common life goals are destinations, the journey is events in the relationship, distance covered is progress made, and the relationship is a vehicle. *Love is a journey* draws upon primary metaphors such as *intimacy is physical proximity* and *purposes are destinations.*

The second example is the metaphor *an argument is a building*, used when speaking of giving support for an argument so that it does not collapse; laying the groundwork for a good argument; the framework for a solid argument; and whether the argument is strong and can withstand criticism. The *argument is a building* metaphor is comprised of two primary metaphors: *logical structure is physical structure* and *persisting is remaining erect.*

In these examples a "source domain" (journey and building) is applied to a "target domain" (love and argumentation). Some aspects of the source domain are used to think about or understand the target domain. But why do we use *these* source domains instead of others? Why, for instance, should we think of arguments as buildings? Though they are extremely common in our culture there is no necessary connection between journeys and love, or buildings and arguments.[13] In fact, the target domain of love was not conceptualized in terms of a journey until that particular source domain was mapped onto it. We created the conceptualization of love in terms of journey; but we need not have, since other cultures have different ways of understanding love relationships.[14] Conceptual metaphors are culturally constrained because not all cultures use the same metaphors to think about abstractions such as love, anger, success, and truth.

---

13. Proponents of the traditional metaphor theory typically claim that metaphors involve a similarity between the source and target domains. Though there are similarities in some cases there need not be any similarities between the two domains. For instance, if we say, "She is a firecracker" it is the source domain that imposes a structure on the target domain. There is no literal similarity between the woman and a firecracker. Rather, it is the application of a firecracker that enables us to understand an abstraction about the woman. See Kövecses, *Metaphor: A Practical Introduction*, 67–77.

14. On the subject of cultural influence on conceptual metaphors see Kövecses, *Metaphor: A Practical Introduction*, 163–97, and Zoltan Kövecses, *Metaphor in Culture: Universality and Variation* (New York: Cambridge University Press, 2006).

Variations of conceptual metaphors among cultures are not the only constraint upon metaphors. I will mention three other constraints. First, metaphors only partially map reality in that they apply only some aspects of the source domain and ignore others.[15] For instance, in the *arguments are buildings* metaphor elements of physical structure, such as foundations and supports, are applied to argumentation but not plumbing or chimneys. If metaphors are used to highlight some specific aspects of a target domain this means that other aspects that could be used are not. In other words, the partial mapping of metaphors filters out some elements while letting others through.

The flip side of this idea is that not every characteristic of the source domain is attributed to the target domain. For example, when it is said, "the Pope is the father of the Roman Catholic church" only some entailments of human fatherhood are applied to the Pope. The fatherhood of the Pope often refers to authority, but his fatherhood certainly does not entail sexual relations to give birth to Catholics. If we say, "Tom is a firecracker" we clearly do not think that Tom explodes and makes a loud noise. Rather, only the aspect of liveliness is taken from the source domain and mapped onto the target domain.[16]

The second constraint is that the use of different sources changes our understanding of the target. If we want to highlight other aspects of the target that a particular metaphor does not involve, then we use other sources because different source domains lead to different entailments in the target. For example, there are several other ways that English speakers conceptualize arguments, and these bring out different features. First, we think of arguments as containers when we say, "your argument has a great deal of content." Second, we understand arguments as journeys when we say, "the reasoning proceeds *step-by-step*," or "we have *covered a lot of ground*." Third, we conceive of arguments as war when we say, "he could not *defend* the point," or, "she *attacked* his major premise." Zoltan Kövecses suggests that each of the ways of conceiving arguments highlights different aspects unavailable in the other sources. The container metaphor highlights the content while the journey metaphor brings out progress and the war metaphor seems to focus on control and persistence. Kövecses observes that while the "*con-*

---

15. Kövecses, *Metaphor: A Practical Introduction*, 79–92.

16. See Gilles Fauconnier and Mark Turner, *The Way We Think: Conceptual Blending and the Mind's Hidden Complexities* (New York: Basic Books, 2002), 141–42.

tainer metaphor highlights issues of content it simultaneously hides such other aspects as progress, control, construction and strength."[17]

The utilization of different sources leads us to the final constraint: we typically need several sources for the same target because a single metaphor does not disclose all that can be understood about a target. Given that different sources highlight different elements in the target domain, it is not surprising that we have employed a variety of conceptual metaphors in order to understand our experiences. Take the experience of love, for example. There are literal elements to love: a lover, the beloved, feelings of affection, and a relationship that has a temporal beginning. This is rather skeletal, however, which is why we have a rich assortment of metaphors for conceptualizing love. In addition to *love is a journey* we think of love as a *nutrient* ("he was *starved* for affection," "her love *sustains* him"); as *fire* ("*burning* with love"); as *physical forces* ("he is strongly *attracted* to her"); as *natural forces* ("he was *swept off* his feet"); as *insanity* ("she's *madly* in love"); as *unity* ("she is my better *half*" or "they are a perfect *fit*"); and as a *game* ("she's *playing* hard to get"). If we had to think of love only in terms of a journey we would sacrifice these other ways of conceptualizing love.

The Traditional Theory of Metaphor versus Conceptual Metaphor Theory

An explanation of the contrast between the "traditional" theory of metaphor and conceptual metaphor theory will show why the foregoing material is important. The traditional way of distinguishing metaphors from literal statements involves several assumptions: that (1) metaphors are figurative ways of stating what could otherwise better be said literally; (2) definitions and conventional everyday language are literal; and (3) only literal language can be true or false.[18]

Conceptual metaphor theory rejects these three assumptions and affirms, instead, that metaphors are used to *conceptualize* and *reason* about our world.[19] They are not used simply to *speak* about the world

---

17. Kövecses, *Metaphor: A Practical Introduction*, 80.
18. George Lakoff, "The Contemporary Theory of Metaphor," in *Metaphor and Thought*, ed. Andrew Ortony, 2nd ed. (New York: Cambridge University Press), 240–41.
19. Ibid., 202–51.

and our experience; they are vehicles for understanding our world—they structure the way we think about our experiences. Our conceptualizations about interpersonal relationships, time, purposes, and categories are largely metaphorical in nature. This does not mean, however, that all statements are metaphorical. For example, the statement "the car is blue" is literal, whereas the statement "Sally is blue today" is metaphorical. The statement "these colors are similar" is literal whereas the statement "these colors are close" is metaphorical since colors are not actually near or far. The statement "these colors are close" uses the *similarity is proximity* metaphor. The problem is that the traditional view of language claims that "these colors are close" and "our relationship hit a dead end" are literal when, in actuality, they are metaphorical ways of conceiving our experience.

Consequently, when Evangelical Calvinist critics of open theism speak about the "clear" texts of scripture they fail to realize that they are using conceptual metaphors. In this case, "clear" utilizes the *knowing is seeing* metaphor (to be discussed more fully below). Here, it is sufficient to observe that windows can be literally clear but texts are not literally clear. Cognitive linguists have discovered an enormous system of such metaphors by which we give meaning to our life experiences. In the words of George Lakoff, "It is a system of metaphor that structures our everyday conceptual system, including most abstract concepts, and that lies behind much of everyday language. The discovery of the enormous metaphor system has destroyed the traditional literal-figurative distinction, since the term 'literal,' as used in defining the traditional distinction, carries with it all those false assumptions."[20]

Thinking About God in the Bible

This section will apply the preceding ideas to biblical depictions of God.[21] I argued above that abstract concepts are largely metaphori-

---

20. Ibid., 204.
21. For a helpful overview of cognitive science and its applicability to theology see Gregory R. Peterson, *Minding God: Theology and the Cognitive Sciences* (Minneapolis: Fortress Press, 2003). For an excellent introduction to conceptual metaphor theory and its application to biblical studies see Bonnie Howe, *Because You Bear This Name: Conceptual Metaphor and the Moral Meaning of 1 Peter* (Atlanta: Society of Biblical Literature, 2008). For the relevance of cognitive linguistics to biblical translation see Kenneth A. McElhanon, "From Simple Metaphors to

cal, and that these are grounded in our embodied experience. Moreover, metaphors are used to conceptualize and reason about our world rather than simply to speak about it. Our conceptualizations about interpersonal relationships, time, purposes, and categories are largely metaphorical in nature. All of this is also true of the way we understand God and our relationship to God.

If God is going to communicate with us and have a relationship with us it will have to be in ways that are comprehensible to us. If we are to think of God in profound and rich ways rather than shallow and skeletal ways then we are going to use conceptual metaphors, and these will be grounded in our embodied experience. Recall that the human face of a caregiver provides security, affirmation, and peace to an infant. Repeated face-to-face interaction with a child helps to develop the child's sense of personhood. This profound human experience in infancy becomes a prototype for the experience of God in the Bible. The biblical writers repeatedly speak of the "face" of God.[22] In the Hebrew Bible the worshippers sought the "face" of Yahweh (Ps. 24:6, 42:4). When God's face is turned toward the worshipper, one experiences affirmation and peace (Num. 6:24–26). When God hides his face the worshipper experiences anxiety (Ps. 13:2, 104:29). In the New Testament Paul writes that the glorified face of Christ manifests the glory of God (2 Cor. 4:6). Also, believers are promised that the eschaton will contain the experience of the face of God (Rev. 22:4). The biblical writers used the powerful human experience of the physical face of the other in order to conceptualize ideas such as *security is the divine face*.

Talk of the "face" of God is closely related to the common metaphors *intimacy is physical proximity* and *emotional distance is physical distance*. Deeply spiritual persons are said to be physically close to God. Enoch walked with God for many years (Gen. 5:22–24). God carried the Israelites in his arms as a father carries a son (Deut. 1:21). Moses had a face-to-face relationship with God (Ex. 33:11; Num. 12:8). When worshippers experience problems in their relationship with God

---

Conceptual Blending: The Mapping of Analogical Concepts and the Praxis of Translation," *Journal of Translation* 2, no.1 (2006): 31–81.

22. See *The New International Dictionary of New Testament Theology* (Grand Rapids, Mich.: Zondervan, 1975), 585–87, and F. LeRon Shults and Steven J. Sandage, *The Faces of Forgiveness: Searching for Wholeness and Salvation* (Grand Rapids, Mich.: Baker, 2003), 105–24.

they ask God to be "near" them (Ps. 22:11, 35:22, 38:21). In the New Jerusalem worshippers will experience a clear presence of God for they will be "close" to God (Rev. 22:4). In passing, it should be noted that these metaphors as well as several others discussed below remain in use in our culture (e.g., "My mom and I are really close").

Biblical writers frequently used basic-level image schemas in order to comprehend religious experience.[23] For example, the *body is a container* image is frequent. The community of believers is the temple of God in which the Spirit of God dwells (1 Cor. 3:16). The heart is a container for good or evil thoughts (Mark 7:21–23) and the Israelites are instructed to put God's word into their hearts (Deut. 30:14). Also, the "up-down" schema is used in a variety of ways. It seems that all cultures share the valuations that *good is up* while *bad is down* and *authority is up* while *submission is down*. In the Bible the prayers of God's people rise up to God (Ex 2:23). Greater security is conceived as up when it is said that God will set the believer securely on high (Ps. 20:1). Higher authority is conceived as up when the Centurion says to Jesus that he is under authority and he has authority over others (Matt. 8:8–9). This explains why biblical writers conceptualize God as looking down from heaven (Ps. 14:2, 102:19) and even descending from heaven (Gen. 18:21). It would be improper to conceptualize God—a greater authority—as coming from below us.

Primary metaphors occur in the Bible as well. For example, *knowing is seeing* is used of both God and humans. God investigates to see if the humans in Sodom are beyond help (Gen. 18:21). God looks down to see if anyone understands (Ps. 14:2, 53:2). Humans are able to see whether God has blessed someone (Ps. 26:28) and see whether God's word is true (Num.11:23). Moses was allowed to see the divine goodness (Ex. 33:18–23). We are asked to see that God is good (Ps. 34:8). Divine "goodness" is not a visible object that can be literally seen. Instead, it refers to complex characteristics of God in relation to creatures. In these texts, the concrete source domain of visual sight is mapped onto God in order to conceptualize the abstract relations of God to creatures.

In the Bible a wide array of metaphors are used to understand what God is like. In an excellent article, Mary Therese DesCamp and Eve Sweetser have cataloged these metaphors and found 44 separate

---

23. The following section is deeply indebted to several unpublished papers by Kenneth McElhanon.

metaphors for God in the Hebrew Bible and 50 in the New Testament.[24] Their interest was to discover which characteristics of God were most important to the biblical writers by cataloging which metaphors were applied to God. A few of the metaphors they list are: father, king, warrior, husband, woman, master, fortress, heat, eagle, bear, potter, smelter, planter, and land owner. They note that some metaphors are sparse (God is a rock) while others are frequent (God is a father). For each metaphor they map the entailments from the source domain that are attributed to the target domain (God). The same six characteristics are found in both the Old and New Testaments. These are (1) protection and sustenance (husband, father); (2) mutual relationship though asymmetric in authority (father, judge); (3) physical control (smelter); (4) the ability to change one's state or essence (king, woman in labor); (5) authority (king, teacher); and (6) the power to punish (father, bear).

DesCamp and Sweetser draw two main conclusions from their detailed study. First, mutual relationships are the ideal form of relationship between God and humans. Even though the relationships are asymmetric in terms of authority (e. g., father-child, king-subject), there is two-way mutuality between the subjects. Each gives and each receives, though not in equal measure. Second, human-to-human metaphors are usually preferred over metaphors of inanimate objects or animals. This is because human metaphors have richer entailments due to the ongoing and dynamic nature of the relationship.

The metaphors used for God do not map every characteristic of the source domain onto the target. Just as "The Pope is the father of the Catholic Church" does not entail sexual relations in order for a person to become a member of the Catholic family, so every aspect of each source domain is not applied to God. Even those metaphors used a great deal, such as "father" and "shepherd," do not map every aspect of human fathers and shepherds onto God. God does not, for example, have a penis to impregnate a goddess in order to give birth to Israel, nor does God shear humans or roast them for a feast. Only those aspects of the source domain that the biblical authors deem fitting are applied to God. In his excellent study of the metaphor "God as

---

24. Mary DesCamp and Eve Sweetser, "Metaphors for God: Why and How Do Our Choices Matter for Humans? The Application of Contemporary Cognitive Linguistics Research to the Debate on God and Metaphor," *Pastoral Psychology* 53, no. 3 (January 2005): 207–38.

king," Marc Brettler notes that the biblical writers frequently used this metaphor for God yet they were highly selective about which aspects of the source domain (human kings) they applied to God.[25] Though some aspects of human kingship are ascribed to God, most aspects are qualified such that God is king in a special way that either surpasses or is contrary to human kings. For example, human kings and God are both called shepherds but only God uses his staff beneficially rather than for punishment. Also, though both have "power," God can use his power for peace and justice. Finally, God uses his strength to forgive and his right hand for righteousness, whereas human kings often use their right hand for bloodshed.

The biblical writers used different source domains in order to change the way we conceptualize the target. For example, conceptualizing God as an eagle produces some entailments that are very different from understanding God as a rock. God's relation to creatures is very complex and rich; hence the need for multiple metaphors. Thus, Yahweh is not only understood as father but also has so-called feminine characteristics: Yahweh gave birth to Israel (Deut. 32:18); Yahweh has a nursing child (Isa. 49:15); and Yahweh is a female vulture (eagle) that hovers over the nest and carries the young on her wings (Deut. 32:11). Conceptualizing God as father helps us understand certain characteristics of God while conceiving God as mother highlights other aspects of God. As father, Yahweh could not give birth to Israel, so in order to apply this deep connection between God and Israel Yahweh had to be understood as a mother.

This leads to a couple of important cautions. First, DesCamp and Sweetser note that, "Theologians should be concerned with the repeated use of 'father' and 'king' because no matter how benevolent those particular metaphors may appear, they nonetheless suppress certain features of God and lead faith communities to inaccurate and inadequate representations."[26] Second, though we need many metaphors in order to understand God's many facets, we must be careful not to mix the entailments from the different metaphors. For example, God as father of Israel and as husband/lover of Israel each have rich entailments, but if

---

25. Marc Zvi Brettler, *God is King: Understanding an Israelite Metaphor*. Journal for the Study of the Old Testament, Supplement Series 76 (Sheffield, England: JSOT Press, 1989).

26. DesCamp and Sweetser, "Metaphors for God," 236.

these two are brought together at the same time we have incest, which, of course, is an inappropriate entailment for God.

Conceptual Metaphor Theory and the Mormon Understanding of God

Mormons believe that God is literally the father of all humans. God the father once lived on an earth but is now "an exalted man, a corporeal being, a personage with flesh and bones."[27] God the Father and his wife (a female deity about whom little has been revealed) produce spirit beings that are then born to human parents. Jesus, also known as Yahweh (Jehovah), is the literal firstborn spirit being of the divine parents. Jesus is special in that he is the Firstborn as well as the one who fashioned the basic elements into our planet and brought about salvation. Yet, all humans are essentially like Jesus in that "men and women are literally the spirit sons and daughters of God" who lived in a premortal existence (the "first estate") prior to our physical births.[28] Consequently, humans "are of the same species as God."[29] Divine parents sired us after Jesus was born in the first estate. This means that Jesus is literally our "elder brother."[30]

I find this sort of literality quite puzzling, as would, I believe, most Christians throughout history for the simple reason that a host of metaphors are used in the Bible to conceptualize both God and our relationship to God. The human situation in relation to God is not only portrayed in terms of children but also in terms of household servants, sheep, branches of a vine, temple, and bride just to name a few. To my knowledge, no one takes these literally. Given the Mormon propensity for highly literal readings of biblical texts it seems to me that they run into a host of difficulties. Consider the statement in 1 John that those who are "born of God" do not continue in sin (3:9). Clearly, this cannot be taken in the Mormon sense that we are all literally born of God since

---

27. Robert Millet, *The Mormon Faith: A New Look at Christianity* (Salt Lake City: Deseret Book Company, 1998), 29. I will draw heavily on Millet's book for he is widely accepted by Mormons as a trusted authority on Mormon theology. See also B. H. Roberts, *The Mormon Doctrine of Deity* (Salt Lake City: Signature Books, 1998).
28. Millet, *Mormon Faith*, 56.
29. Ibid., 34.
30. Ibid., 57.

there are many humans who do continue in sin. Moreover, Paul refers to Christians as "sons of God" who now call God "Abba" (father). This is because we have been "adopted" rather than because we are natural born children of God (Gal. 4:5–6; Rom. 8:14–17). It seems to me that adoption is just as metaphorical as being a "son" of God. I do not know if Mormons take the statement that Jesus is the "only begotten of the father" (John 1:14, 3:16) literally, but if they do, such literality would seem to create a problem for them in that Jesus is not, in fact, the *only* begotten but only the *first* begotten.[31]

In the previous section it was noted that Yahweh is identified as the father, mother, and husband of Israel.[32] If, as Mormons believe, Jesus is Yahweh then it is difficult to see how Jesus can be father, mother, and husband except as conceptual metaphors.[33] If Jesus is literally our elder brother then he cannot literally be our mother as well. Yahweh is portrayed as the husband of Israel in the Old Testament and Jesus is the bridegroom of the church in the New Testament (Rev. 19:7). Thus, Israel and the church are understood as female, but if these verses are taken literally, it becomes difficult to understand since there are also males in both Israel and the church. Also, the Mormon teaching that God the Father is not Yahweh (Jesus) seems to lead to the following problem: If God the father is our literal father then what is to be made of the biblical statements that Yahweh is our father? These seem contradictory assertions unless interpreted as conceptual metaphors.

Mormons, of course, have a long history of explaining and defending their religion and they may have already developed answers to the problems I raise. Mormons are, I believe, on target in so far as they draw connections between our embodied experiences and our understanding of God. However, I believe that conceptual metaphor theory is correct, and inasmuch as Mormonism interprets scriptural texts literally, I

---

31. Many Mormons believe that the body of Jesus was literally "sired" by God the Father with Mary (though the Holy Ghost is somehow involved in the process) and had no human father (see Millet, *Mormon Faith*, 31). Perhaps (and here I speculate) Mormons would explain the appellation of "only begotten" to Jesus by claiming that whereas our earthly bodies are from two human parents, Jesus's earthly body was only from one human parent.

32. On Yahweh as husband see the excellent study by Nelly Stienstra, *YHWH is the Husband of His People: An Analysis of a Biblical Metaphor with Special Reference to Translation* (Kampen, Netherlands: Kok Pharos, 1993).

33. Millet, *Mormon Faith*, 30.

simply cannot agree with the highly literal Mormon understanding of God. In my view, the biblical depictions of God in terms such as father, mother, rock, vulture, and shepherd are all metaphors and should not be taken literally. This is not to "demote" the biblical language because conceptual metaphors are the normal means we use to reason about abstract relations such as love, argumentation, and the economy. The process by which we reason about biblical texts and God is the same.

11

David Paulsen on Divine Embodiment

Stephen T. Davis, *Claremont McKenna College*

It is a pleasure to participate in this *festschrift* for my long-time friend and fellow philosopher of religion, David Paulsen. I have known David for many years. We originally became acquainted at conferences of the American Philosophical Association and the Society of Christian Philosophers. My own limited engagement with Mormon thought[1] originated one day (I think it was in 2001) when David casually asked me—he knew I was a Presbyterian with Evangelical leanings—whether I might accept an invitation to give a paper at Brigham Young University. I said I would love to do so, and a few months later gave two presentations at the invitation of the philosophy department.

David is a first-rate philosopher of religion and theologian. His work is always clear, well argued, and eminently fair. He is an excellent ambassador and apologist for Latter-day Saint thinking. His intellectual honesty is apparent in his writings, as well is his deep and active faith. As everyone who knows him would undoubtedly agree, he is also a fine human being with whom it is a pleasure to associate as a friend and colleague.

I have divided the present paper into three parts. In Section I, I will make a preliminary biblical case for divine immaterialism. This is

---

1. This limited engagement has led me to writing, apart from the current piece, four essays thus far engaging with Mormonism: "Are Mormons Christians? Theological Impressions After a Visit to Zion," *Perspectives* 18, no.1 (January 2003); Roger R. Keller and Robert L. Millett, eds., "Bodily Redemption: A Reformed Perspective," in *Salvation in Christ: Comparative Christian Views* (Provo, Utah: Brigham Young University Press, 2005); "The Mormon Trinity and Other Trinities," *Element: The Journal of the Society for Mormon Philosophy and Theology* 2, no. 1 (Spring, 2006); and "Philosophical Theology for Mormons: Suggestions from an Outsider," *Element* 3 (Spring and Fall 2007). As for this chapter, I would like to thank Professors Brian Birch, Craig Blomberg, and Charles Taliaferro for their helpful comments on an earlier draft.

the notion that God—except, of course, for the Second Person of the Trinity in His incarnation—is not a physical object, does not have a body, and is an invisible and incorporeal "spirit." This is the opinion of virtually all mainstream Christians (by which I mean Roman Catholics, Eastern Orthodox Christians, and Protestant Christians). In Section II, I will analyze Paulsen's case for divine materialism. This task is not easy because he has written about this topic on many occasions and at some length.[2] Moreover, his arguments are carefully and subtly made. Finally, in Section III, I will argue on philosophical and theological grounds in favor of divine immaterialism.

Before I proceed with my analysis, I feel it necessary to make a point about LDS theology in general and LDS theological terminology in particular. I simply want to note that LDS thinkers, and possibly Paulsen himself, need to do some work in the area that philosophers call the "mind/body problem." Perhaps it is just a matter of defining terms clearly. For example, given the way Mormons use the word "spirit" (see note 4 below), I am not clear whether or not they are committed to some version of mind/body dualism. This is the theory that asserts: (1) human beings consist of both material bodies and immaterial souls, and (2) the soul is the essence of the person. I suspect that Mormons would affirm the first conjunct of that sentence (although they would prefer the word "spirit" to the word "soul") and not the second, but I am not sure. Moreover, I would like to know more about the Mormon concept of "refined matter." Is it meant to be the same thing as the new body or resurrection body (*soma pneumatikon*) that Paul speaks

---

2. The sources from Paulsen that I have consulted are as follows: "Must God Be Incorporeal?" *Faith and Philosophy* 6, no. 1 (January 1989): 76–87; "Early Christian Views of a Corporeal Deity: Origin and Augustine as Reluctant Witnesses," *Harvard Theological Review* 83, no. 2 (1990): 105–16; "Reply to Kim Paffenroth's Comment," *Harvard Theological Review* 86, no. 2 (1993): 235–39; "The Doctrine of Divine Embodiment: Restoration, Judeo-Christian, and Philosophical Perspectives," *BYU Studies* 35, no. 4 (1995–1996): 6–94; and "Divine Embodiment: The Earliest Christian Understanding of God," in *Early Christians in Disarray: Contemporary LDS Perspectives on the Christian Apostasy*, ed. Noel B. Reynolds (Provo, Utah: Brigham Young University Press/FARMS, 2005), 239–94. I also consulted the following works co-authored by Paulsen: Carl W. Griffin and David L. Paulsen, "Augustine and the Corporeality of God," *Harvard Theological Review* 86 (2002): 97–118; and Clark H. Pinnock and David L. Paulsen, "A Dialogue on Openness Theology," in *Mormonism in Dialogue with Contemporary Christian Theologies*, eds. Donald W. Musser and David L. Paulsen (Macon, Ga.: Mercer University Press, 2007), 489–554.

of in 1 Corinthians 15, or is it something else? And is having a body consisting of refined matter the same thing as having a "spirit body," which the Holy Spirit has according to Mormonism (D&C 130:22)? (Mainstream Christians do not affirm that the Holy Spirit has any sort of body.) I would also like to know more about the Mormon view of "intelligence." What do these terms mean and how are they related?[3] I believe that a more comprehensive and definitive treatment of these questions in Mormon theology would provide clarity that Mormon and non-Mormon philosophers and theologians could appreciate and utilize to more effectively communicate with one another.

I

Quite apart from the arguments of Paulsen and other Mormons, how might mainstream Christians argue on behalf of the idea that God is immaterial? Limiting ourselves for now to the biblical evidence, I suspect most of them would do so roughly and briefly in the following way.

There is no question that God is frequently described in the Bible, and especially the Old Testament, as if he were an embodied being. For example, references to God's face (Gen. 32:30; Ex. 33:11, 20), eyes (2 Chron. 16:9), arms (Ex. 6:6; Ps. 44:3, 89:13), feet (Ex. 24:10; Ps. 18:9), hands (Deut. 4:34, 7:19; Ps. 44:2), fingers (Ex. 33:23), and nostrils (Ps. 18:15) are common. In addition, God is said to see (Gen. 11:5; Deut. 7:19), hear (Gen. 21:17; Num. 11:1, 12:2), walk (Gen. 3:8), grieve (Gen. 6:6), repent (Gen. 6:6–7), and be jealous (Deut. 29:20). Mainstream Christians do not doubt that God can take bodily form and has done so (definitely in the incarnation of Christ and perhaps as "the angel of the Lord" in the Old Testament), but the dominant Christian tradition has rejected the idea that God is a material being.

The hermeneutical key for mainstream Christians on this issue is John 4:24, where Jesus says, "God is spirit [*pneuma*], and those who

---

3. Brigham Young University professor of philosophy James E. Faulconer makes a helpful beginning toward an LDS view of the mind/body problem in "Divine Embodiment and Transcendence: Propaedutic Thoughts and Questions," *Element: The Journal of the Society for Mormon Philosophy and Theology* 1, no. 1 (Spring 2005). Available at http://smpt.org/docs/faulconer_element1-1.html (accessed April 24, 2012).

worship him must worship in spirit and truth."[4] The Greek work *pneuma* and the corresponding Hebrew word *ruach* are multi-faceted terms that are difficult to translate precisely;[5] however, *pneuma* is also used in Luke 24:39 ("A ghost does not have flesh and bones as you see that I have"), and that text constitutes strong evidence for the claim that the statement, "X is spirit," implies that X is immaterial. In addition, the Bible affirms that God is not located in any one place (1 Kgs. 8:27; Acts 7:48–50, 17:24–25), as physical objects such as human bodies always are. Moreover, God is also said to be invisible (John 1:18, 5:37; Col. 1:15; 1 Tim. 1:17). We will return to these points in Section III.

If God is immaterial, then what about these many biblical texts that seem to imply that God has bodily parts? The dominant tradition would take most of them as examples of anthropomorphism. This term refers to the treating of something that is not human as if it were human. We often see anthropomorphism in cartoons, in newspapers, or on television (e.g., when animals or trees are made to talk). In the Bible, it is quite understandable and perfectly acceptable that the biblical writers frequently depicted God as they were best able to understand God—in human terms. In such cases, their descriptions are not to be taken literally. God does not literally have hands, feet, and a face. In general, the hermeneutical rule is that any depiction of God in the Bible is not to be taken literally if it entails that God has human limitations.

In many texts, the Bible insists that human beings cannot see God (Gen. 32:30; Ex. 33:20; Isa. 6:5), or that only the righteous and pure of heart can do so (Ps. 11:7; Matt. 18:10; Heb. 12:14; Rev. 22:3–4). Those few places in the Bible where people are said to see God or parts of God (e.g., Ex. 24:10, 33:18–23) are accordingly to be understood either as examples of anthropomorphism or as situations where God did indeed take physical form (John 1:32).

The ancient Israelites were convinced that their God, the Lord, was not like anyone or anything else. They lived in a religious envi-

---

4. All biblical quotations in the present paper are taken from the New Revised Standard Version (NRSV) translation. I should also note that the Joseph Smith Translation of the Bible (JST) renders John 4:24, "for unto such hath God promised his Spirit." This, however, is not an accurate translation of the Greek.

5. I should note that Latter-day Saints do not hold that being a "spirit" entails being incorporeal. They believe that spirits are embodied, human-like persons, although possibly less tangible than human persons because they are composed of "refined matter" (see Ether 3:16, D&C 131:7).

ronment in which other nations worshipped gods made in images of human beings or animals. But the Israelites insisted that God was incomparable in wisdom, power, and majesty (see Isa. 40:12–26). This is why they were strictly prohibited from making graven images or worshipping idols (Ex. 20:4; Deut. 4:12–23). In other words, they drew a strong connection between God not having any sort of physical form and the prohibition of idolatry.

Mainstream Christians certainly know and affirm the biblical notion that human beings are created "in the image of God" (Gen. 1:27). A great deal has been written in Christian history about just what the "image of God" consists. But mainstream Christians deny the LDS notion that the "image of God" is a physical image or likeness. Their denial of God's physical likeness is not due to any Platonic or Gnostic desire to impugn bodily existence, but rather because of their interpretations of scripture. For example, Colossians 3:10 implies that the image of God has primarily to do with spiritual knowledge. 2 Corinthians 3:18 implies that God's image is related to the glory of God. Ephesians 4:24 suggests that it has to do with "true righteousness and holiness." Finally, Colossians 1:15 refers to Christ as "the image of the invisible God," which seems to clearly rule out the idea that an "image" is a physical likeness. Since God is invisible, Christ must be the image of God in some non-visible sense.

I believe that something like this account would be accepted by the vast majority of mainstream Christians. Their notion is that, except for occasional epiphanies and the incarnation of Christ, God is not an embodied being. Rather, God is an immaterial spirit.

II

As noted above, David Paulsen has written about divine embodiment on many occasions. Indeed, he has probably written about this subject more than any other single topic in theology or the philosophy of religion. And it is clear (as Paulsen himself admits[6]) that Latter-day Saints believe that God is embodied, not primarily because of philosophical or even biblical arguments, but because of modern revelation. Latter-day Saints affirm that the doctrine of divine embodiment was revealed to Joseph Smith. Indeed, in the prophet's First Vision, in 1820

---

6. Pinnock and Paulsen, "A Dialogue on Openness Theology," 519.

in a grove of trees near Palmyra, New York, God the Father and Jesus Christ appeared to Joseph Smith as embodied persons. On April 2, 1843, in Ramus, Illinois, Joseph Smith taught:

> The Father has a body of flesh and bones as tangible as man's; the Son also; but the Holy Spirit has not a body of flesh and bones, but is a personage of Spirit. Were it not so, the Holy Ghost could not dwell in us. (D&C 130:22)[7]

Similarly, on April 7, 1844, in Nauvoo, Illinois, Joseph Smith made the following statement to his followers:

> It is the first principle of the Gospel to know for a certainty the Character of God, and to know that we may converse with him as one man converses with another ... and ... if you were to see him today, you would see him like a man in form—like yourselves in all the person, image, and very form as a man.[8]

Moreover, as Paulsen points out, the notion of divine embodiment is crucially connected to other important LDS doctrines, such as the purpose of life, bodily resurrection, and the eternal progression of men and women toward Godhood.[9]

But quite apart from modern revelation, let me now discuss five arguments that Paulsen raises in favor of divine materiality.

A. The Biblical Argument

Here Paulsen clearly has in mind the numerous places in the Bible (many of them mentioned above) where God seems to be depicted as embodied. However, he differs from mainstream Christians in that, like most Mormons, Paulsen wants to interpret these texts in a straightforward, literal sense. Indeed, he applauds the attempt "to release explicitly anthropomorphic and anthropopathic biblical messages from the shackles of merely figurative interpretation."[10] God really does have a

---

7. It should be noted that D&C 130 is somewhat unusual in that it is presented as "items of instruction" rather than a revelation given to (or given through) Joseph Smith. The LDS Church certainly considers it revelatory, however.

8. The quotation is taken from Joseph Smith's "King Follett Sermon." See Joseph Fielding Smith, comp., *Teachings of the Prophet Joseph Smith* (Salt Lake City: Deseret Book Company, 1976), 342–62.

9. Paulsen, "The Doctrine of Divine Embodiment," 7–8 note 2.

10. Pinnock and Paulsen, "A Dialogue on Openness Theology," 516.

face, hands, and fingers because God is embodied. Or, perhaps more astutely, God is embodied because God has a face, hands, and fingers.

The only objection that I will raise here is this: why do Latter-day Saints take *these* anthropomorphisms literally but not others in the Bible? For example, why not affirm that God is forgetful (Gen. 8:1), impatient (Ex. 32:7–14), full of rage (Deut. 29:28), has wings (Ps. 17:8, 36:7, 57:1, 61:4, 91:4), or lives in a tent (Ps. 61:4)? Indeed, why not affirm that God is a fire (Deut. 4:24), a rock (2 Samuel 22:47), or bread (John 6:51)? Do Latter-day Saints have a coherent hermeneutic that allows them to take the divine embodiment texts literally but not the God-as-mother-hen texts literally?

B. *The Historical Argument*

In several of his essays Paulsen argues strongly for the claim that divine embodiment was the default view of God for many ordinary Christians in the first three centuries of the early church, and that even at the time of Augustine (CE 354–430) there were Christian communities whose members held that God was embodied.[11]

I have no problem conceding much of this point, but I do wish to make two comments about it. First, I reject Paulsen's claim that Christianity moved to the idea of divine immateriality because of the influence of "Greek philosophy" and especially Platonism.[12] This is a charge that Mormons often make about mainstream Christian doctrines that they reject, but the assertion is usually left at the level of vague generality, even sloppiness.[13] I accept that intellectual or theological influence is not always easy to substantiate, but in my opinion no Mormon scholar has made this claim stick.[14] I do not deny that Greek philosophy had an influence on early Christian thought, but my own view is that

---

11. Most notably, see Paulsen, "Early Christian Views of a Corporeal Deity," "The Doctrine of Divine Embodiment"; Griffin and Paulsen, "Augustine and the Corporeality of God," and "Divine Embodiment."

12. Paulsen, "Divine Embodiment," 2, 4 and RES, 518.

13. See, for example, Stephen E. Robinson's many statements to this effect in Craig L. Blomberg and Stephen E. Robinson, *How Wide the Divide? A Mormon and an Evangelical in Conversation* (Downers Grove, Ill.: InterVarsity Press, 1997).

14. This point is made compellingly in Paul Owen and Carl Mosser, "How Wide the Divide? A Mormon and an Evangelical in Conversation," *FARMS Review of Books* 11, no. 2 (1999): 1–102.

Christians held (and still hold) the belief that God is immaterial primarily because that is the way in which they interpret the scriptures.[15] Moreover, several of the Greek Fathers were well versed in the Greek classics and went to great pains to argue that Christianity is superior to Greek philosophy.[16]

Second, I must note that it is puzzling to find a Latter-day Saint scholar arguing for the truth of an important Mormon doctrine on the grounds that many people in the first few centuries of church history believed. This puzzlement results from the fact that it is also a crucial LDS doctrine that, at the end of the apostolic age, the Christian church went radically wrong and fell into "the Great Apostasy," which was only corrected in the nineteenth century. The strong language in the Mormon scriptures about the mainstream church (see 1 Ne. 13:5–6; D&C 29:21) makes one wonder why Mormons would be interested in *anything* that these apostates believed.

On the other hand, some contemporary LDS scholars seem willing to concede that they have much to learn from the early church, and that the "Great Apostasy" was not as sudden or absolute as Mormons once thought.[17] Indeed, Paulsen can claim that some of the apostates of the first few centuries of the Christian church probably held correct opinions on some points, with divine embodiment being one of them. Fair enough.

However, there does remain a curious double standard in the way that Mormons appeal to the Hellenization or Platonization of the early church. Where the early church teaches something that Mormons reject, it constitutes confirmation of the growing apostasy and corruption of the pure Jewish gospel. But when the early church supports something that Mormons accept, it is understood as vestiges of the original,

---

15. In another sense, it is surprising for LDS scholars to claim that early Christian thought was corrupted by Platonistic influences, since the LDS view of human pre-existence in a spirit world is remarkably similar to views that Plato espoused in several of his dialogues (the *Phaedo* and the *Meno*, for example). Both Plato and Mormons hold that there is, in addition to this present spatio-temporal world, another realm of spirit from which we came.

16. See Jaroslav Pelikan, *Christianity and Classical Culture: The Metamorphosis of Natural Theology in the Christian Encounter With Hellenism* (New Haven, Conn.: Yale University Press, 1993), 3–21.

17. Among others, see Roger Keller, *Reformed Christians and Mormon Christians: Let's Talk* (Sandy, Utah: Pryor Pettengill, 1986).

pure gospel—even if that element is not at all Jewish. Thus, their position becomes unfalsifiable.

C. The Deductive Argument for Divine Materiality

Paulsen offers a deductive argument for the conclusion that God is embodied:[18]

1. Jesus Christ is God.
2. Jesus Christ was resurrected with an incorruptible body.
3. The separation of the spirit from the body is death.
4. Jesus Christ will never die again.
5. Thus, Jesus Christ will be embodied everlastingly (from 2–4).
6. Therefore, Jesus Christ is both God and embodied everlastingly (from 1, 2, 5).
7. Jesus is the express image of the Father (Heb.1:1–3).
8. Therefore, God the Father is embodied everlastingly (from 5 and 7).

The argument looks perfectly acceptable to me down through premise (7). I certainly believe that Jesus Christ is permanently embodied in his resurrected body, but why must the "image of the Father" spoken of by the writer to the Hebrews be a physical image? If that point could be substantiated, Paulsen's argument might be probative.

Paulsen knows that mainstream Christians accept the present and permanent embodiment of Christ. He tries to turn that fact into an inconsistency in their position. They are committed, he says, to an inconsistent triad—a set of three propositions where the truth of any two entails the falsity of the third.[19] It consists of (a) Jesus of Nazareth exists everlastingly with a resurrected body, (b) Jesus of Nazareth is God, and (c) necessarily, if x is God, then x is incorporeal.[20] However, I would respond that *because* mainstream Christians accept (a), they reject (c). They do not hold that God is *essentially* or *necessarily* incorporeal. They certainly do hold that God the Father and God the Holy Spirit are *in fact* incorporeal, but that does not lead to any inconsistency.

---

18. Pinnock and Paulsen, "A Dialogue on Openness Theology," 517.
19. For example: (1) A is taller than B, (2) B is taller than C, and (3) C is taller than A.
20. Paulsen, "The Doctrine of Divine Embodiment," 81 note 208.

D. *The "Body is Not Evil" Argument*

Surprisingly, Paulsen argues, "belief in an embodied God replaces the duality of Greek philosophy wherein the body is relegated to an evil regression from the purely spiritual."[21] This argument goes nowhere, in my opinion, because mainstream Christians do not hold—as did Plato and others in the ancient world—that the body is inherently evil and inferior to spirit. The long-running battle that many of the Church Fathers fought against the Gnostics—who *did* hold to this view—is proof of that fact. Mainstream Christians hold that the body, like the rest of creation, is good. Of course, sin has corrupted everything human, including both our bodies and our souls, leaving them in need of redemption. However, we do not hold that the body is an evil regression from the spirit.

E. *The Pastoral Argument*

Finally, Paulsen offers a practical argument on behalf of divine materiality. He says, "Understanding the literalness of [humans] being created 'in the image' of God is tremendously ennobling and empowering as one seeks to overcome the trials and temptations of the flesh." He adds that this doctrine motivates us and enables us to do great things.[22] In this connection, Paulsen quotes LDS figures Truman Madsen and Charles W. Penrose on the importance of *human* embodied existence—though I will not comment on this point since it is irrelevant to the issue of divine immateriality. With this point, mainstream Christians would not disagree.

Now Paulsen is surely aware that we cannot settle matters of truth by appeals to benefit; whether one holds that God is material or immaterial should not be decided on the basis of which theory is more helpful to human beings as they travel the road of life. Moreover, Paulsen and the LDS figures that he cites seem to be targeting those who deny that human beings are literally created in God's image. However, I can assure him that mainstream Christians are not members of that group. I certainly affirm that we are *literally* (not figuratively or metaphorically) created in the image of God and I agree that that affirmation

---

21. Pinnock and Paulsen, "A Dialogue on Openness Theology," 518.
22. Ibid., 519.

is essential to Christianity. The difference is that we do not think the "image" is a matter of physical likeness. Latter-day Saints understand "image" to mean "bodily image," while mainstream Christians do not.

One problem for the Mormon view of the image of God is the Christian doctrine that human beings are fallen, and that the Fall severely damaged, but did not entirely eradicate, the image of God in us. Perhaps Mormons will simply deny much or all of this doctrine.[23] In one sense they must since they believe that the image of God in us is a visible, bodily image that is still very much intact. As Joseph Smith said, if you met God "you would see him like a man in form."[24] This is challenged, however, by the traditional view that the fallen image of God is being rebuilt in us through the Holy Spirit—which seems a clear implication of Biblical passages, such as Psalm 51:5, Romans 5:12, 2 Corinthians 4:16, Ephesians 4:22–24, and Colossians 3:10.

III

Having presented a more overtly biblical analysis in favor of divine immaterialism in Section I, I will now mount three arguments on philosophical and theological grounds in favor of divine immaterialism.

A. Invisibility

The most convincing aspects of the biblical argument for divine immateriality, in my opinion, concern divine invisibility and omnipresence. Let's consider invisibility first. As noted above, Colossians 1:15 refers to "the invisible God." Timothy 1:17 refers to "the King of the ages, immortal, invisible, the only God" (see also 1 Tim. 6:16). Accordingly, mainstream Christians hold that God is inherently invisible but does at times become embodied or visible. Mormons reverse the idea: they argue that God's invisibility is a matter of choice, not nature; while God's default status is embodiment he can become invisible at will.[25]

In this connection, I have heard Mormon scholars refer to John 14:9 in support of divine materiality. In this text, Jesus says to Philip: "Who-

---

23. I should note that although I affirm original sin, I reject the idea that people are guilty for, and can be condemned for, sins that other people committed.
24. See note 8.
25. Paulsen, "Divine Embodiment," 3.

ever has seen me has seen the Father." However, that is not a good argument. Suppose I was to say, "Whoever has seen me has seen the Russell K. Pitzer Professor of Philosophy at Claremont McKenna College." It is clear that both uses of "seen" in this sentence can refer to literal sight because I am numerically identical with the Russell K. Pitzer Professor of Philosophy at Claremont McKenna College. But it cannot be the case that the second use of "seen" in Jesus's sentence refers to literal vision because, as both mainstream Christians and (especially) Mormons hold, God the Father is *not* numerically identical to God the Son.

B. Omnipresence

That God is omnipresent or ubiquitous is implied in many biblical texts. In 1 Kings 8:27, Solomon says to God, "Even heaven and the highest heaven cannot contain you, much less this house that I have built!" (see also Isa. 66:1). Psalm 139:7–10 says, "Where can I go from your spirit? Or where can I flee from your presence? If I ascend to heaven, you are there; if I make my bed in Sheol, you are there; If I take the wings of the morning and settle at the farthest limits of the sea, even there you hand shall lead me, and your right hand shall hold me fast." And Luke quotes Paul, in his speech on the Areopagus, as insisting that God "does not live in shrines made by human hands" (Acts 17:24).

Omnipresence does not mean being simultaneously located at every spatial point. Embodied beings cannot be omnipresent in that sense because they are located in only one place at a time; nor can immaterial things be omnipresent in the same sense because they lack any spatial location. The claim that God is omnipresent means, I take it, that God is always aware of all that is going on at all spatial points and that God is always able directly to influence what is going on at all spatial points. Human beings are able to indirectly influence events at a distance—for example, by shouting, sending a message, or naming an appointee who acts on one's behalf in another location. God, however, is able to influence things at any spatial point without the use of intermediaries or intermediate steps. Throughout the creation, God knows and acts, as we might say, directly. Moreover, human powers to influence events are greatly limited, while God's powers (since God is also omnipotent) are only limited by logical considerations. If God is embodied, however, then there is a physical location from which God looks out on the world (i.e., the place where his body is located). This places, what I would consider, an unacceptable limitation on God.

An additional point: I wonder about the Mormon view of God's relation to his own body. Does God depend on his body, as we do on ours? It seems clear to me that we need our bodies to exist, but does God also need a body to exist?[26] If the LDS view is that God depends upon his body for his own existence, I would have to disagree—even if it is held with the belief that God's body is indestructible.

C. Can an Embodied God Be God?

My own view is that a price must be paid by anyone who holds that God is embodied. For one thing, if God is a material being, it seems that God must be dependent upon the fundamental laws of physics—gravity, thermodynamics, inertia, etc.—and can thus hardly be the creator or explanation of those laws. It follows from this that God is in some ways a contingent being (i.e., a being who depends on other things for its status and identity—whether those things be conditions, laws, beings, or whatever).[27]

From divine embodiment, it also follows that God cannot be a truly omnipotent being (where "X is omnipotent" means roughly that "X has the ability to bring about any non-contradictory state of affairs").[28] If God is located somewhere in space, the speed of light will limit what God can do in distant areas of space. How can God experience all spaces at once, let alone influence them? Even if God can move faster than 186,000 miles per second—like hypothetical tachyons—as an embodied being subject to the laws of physics, he will still be limited in velocity. He will be quite unable to have a God's eye view of all reality at once. In other words, if God is limited in velocity and position,

---

26. Richard Swinburne, *The Christian God* (Oxford, England: Oxford University Press, 1994), 127.
27. I say "in some ways" because Mormons hold that all beings, Gods and humans, are in some primordial sense uncreated.
28. Some LDS scholars are prepared to admit that because of their view of God, divine omnipotence and omniscience must be understood differently than it is in mainstream Christianity. See, for example, Faulconer, "Divine Embodiment and Transcendence," 9.

as embodied beings must be, then God is limited in what I consider a theologically unacceptable way.[29]

Mormons may reply to these sorts of points by claiming that God is not a *purely* material being, that God is not exhausted by his body, or that God is a being composed of both spirit and body. Indeed, the late President Gordon B. Hinckley wrote, "I said, 'Of course God is a spirit, and so are you, in the combination of spirit and body that makes you a living being, and so am I.' Each of us is a dual being of spiritual entity and physical entity."[30] If this is the official LDS position, then perhaps Mormons might be able to evade at least some of the points that I have just been making.

In this connection, I have heard Mormons scholars give the example of the earthly Jesus. He surely was both body and spirit, they say. And that is certainly true. However, this example will not help them in the present connection, because the earthly Jesus was not omnipresent, either in terms of knowledge (see Mark 13:32) or in terms of power (Mark 6:5). Moreover, despite his ability to perform miracles, his body clearly limited him by such natural laws as the speed of light.

Mainstream Christians place great emphasis on the transcendence of God. They note such texts as Isaiah 55:8–9: "For my thoughts are not your thoughts, nor are your ways my ways, says the Lord. For as the heavens are higher than the earth, so are my ways higher than your ways and my thoughts than your thoughts" (see also Isa. 46:5). According to 1 Timothy 6:16, "It is he alone who has immortality and dwells in unapproachable light, whom no one has ever seen or can see; to him be honor and eternal dominion" (see also Num. 23:19; 1 Sam. 15:29; Hosea 11:9). To say that God is transcendent is to say that God is other than and superior to the created order, and that God, in his essence, is unknowable to us. Apart from God's revelation of himself to us, God would be entirely mysterious to us. Mainstream Christians see a strong connection between God's transcendence and God's worthiness of worship. Like the ancient Hebrews, we are loath to worship a creature.

---

29. Paulsen might well respond at this point by asking about Jesus Christ. Since he is presently embodied in heaven, is he also to be limited in these same ways? Not at all, I would say. The Trinitarian doctrine of *perichoresis* rules that out. See Stephen T. Davis, *Christian Philosophical Theology* (Oxford, USA: Oxford University Press, 2006), 60–78.

30. Gordon B. Hinckley, "The Father, Son, and Holy Ghost," *Ensign*, March 1998, 2.

Can the LDS God be transcendent? Well, certainly not in the same sense that the God of mainstream Christianity is. There are of course senses in which Latter-day Saints can affirm that God transcends the world. However, their doctrine of divine embodiment plus the notion that God and human beings are members of the same Species rule out anything like the mainstream notion of divine transcendence. While Latter-day Saints may be willing to pay the price of affirming this type of divinity, mainstream Christians are certainly not. Instead, mainstream Christians hold that God is an independent and transcendent being, not dependent for his identity and status on anything else. Furthermore, they hold that God is omnipotent, omniscient, and infinitely superior to humans.

Conclusion

Although I reject it, I admit that I cannot disprove the general claim that Latter-day Saints are recipients of modern revelation. Nor can I disprove their particular claim that God's embodiment is a part of that. For those who accept that revelation, the matter is decisively settled. But apart from those claims—i.e., based on biblical revelation and philosophical argumentation alone—the case for divine immaterialism seems to me to be decisive. In my opinion, while David Paulsen has done as good a job of defending his church's position on this issue as can be done, it is a case that has little hope of convincing non-Mormons.

12

Does Divine Passibility Entail Divine Corporeality?

Clark H. Pinnock, *McMaster Divinity College*

I wish to honor my friend David Paulsen with this essay. He is an outstanding Mormon philosopher and theologian, one who deserves to be honored and even better known. We have had fruitful conversations over the years and I happily admit that I have learned a good deal from him. I think that his students would agree with me that he has a beautiful mind, not to mention a godly disposition.

Some Evangelical readers, noting the topic that I have chosen to discuss, may not understand it. What it means, briefly, is whether God can be affected by events in the world and, if so, if this entails that God has a bodily dimension that handles sensory and corporeal input. Otherwise, how does God speak, act, and breathe?[1]

Other readers may be taken aback, not because they do not understand the question but because they understand it quite well. They might wonder why this matter is up for discussion at all. Is it not a core Christian doctrine, hardly debatable among mainstream Christians, that God is a spiritual being who is immaterial, invisible, and intangible? As Christians, are we not encouraged to think that the very idea of God having a body is a non-starter? Here I must disagree. Divine embodiment is an important category for Christian theology generally and for Mormon theology in particular, and it must be considered and discussed in order for any meaningful future dialogue with Mormons to take place. If one accepts the divine pathos (as most Evangelicals do), the question of divine embodiment arises: how can an incorporeal God have passions?[2]

---

1. Consider the treatment of this topic by Marcel Sarot, *God, Passibility, and Corporeality* (Kampen, Netherlands: Kok Pharos, 1992).

2. Tertullian and a few other Church Fathers believed that God has a body. See Grace Jantzen, "Theological Tradition and Divine Corporeality," chap. 3 in *God's World, God's Body*, ed. Grace Jantzen (Philadelphia: The Westminster Press, 1984).

According to David Paulsen, "Latter-day Saints have waited a long time for some competent Christian theologian to release the explicitly anthropomorphic biblical passages from the shackles of merely figurative interpretation."[3] This contribution can be seen as part of the Openness of God project in which we pull on the strings of the classical model of God to see where the tradition may have got things right and where it got them wrong.

The Passibility of God

Let me begin where David and I are in agreement. Mormons and most Evangelicals agree that God is capable of loving, feeling, and, therefore, suffering. We serve a passionate deity. Classical theists, on the other hand, worry about God being made vulnerable in this way and less than perfect. However, thinking on this matter has changed noticeably! It has become much more common among Christians to hear the following: "If God loves, God must be able to suffer, because love involves risk. We wonder: will our love be received or not?" (God wonders about it too!)

God experiences pathos. God's life is influenced by what happens in the world. He can be delighted or dismayed in relation to it. In Isaiah we read that God "cries out like a woman in travail. She gasps and pants" (Isa. 42:14). Hosea hears God say, "My heart recoils within me and my compassion grows warm and tender" (Hosea 11:8). The pathos of God is central to his identity. God is moved by what happens in the world. Worldly events arouse in him joy or sorrow, pleasure or wrath. The God of the Bible is passible. Only such a God is credible to Christian scripture and tradition, and only such a God can be redemptive. This is a positive development in Christian doctrine for our time.[4]

---

3. Clark H. Pinnock and David L. Paulsen, "A Dialogue On Openness Theology," in *Mormonism in Dialogue with Contemporary Christian Theologies*, ed. David L. Paulsen and Donald W. Musser (Macon, Ga.: Mercer University Press, 2007), 515–16. What little I have contributed to this topic can be found in Clark Pinnock, *Most Moved Mover: A Theology of God's Openness* (Grand Rapids, Mich.: Baker Academic Press, 2001), 79; and Clark Pinnock, "A Dialogue On Openness Theology," in *Mormonism in Dialogue with Contemporary Christian Theologies*, eds. David L. Paulsen and Donald W. Musser (Macon, Ga.: Mercer University Press, 2007), 500–553.

4. Warren McWilliams, *The Passion of God: Divine Suffering in Contemporary*

The Corporeality of God

Allow me to explain the link between passibility, which is widely accepted, and corporeality, which is not. Persons as we know them come to us embodied. They are not ghosts or statues. They have characteristics that make them persons. They have emotions, they communicate, and, above all, they love. They would not be persons if they did not manifest such characteristics. Neither would God be personal, if he did not also manifest them. God and man both need bodies to be persons. Thus, it is necessary that in God there is a corporeal and embodied dimension. The experiences that we ascribe to God cannot reasonably be ascribed to an incorporeal deity!

Aquinas reasoned in the opposite direction—that a pathos cannot be ascribed to God, in part because of his incorporeal nature. Nevertheless, Aquinas unwittingly helps me illustrate the point. The Bible appears to say very clearly that emotion and the divine nature are not incompatible. However, emotions require corporeality. Were God to have emotions, he would have to be corporeal. But, the presupposition of incorporeality forbids it. Thus, we are forced to say that God has no emotions. Nevertheless, passibility entails corporeality because an incorporeal God would not be able to have emotions, experience bodily sensations, and other important functions. It would seem that, if God lacks a body, considerable limitations are imposed on what God can experience or do.[5]

Scripture is supportive of the idea of divine embodiment on a number of levels. Human beings have been made in the image and likeness of God. There is a resemblance between the two. The Word was made flesh and dwelled among us. God can be incarnated in human flesh. The body is not foreign to God. We are not dualists. Beyond this, many scriptures suggest divine embodiment.[6] In the Old Testa-

---

Protestant Theology (Macon, Ga.: Mercer University Press, 1985). Cf. Blake T. Ostler, "Immutability and Impassibility," in *Exploring Mormon Thought: The Attributes of God* (Salt Lake City: Greg Kofford Books, 2001), 365–408.

5. Abraham Heschel, "The Theology of the Pathos of God," chap. 12 in *The Prophets* (New York: Harper & Row, 1962).

6. Interestingly enough, Mormons often minimize this point because, as I note in this essay, they do not rest their confidence in divine embodiment on the Bible but on the visions of Joseph Smith. Let them be amused that a non-Mormon Evangelical (me) would like to help them ground their faith in divine corporeality

ment we learn that God comes to his people in both human form and as an angel. God allows himself to be seen and touched.[7] Amos speaks of God "standing" (Amos 7:7); Isaiah sees God "sitting" (Isa. 6:1). Jeremiah feels God's hand "touch" his mouth (Jer. 1:9). Ezekiel sees God sitting on a throne in the likeness of a human form (Ezek. 1:26.) The point is that God in the Old Testament is often presented in human terms. Not as something foreign to humankind, God comes to us in personal and humanly vulnerable ways. Incarnation or embodiment is something that God regularly experiences. One might say that the God of the Old Testament is comfortable with incarnating himself.

Here it would be quite natural to ask if God assumes human form for the sake of humans or if there is actually a human form that God has. Is God's coming in human form appropriate for God, or is it just an anthropic act where God merely stoops to our level of ignorance, revealing nothing? After all, God made man in his image—that is, God made us "theomorphically," such that there is real continuity between God and humanity. Being human is not foreign to God. Coming in human form does not compromise his deity. God is in fact like us! The human form and way of being is not alien to deity. God can take the form of the human without compromising the "God-ness" of God.

Divine Embodiment

God is certainly passible and probably corporeal. Though, while we know much about what it means to be corporeal as humans, what it would mean for God is a great mystery. We can, however, try to understand what divine corporeality might entail. C. S. Lewis once asked, "What soul ever perished for thinking that God had a beard?"[8] Let us ask the question: If God has a body, what kind of body might it be?

---

securely in the Bible also.

7. Terence E. Fretheim, "God in Human Form," in *The Suffering of God: An Old Testament Perspective* (Philadelphia, Penn.: Fortress Press, 1984), ch. 6. God is presented almost indisputably as corporeal in the Old Testament. We hear about his arms and legs, his ears and hands, his lips and mouth, his eyes and voice. Among the rabbis there are literalists who hold that God has a human shape while others prefer divine incorporeality vis-à-vis a metaphorical approach. The majority of Evangelicals today are with the latter group. Logically, though, they should not buy into the pathos of God, which would take them where they theologically do not want to go.

8. C. S. Lewis, *Letters to Malcom: Chiefly on Prayer* (New York: Harvest-Harcourt

A. *How do Latter-day Saints think about God's body?*

Mormons were the first modern ecclesial fellowship to treat the question seriously, and they deserve to be heard on this matter. Epistemologically, Mormonism embraced the doctrine from the visions and revelations of Joseph Smith rather than from the Bible *per se*. For Latter-day Saints, revelation continues, and this fact generates no embarrassment. They do not hold to the doctrine solely because the Bible teaches it, but because Joseph Smith experienced it. As to the content of the doctrine, they come down on the literal side of its interpretation. God the Father has "a body of flesh and bones, as tangible as man's" (D&C 130:22). This may sound intransigent and fundamentalist; however, we must remember that reason is a source for theology alongside other sources for Mormons. In this light, consider this insight from LDS author Stephen Robinson who writes, "Latter-day Saints affirm only that the Father has a body, not that his body has him. The Father is corporeal and infinitely more . . ."[9] Certainly, a useful dialogue could be realistically pursued with LDS theologians like this.[10]

B. *How might Evangelicals think about God's body?*

Evangelicals' conservatism, I fear, may make it unlikely that they will consider divine embodiment. Nevertheless, how might an Evangelical understand divine embodiment? In the quotation from Lewis, he puts the issue in perspective. There is scripture that supports divine embodiment and scripture that does not; nevertheless, it is not a Church-dividing issue. In addition, several of the Church Fathers espoused it and many more believed it was worthy of debate.[11] In our day, leading Evangelical theologian Donald G. Bloesch alludes to God's "supernatural body" as something that God could assume, and Richard Swinburne, a leading Christian philosopher, writes that God may have

---

Brace Jovanovich, 1964), 22.

9. Craig L. Blomberg and Stephen E. Robinson, *How Wide the Divide? A Mormon and an Evangelical in Conversation* (Downers Grove, Ill.: InterVarsity Press, 1997), 88.

10. I find that Mormons are generally less touchy about strict orthodoxy in their church than Evangelicals are in churches. A great deal is still open to discussion.

11. Jantzen, "Theological Tradition and Divine Corporeality."

a body but is not dependent on it.[12] Paul taught that there are "many different kinds of bodies in this world" (1 Cor. 15:35–36). Our task should be to study these phenomena in order to formulate a theory of divine corporeality. Certainly God's body would be blindingly glorious, and unlike any kind of body with which we are familiar. It would be a mysterious body and not something one would be able to adequately describe. However, the possibility of God's embodiment is deeply relevant, given the fact that human beings are destined to share in the glory of God and become partakers of the divine nature (Rom. 5:2; 2 Pet. 1:4). Notwithstanding, if human deification and divine embodiment turn out to be part of a "restored Christian faith," we will need an extra century or two to comprehend it, if we ever do.

C. *Can philosophers help?*

Philosophers can often be helpful because they are very good at clarifying concepts and are relatively independent of the clerical harassment that theologians sometimes suffer. They can often also be Christian scientists, like Wolfhart Pannenberg and John Polkinghorne, who can handle the scientific metaphysics of our time. One voice that has helped me is a former colleague and fellow Canadian, the late Dr. Grace Jantzen, who spoke of the world as God's body. Her contribution is that of a speculative theory of divine corporeality, similar to but independent of, the work of Charles Hartshorne. The world is viewed as the body of God. She gives us a holistic and non-dualistic way to think about God's relationship to the world. God, for Jantzen, is very much personal, which has some important implications. God should be viewed as corporeal because of his ability to perceive things. Perception implies sensation, and therefore embodiment. A personal God also has to be able to act and be present everywhere and at all times. The ability to be present everywhere is vitally related to God's ability to perceive and to act everywhere. If God is a person, it might be better to imagine God as corporeal rather than incorporeal.[13]

---

12. Cited in Pinnock and Paulsen, "A Dialogue on Openness Theology," 502.

13. Should any Mormons and/or Evangelicals aspire to improve their theology in this matter, Grace Jantzen is most definitely one who can help them. See Jantzen's *God's World, God's Body* and Sarot's discussion of her work in *God, Passibility, and Corporeality*, 219–36.

Conclusion

The old proverb says that curiosity killed the cat. But equally, I would say, curiosity is a theological virtue that makes theology a fulfilling journey of discovery. I hope that this modest meditation on an important theological concept proves enriching and thought provoking to all who read it. I believe that with regard to theological concepts, such as the potential embodiment of God, Mormonism has much to contribute to emerging Evangelicalism. I know from personal experience that dialogue with Latter-day Saints on topics such as this can be a very fruitful and mutually enriching experience.

13

Transascendence: Transcendence in Mormon Thought

James E. Faulconer, *Brigham Young University*

Speaking as the mouthpiece of God, Isaiah says, "For my thoughts are not your thoughts, neither are your ways my ways, saith the Lord. For as the heavens are higher than the earth, so are my ways higher than your ways, and my thoughts than your thoughts" (Isa. 55:8–9). Only Anselm's fool would think otherwise. God's way of being is so much beyond our own that we cannot understand divine being. What would it be like to have all the power there is, or to know all knowable things, or to bring a world into being? We cannot answer such questions. We stand in awe of God's incomprehensible majesty, power, and condescending love. That is part of what it means to worship him, and I presume that no Latter-day Saint thinks otherwise. But Mormon theological responses to this difference between God and human beings—and there are several possible responses—differ considerably from the theological responses of other Christians.

Two Traditional Positions on God's Transcendence

When traditional Christian theologians have turned their thought to this inescapable facet of belief and worship, they have said that God is *transcendent*. His being exceeds ours, transcends ours. And, believing in creation *ex nihilo*, they have often explained this transcendence by saying that the Creator is not himself created, so he cannot share the being of anything created. The source of being cannot be the same as being. In his very essence God is absolutely other than any creature, so one can reasonably say—indeed *must* say—that he is beyond or without being since "being" in phrases such as "beyond being" and "without being" means the being of created things. The word "being" does not mean the same in reference to God as it does in reference to his creation, so as

Thomas Aquinas (1225–74) says, for example, it is equivocal. "Beyond being" is what "transcendence" means in much Christian theological writing. God transcends human beings by virtue of the fact that the Creator is infinitely different than his creations.

The position that "being" is equivocal was the usual position in theology until John Duns Scotus (1266–1308), who argued that "being" could have only one meaning, whether we are speaking of created beings or of God. Scotus argued that "being" is univocal—means the same thing in each case—rather than equivocal. According to Scotus the difference between God and human beings is not that God has a different kind of being than we, but that he has the same kind of being to an infinite degree: human beings have love; God has the *same* love, but whereas human love is limited, God's love is infinite. The transcendence of God is the transcendence of the infinite over the finite rather than an ontological transcendence. Since Scotus articulated this position it has been an important understanding of God's transcendence (probably the majority position), though Aquinas's position has also had a significant following. Indeed, today the older position—that "being" is equivocal—has seen a renaissance among some thinkers, such as those associated with Radical Orthodoxy[1] and thinkers like Jean-Luc Marion.[2] In practical terms, however, the difference is insignificant. God is either ontologically transcendent of us or he is transcendent of us because he is infinite and we are not. In either case, he is incomparable, perhaps even unthinkable.

---

1. Catherine Pickstock's book, *After Writing: The Liturgical Consummation of Philosophy* (Oxford, England: Blackwell, 1998), has a good discussion of the issue of the equivocity and univocity of being, explaining both Duns Scotus's position and the Radical Orthodoxy rejection of that position. For an excellent overview of the older view and the change to the newer, see Louis Dupré, *Passage to Modernity: An Essay on the Hermeneutics of Nature and Culture* (New Haven, Conn.: Yale University Press, 1995).

2. Though Jean-Luc Marion has written later books that give more philosophical structure to his thinking about the issue of being, for instance *Being Given*, trans. Jeffrey L. Kosky (Palo Alto, Calif.: Stanford University Press, 2002), and *The Erotic Phenomenon*, trans. Stephen E. Lewis (Chicago: University of Chicago Press, 2007), the most obvious place to see him thinking along these lines is *God Without Being*, trans. Thomas A. Carlson (Chicago: University of Chicago Press, 1991).

What "Transcendence" Does Not Mean

When we are not sufficiently critical, we sometimes assume that to believe that God is beyond being is tantamount to saying that there is no God: if he is beyond being, then he must not exist. We can occasionally hear such an argument, for example, in Mormon Sunday School classes, and I will later examine more closely one such version of the argument. But that criticism is mistaken. Because "without being" in theology means "outside of creation" or "otherwise than creation," rather than "nonexistence," the traditional understanding of God's transcendence does not imply that there is no God. Equally, it does not imply that we can know nothing of him. For traditional Christians, of course, we know him through Jesus the Messiah. However, for most Christian theologians we can also know him *because* he is the Creator.[3] His act of creation has left its imprint on that creation. Some believe that reason can reflect on creation and, detecting the imprint of God in created beings, reason can come to a knowledge of God.[4] Others believe that reason cannot know God unaided. According to those who think this way, the knowledge of God may need reason, but it cannot be complete without revelation.[5] There are also other positions, but if understood as general descriptions these two—that reason can come to know God or that it can only know God with the aid of revelation—cover most of the ways that Christians have thought about how one can know God. "Beyond being" means neither that there is no God nor that we cannot know him.

A Third Meaning of "Transcendence"

There is an additional way of understanding "beyond being." Many contemporary thinkers who use that phrase to describe God do so because they use the word "being" in the way that the Lithauanian-French philosopher Emmanuel Levinas (1906–95) used it, to refer to the understood and understandable totality of what is, to the comprehensible

---

3. Thomas Aquinas, *Summa Theologica*, 1.8. The twentieth-century theologian Hans Urs von Balthasar takes a more-or-less Thomistic position, but he argues that we come to know God only in Christian life. See Hans Urs von Balthasar, *Theo-Drama: Theological Dramatic Theory, Vol. 2: Dramatis Personae: Man in God* (San Francisco: Ignatius Press, 1991), 272.

4. Again, Aquinas is perhaps the most well known example. See *Summa Theologica*, 1.2.

5. See, for example, Augustine, *City of God*, 11.2.

essences.⁶ God is outside that totality—beyond what can be represented in a conceptually comprehended totality—so he is beyond being. However, because those who follow Levinas's usage argue that persons are also outside the conceptual totality, what they mean when they say that God is beyond being does not necessarily fall into the camp either of Thomas Aquinas or of John Duns Scotus. In fact, these thinkers are not particularly concerned about the metaphysical question of whether being is univocal or equivocal. Rather, they are concerned to argue that God's being is not something that can be comprehended in a rational totality (and neither is the being of mortal persons).

It is possible, therefore, to hold to the third meaning of "transcendence" and to ignore the metaphysical question of the equivocity or univocity of being, to think productively about transcendence without taking up that question. I assume, however, that if one were to place these thinkers in one camp or the other, they would be on the side of Aquinas: being is equivocal. Using that terminology (though it does not fit well), for Levinas being is not only equivocal with regard to God and the individual person, it is also equivocal with regard to other persons. Explaining what "beyond being" means, he says that in the relationship with the other person I have "access to being that is external to me."⁷ "Being" does not mean the same thing for the ego that it means when applied to the other person.

This is the position I will argue for as the most satisfying for understanding the Mormon concept of God's transcendence. Before turning to that argument, however, consider why transcendence is a problem in Mormon theology.

The Mormon Contrast:
The Same Form, the Same Relations, a Becoming God

In contrast to the tradition, Joseph Smith is explicit about the sameness of divine and human beings. The different transcriptions of

---

6. One can see that this is what Emmanuel Levinas means by "being" from the title of his second major work, *Otherwise than Being or Beyond Essence*, trans. Alphonso Lingis (The Hague: Martinus Nijhoff, 1981). Clearly "being" and "essence" are used there as synonyms.

7. Emmanuel Levinas, "Signature," in *Difficult Freedom: Essays on Judaism*, trans. Seán Hand (Baltimore: Johns Hopkins, 1990), 293; translation slightly revised by author.

his April 1844 sermon, commonly referred to as "the King Follett discourse," record him as saying:

> God who sits in yonder heavens is a *man like yourselves.* That God if you were to see him to day, that holds the worlds, you would see him like a man in form, like yourselves.[8]

> God himself who sits enthroned in yonder Heavens is a man like unto one of yourselves who holds this world in its orbit & upholds all things by his power if you were to see him today you would see him a man.[9]

> If the veil was rent to day & the great God who holds this world in its sphere or its orbit—the planets—if you were to see him to day you would see him in all the person image, very form of man.[10]

> God: a man like one of us, even like Adam.[11]

Each of these accounts except, perhaps, the last—which is by far the most abbreviated—tells us that when Smith said that God and human beings are the same, he said that they have the same form. Thus, the first thing we are told about what it means to be the same as God is having the same form as God. In their larger contexts, each but, perhaps, the last of these also tells us that Smith preached that God is a being one can walk and talk with, as Adam did. Our sameness with God means that we can have relations with him that are like the relations we have with mortal persons. Finally, each of the fuller accounts tells us that God was not God from all eternity, but became God. Being the same as God means that God was once like us. So Smith's teaching about the being of God includes at least three things:

1. God has the same form as human beings;
2. The relations of human beings to God are like the relations of human beings to each other;
3. God has not always been God. He *became* who he is having once been like us.

---

8. Andrew F. Ehat and Lyndon W. Cook, eds., *The Words of Joseph Smith: The Contemporary Accounts of the Nauvoo Discourses of the Prophet Joseph Smith* (Provo, Utah: Religious Studies Center, 1980), 344. This is Willard Richards's transcription.
9. Ibid., 349. Thomas Bullock transcription.
10. Ibid., 357. William Clayton transcription.
11. Ibid., 361. Samuel W. Richards note.

Mormons believe that God and humans are, to use the language of B. H. Roberts, "of the same species."[12] Whether this is the same as believing that "being" is univocal for all entities is another question, a question on the plain of philosophical theology rather than that of religious discourse. I assume, though, that the answer is probably "Yes."

"Transcendence" in Mormonism

The extracts I have inserted from the King Follett discourse reveal a philosophical problem: How is it possible to say that God is transcendent *and* to say these things about him? How can a being that is like us in form and relationships, and indeed, who was once like ourselves be described as transcendent? For Mormons does "transcendent" mean anything more than "very great" or "wonderful"? If we take seriously the description of God as infinite, how is it possible for a finite being to become infinite over some finite period of time?

A perusal of LDS General Conference addresses, articles in the official church magazine, the *Ensign*, and books published by Mormon presses suggest that in most cases Latter-day Saints use "transcendent" or a related word to use it as a synonym for "indescribable" or "superlative": transcendent landscape, transcendent sinlessness, transcendent genius, transcendent beauty. In most cases, the word functions as a rhetorical gesture toward greatness rather than as part of a doctrinal claim. If the usage has a doctrinal implication, it is that Latter-day Saints take transcendence to be a matter of magnitude: God is infinitely what we are finitely.

There are a few exceptions. For example, Orson F. Whitney, a member of the Quorum of the Twelve Apostles in the early twentieth century, implied that God's being is transcendent when he speaks of the "transcendent height" of God's existence:

> It is His superior intelligence which makes Him the Supreme being that He is. He acquired the transcendent height whereon He stands, by educating-developing, through study, labor and experience,

---

12. B. H. Roberts, *The Mormon Doctrine of Deity: The Roberts-Van Der Donckt Discussion, to Which is Added a Discourse, Jesus Christ: The Revelation of God* (Salt Lake City: The Deseret News, 1903), 255.

the godlike powers inherent within Him; by battling with evil and overcoming it, and rising superior from every contest therewith.[13]

Accepting Smith's teaching, Whitney makes this "transcendent height" a matter of divine progression, the development of "the godlike powers inherent within Him." Whitney seems not to have considered the problem of how to understand development as a movement from finitude to transcendent infinitude.

More recently Gordon B. Hinckley spoke explicitly of "the great and transcendent nature of God Himself."[14] Hinckley was not making a pronouncement of philosophical theology, but his statement at least opens the possibility that Mormons consider God to be transcendent by nature.

When we speak of things that devolve on a being by nature we can mean things that are given and unchangeable (like right- or left-handedness in the biological realm of thought), the rationality of human beings in the philosophical, or the omniscience of God in traditional Christian theology. But we can also mean, as Aristotle argues, that which unfolds in us only by learning and education.[15] According to Aristotle it is in our nature to seek happiness, but only by education and habituation will the virtues that bring happiness become manifest in our lives. Whitney clearly understands transcendence in the latter way, a way that is important for Latter-day Saint thinking: God had the character of godliness as part of his nature from the beginning, but it became manifest in him only by study, labor, experience, and battling with evil. In contrast, Hinckley's statement does not decide between whether God's transcendent nature is acquired and whether it is the same from the beginning.

What "by nature" means for Mormons remains an open question and, as a result, so does the meaning of "transcendence." Though one can find authoritative Mormon speakers and writers who appear to use "transcendent" to describe the being of God rather than as a rhetorical recognition of his majesty, the more theological use of the word is infrequent and insufficient for a conclusion about the meaning of "transcendence," though Whitney's use offers perhaps more possibilities than others.

---

13. Transcription of a lecture by Orson F. Whitney, "What is Education," *The Contributor* 6, no. 9 (June 1885).
14. Gordon B. Hinckley, "Loyalty," *Ensign*, May 2003, 58.
15. Aristotle, *Nicomachean Ethics* 1103a24–1103b1.

N. L. Nelson on Divine Transcendance

The infrequent use of "transcendent" to describe God's nature is probably because theological reflections on God's transcendence are even more infrequent than explicit statements of the transcendent nature of God's existence. Indeed, where we find such reflections—as is the case with most explicitly theological reflections among Mormons—they seem mostly to be arguments *against* the traditional understanding of divine transcendence rather than *for* a particular Latter-day Saint understanding of it.

An excellent example of this kind of argument is from a 1905 essay by N. L. Nelson, "Heaven Versus Nirvana 1."[16] Nelson offers an argument that seems to have been well-accepted by Mormons at the turn of the twentieth century[17] and which continues to be repeated in some version or another:

> To assume that God is absolute, i.e. transcends all limitation, what is it but putting an eternal barrier between him and man? If he has no limitation, then he is inconceivable, and therefore cannot enter into the life of man. For how can man be influenced by that of which he can form no conception? To pretend that a formulary of doctrine and ritual comes from a Being whom you have just denied the power to

---

16. N. L. Nelson, "Heaven Versus Nirvana 1," *Improvement Era* 3 (May 1905). Nelson was a popular professor of English at Brigham Young University from 1887–1920, perhaps on a par with someone like B. H. Roberts, though we have forgotten Nelson and remembered Roberts. Nelson was so popular that at the dedication of BYU's Maeser Building his were the only books on church doctrine chosen by the president of the Church, Joseph F. Smith, to be interred in the cornerstone.

For my information on and understanding of Nelson and his work I have relied primarily on the unpublished paper of Michael Tiedeman, "A Faithful Thomas: Reinstating N. L. Nelson on the Early Twentieth-Century Mormon Intellectual Landscape," produced for the symposium on early Mormon intellectual history led by Richard L. Bushman and Terryl Givens at Brigham Young University, June–August 2007. See also Davis Bitton, "N. L. Nelson and the Mormon Point of View," *BYU Studies* 13, no. 2 (Winter 1973): 157–71.

17. That it was not uncommon for people to complain about Nelson's writing style may count against my claim that his argument was well-accepted, but the appearance of "Heaven and Nirvana 1" in the Church's official organ and the imprimatur of President Joseph F. Smith suggests otherwise. See Bitton, "N. L. Nelson," 162; Tiedemann, "A Faithful Thomas," 12

enter into man's conception is surely not more moral than to assume that He is pure negation.

From such a consideration, it becomes evident that man can have no God save as he is comprehensible; which means, in other words, that God must be in the same universe of time and space with man. Indeed, he is God little or much to man in proportion as he presents aspects that can be reflected in the soul of man.[18]

I outline Nelson's argument like this:

1. If God transcends all limitation, then he is inconceivable.
2. If he is inconceivable, then he cannot influence human beings.
   a. It is not possible to be influenced by something of which one has no conception.
   b. To believe that one's religion comes from a God who does not have the power to make himself conceivable is tantamount to asserting that God is pure negation.
3. So, God must be conceivable.
4. If God is conceivable, then he must be part of the space-time universe in which human beings dwell.
5. So, God is God to the degree that he has aspects that can be reflected in human souls.

For my purposes we can further reduce the first part of Nelson's argument (points 1–3) to this syllogism:

1. If God is inconceivable, then he cannot influence human beings.
2. God can influence human beings.
3. So, God is not inconceivable.

Obviously this syllogism is valid and the second assumption seems inarguable for any Christian: God can influence human beings. So it remains to decide the truth of the first assumption, "If God is inconceivable, then he cannot influence human beings." Nelson argues for that with two claims, points 2.a and 2.b of the outline. The first, 2.a, tells us that we cannot be influenced by something of which we have no conception, but I see no reason to grant that. Presumably, a person in the sixteenth century had no conception of microbes, yet it is undoubtedly true that many people were influenced by them.

---

18. Nelson, "Heaven and Nirvana 1."

Perhaps by "influence" Nelson means something narrower such as "spiritual influence": one cannot be influenced spiritually by something of which one has no conception. But this seems no more likely to be true. Surely God influences even those who have no conception of him. What is the Light of Christ if not that kind of influence, an influence of which some may have no conception? Confucian cultures are an example: millions of those living in Confucian cultures have had no conception of God, but surely he has influenced them, guiding them spiritually.[19] Thus 2.a does not support Nelson's assumption that if God were inconceivable, then he could not influence us.

What about the second claim, 2.b? Does it support the assumption that if God is inconceivable, then he cannot influence human beings? That is difficult to decide because it is difficult to know what to make of 2.b—"To believe that one's religion comes from a God who does not have the power to make himself conceivable is tantamount to asserting that God is pure negation." It is unclear what belief Nelson is refuting. The first part of the statement appears to imply: "If God exists, then he must be able to make himself conceivable." Perhaps that means that to have the power of God is to have the power to make oneself conceivable. But it is not at all clear that divine power would have to include that particular power. I do not see why that particular power would be god-making, something necessary to a being worthy of worship.

Further, whatever the meaning of the first clause, the claim as a whole is dubious. Its import is that denying the conceivability of God is tantamount to denying his existence. If one were to say, "God is a being of which I have no conception whatsoever," then Nelson's point would follow. There is no substantive difference between saying that and saying that there is no God at all or, as Nelson says "that He is pure negation." But as we have seen, Christian theologians do not claim that they have no conception of God whatsoever. They claim only that no conception of God is adequate to him, which is not problematic. We are familiar with that kind of language in other circumstances. A lover might say "No concept is adequate to the feelings I have for my beloved," and we would think it odd if someone responded, "That is

---

19. The First Presidency of the Church has officially declared that, among others, Confucius "received a portion of God's light." Quoted in Spencer J. Palmer, "World Religions (Non-Christian) and Mormonism: Overview," in *Encyclopedia of Mormonism*, ed. Daniel H. Ludlow (New York: Macmillan, 1992), 1589.

tantamount to saying that your love for your beloved is nothing at all." Being beyond adequate conception does not imply nonbeing.

That means that neither 2.a nor 2.b supports Nelson's assertion "If God is inconceivable, then he cannot influence human beings." His argument against the inconceivability of God fails.

The Mormon Contrast Again: God Within Being

Recall that in the concluding part of the quotation from Nelson's essay he explains God's relation to human beings by reverting to an inference from the three claims we saw in the King Follett discourse. Nelson tells us "God must be in the same universe of time and space with man. Indeed, he is God little or much to man in proportion as he presents aspects which can be reflected in the soul of man."[20]

What Nelson says here is important because, whatever the philosophical problems with his arguments against the traditional understanding of divine transcendence, he plainly believes with Joseph Smith that God is not beyond being in the first sense we examined for that term. God is not of a different order of being, that of the Creator rather than of the creature. So one way to make sense of God's transcendence is to say that Mormons agree with John Duns Scotus that being is univocal and that divine transcendence is a difference of degree rather than of kind. That would explain what appears to be the usual Mormon usage of "transcendent" to mean "superlative": God is infinitely what we are only finitely.

For Mormons, however, this solution may be more complicated than it is for others. It is at least differently complicated. For traditional Christians the difference between human beings and God is located in creation—even if "being" means the same for both God and human beings. God is uncreated, infinitely being from all eternity, and as created

---

20. I presume that by "soul" Nelson means "the spirit and the body" as per Doctrine and Covenants 88:15. One might quarrel with the theology of this claim that God is God only to the degree that his being is reflected in the being of humans. It appears to say that the divine attributes of God are only divine if they manifest themselves in human beings in some way. It is one thing to say that the attributes of divinity *do* appear in the human soul. It is something else to say, as Nelson does, that they are divine *because* they appear in the human soul. I am not sure what to make of the latter, but since its examination would not contribute to the question of how to understand transcendence, I will ignore it.

beings humans are finite from the creation and for eternity afterward. Except in theologies of mystical union, that distance cannot be overcome because it exists as an effect of creation *ex nihilo*. What does it mean to say, as Mormons do, that the difference between the infinity of divine being and mortal finitude can be overcome? The problem is an old one: it is impossible to get to infinity by counting one number at a time. One can argue that, similarly, it is impossible for a finite being to become infinite in a step-wise fashion, by adding one improvement to another. No matter how many times one takes a step toward infinity it will never be reached.

One response is the Aristotelian one: we have within us already the possibilities of godhood. Becoming like God is a matter of the divine attributes within us unfolding to their full potential. As Whitney said, it is a matter of "educating-developing, through study, labor and experience, the godlike powers inherent within." The Aristotelian view has much to recommend it because it gives us a way of understanding how God and humans can be alike, but it doesn't solve the problem of crossing an infinite distance in a finite amount of time. Even on the Aristotelian view, and even if we understand God as bounded in ways that the traditional Christian God is not, the distance between the character and majesty of God and that of humans is infinite and we must move across that infinite gap.

The best answer mimics the doctrine taught by Paul in his letter to the Romans: we do not reach the infinity of divine being in a step-wise way. We do not make ourselves like God. Instead, being like God is a gift he gives those who will accept it. God has the power to overcome our finitude, to make us like himself. Christ's resurrection has done so with regard to the finitude imposed by death: all will have eternal life, life of infinite duration if not of infinite quality.[21] God's gift of adoption (Rom.

---

21. D&C 76:69–86 describes the difference in quality of life for the different kinds of resurrection. Nevertheless even this difference in quality might be understood in terms of infinity since both the terrestrial and the telestial kingdoms receive the ministration of a member of the Godhead (D&C 76:86). The question is how to understand these kingdoms—kingdoms of glory—as kingdoms of divine being though not a fullness of that being (D&C 76:71, 78, 81, 97–98). D&C 76:89 explicitly says that the glory of the lowest kingdom, the telestial, "surpasses all understanding," (i.e., is transcendent). So an argument that salvation in *any* kingdom is salvation to transcendent eternal life seems possible. If so, then the conclusion would be either that there are degrees of divine transcendence or

8:15) overcomes our finitude. Those adopted into the family of God will receive everything that God has; they will no longer be finite, but infinite.

On this view, God's transcendence is a matter of magnitude rather than of being, the meaning of which is univocal. The magnitude of his love is infinite whereas ours is finite. But that difference in magnitude can be overcome by an act of God.

God and Others Without Being: Transascendence

Though I think the explanation that I have just given of what "transcendence" can mean in a Mormon context hangs together, I do not find it satisfying. Except perhaps in the discussion of how our finitude is overcome by God's grace, I do not think it gets at the very thing that talk of God's transcendence is supposed to get at: the majesty and awe that inspires our worship. The question of the equivocity or univocity of being and the metaphysical answers to that question, Mormon or otherwise, anesthetize the discussion of God's transcendence.

But I believe it is possible to locate a less anesthetic way of thinking about transcendence. We find it in the third possible way of understanding "beyond being" that I discussed briefly at the beginning of the chapter, namely, understanding "transcendence" to mean "what is beyond representation in a conceptually comprehended totality." That understanding avoids entirely the question of equivocity and univocity.

As mentioned, the philosopher most known for introducing this understanding of transcendence is Levinas. But the philosopher who has developed the notion most fully is Jean-Luc Marion (1946–). Marion argues that we find transcendence all about us:

> In every perception, the referent or the thing-in-itself remains invisible: I really see only certain aspects, certain parameters, in virtue of which I infer a totality that, in fact, I have never had before my eyes. ... [W]e live and move, not in the milieu of that which we see, but in relation with that which we do not see, a relation visible in that which we see.[22]

---

that there are other kinds of transcendent life than divinely transcendent life. In such an argument the problem would be to clarify the difference between fullness of transcendence and non-fullness of it.

22. Jean-Luc Marion, *La croisée du visible* (Paris: Presses Universitaires de France [PUF], 1996), 100.

My conceptual grasp of the world is a necessary abstraction from that world. Without conceptual abstraction I would remain encased in what William James (1842–1910) called a "blooming buzzing confusion."[23] But because it is an abstraction, my conceptual grasp is also always inadequate to the things of the world themselves; those things remain invisible to our sight—a metonymy for all comprehended sense perception. Our relation to the things of the world is a relation to things transcendent.

The transcendence and invisibility of things does not mean that we do not know (by acquaintance—in experience rather than conceptually) the things themselves. Of course in much of our ordinary experience of the world, we do not relate to the things themselves. I use *a* computer, one of many and an object in my world that is determined by its function, a function shared by other computers. I never experience my computer as it is in itself rather than as a tool for my use, a tool that could be replaced by another tool like it without my even noticing. I relate to the computer I use as a function, as something determined by my use and understanding. Its place in my world is its being. The same is true for the other objects of my ordinary world, sometimes including other persons. I encounter them as tools for accomplishing the things I wish to do rather than in themselves. If I did not, if I were constantly dealing with things themselves rather than with them as tools, I would be unable to function. I would find myself back in the blooming buzzing confusion. The being of things is their being in my world rather than their being in themselves. Nevertheless, there are moments in which I encounter things themselves—and people themselves—rather than mere instruments for accomplishing the task at hand.

Marion identifies five categories of experience when I encounter what transcends being: the experience of the historical event, of things such as paintings, of the affectivity of my body, of the other person, and of revelation.[24] Each of these categories is a grouping of phenomena in which something overpowers us, amazes and bedazzles us, exceeding our understanding. In such cases, I cannot *see* clearly; I can have no adequate concept of the experience. Marion argues that phenomena like

---

23. William James, *The Principles of Psychology* (Cambridge, Mass.: Harvard University Press, 1981), 462.

24. See Jean-Luc Marion, *Étant donné. Essai d'une phénoménologie de la donation* (Paris: Presses Universitaires de France, 1997), 318–35.

these "cannot be borne by any gaze that would measure up to it ('objectively'), it is perceived ('subjectively') by the gaze only in the negative mode of an impossible perception, the mode of bedazzlement."[25] This experience of bedazzlement is an experience of transcendence, of that which goes beyond my understanding, beyond the world of being. It is an experience of awe, of wonder.

Thus, on Marion's view, we deal with—organize—what would otherwise be the confusion James describes by constituting atemporal events: what we could call objective things, using Kantian-like language, intuitionally impoverished phenomena.[26] As with Martin Heidegger (1889–1976), for whom the art work makes visible what transcends and grounds our ordinary relations to things,[27] for Marion the fundamental experience of things is that of transcendence. Other ways of relating to the things are built on the experience of the transcendence of things: "the object . . . is the simple illusion of an atemporal event."[28] Beneath or behind that objectification of things are experiences of transcendence—experiences of bedazzlement that take the forms of the historical event, art works, bodily affectivity, the other person's interruption of my being, and revelation.

How does the experience of God—that is, revelation—differ from the experience of other transcendent things? To think about that question consider that the experience of God is analogous to the experience

---

25. Jean-Luc Marion, "The Saturated Phenomenon," trans. Bernard G. Prusak and Jeffrey L. Klosky, in *Phenomenology and the "Theological Turn": The French Debate*, ed., Dominique Janicaud et al. (New York: Fordham University Press, 2000), 201. The words "objectively" and "subjectively" are between quotation marks because bedazzlement is not exactly something constituted by the subject; in other words, that which bedazzles us is not an object of a subject. Thus, the language of subjectivity and objectivity is inadequate.

26. In terms of his understanding of ordinary experience, Marion is a Kantian. See the discussion of Kant in "Saturated Phenomenon," 177–78, 189–98, 202–9, 214–16.

27. Cf. Martin Heidegger, "The Origin of the Work of Art" in *Off the Beaten Track*, eds. and trans. Julian Young and Kenneth Hayes (Cambridge: Cambridge University Press, 2002), 1–56. For his understanding that the ordinary object is grounded in a transcendent thing, see Martin Heidegger *Basic Problems of Phenomenology*, trans. Albert Hofstadter (Indianapolis: University of Indiana Press, 1975), 321.

28. Jean-Luc Marion, "The Event, the Phenomenon, and the Revealed" in *Transcendence in Philosophy and Religion*, ed. James E. Faulconer (Bloomington: Indiana University Press, 2003), 94.

of another person. Marion says that the philosopher who has dealt best with the experience of the other person is Levinas;[29] so let us turn to him. According to Levinas when I experience the other person as a person (rather than as one more tool in my world), she breaks through the sphere of my otherwise solitary, ego-centered conceptual world (through what Levinas calls "being"). Exposure to another person disengages me from my participation in this objective world, the world of objects, my objects. It makes me disinterested in the root sense of that word: "not in and among things," "not within the realm of essences."[30] As person, the other person overflows my intention—my directed consciousness that takes her as an object—and by overflowing it interrupts that intention, shows its limitation, interrupts it. Her overflow marks my finitude and produces her infinition.[31] My encounter with the other person as person is an encounter with infinity, a breaking or interruption of limits, a figure of my encounter with God.

Because the other person is not within the realm of my interests (Levinas's realm of being) another way to speak of the infinity of the other person is to say that he or she is otherwise than being. Levinas says:

> Moral consciousness is not an experience of values, but access to being that is external to me.[32]

> Transcendence is passing over to being's other, otherwise than being. Not to be otherwise, but otherwise than being. And not to not-be.[33]

In the relationship with another person I find myself related to a being-otherwise.

But my encounter with the otherwise-than-being, infinite being, is not the only way that my encounter with the other person figures God. In this experience of interruption, the other person is not only infinitely other than me; in other words, she is not only irreducible to my wants, needs, goals, intentions, or conceptions. She is also someone to whom I am obligated. I must respond to her interruption. Her inter-

---

29. Marion, *Étant donné*, 318–25.

30. Levinas, *Otherwise than Being or Beyond Essence*, 55. The root of "interest" is *interesse*: "among essences."

31. Levinas, *Totality and Infinity*, 25.

32. Levinas, "Signature," 293.

33. Levinas, *Otherwise than Being*, 3.

ruption of being, of the world I have made for myself in answer to my projects,[34] demands my recognition and response.

That demand of recognition is most obvious in language. I find myself under the judgment of the other person,[35] for I communicate with her in order to explain myself and for her to decide whether my explanation is adequate. Her judgment of what I say may consist only in "I understand" or "I don't understand," but it is a judgment to which I must submit if I speak. Submission to judgment is the essence of language. (Meaning is not the function of a solitary ego, but of social relation and the obligation to give an account of myself and my doings that comes with social relation.[36]) That necessity, the necessity of explanation, is emblematic of my relationship with the other person: the relationship with the infinite other is a relationship of obligation and being-under-judgment. These things—the interruption of being by the other, the necessity of explaining myself, the expectation of judgment—are the experience of something transcendent of me and higher than me.

Borrowing the vocabulary of Jean Wahl (1887–1974) and Gabriel Marcel (1889–1973), Levinas calls that relationship to the other person in her infinity "transascendence,"[37] a word that I take to also describe our relation to God. In relation to God, we are drawn out of ourselves toward and by someone infinitely higher, someone to whom we are indebted and someone by whom we are judged. The other person is the figure of God toward whom we transascend.

For a Mormon thinking in these terms neither "equivocity" nor "univocity" properly describes how to think about the being of God and the being of human beings. For *each* other person, mortal or divine, is being-otherwise (in other words, otherwise-than-being) and has been so eternally.[38] The distance or difference between persons of every sort is infinite in the relevant sense—irreducible merely to an object of cognition—existing in a difference that cannot be undone and that difference

---

34. "The world I have made" need not have been consciously made. Marion agrees that the Kantian transcendental ego is an excellent explanation of how Levinas's being comes to be.
35. Ibid., 231.
36. Ibid., 206–7.
37. Levinas, *Totality and Infinity*, 35.
38. Among Latter-day Saints, this is the common interpretation of what Joseph Smith is reported to have said. See Ehat and Cook, *The Words of Joseph Smith*, 352, 359–60, and Abraham 3:18. I am assuming that common interpretation.

has been from eternity and will be forever. In theological language, each other intelligence is transcendent of me as an intelligence. Using Levinas's language, in relation to the other person (and I can be an I only in relation to another person) I am transascendent: the other person interrupts my interiority and brings me outside myself and my world.[39] But, returning to LDS belief, God is the *first* of the intelligences. It is he who brings us into spiritual and then mortal life. Though he does not create intelligences *ex nihilo* in the traditional sense of the phrase, they are nothing without his creation, mere "matter,"[40] neither a me nor an I, neither affected nor affecting.[41] God creates us from outside ourselves and from an infinite distance—the distance between the ones who are brought into life and the one who brings them.

Mormons recognize the analogy between humanity and God by saying that we and God are of the same species. But saying that runs the risk of idolatry—the idolatry of bringing God down from his majesty and making him merely another person or thing in our world. Although this potential God may be a very powerful person or thing, perhaps even an infinitely powerful one, he is nevertheless an idol. How can we avoid that idolatry when we go as far as we do in the direction of making God and humans the same? Can understanding other persons as infinitely other and, so, more like God, rescue us from this potential idolatry?

The answer is what we have seen: I can void idolatry if I understand the distance between myself and the other person to be infinite and recognize the elevation of the other person in relation to me. I recognize the other as a person who is not an object in my world, the product of my concepts, but who necessarily exceeds my world and concepts (i.e., is infinite), demanding my transascendence (i.e., is higher than me in that he or she obliges me). I am called out of my world to something other. The other person is not an object brought down into my world, a thing that I can manipulate. Taking her to be so is analogous to idolatry, so that we avoid objectification in the transascendence of ethical relations shows us the possibility of avoiding idolatry in a

---

39. I can, of course, refuse, but even refusal is a recognition of what is beyond. Even refusal has gone beyond the ego to what is outside because I refuse what is other than me, and I can only refuse what strikes me as a demand, an obligation. In other cases, I would fail to recognize the thing in question rather than refuse it.

40. Cf. D&C 131:7.

41. Cf. 2 Nephi 2:26.

similar fashion. The infinite relationship with the other person is an analogy to the infinite distance between myself and God, though the latter is an infinite distance of another order, the order of the Divine Infinite rather than the human infinite. The other person demands my transascendence. God demands it analogously. Ultimately the other person cannot be made an object in my world. Analogously, God cannot be made an idol. Understanding our relation to the other and to God in terms of transascendence preserves both the "sameness" of God and human beings taught in Smith's King Follett discourse and the majesty of God that worship requires.

That each intelligence is without-being from eternity allows Mormon thought to understand human relationships as figures of our relationship with God: an infinite relationship of both obligation and judgment. Understanding the infinite distance between ourselves and the being-otherwise of other persons as a figure of the infinite distance between ourselves and the being-otherwise of God allows us to understand that infinity by analogy and, at the same time, to respect the distance that reverence for divinity demands.

Conclusion

To worship God is to recognize his incomprehensible majesty, power, and condescending love, a recognition that we give in our awe more than in our conceptual understanding. The Christian tradition has understood our recognition of God's transcendence of human beings either by describing him as ontologically transcendent or by describing him as ontologically the same but infinitely greater. A third possibility, one found perhaps only in Mormonism, though one closely related to the claim that God is ontologically different, has been to argue that *every* other person, divine or not, is "otherwise than being." On this third view not only are the qualities such as human love analogous to those same divine qualities, more importantly the transcendence of God is analogous to the transcendence of other persons.

Latter-day Saint belief does not fit well into either of the first two views of transcendence (the views of Aquinas and Scotus) because we believe that God has the same form as human beings and the same relations, and that he is becoming. At first glance it appears that Mormons take being to be univocal. Indeed, I think that if pressed and given an understanding of the vocabulary, most Mormons would say that being is univocal. That is why when Mormons use the term "transcendent" they almost always mean "superlative": transcendence is a matter of exceptional degree. However, that way of understanding God's transcendence runs the risk of idolatry when combined with Mormon theomorphism. We may understand God to be like humans to such a degree that we blaspheme, bringing him down from his transcendent glory to our mundanity.

A resolution of that risk can be found in a Mormon version of the third possibility for thinking about the being of God. Levinas calls that third possibility "transascendence": existing within our conceptually constructed world (being), we are interrupted by another person—someone higher, someone to whom we are indebted, someone who will judge us—and we are drawn toward that person. That describes our relation to other persons, and it is an analogy for thinking about God, making the other person, in his transcendence and our transascendence toward him, a figure for God.

Mormons can appropriate this way of thinking about transcendence: every intelligence is uncreated and irreducibly other than every other intelligence, so that the experience of the person is an experience of something absolutely—irresolvably—other, the experience that Levinas describes. In turn, that experience of otherness is an analogue of our experience of God, whose infinite distance is qualitatively different than the infinite distance of one person to another. In both cases, our relation to the other person and to God is a matter of transascendence, moving upward from the ego-centered world to another person or Person. Mormons can understand divine transcendence in terms of transascendence rather than merely as supreme greatness.

14

"We Shall Be Like Him": Explorations into the LDS Doctrine of Deification

Robert L. Millet, *Brigham Young University*

Few teachings found within LDS writings and culture have proven to be more provocative, sensitive, and controversial than the concept that men and women have the capacity to become as God is. Critics of this view are quick to point out that such a notion lessens God in the eternal scheme of things. Others, such as Ed Decker, who produced the video, *The Godmakers*, contend that such a grand and unreachable ideal leads to frustration, exasperation, and spiritual burnout among Mormons far and wide. In this essay I will respond to some of the objections to this doctrine by suggesting what Latter-day Saints know and believe, and what we do not.

We Become What We Worship

God the Father and His Son Jesus Christ are glorified, exalted, and perfect personages. They yearn to forgive our sins and purify our hearts and delight to honor those who serve Them in righteousness and in truth to the end (D&C 76:5). That is, They are not possessive of Their powers, nor are They hesitant about dispensing spiritual gifts or sharing Their divine attributes. In the words of the famous Christian writer, Max Lucado, "God loves you just the way you are, but he refuses to leave you that way. He wants you to be just like Jesus."[1] Dallas Willard, a Christian philosopher at the University of Southern California, likewise noted, "Jesus offers himself as God's doorway into the life that is truly life. Confidence in him leads us today, as in other times, to be-

---

1. Max Lucado, *Just Like Jesus* (Dallas: W. Publishing Group, 2003), 3.

come his apprentices in eternal living."[2] In the *Lectures on Faith* we learn that all those who keep God's commandments "shall grow up from grace to grace, and become heirs of the heavenly kingdom, and joint heirs with Jesus Christ; possessing the same mind, being transformed into the same image or likeness."[3]

New Testament scholar and Bishop of Durham N. T. Wright writes of "two golden rules at the heart of spirituality." First, "You become like what you worship. When you gaze in awe, admiration, and wonder at something or someone, you begin to take on something of the character of the object of your worship." Second, "Because you were made in God's image, worship makes you more truly human. When you gaze in love and gratitude at the God in whose image you were made, you do indeed grow. You discover more of what it means to be fully alive."[4]

"It is becoming less necessary in the English-speaking world to apologize for the doctrine of deification." This is the opening line of the preface in Norman Russell's important book, *The Doctrine of Deification in the Greek Patristic Tradition*. Russell continues:

At one time it was regarded as highly esoteric, if it was admitted to be Christian at all. But since the appearance in 1957 of the English version of Lossky's brilliant book on the Eastern Church's mystical theology, steady progress in the translation of modern Greek theologians . . . have brought the importance of deification (or theosis) in Orthodox soteriology to the attention of a wide readership. In recent years a succession of works on deification in individual Fathers from Irenaeus to Maximus the Confessor has confirmed the patristic basis of the doctrine. Since the 1950s several studies have shown how deification, in a more muted way, is also at home in the Western tradition.[5]

---

2. Dallas Willard, *The Divine Conspiracy: Rediscovering Our Hidden Life in God* (San Francisco: Harper San Francisco, 1998), 12.

3. *Lectures on Faith, Delivered to the School of the Prophets in Kirtland, Ohio, 1834–35* (Salt Lake City: Deseret Book Company, 1985), 5:2.

4. N.T. Wright, *Simply Christian: Why Christianity Makes Sense* (San Francisco: Harper San Francisco, 2006), 148.

5. Norman Russell, *The Doctrine of Deification in the Greek Patristic Tradition* (New York: Oxford University Press, 2004), vii.

Scripture, Church Fathers, and Eastern Orthodoxy

All men and women, like Christ, are made in the image and likeness of God (Gen. 1:27; Moses 2:27). Consequently, Latter-day Saints feel it is neither audacity nor heresy for the children of God to aspire to be like God. Consider the implications of the following scriptural passages:

"Be ye therefore *perfect, even as your Father which is in heaven is perfect.*" (Matt. 5:48; emphasis added)

"For as many as are led by the Spirit of God, they are the [children] of God. For ye have not received the spirit of bondage again to fear; but ye have received the spirit of adoption, whereby we cry, Abba, Father. The Spirit itself beareth witness with our spirit, that we are the children of God: and *if children, then heirs: heirs of God, and joint-heirs with Christ*; if so be that we suffer with him, that we may be also glorified together." (Rom. 8:14–17; emphasis added)

"Where the Spirit of the Lord is, there is liberty. But we all, with open face beholding as in a glass [mirror] the glory of the Lord, are changed into the same image [of Christ] from glory to glory, even as by the Spirit of the Lord." (2 Cor 3:17–18)

"Grace and peace be multiplied unto you through the knowledge of God, and of Jesus our Lord. According as his divine power hath given unto us all things that pertain unto life and godliness, through the knowledge of him that hath called us to glory and virtue: whereby are given unto us exceeding great and precious promises: that by these *we might be partakers of the divine nature*, having escaped the corruption that is in the world through lust." (2 Pet. 1:2–4; emphasis added)

"Behold, what manner of love the Father hath bestowed upon us, that we should be called the [children] of God: therefore the world knoweth us not, because it knew him not. Beloved, now are we the [children] of God, and it doth not yet appear what we shall be: but we know that, *when he shall appear, we shall be like him*; for we shall see him as he is." (1 Jn. 3:1–2; emphasis added)

Veli-Matti Karkkainen at Fuller Theological Seminary has described this doctrine as "the most profound question of human life, namely, what is the way back to God, to live with God, to live in God and share in the divine? Christian theology from the beginning has offered an answer to the world and its followers in the form of the doctrine of deification and/or union with God."⁶ Hence, early Christian leaders⁷ wrote definitive statements about the doctrine of deification:

> Irenaeus (ca. CE 130–200): "Do we cast blame on [God] because we were not made gods from the beginning, but were at first created merely as men, and then later as gods?" Also: "But man receives progression and increase towards God. For as God is always the same, so also man, when found in God, shall always progress toward God."

> Clement of Alexandria (ca. CE 150–215): "If one knows himself, he will know God and knowing God will become like God."

> Athanasius, bishop of Alexandria (ca. CE 296–373): "The word was made flesh in order that we might be enabled to be made gods. . . . Just as the Lord, putting on the body, became a man, so also we men are both deified through his flesh, and henceforth inherit everlasting life."

> Augustine of Hippo (ca. CE 354–430): "But he himself that justifies also deifies, for by justifying he makes sons of God. 'For he has given them power to become the sons of God' (John 1:12). If then we have been made sons of God, we have also been made gods."

German Cardinal and influential medieval theologian Nicholas of Cusa (1400–1464) built upon Gregory of Nyssa's theological contributions by taking a much more optimistic approach to the natural world. His teachings might be distilled as follows: "The ultimate destiny of humanity is *theosis*, rather than merely *redemption*, because it is directed by an original divine intentionality instead of the retrieval of a fallen spiritual universe. Humankind is not just restored to an original condition but is exalted to a point of deification."⁸ Moreover, "just as theology is defined by *relationship* with God, deification is defined by *union* with God."⁹

---

6. Veli-Matti Karkkainen, *One With God: Salvation as Deification and Justification* (Collegeville, Minn.: Liturgical Press, 2004), 1.

7. These four statements are cited in Stephen Robinson, *Are Mormons Christians?* (Salt Lake City: Bookcraft, Inc., 1991), 60–61.

8. Nicholas of Cusa, as paraphrased in Nancy J. Hudson, *Becoming God: The Doctrine of Theosis in Nicholas of Cusa* (Washington, D. C.: The Catholic University of America Press, 2007), 15; emphasis in original. See also Vladimir Lossky, *In the Image and Likeness of God* (Crestwood, N.Y.: St. Vladimir's Seminary Press, 2001), 103.

9. Hudson, *Becoming God*, 29; emphasis in original.

Theosis or deification has remained a significant doctrine within Eastern Orthodoxy. Archimandrite Christoforos Stravropoulos observed, "There is hardly a person alive who has not asked himself, 'Why do we live upon this earth?' In the last analysis there is only one answer. We live on earth in order to live in heaven, in order to be 'divinized,' in order to become one with God. This is the end and the fulfillment of our earthly destiny." Then, after quoting Psalms 82:6 and John 10:34 ("Ye are gods, sons of the Most High—all of you"), he says,

Do you hear that voice? Do you understand the meaning of this calling? *Do we accept that we should in fact be on a journey, a road which leads to Theosis? As human beings we each have this one, unique calling, to achieve Theosis. In other words, we are each destined to become a god, to be like God Himself, to be united with Him.* . . . *This is the purpose of your life*; that you be a participant, a sharer in the nature of God and in the life of Christ, a communicant of divine grace and energy—*to become just like God, a true god.*[10]

In short, "Man's growth to full stature coincides for Paul with his Christification."[11] This is no "external imitation or a simple ethical improvement but a real Christification."[12]

Bishop Kallistos of Diokleia has written: "In the Orthodox understanding Christianity signifies not merely an adherence to certain dogmas, *not merely an exterior imitation of Christ through moral effort, but direct union with the living God, the total transformation of the human person by divine grace and glory*—what the Greek Fathers termed 'deification' or 'divinization.' In the words of St. Basil the Great, man is nothing less than a creature that has received the order to *become god*."[13] Indeed, theosis "is like a continuous golden thread running throughout the centuries of Orthodoxy's ancient theological tapestry."[14] We "become gods

---

10. Christoforos Stavropoulos, *Partakers of the Divine Nature* (Minneapolis: Life and Light Publishing Company, 1976), 11, 17–18; emphasis added.

11. Panayiotis Nellas, *Deification in Christ: The Nature of the Human Person* (Crestwood, N.Y.: St. Vladimir's Seminary Press, 1987), 34.

12. Ibid., 39.

13. Bishop Kallistos of Diokleia, quoted in Karkkainen, *One With God*, 17; emphasis added.

14. Daniel B. Clendenin, *Eastern Orthodox Christianity: A Western Perspective* (Grand Rapids, Mich.: Baker Books, 1994), 120.

by adoption by grace."[15] In other words, "Although Jesus Christ alone is by nature God, all people are called to become God 'by participation.'"[16] Finally, Vladimir Lossky profoundly concluded, "The redeeming work of Christ is an indispensable pre-condition of the deifying work of the Holy Spirit."[17]

One grand manifestation of the fact that people are being divinized is the extent to which they begin to grow in love, and more especially in Godly love or charity:

> The natural human capacity for reason, itself a divine gift, is used to approach God as far as it is able. Eventually, however, the mind is stilled when it is struck by the 'blazing light' of God. Deification is a result of the engulfing fire of divine love, not of philosophical discipline. God, 'because of his love for humanity ... has designed to come down to us and ... like a fire, he has made one with himself all those capable of being divinized.' Only because of this is the human being able to grow into divine likeness.[18]

According to Stavropoulos,

> He who loves sees God with his mind and is united with Him.... The God who is totally un-knowable in the sphere of human knowledge, He who is unapproachable in His essence, is revealed to the heart which loves Him... Love is the door through which human beings pass in order to find themselves in the holy of holies.... The perfect work of God is the union of God with humanity, to that point on the one hand that God becomes human, and human beings—who were created in the image of God—become gods.... Other than love, there is nothing more divine-like, or more mystical, which leads toward Theosis. Love is the *telos* of all good things, the first and unique good, since it binds God with human beings. It is inseparably bound with the other two theological virtues, faith and hope, which it completes, overshadows, and supersedes so as to reach the Kingdom of God.[19]

This will no doubt have a familiar ring to those acquainted with Nephi's words in the Book of Mormon: "My God hath been my support;

---

15. Peter of Damascus, commenting on "John the Theologian," in Clendenin, *Eastern Orthodox Christianity*, 126.
16. Clendenin, *Eastern Orthodox Christianity*, 128.
17. Lossky, *In the Image and Likeness of God*, 109.
18. Nicholas of Cusa, quoted in Hudson, *Becoming God*, 41.
19. Stavropoulos, *Partakers of the Divine Nature*, 83–84.

he hath led me through mine afflictions in the wilderness; and he hath preserved me upon the waters of the great deep. He hath filled me with his love, even unto the consuming of my flesh" (2 Ne. 4:20–21). Further, it was Mormon who encouraged his listeners and readers to "pray with all the energy of heart, that ye may be filled with [charity], which he hath bestowed upon all who are true followers of his Son, Jesus Christ; that ye may become the sons [and daughters] of God; that when he shall appear we shall be like him, for we shall see him as he is; that we may have this hope; that we may be purified even as he is pure" (Moro. 7:48).

C. S. Lewis on Deification

The idea of the ultimate deification of humankind has not been completely lost from everyday Christian thinking in our own time. "The Son of God became a man," C. S. Lewis pointed out, "to enable men to become sons of God."[20] Further, Lewis explained,

> God said (in the Bible) that we were "gods" and He is going to make good his words. If we let Him—for we can prevent Him, if we choose—He will make the feeblest and filthiest of us into a god or goddess, dazzling, radiant, immortal creature, pulsating all through with such energy and joy and wisdom and love as we cannot now imagine, a bright stainless mirror which reflects back to God perfectly (though, of course, on a smaller scale) His own boundless power and delight and goodness. The process will be long and in parts very painful; but that is what we are in for. Nothing less. He meant what He said.[21]

Lewis wrote elsewhere:

> It may be possible for each to think too much of his own potential glory hereafter; it is hardly possible for him to think too often or too deeply about that of his neighbor. . . It is a serious thing to live in a society of possible gods and goddesses, to remember that the dullest and most uninteresting person you can talk to may one day be a creature which, if you saw it now, you would be strongly tempted to worship. . . There are no ordinary people.[22]

From *Miracles*, Lewis writes, "Christ, re-ascending from his great dive, is bringing up Human Nature with Him. Where He goes, it goes

---

20. C. S. Lewis, *Mere Christianity* (New York: Touchstone, 1996), 155.
21. Ibid., 176.
22. C. S. Lewis, *The Weight of Glory* (New York: Touchstone, 1996), 39.

too. It will be made 'like him' (Philip. 3:21; 1 Jn. 3:1–2)." Lewis went on to say that eventually those who are redeemed in Christ would have the power to perform miracles, just as Christ did. "Christ's isolation," he continued, "is not that of a prodigy but of a pioneer. He is the first of His kind; He will not be the last."[23]

Furthermore, from *A Grief Observed*, Lewis writes:

> Sometimes, Lord, one is tempted to say that if you wanted us to behave like the lilies of the field you might have given us an organization more like theirs. But that, I suppose, is just your grand experiment. Or no; not an experiment, for you have no need to find things out. Rather your grand enterprise. To make an organism which is also a spirit; to make that terrible oxymoron, a 'spiritual animal.' To take a poor primate, a beast with nerve-endings all over it, a creature with a stomach that wants to be filled, a breeding animal that wants its mate, and say, 'Now get on with it. Become a god.'[24]

I do not claim to fully know what Lewis meant (nor certainly know what he intended) by these statements. The doctrine of the deification of man did not originate with Lewis, nor with the Latter-day Saints; it is found throughout Christian history and within Orthodox Christian theology today. Whether Lewis would have agreed fully with the teachings of early Christian leaders on deification—or, for that matter, with what the Latter-day Saints teach—I cannot tell.

Revealed Anew

It appears that the first revelation of the doctrine of deification to the restored Church came in "the Vision" on February 16, 1832, at John Johnson's home.[25] Those who attain unto the highest heaven are described as people whom "overcome by faith, and are sealed by the Holy Spirit of promise, which the Father sheds forth upon all those who are just and true. They are they who are the church of the Firstborn. They are they into whose hands the Father has given all things—they are they who are priests and kings, who have received of his fulness and of

---

23. C. S. Lewis, *Miracles* (New York: Touchstone, 1995), 178.
24. C. S. Lewis, *A Grief Observed* (San Francisco: Harper Collins, 1994), 84–85.
25. For the background of the Vision, see Mark Lyman Staker, *Hearken O Ye People: The Historical Setting of Joseph Smith's Ohio Revelations* (Salt Lake City: Greg Kofford Books, 2009), 319–42.

his glory; . . . wherefore, as it is written [presumably in Psalms 82:6 and John 10:34], *they are gods, even the sons [and daughters] of God*" (D&C 76:53–58; emphasis added).

I say that the Vision "appears" to be the first revelation of this doctrine, but I do so cautiously. We know that many parts of the revelation on eternal marriage, known to us as section 132 of the Doctrine and Covenants, were made known to the Prophet during his inspired translation of the Bible in 1831.[26] In that revelation we are told that those whose marriages and lives are sealed by the Holy Spirit of Promise, who receive the two major blessings of eternal life—the fullness of the Father and the eternal continuation of the family, eternal lives (D&C 132:19, 24)—are "gods, because they have no end; therefore shall they be from everlasting to everlasting, because they continue; then shall they be above all, because all things are subject unto them. Then shall they be gods, because they have all power, and the angels are subject unto them" (D&C 132:20).

Between the time of the Vision in 1832 and the King Follett Sermon on April 7, 1844, Joseph Smith and other early church leaders took part in a training program known as the School of the Elders. It is here, during the winter of 1834–35 in Kirtland, that the Lectures on Faith were delivered. In Lecture Five we have not only a deep and profoundly significant discussion of the Godhead but also a specific reference to human beings becoming like God through being graced and endowed with the power, might, glory, and mind of Deity.[27]

"Man is made an agent to himself before his God," President Brigham Young declared; "he is organized for the express purpose that he may become like his Master. You recollect one of the Apostle's sayings, that when we see Him, we shall be like him [1 Jn. 3:1–2]; and again, 'We shall become gods, even the sons of God' [D&C 76:88]. . . We are created, we are born, for the express purpose of growing up from the low state of manhood, to become gods, like unto our Father in heaven."[28]

---

26. See the preface to D&C 132 in *The Doctrine and Covenants of the Church of Jesus Christ of Latter-day Saints* (Salt Lake City: The Church of Jesus Christ of Latter-day Saints, 1981), 266.

27. *Lectures on Faith*, 5:3.

28. Brigham Young, August 8, 1852, *Journal of Discourses*, 26 vols. (London and Liverpool: LDS Booksellers Depot, 1854–86), 3:93.

On the one hand, we worship a divine Being with whom we can identify. That is to say, His infinity does not preclude either His immediacy or His intimacy. "In the day that God created man," the Prophet's inspired translation of Genesis attests, "in the likeness of God made he him; in the image of his own body, male and female, created he them" (Moses 6:8–9). We believe that God is not simply a spirit influence, a force in the universe, or the Great First Cause; when we pray "Our Father which art in heaven" (Matt. 6:9), we mean what we say. We believe God is comprehendible, knowable, approachable, and, like his Beloved Son, touched with the feeling of our infirmities (Heb. 4:15).

On the other hand, our God is God. There is no knowledge of which He is ignorant and no power He does not possess. Scriptural passages that speak of him being the same yesterday, today, and forever clearly have reference to His divine attributes—His love, justice, constancy, and willingness to bless His children.

Eternal life consists in being *with* God; in addition, it entails being *like* God. "People who live long lives together," Max Lucado observed, "eventually begin to sound alike, to talk alike, even to think alike. As we walk with God, we take on his thoughts, his principles, his attitudes. We take on his heart."[29] That is, we begin to become more and more like God.

God is our Heavenly Father, the Father of our spirits (Num. 16:22, 27:16; Heb. 12:9). He is a glorified, exalted man, a Man of Holiness (Moses 6:57), possessing a body of flesh and bones as tangible as our bodies (D&C 130:22). We are created in His image and likeness. God is in every way a divine Being. He possesses in perfection every godly attribute. There is no truth He does not know and no power He does not possess. He is omnipotent, omniscient, and, by the power of His Holy Spirit, omnipresent.

Joseph Smith taught in the King Follett Sermon that God was once a man and lived on an earth.[30] Other than the Prophet's statement in that particular address, this is all we know. When and how and in what manner He became God is unknown. We do know that He is infinite and eternal. God has the power and the desire to extend His grace, including the gifts, fruit, and blessings of the Spirit to His children. He does not hesitate to do so. The scriptures do not speak of a barrier beyond which

---

29. Lucado, *Just Like Jesus*, 61.

30. Joseph Fielding Smith, comp., *Teachings of the Prophet Joseph Smith* (Salt Lake City: Deseret Book Company, 1976), 342–62.

human beings may not progress spiritually. Followers of the Christ are not told by the writers and speakers, in either ancient or modern scripture, that they can progress and grow and mature and develop "thus far and no more." Eternal life, exaltation, salvation—all are equivalent terms. In the words of Elder Bruce R. McConkie, "To be saved, to gain exaltation, to inherit eternal life, all mean to be one with God, to live as he lives, to think as he thinks, to act as he acts, [and] to possess the same glory."[31] To gain eternal life or exaltation is to gain godhood.

Joseph explained that as men and women live in such a way as to cultivate the gift and gifts of the Spirit, they eventually receive the assurance of eternal life—they make their calling and election sure.[32] That is, the Lord seals an exaltation upon them, seals them up unto eternal life. In receiving the promise of salvation, the individual has thereby passed the tests of mortality and qualified for exaltation and godhood hereafter. King Benjamin closed his magnificent sermon with this invitation: "Therefore, I would that ye should be steadfast and immovable, always abounding in good works, *that Christ, the Lord God Omnipotent, may seal you his, that you may be brought to heaven, that ye may have everlasting salvation and eternal life*" (Mosiah 5:15; emphasis added).

While laboring tirelessly with the people of the Church, particularly those in transgression, Alma the elder received the following commendation and promise from God: "Blessed art thou, Alma, and blessed are they who were baptized in the waters of Mormon. Thou art blessed because of thy exceeding faith in the words alone of my servant Abinadi. . . . And blessed art thou because thou hast established a church among this people; and they shall be established, and they shall be my people. . . . And because thou hast inquired of me concerning the transgressor, thou art blessed. Thou art my servant; and *I covenant with thee that thou shalt have eternal life*." (Mosiah 26:15, 17, 19–20; emphasis added.) In our dispensation, the Lord made a similar promise to the prophet Joseph: "I am the Lord thy God, and will be with thee even unto the end of the world, and through all eternity; for verily *I seal upon you your exaltation*, and prepare a throne for you in the kingdom of my Father, with Abraham your father" (D&C 132:49; emphasis added).

---

31. Bruce R. McConkie, *The Promised Messiah: The First Coming of Christ* (Salt Lake City: Deseret Book Company, 1978), 129–30.
32. Smith, *Teachings of the Prophet Joseph Smith*, 150.

Those who grow up in the Lord (Hel. 3:21) and receive "a fulness of the Holy Ghost" (D&C 109:14–15) prepare themselves for association with holy beings. The role of the Holy Spirit is to lead men and women to the point of illumination and inspiration at which they are ready to be ushered into the presence of the Father and the Son. That is, the Spirit "shall bring all things to remembrance, whatsoever things I [the Lord] have said unto you; he shall teach you until ye come to me and my Father."[33] In the *Lectures*, it was taught that "after any portion of the human family are made acquainted with the important fact that there is a God, who has created and does uphold all things, the extent of their knowledge respecting his character and glory will depend upon their diligence and faithfulness in seeking after him, until, like Enoch, the brother of Jared, and Moses, they shall obtain faith in God, and power with him to behold him face to face."[34]

The scriptures speak of those who qualify for exaltation and godhood as being the Church of the Firstborn (D&C 76:54, 67, 102). The Church of the Firstborn is the "inner circle" of faithful Saints who have proven true and faithful to their covenants. As baptism is the gate to membership in the church of Jesus Christ on earth, celestial marriage opens the door to membership in the heavenly church.[35] The Church of the Firstborn is the church beyond the veil, the organized body of Saints who qualify for exaltation. It is made up of those who qualify for the blessings of the Firstborn. Jesus is the Firstborn of the Father and as such is entitled to the birthright. As an act of consummate mercy and grace, our blessed Savior makes it possible for us to inherit, receive, and possess the same blessings He receives, as though we were the Firstborn. We become heirs of God, joint heirs or co-inheritors with Christ to all the Father has, including eternal life. "Wherefore, as it is written, they are gods, even the sons of God" (D&C 76:58). President Brigham

---

33. Andrew F. Ehat and Lyndon W. Cook, eds., *The Words of Joseph Smith* (Provo, Utah: BYU Religious Studies Center, 1980), 14–15; spelling and punctuation updated.

34. *Lectures on Faith*, 2:55.

35. See Joseph Fielding Smith, *Doctrines of Salvation: Compiled Sermons of Joseph Fielding Smith*, comp. Bruce R. McConkie, 3 vols. (Salt Lake City: Bookcraft, 1954–56), 2:42; *Man: His Origin and Destiny* (Salt Lake City: Deseret Book Company, 1954), 272; *The Way to Perfection* (Salt Lake City: Deseret Book Company, 1970), 208. See also McConkie, *The Promised Messiah*, 47; Bruce R. McConkie, *A New Witness for the Articles of Faith* (Salt Lake City: Deseret Book Company, 1985), 337.

Young therefore stated, "The ordinances of the house of God are expressly for the Church of the Firstborn."[36]

These blessings do not come to the sign-seeker, the curious, or the man or woman possessed of excessive zeal. Those who have come unto Christ by covenants and saving ordinances seek for the certain assurance of salvation before the end of their mortal lives. However, if one does not formally receive the glorious promise in this life, the scriptures attest that faithfully enduring to the end eventuates in eternal life, whether that assurance is received here or hereafter (see 2 Ne. 31:20; D&C 14:7, 50:5, 53:7). Truly, "If we die in the faith, that is the same thing as saying that our calling and election has been made sure and that we will go on to eternal reward hereafter."[37]

The gospel is "the power of God unto salvation" (Rom. 1:16), the power to renew and revitalize men and women. God is our Father and wants all of his children to become as He is. Thus, the plan of salvation is a developmental process whereby we learn to exercise faith in God and Christ unto life and salvation. Elder B. H. Roberts summarized:

[A] union of . . . three elements, that is, a belief in the existence of God, a correct conception of his character, and a knowledge that the course of life pursued is approved of him—will render faith perfect, will constitute it a principle of power, the incentive to all action . . . leading from one degree of knowledge or excellence to another, from righteousness to righteousness, until the heavens will be opened to them and they will hold communion with the Church of the First Born, with Jesus Christ, and with God the Father, and thus will they make their calling and election sure—through faith ripening into knowledge.[38]

Reaction and Response

Many Christians find the LDS concept of deification to be problematic at best and perverse at worst. They do not seem to be too put off by the Eastern Orthodox teachings on the matter, but then, I do not see large numbers of Evangelicals rushing to adopt them. When it comes

---

36. Brigham Young, August 26, 1860, *Journal of Discourses*, 8:154.

37. Bruce R. McConkie, address delivered at the funeral of Elder S. Dilworth Young, July 13, 1981, typescript, 5. Copy in author's possession.

38. B. H. Roberts, *The Gospel and Man's Relationship to Deity*, 11th ed. (Salt Lake City: Deseret Book Company, 1966), 111.

to the Latter-day Saints, however, it is a different story. Why? It is simply because of our belief that God is not the "Wholly Other" or the distant Deity, but rather that God is our literal Father in heaven. Our belief that finite human beings may relate to and come to be like an infinite and eternal Being borders on blasphemy, they contend, for it shortens the otherwise infinite chasm between Creator and creation. I think it is fairly evident that one of Joseph Smith's most significant efforts was to make the Father of the universe more accessible to His family members within that universe—to be able to retrieve the unreachable, unknowable, timeless, and impossible Deity that had been pushed to the grand beyond by traditional Christians. As Richard Mouw of Fuller Seminary observed,

> While Joseph [Smith] and Mary Baker Eddy espoused very different—indeed opposing—metaphysical systems, with Joseph arguing for a thorough-going physicalism and the founder of Christian Science insisting on a thorough-going mentalism—they each were motivated by a desire to reduce the distance between God and human beings.... These two reduce-the-distance theologies emerged in an environment shaped significantly by the high Calvinism of New England Puritanism. I think it can be plausibly argued that New England theology, while rightly, from an orthodox Christian perspective, stressing the legitimate *metaphysical* distance between God and his human creatures, nonetheless at the same time fostered an unhealthy *spiritual* distance between the Calvinist deity and his human subjects.[39]

More than once I have heard our view of Deity described as a belief in a "finite God." I suppose because of the one statement by Joseph Smith that God was once a man, people jump to the conclusion that the God in whom Latter-day Saints put their complete trust in is not the same Being Christians know as the God of the "omnis." I am one, however, who is very uncomfortable with stating that we believe in a finite God; all of the scriptures state otherwise. From the Doctrine and Covenants, for example, we learn that Latter-day Saints worship "a God in heaven, who is infinite and eternal, from everlasting to everlasting, the same unchangeable God, the framer of heaven and earth, and all things which are in them" (D&C 20:17). Our Father

---

39. Richard Mouw, "The Possibility of Joseph Smith: Some Evangelical Probings," in *Joseph Smith: Reappraisals after Two Centuries*, eds. Reid L. Neilson and Terryl L. Givens (New York: Oxford University Press, 2008), 195.

in heaven is indeed omnipotent, omniscient, and, by the power of His Holy Spirit, omnipresent. He is a gloried, exalted, resurrected being, "the only supreme governor and independent being in whom all fullness and perfection dwell . . . in Him every good gift and every good principle dwell; He is the Father of lights; in Him the principle of faith dwells independently, and He is the object in whom the faith of all other rational and accountable beings center for life and salvation."[40] The Almighty sits enthroned, "with glory, honor, power, majesty, might, dominion, truth, justice, judgment, mercy, and an infinity of fullness" (D&C 109:77). He is not a student, an apprentice, nor a novice.

As late as 1840, Matthew S. Davis, a non-Mormon, heard Joseph Smith preach in Washington, D.C. In a letter to his wife, he quotes Joseph preaching, "I believe that there is a God, possessing all the attributes ascribed to Him by all Christians of all denominations; that He reigns over all things in heaven and on earth, and that all are subject to his power." Davis also reported that he heard the Mormon prophet say, "I believe that God is eternal. That He had no beginning, and can have no end. Eternity means that which is without beginning or end."[41]

Further, while Latter-day Saints certainly accept the teachings of Joseph Smith regarding humankind becoming like God, we do not fully comprehend all that is entailed by such a bold declaration. Subsequent or even current Church leaders have spoken very little concerning which of God's attributes are communicable and which are incommunicable.

Not long ago I was traveling with a general authority of the LDS Church; there we met with about twenty prominent pastors in the area. This leader of the Church made a few remarks and then opened the meeting for questions. The spirit there was amiable and respectful, and the questions were fair and authentically seeking for information. One of the questioners asked, "Is it true that you folks believe that you will one day be like God, create worlds, preside over those worlds, travel and govern throughout the cosmos, etc.?" The Church leader smiled and answered, "Well, I don't know anything about that planetary stuff. What I do know for sure, and the scriptures confirm this, is that through the Atonement of Jesus Christ and the sanctifying power of the Spirit, we may develop and

---

40. *Lectures on Faith*, 2:2.
41. Joseph Smith, et. al., *History of the Church of Jesus Christ of Latter-day Saints*, ed. B. H. Roberts, 2nd ed., 7 vols. (Salt Lake City: Deseret Book Company, 1948), 4:78–79.

mature in Christ-like attributes, the divine nature, until we are prepared and comfortable to dwell in the presence of God and Christ, together with our families, forever. To me, that is eternal life or godhood."

While we believe that becoming like God is entailed in the meaning of eternal life (D&C 132:19–20), we do not believe we will ever, worlds without end, unseat or oust God the Eternal Father or his Only Begotten Son, Jesus Christ; those holy beings are and forever will be the Gods we worship. Even though we believe in the ultimate deification of man, I am unaware of any authoritative statement[42] in LDS literature that suggests that men and women will ever worship any being other than the ones within the Godhead.

Parley P. Pratt wrote one of the first theological treatises within Mormonism, *Key to the Science of Theology*. In describing those who are glorified and attain eternal life, Parley states, "The difference between Jesus Christ and another immortal and celestial man is this—the man is subordinate to Jesus Christ, does nothing in and of himself, but does all things in the name of Christ, and by his authority, being of the same mind, and ascribing all the glory to him and his Father."[43] We believe in "one God" in the sense that we love and serve one Godhead, one divine presidency, each possessing all of the attributes of Godhood (Alma 11:44; D&C 20:28). While we do not believe that God and man are of a different species, we readily acknowledge that the chasm between a fallen, mortal being and an immortal, resurrected, and glorified Being is immense (see D&C 20:17, 109:77).

Many critics of Mormonism have been eager to question the famous couplet of Lorenzo Snow, the fifth president of the Church:

> As man is, God once was.
> As God is, man may become.[44]

---

42. For more on what I believe qualifies as an authoritative statement, see my essay, "What Do We Really Believe? Identifying Doctrinal Parameters within Mormonism," in *Discourses on Mormon Theology: Philosophical and Theological Possibilities*, eds. James M. McLachlan and Loyd Ericson (Salt Lake City: Greg Kofford Books, 2007), 265–81.

43. Parley P. Pratt, *Key to the Science of Theology* (Salt Lake City: Deseret Book Company, 1978), 21–22.

44. Lorenzo Snow, *Teachings of Lorenzo Snow*, ed. Clyde J. Williams (Salt Lake City: Bookcraft, 1996), 1.

First, we know little or nothing about God's life before he was God. As to the second issue raised within Brother Snow's words, I ask: What if this couplet read differently?

> As man is, Christ once was.
> As Christ is, man may become.

Beloved Christian churchman and writer John Stott recently explained, "I want to share with you where my mind has come to rest as I approach the end of my pilgrimage on earth and it is—God wants his people to become like Christ. Christ-likeness is the will of God for the people of God. . . . In other words, if we claim to be a Christian . . . God's way to make us like Christ is to fill us with his Spirit."[45]

And so what of Ed Decker and other aggressive critics referring to the Latter-day Saints as "the God-makers?" Jordan Vajda, formerly a Roman Catholic priest and now a Mormon, has noted,

> What was meant to be a term of ridicule has turned out to be a term of approbation, for the witness of the Greek Fathers of the Church . . . is that they also believed salvation meant "becoming a god." It seems that if one's soteriology cannot accommodate a doctrine of human divinization, then it has at least implicitly, if not explicitly, rejected the heritage of the early Christian church and departed from the faith of first-millennium Christianity. However, if that is the case, those who would espouse such a soteriology also believe, in fact, that Christianity, from about the second century on, has apostatized and "gotten it wrong" on this core issue of human salvation.[46]

Hyrum Mack Smith and Janne M. Sjodahl offered the following commentary on Joseph Smith's revelation that God's exalted children "shall be gods" (D&C 132:20):

What a wonderful revelation this is when compared with the narrow ideas held in the world! Children of kings are princes and princesses, associating on terms of equality with their royal parents, and having a good chance of becoming kings and queens themselves. But when we say that the privilege of God's children is to associate with

---

45. John Stott, "The Model: Becoming More Like Christ," sermon delivered at the Keswick Convention, July 17, 2007.

46. Jordan Vajda, *Partakers of the Divine Nature: A Comparative Analysis of Patristic and Mormon Doctrines of Divinization*, FARMS Occasional Papers, ed. William J. Hamblin (Provo, Utah: FARMS, 2002), 56–57.

Him in the eternal mansions, and that they may become gods, then the world does not understand us, and many deem us guilty of blasphemy. *They seem to think that they honor God by supposing that His children are infinitely inferior to Him. What kind of father is He, then, that He should feel it an honor to be the progenitor of an inferior offspring?* Is there a king in earth that would feel honored by having degenerates and beggars for children? Do not fathers and mothers rejoice in the progress of their children? Is it not their ambition to educate and train their loved ones, until these shall reach the highest possible degree of intelligence and efficiency? Surely, we can do no greater honor to God, our Father, than to admit the divine possibilities which He has planted in His offspring, and which will be developed under His tuition in this life and hereafter, until His children are perfect as He is perfect.[47]

> We do not believe we can work ourselves into glory or godhood, nor can we gain eternal life through human effort alone. One does not become more and more Christ-like through sheer grit and will power. Central to any and all spiritual progress is the Atonement of Jesus Christ, and it is only by and through his righteousness that we may be declared righteous. It is only by the power of his precious blood that we may be cleansed and sanctified from the taint and tyranny of sin. And it is only by and through the power of his everlasting life that we receive life—energy, strength, vitality, renewal, enabling power—to accomplish what we could never, worlds without end, accomplish on our own.

Just how strange, then, is the LDS doctrine of deification? How unscriptural is it? In connection with these questions it is fascinating to read two statements made by Martin Luther. The first, written in his Christmas sermon of 1514, affirms, "Just as the word of God becomes flesh [Jesus becomes man], so it is certainly also necessary that the flesh become word [that man become like Christ]. For the word becomes flesh precisely so that the flesh may become word. In other words: God becomes man so that man may become God. Thus power becomes powerless so that weakness may become powerful."[48] In 1519 Luther wrote, "For it is true that a man helped by grace is more than a

---

47. Hyrum M. Smith and Janne M. Sjodahl, *Doctrine and Covenants Commentary* (Salt Lake City: Deseret Book Company, 1965), 826–27; emphasis added.
48. Martin Luther, cited in Karkkaienen, *One With God*, 47.

man; indeed, the grace of God gives him the form of God and deifies him, so that even the Scriptures call him 'God' and 'God's son.'"[49]

Vladimir Lossky taught, "Redemption has our salvation from sin as an immediate aim, but that salvation will be, in its ultimate realization in the age to come, *our union with God, the deification of the created beings whom Christ ransomed*."[50] Similarly, Nicolas Kavasilas pointed out, "How wonderful will that sight be: to see a countless multitude of luminaries upon the clouds, to be led up as chosen people to a festive celebration beyond any comparison, to be *a company of gods surrounding God*, of the beautiful surrounding Him who is perfect Beauty, or servants surrounding the Master." That is, "The saints in the age to come will be 'gods surrounding God, fellow-heirs with Him of the same inheritance, co-rulers with Him of the same Kingdom.'"[51]

In the fifteenth century Nicholas of Cusa taught, "Every creature is, as it were, a finite infinity or a created god, so that it exists in the way in which this could best be. It is as if the Creator had spoken: 'Let it be made,' and because God, who is eternity itself, could not be made, that was made which could be made, which would be as much like God as possible. The inference, therefore, is that every created thing as such is perfect, even if by comparison to others it seems less perfect."[52] In the twentieth century Panayiotis Nellas has written that the precise meaning of being created in the image of God is "*to transcend the limited boundaries of creation and to become infinite*. This relates to all the elements of his being from the most peripheral to the very core of his existence."[53]

To summarize, Latter-day Saints teach that through the cleansing and transforming power of the blood of Jesus Christ, and through the sanctifying and divinizing power of the Holy Spirit, men and women may over time mature spiritually, a process that is referred to variously as participation, transformation, union, intermingling, partaking, elevation, kingship, interpenetration, joint-heirship, son and daughterhood, adoption, re-creation, and realization.[54] And so I ask again: Just how odd, how unusual, how unorthodox, how unfathomable, how un-

---

49. Ibid.
50. Lossky, *In the Image and Likeness of God*, 103; emphasis added.
51. Nicolas Kavasilas, quoted in Nellas, *Deification in Christ*, 158–59; emphasis added.
52. Nicholas of Cusa, in Hudson, *Becoming God*, 70.
53. Nellas, *Deification in Christ*, 28; emphasis added.
54. See, for example, Clendenin, *Eastern Orthodox Christianity*, 131.

Christian *are* the words of Joseph Smith and the doctrine of the Latter-day Saints? How strange is it to believe that eternal life consists of knowing "the only wise and true God; and you have got to learn how to be Gods yourselves, and to be kings and priests to God, the same as all Gods have done before you, namely, by going from one small degree to another, and from a small capacity to a great one; from grace to grace, from exaltation to exaltation, until you attain to the resurrection of the dead, and are able to dwell in everlasting burnings, and to sit in glory, as do those who sit enthroned in everlasting power?"[55]

Conclusion

Whether the LDS doctrines of exaltation and deification are the same as those delivered by the Church Fathers, by Eastern Orthodox thinkers of the past and present, or with modern Christians is absolutely immaterial. Joseph Smith did not organize The Church of Jesus Christ of Latter-day Saints by drawing upon ideas that consisted of "doctrinal debris left over from another age."[56] Nor did the Mormon leader become a prophetic packrat and collect practices and beliefs of his day in order to gain legitimization. Nor do we in the twenty-first century; we do not seek nor require a theological imprimatur from Catholic, Orthodox, or Protestant Christians. The intent of this contribution is not to suggest that others ought to accept Mormonism because bright and inspired minds of other faiths have used language or ideas similar to our own. Rather, my intent is to instead point out what should be more obvious than it is to many—that the doctrine of deification, divinization, and *theosis* has been around for a long, long time, and that therefore it should require more than a tiny bit of cognitive and spiritual dissonance to dismiss or ignore it outright. President Gordon B. Hinckley declared:

> The whole design of the gospel is to lead us onward and upward to greater achievement, even, eventually, to godhood. This great possibility was enunciated by the Prophet Joseph Smith in the King Follett sermon and emphasized by President Lorenzo Snow . . . Our enemies have criticized us for believing in this. Our reply is that this

---

55. Smith, *Teachings of the Prophet Joseph Smith*, 346–47.
56. Neal A. Maxwell, *Things As They Really Are* (Salt Lake City: Deseret Book Company, 1978), 46.

lofty concept in no way diminishes God the Eternal Father. He is the Almighty. He is the Creator and Governor of the universe. He is the greatest of all and will always be so. But just as any earthly father wishes for his sons and daughters every success in life, so I believe our Father in Heaven wishes for his children that they might approach him in stature and stand beside him resplendent in godly strength and wisdom.[57]

We might well ask: Does God want His children to be like Him? Or is this something that is repulsive to Him? Is it something that is inappropriate? Does God possess the power to re-create men and women in his own image? What parts of the "divine nature" or "being like Him" are out of bounds, off base, and so forth? And what scriptural injunctions preclude the children of God from aspiring to be like Him in every way possible?

As Latter-day Saints we glory in the reality that through the Savior's blood, we "have a forgiveness of sins, and also a sure reward laid up for [us] in heaven, even that of partaking of the fulness of the Father and the Son through the Spirit. As the Son partakes of the fulness of the Father through the Spirit, so the saints are, by the same Spirit, to be partakers of the same fulness, to enjoy the same glory; for as the Father and the Son are one, so, in like manner, the saints are to be one in them. Through the love of the Father, the mediation of Jesus Christ, and the gift of the Holy Spirit, they are to be heirs of God, and joint heirs with Jesus Christ."[58]

---

57. Gordon B. Hinckley, "Don't Drop the Ball," *Ensign*, November 1994, 48.
58. *Lectures on Faith*, 5:3.

15

Kalam Infinity Arguments and the Infinite Past

Blake T. Ostler, *Salt Lake City, Utah*

1.0 Introduction

In their contribution to *The New Mormon Challenge: Responding to the Latest Defenses of a Fast-Growing Movement* (NMC) entitled "Craftsman or Creator: An Examination of the Mormon Doctrine of Creation and a Defense of *Creatio Ex Nihilo*," Paul Copan and William Lane Craig (C&C) raise two logical arguments in order to establish that the universe, in the sense of all that exists in any sense, must have begun to exist from absolute nothing a finite time ago.[1] They argue that an actual infinite series is impossible and therefore the universe cannot

---

1. Paul Copan and William Lane Craig, "Craftsman or Creator: An Examination of the Mormon Doctrine of Creation and a Defense of Creatio Ex Nihilo," in Francis Beckwith, Carl Mosser, and Paul Owen, eds., *The New Mormon Challenge: Responding to the Latest Defenses of a Fast-Growing Movement* (Grand Rapids, Mich.: Zondervan, 2001), 113–77. Though I focus on NMC, I will also discuss the extensive defense of the argument by Craig in *The Kalam Cosmological Argument* (New York: Harper & Row, 1979); with Quentin Smith, *Theism, Atheism, and Big Bang Cosmology* (Oxford, England: Clarendon Press, 1993); "God and Real Time," *Religious Studies* 26, no. 3 (1991): 335–47; "Time and Infinity," *International Philosophical Quarterly* 31, no. 4 (1991): 387–401; "Professor Mackie and the Kalam Cosmological Argument," *Religious Studies* 20, no. 3 (1985): 367–75; "The Kalam Cosmological Argument and the Hypothesis of a Quiescent Universe," *Faith and Philosophy* 8 (1991): 104–8; "A Swift and Simple Refutation of the *Kalam* Cosmological Argument?" *Religious Studies* 35, no. 1 (1999): 57–72; "Graham Oppy and the Kalam Cosmological Argument," LeadershipU, Novermber 8, 2005, http://www.leaderu.com/offices/billcraig/docs/oppy.html (accessed May 2, 2012); "Reply to Smith: On the Finitude of the Past," *International Philosophical Quarterly* 33, no. 2 (1993): 225–31.

be eternal. They also argue that it follows that the universe was created *ex nihilo* by a nonmaterial and yet personal being.

I argue, in response, that C&C's arguments do not apply to the order of infinity involved in an infinite past. Therefore, the two infinity arguments proposed by C&C are not sound. The first argument turns on an equivocation in the use of terms such as "number," "more than," and similar terms. In particular, the first argument mistakenly applies the meaning of terms used for finite mathematics such as "number," "equal to," and "more than" to transfinite set logic where these concepts mean something quite different. The first argument commits the fallacy of equivocation by adopting the logic that applies to individual members in finite collections to infinite sets. I also argue that neither premise of the second argument applies to the order of infinity involved in the infinite past and is, therefore, based on two false premises.

I further argue that the two infinity arguments do not establish a logical contradiction in the concept of an actually infinite series that has no first term—as C&C readily admit. However, I show that their arguments can be sound only if the coherence of Cantor's theories of infinite set logic is called into question. I then argue that it can be demonstrated that it is *logically possible* that a material universe has always existed without beginning. I argue that the alleged "absurdities" claimed by C&C are perhaps unusual—given the fact that our experience is limited—but that they are neither impossible nor absurd.

Finally, I argue that, even if they were sound, the infinity arguments do not apply to temporally discontinuous temporal epochs, each of which is finite but infinite as a collection. Thus, the arguments do not apply to the discontinuous temporal epochs posited by the quantum vacuum and chaotic inflationary theories of the universe.

2.0 The Nature of Infinities

C&C do not argue that the notion of infinity is incoherent. They admit that Cantor's mathematical logic of infinite sets is self-consistent. Indeed, they acknowledge that "the actual infinite may be a fruitful and consistent concept within a postulated universe of discourse." However, they claim that, "it cannot be transposed into the real world, for this would involve counter-intuitive absurdities."[2]

---

2. NMC, 150.

Mathematicians have been comfortable reasoning about the infinite for some time. However, prior to the breakthrough work of Georg Cantor, mathematicians refused to consider infinities in their theories.[3] The reason for this reluctance was simple and straightforward: for any inductive[4] finite number n, the number n + 1 has two certain properties: First, n $\neq$ n + 1. Second, n < n + 1 and n > n − 1. However, they refused to accept mathematical infinities because infinite collections violate these simple rules, which seemed to be both contrary to logic and absurd. As Bertrand Russell notes,

> The difficulties that so long delayed the theory of infinite numbers were largely due to the fact that some, at least, of the inductive properties were wrongly judged to be such as *must* belong to all numbers; indeed it was denied without contradiction. The first step in understanding infinite numbers consists in realizing the mistakenness of this view.[5]

The most amazing difference between an inductive number and an infinite number is that the rules that apply to finite "numbers" do not apply to infinite "numbers." The word "number" is thus equivocal when used for infinite sets rather than finite sets. Consider the set of all cardinal numbers: 0, 1, 2, 3, 4, 5 ... This set has a first member but no last member. It is infinite. Cantor called the smallest of infinite cardinals $\aleph_0$ (aleph-zero). This "transfinite number" has some very different properties from finite inductive numbers. We can add or subtract 100,000 to or from $\aleph_0$ and it is the same transfinite number! That is, it still has the property of being an infinite set. Indeed, we can add any finite number to $\aleph_0$ and it is still the same transfinite number. Indeed, we can add $\aleph_0 + \aleph_0 = \aleph_0$. Cantor adopted the fact that 1 can be added to $\aleph_0$ as a definition of transfinite numbers, so $\aleph_0 + 1 = \aleph_0$. However, as I will discuss below, it is better to include within the definition of transfinite cardinal numbers the recognition that they are "numbers" that do not possess all proper-

---

3. Georg Cantor, *Contributions to the Founding of the Theory of Transfinite Numbers*, trans. O. Jourdain (Chicago: Open Court, 1915).

4. By "inductive number" I mean any number that has the inductive properties of mathematics roughly in the sense argued by Bertrand Russell and Alfred North Whitehead in *Principia Mathematica* (Cambridge: Cambridge University Press, 1910–13).

5. Bertrand Russell, *Introduction to Mathematical Philosophy* (1919; rpt., New York: Dover Publications, 1993), 78–79.

ties of inductive numbers (i.e., transfinite numbers are not inductive numbers).

This fact is important because C&C attempt to exploit our intuitions about finite numbers and argue that it is absurd that infinite numbers do not act like finite numbers. Indeed, they refuse to accept the possibility of an actual infinite for the same reason that mathematicians so long refused to accept transfinite numbers: they do not obey the rules that apply to finite sets. But this difference between properties of finite numbers and transfinite numbers arises because transfinite numbers actually define properties of sets and not of individual members of sets, as do inductive numbers. Sets often have different properties than their individual members. Thus, we might say that a large crowd of people is not the same as a crowd of large people.

However, not all transfinite numbers have the same "number" of terms or the same properties. That is, not all transfinite number have $\aleph_0$ terms. The number of the set of real numbers is "greater than" $\aleph_0$; in fact, it is $2\aleph_0$. This result follows by considering all of the subclasses of $\aleph_0$. If a class has n members, it contains 2^n subclasses—that is, there are 2^n ways of configuring its subclasses. Further, there is no maximum to the infinite cardinal numbers. However great the number in any infinite set n, the number 2^n will always be greater.

Now the arithmetic of transfinite numbers is a bit surprising until it is grasped that it is the property of infinity that generates these interesting results:

$\aleph_0 + 1 = \aleph_0$
$\aleph_0 + n = \aleph_0$ for any n that is a finite inductive number
$\aleph_0^2 = \aleph_0$

However, it must be noted that

$2^{\aleph_0} > \aleph_0$

Further, although addition and multiplication work well for transfinite numbers, we cannot obtain definite results for subtraction and division. Because transfinite numbers have different properties than finite numbers, we obtain different results. Subtraction of a finite number from an infinite number is straightforward:

$\aleph_0 - n = \aleph_0$ for all n that are inductive numbers

However, $\aleph_0 - \aleph_0 = 0 \ldots \aleph_0$

That is, when we subtract $\aleph_0$ from itself, the result is not definite. Consider the results of subtracting the collection of $\aleph_0$ from the following:

a) All inductive numbers − $\aleph_0$ = 0
b) All inductive numbers from n onwards − $\aleph_0$ = remainder in numbers 0 to n − 1
c) All odd numbers − $\aleph_0$ = all even numbers

All of these ways of subtracting $\aleph_0$ from $\aleph_0$ give different results. Division is similar. Whenever $\aleph_0$ is multiplied by any finite number, the product is always $\aleph_0$ terms. However, $\aleph_0$ divided by $\aleph_0$ may have values ranging from 1 to $\aleph_0$. It follows that negative numbers and ratios do not apply to transfinite numbers. C&C complain that to "avoid the contradictions involved in subtraction of infinite quantities, transfinite arithmetic simply prohibits such inverse operations by fiat."[6] But this assertion is simply erroneous, for transfinite mathematics does not simply prohibit subtraction and division by fiat; rather, transfinite mathematics shows why operations that can be done with finite numbers sometimes give indefinite results for transfinite numbers. It should be noted that Cantor's theory is not the only systematic exposition of transfinite logic. Graham Oppy has pointed out that there are a number of other developed theories of transfinite numbers that deal with inverse operations with transfinite numbers without contradiction.[7]

There are also different orders of transfinite numbers. In fact, the ordinal series of the form 1, 2, 3, 4 . . . n . . . represents the smallest of transfinite serial or ordinal numbers, which Cantor called w. Moreover, various serial successions may be greater than others. The ordinal number of the series of all ordinals that can be made out of a $\aleph_0$ collection, taken in order of magnitude, is called ω_1. Moreover, it can be shown that $1 + w \ne w + 1$. Such a rule is true of all relation-numbers and not merely transfinite numbers. If m and v are two relation-numbers, the general rule is that $m + v \ne v + m$. Thus, when discussing transfinite orders, it is essential to note that differing orders have different values. The infinite order collection beginning with {1 + 0, 1, 2, 3 . . .} has a different value than the set (. . . −3, −2, −1, 0 + 1). Thus, the order of the

---

6. NMC, 155.

7. Graham Oppy, "Reply to Craig: Inverse Operations with Transfinite Numbers and the Kalam Cosmological Argument," *International Philosophical Quarterly* 35, no. 2 (1995): 219–21.

past without a beginning to which it is added has a different order value than the infinite past that is counted down to zero.

The series of, first, all odd numbers, and then all even numbers, has a serial number of 2w. This number is "greater than" $\aleph_0 + n$, where n is any finite number.

There is also a crucial distinction between a "well-ordered" series and a "not-well-ordered" series. A well-ordered series has a *beginning*, and has *consecutive terms*, or has a *next term* after any selection of terms, like {1/2, 1/4, 1/8, 1/16, 1/32 ...}. A "not-well-ordered" series is one that *has no first term or is discontinuous*. The series of negative numbers beginning with –1 and counting backward {–1, –2, –3 ...} is well-ordered. However, the series *ending in* –1 in a series {... –4, –3, –2, –1} is not-well-ordered. The reason this is important is that not-well-ordered series do not have the same properties as well-ordered infinite series. The infinite past has the cardinal number $\aleph_0$ and the order type ω_0. Not-well-ordered series do not obey the commutative law [(a + b = b + a) and (a + b = b x a)] or the distributive law [a (b + c) = ab + ac]. The distributive law holds for transfinite ordinals in the form

(b + c) a = ba + ca

but does not hold for the form

a (b + c) = ab + ac

Now we must ask, what does it mean for two sets to have the same number of members? For finite numbers, the two sets simply have the same finite number, say 4. That tells us how many are in each set. However, for set theory, two sets have the same "number" of members if they can be put into a one-to-one correspondence with one another. Thus, these two sets have the same number of members:

a	b	c	d
w	x	y	z

An infinite set is one whose proper subset can be put into a one-to-one correspondence with the whole of the set. Consider the set of count numbers and odd numbers:

Count numbers: 1 2 3 4 5 6 7 8 ...
Odd numbers: 1 3 5 7 9 11   13   15 ...

Note that no count numbers are left over, so no odd number is paired with more than one count number. There is a one-to-one correspondence. Thus, the sets of count numbers and of odd numbers are both infinite sets. However, take any finite collection of numbers:

{2, 4, 6, 8}

No proper subset of this set can be put into a one-to-one correspondence with the whole. Thus, the set is finite. In other words, the set {2, 6, 8} cannot be put into a one-to-one correspondence with the set: there will always be something remaining. Thus, we can adopt the following rules regarding finite and transfinite numbers:

> *R1* = A finite set has more members than any of its proper subsets
>
> *R2* = An infinite set does not have more members than any of its proper subsets, and each member of an infinite set can therefore be placed into a one-to-one correspondence

For finite sets, the whole set is always "greater than" a subset consisting of only some but not all of the set's members. For an infinite set, the whole set is not "more than" a proper infinite subset consisting of only some but not all of the set's members.

It is imperative to see that transfinite sets have different properties than finite sets. Thus, when we use terms like "number," "greater than," and "equal to," they mean something different for a transfinite series than for a finite series. In transfinite logic, for two transfinite sets to have the same number of members means that the members of each infinite collection can be placed in a one-to-one correspondence. However, for two inductive numbers to be equal means that they are "the same number."

3.1 The First Infinity Argument

C&C begin by distinguishing between a potential infinite and an actual infinite. A potential infinite is one that is always actually finite but open-ended without limit. All of the members of the collection do not yet actually exist (and thus technically do not form a set). An actual infinite series is one that has an actually infinite number of members. C&C maintain that if the universe has always existed, then, for example, the series of events up to the birth of Cantor constitutes an *actual* infinite. However, the series of events since Cantor's birth and stretching into the future, *provided that* the future is unending, constitutes only a *potential* infinite. C&C argue that a potential infinite can exist in the real world, but an actual infinite cannot. The distinction is one of the ontological statuses of events.[8] Given these distinctions, C&C's first argument runs as follows:

    1.1 An actual infinite cannot exist.
    1.2 An infinite temporal regress is an actual infinite.
    1.3 Therefore, an infinite temporal regress of events cannot exist.

The first premise is obviously the important premise in the argument—although I want to begin by arguing that premise 1.2 is ambiguous and problematic. We may ask what it means for a series of past events to "be actual," for it seems that the past is not still actual, and an infinite series can be *actually infinite* only if all of its temporal moments are actual at once. Those who adopt an A-theory of time maintain that there is a genuine distinction between past, present, and future and that the past and future are not actual but only the present moment is actual. On the other hand, those who adopt a B-theory of time maintain that the past, present, and future are equally real or actual. C&C seem to want to make an ontological distinction between a potentially infinite series and an actually infinite series. The difference is that the events in an actually infinite series are ontologically real; they actually exist in the real world are not merely mental or mathematical constructs—as C&C take numbers and mathematics to be. However, an infinite temporal regress is not the same as a beginningless series of events in time. An infinite temporal *regress* constitutes a "well-formed" infinite series. It has a beginning term, 0 (or −1, depending on how the set is constructed), and then counts backwards $\{0, -1, -2, -3 \ldots\}$. An infinite temporal regress has the same mathematical properties as the set of real numbers beginning with 0 (or 1) and counting forward. However, because a be-

---

    8. The distinction between an actual and a potential infinite is made by virtually every proponent of kalam infinity arguments. See G. J. Whitrow, *The Natural Philosophy of Time*, 2nd ed. (Oxford, England: Clarendon Press, 1980), 200; "Time and the Universe," in *The Voices of Time*, ed. J. T. Fraser (New York: George Braziller, 1966); and "On the Impossibility of an Infinite Past," *British Journal for the Philosophy of Science* 29, no. 1 (1980): 31–32; Pamela Huby, "Kant or Cantor: That the Universe, If Real, Must Be Finite in Both Space and Time," *Philosophy* 46, no. 176 (1971): 127; David A. Conway, "Possibility and Infinite Time: A Logical Paradox in St. Thomas's Third Way," *International Philosophical Quarterly* 14, no. 2 (1974): 201–8.

ginningless series of events is a "not-well-formed series," it has different mathematical properties. Recall that the series of past events *ending* with {... −4, −3, −2, −1, 0} has different mathematical properties than the set *beginning* with {0, −1, −2, −3, −4 ...}.

Perhaps C&C would maintain that since the past has been real—it has actually existed in reality—it constitutes an *actual infinity* of events even as regress. However, this assertion is ambiguous. An "actual infinity" can mean that (a) an infinite set of events are all actual at once; or (b) an infinite set of events, some of which have been, are no longer actual. The infinite past does not constitute an infinity of *actual events*. In particular, the set of past events does not constitute a set of *actual events* because the past events are no longer actual (assuming an A-theory of time). This distinction becomes important when setting up stories that supposedly show that a beginningless reality is absurd. After all, if the universe (in the sense that it constitutes all that is) has always existed, then it constitutes a beginningless series but in actuality is not a regress of events.

Nevertheless, premise 1.2 is easily repaired by replacing it with one that accurately mirrors the conditions of a beginningless reality:

1.2* A beginningless series of events in time is an actual infinite.

From 1.1 and 1.2*, it follows that:

1.3* A beginningless past series of events in time cannot exist.

With this correction, we can assess the first argument. C&C attempt to show that premise 1.1 is true by a *reductio ad absurdum*. They suppose for the sake of argument that an actual infinite series exists and then proceed to attempt to derive absurdities from that assumption. In NMC, they use the example of Hilbert's Hotel, derived from the work of the mathematician David Hilbert. Suppose we have a Hotel with an infinite number of rooms and that "all" of the rooms are "full." Now suppose that a new guest arrives and asks for a room. Is there room? Of course, because remember that $\aleph_0 + 1 = \aleph_0$. C&C protest: "But remember, before he arrived, all of the rooms were full! Equally curious, according to the mathematicians, there are now no more persons in the hotel than there were before: the *number is just infinite*. But how can this be? The proprietor just added the new guest's name to the register and gave him the keys—how can there not be one more person in the hotel than before?"⁹ C&C then suggest that we subtract one guest, or move all of the occupants to only even-numbered rooms and thus open up an infinite "number" of rooms for an infinite number of new guests in odd-numbered rooms, or have the odd-numbered guests move out and move the even-numbered guests back again—and we always end up with the same "infinite" number of guests. C&C quip: "Can anyone believe that such a hotel could exist in reality?" C&C conclude that the existence of an actual infinite is absurd and therefore impossible. However, these absurdities are all in their own minds.

We may ask if the example of Hilbert's Hotel is really an analogy for the type of infinity involved in a beginningless past? The answer is that it is not. It does not mirror the infinite past. First, Hilbert's Hotel has a first room, a beginning term, that is followed by consecutive terms and therefore is a well-formed series. The infinite past is a *not-well-formed* infinite series because it has no first term. Second, the rooms in the Hotel all exist at once and are actual in the same moment. That is not true of the infinite past. Only the present moment is actual or ontologically real, assuming an A-theory of time (which C&C accept). Thus, the past events do not actually exist to be transposed and reordered, as the story of Hilbert's Hotel requires. If Hilbert's Hotel were like the past, it would have only one room that has been occupied by an infinite number of guests in consecutive order. Further, the past cannot be jumbled around like the persons in Hilbert's Hotel for reasons quite unrelated to the problems of infinities—*the past is fixed and unchangeable once it occurs.* Year 351,067 B.C. cannot be exchanged for year 465,789 B.C. Thus, we cannot take away all of the odd years. We have the infinite series of past events just as they have occurred and in the very order they occurred, and we cannot alter them in the way C&C suggest for Hilbert's Hotel to create a supposed absurdity.

For these reasons, the supposed "absurd" stories used by C&C to demonstrate that an actual infinite is absurd simply have no application to the type of infinite order involved in the past without a beginning. All of the supposedly absurd stories—like Hilbert's Hotel, or the Tristram Shandy autobiography¹⁰—depend critically upon properties of the

---

9. NMC, 151.

10. See the discussions of the Tristram Shandy paradox in Craig and Smith, *Theism, Atheism, and Big Bang Cosmology,* 33–35. A. R. Small notes that the Tristram Shandy story only gives us half of the supposed paradox. See A. R.

order that the infinite past does not possess. The past events are not like an infinite number of guests in an infinite number of existing rooms, all of which actually exist in the same moment that can be shuffled around and transposed and still maintain the same order of infinite numbers.

Further, the supposed absurdity is contrived. Take the first supposed absurdity—that the number of occupied rooms equals the number of rooms plus one for a new occupant, and that there are no "more" occupied rooms than there were before the new occupant arrived. Absurd? Not really. C&C illicitly use the concepts of "number" and "more" to trade on our intuitions about finite numbers and then apply them to transfinite numbers where such intuitions do not apply. It *is* absurd to suggest for a finite number that 99 rooms plus 1 more room equals the same number of rooms as before. However, in the context of infinite set logic, all infinite collections can be put into a one-to-one correspondence with proper subsets of themselves, and so our ordinary expectations about the way finite numbers behave do not apply in this new context. To say that the "number" of rooms is "infinite," even after a new guest has checked in, is to say only this and nothing more: the occupied rooms before the new guest arrived can be put into a one-to-one correspondence with all counting numbers, and so can the number of occupied rooms after a new guest arrives and one more room is occupied.

Is it absurd to suggest that we can have a Hotel that is full and then move all of the occupants to even-numbered rooms and leave an infinite number of odd-numbered rooms for an infinite number of new guests? Hardly. Conceive of the Hotel as extending into infinity from a certain point in Denver, which is the beginning of the rooms. There is a first *even*-numbered room, a second even-numbered room, a third even-numbered room, and so forth without limit. But there is also a first *odd*-numbered room, a second odd-numbered room, and so forth without limit. There is also an even-numbered room that can be placed into a one-to-one correspondence with every counting number—and the same for all odd-numbered rooms. But that is just what it means to say the number of even-numbered rooms equals the num-

---

Small, "Tristram Shandy's Last Page," *Bristish Journal for the Philosophy of Science* 37 (1986): 213–16. The response to Craig in Craig and Smith in found in *Theism, Atheism, and Big Bang Cosmology*, 88–89. Wes Morriston also responds to Craig's Tristram Shandy argument in "Must the Past Have a Beginning?" *Philo* 2, no. 1 (1999): 5–9.

ber of odd- and even-numbered rooms together. Perhaps a better word than "number" could be used, for we can say instead that the number of even-numbered rooms alone *corresponds* to the number of even- and odd-numbered rooms taken together. Once we clear up the equivocal use of the word "number," the supposed absurdity evaporates. C&C suggest that it is absurd that the "number" of occupied even- and odd-numbered rooms can correspond to just the odd-numbered rooms, but that is the way that transfinite numbers work. In fact, once we state that even-numbered rooms can be put into one-to-one correspondence with even- and odd-numbered rooms taken together, the assertion becomes quite ordinary and mundane. Indeed, one could not reject such a statement without simply objecting to Cantor's theory of transfinite mathematics altogether.

Yet there is a remaining feature that may make us feel uncomfortable. If there are "more" rooms than there are just even-numbered rooms, then the even-numbered rooms are a proper subset of the set of all rooms. Not every room in the Hotel is an even-numbered room. However, it is simply an error to assert that there are "more" rooms than even-numbered rooms because transfinite numbers follow different rules than finite numbers. Unless Cantor is simply mistaken, the number of rooms is not "more than" the number of even-numbered rooms for infinite sets. C&C claim that they have no objection to the abstract mathematical notions of an infinite series of numbers; they only object that such things cannot exist in reality. But the objection made by C&C is valid only if the theory of abstract transfinite numbers is wrong as well. When we subtract all odd numbers from all counting numbers, we have a set that has the same number of terms. Why is this not absurd when applied to abstract numbers of rooms but somehow becomes absurd and unthinkable when applied to real rooms? C&C's objections are really objections to the very notion of infinite numbers and not merely to whether such numbers can be mirrored in reality.

In effect, C&C are suggesting that an actual infinite is impossible because we can derive a violation of the following principle:

R_1 = A set has more members than any of its proper subsets.

They argue that a Hotel that has an infinite number of rooms that are all full and then has room to add an infinite number of guests is impossible. The reason it seems impossible is that, for finite numbers, a set has "more members" than any of its proper subsets. But what does it mean to claim that actually infinite sets have a "number" of members? An actually infinite set does not have an inductive number, or a natural number, or a real number of members. Thus, it is simply mistaken to assert that the Hotel has a "greater inductive number," or a "greater natural number," or a "greater real number" of occupants. Actual infinities have a *transfinite number* of members, and transfinite numbers do not obey R_1, for R_1 is a rule that applies only to finite numbers. Rather, transfinite numbers obey:

R_2 = An infinite set does not have more members than any of its proper subsets.

Thus, it is not true that actually infinite sets have a greater *transfinite* number than all of their proper subsets.

Now, C&C may claim that it is simply impossible for "a set Z to have every member that another set Y has, and also has some 'more' members that the set Y doesn't have, and yet set Z does not have 'more members' than set Y." Yet this assertion is true for transfinite numbers and not for finite numbers. There is a sense in which set Z has "more" members than set Y, but it is a sense that applies only to finite numbers and does not affect the fact that both Z and Y are infinite sets. When we say that an infinite set has every member that another set has and some "more" members in addition, "more" means only that "set Z has all of the members of Y and some members that Y doesn't have and both are infinite sets." The fact that set Z has all of the members of set Y and also some members that Y doesn't have does not preclude the members of set Y and of set Z from being placed into a one-to-one correspondence if Y and Z each has an infinite number of members. When infinite sets are compared, the word "more" does not mean the same thing that it does when finite sets are compared.[11]

Thus, this first argument commits the fallacy of equivocation in the sense that it imputes the properties of individual members of a

---

11. Wes Morriston, John Taylor, and Paul Draper have also noted that Craig surreptitiously imputes the properties applying to finite numbers to transfinite numbers. See Wes Morriston, "Must the Past Have a Beginning?" *Philo* 2, no.1 (1999): 5–19; and "Craig on the Actual Infinite," *Religious Studies* 38, no. 2 (2002): 147–66; John Taylor, "Kalam: A Swift Argument from Origins to First Cause?" *Religious Studies* 33, no. 2 (1997): 167–79; and Paul Draper, "A Critique of the Kalam Cosmological Argument," in *Philosophy of Religion*, ed. Louis Pojman, 3rd ed. (Belmont Calif.: Wadsworth, 1997), 42–47.

finite set to infinite sets as a whole. Finite sets obey Rule R_1. However, it is a mistake to impute this same rule to the properties of infinite sets. Sets do not necessarily obey the same rules that apply to individual members of sets.

3.2 The Second Infinity Argument

C&C offer a second infinity argument that is even weaker than the first:

> 2.1 The temporal series of events is a collection formed by successive addition.
> 2.2 A collection formed by successive addition cannot be an actual infinite.
> 2.3 Therefore, the temporal series of events cannot be an actual infinite.

Premise 2.1 is not true of all temporal series and certainly is not true of a beginningless past series that terminates in the present. An actual past infinite collection is not "formed by successive addition," as if we could add a finite number of terms together and somehow they add up to an infinite number. Rather, for any term added to the past at any given point in the past, the past is *already* an infinite collection at that past time and therefore is not *formed as an infinite* collection by such addition. Indeed, C&C have assumed in premise 2.1 that the "temporal series" of past events has the same properties as a potential infinity rather than an actual infinity, for they assume that an infinity is open-ended and completed by adding to it rather than being a completed infinity without a beginning term. One cannot form a collection by adding to it if the collection already exists *before* the addition. The infinite past already exists as an infinite temporal series before the addition of any term and therefore cannot be formed as an infinite temporal series by addition. I accept that one cannot *by beginning with any one member* of an infinite set complete an infinite set by successively adding new members to the set. But what follows from this is only that a set *that has a first member*, that is, one that could be a "well-formed set," cannot be completed as an actual infinite by successive addition. However, premise 2.1 is not true for "not-well-formed" sets that have no first member. The view that the past consists of an infinite series without beginning does not imply that it can become or "be formed as" an infinite collection by successive addition.

Indeed, C&C quote Bertrand Russell: "Classes which are infinite are given all at once by the defining properties of their members, so there is no question of 'completion' or of 'successive synthesis.'"[12] They take this to support premise 2.2. However, they miss the entire point of Russell's statement. Russell is saying that it is a mistake to assert that infinities of any sort are created or completed by successive addition, which is precisely what premise 2.1 implies. Premise 2.1 is false because it mischaracterizes the properties of an actual past infinite. The past is not "formed" as infinite by adding new days or years to it—it is already infinite at any given moment a new day or year is added! While there is never enough time to add up finite numbers to an infinite in a finite amount of time, the number of times is always already infinite if there is no beginning term—and thus the events constitute members of an actually infinite series. However, there is no time at which the temporal series of events *became* or were *formed* as an infinite collection. There is no sense in which an infinite is "formed" or "completed" by addition, just as Russell says. We cannot form an infinite set by adding 1 or 1,000,000 to it unless the set to which the new number is added is already infinite. Thus, premise 2.1 is false and the argument fails.

However, C&C may claim that the fact that an infinite series cannot be formed by successive addition merely shows that it cannot be a temporal series that can be added to by temporal succession. This is because temporality is essentially defined by the fact that one event is preceded and followed by another. Why should we accept that an infinite temporal series must be formed by successive addition? Craig claims that it is the very nature of all temporal series that they must be formed by successive addition:

> The only way a collection to which members are being successively added could be actually infinite would be for it to have an infinite "core" to which additions are made. But then it would not be a collection *formed* by successive addition, for there would always exist a surd infinite, itself not formed successively but simply given, to which a finite number of successive additions have been made. But clearly the temporal series of events cannot be so characterized, *for it is by its very nature successively formed throughout*. Thus, prior to any arbitrarily

---

12. NMC, 156–57.

designated point in the temporal series, one has a collection of past events up to that point which I successively formed and completed and cannot, therefore, be infinite.[13]

This assertion is no response at all. First, note that the proponent of the infinite past accepts the first three statements made by Craig. As Craig admits, an infinite collection can be added to by successive addition if it has a core that has always existed as an eternal past. Second, the collection is not formed as an infinite by successive addition but exists as an infinite past without some prior explanation for some first event. Further, a temporal series is such that it has events, and for each event there are events prior to and also events subsequent to the event. Even so, Craig argues that this cannot be because it is in the nature of an infinite past that it must be *formed as a series of events* by successive addition if it is a temporal collection. But he merely asserts this without further proof or argument. In fact, as Bertrand Russell states, this last assertion is false. It is in the very nature of the infinite past that it is always already infinite at any point it is added to. Thus, it is the nature of the infinite past that it is not formed as an infinite temporal collection by successive addition. Moreover, it won't do to observe that this view commits a person to the view that the eternal past has just always existed as an infinite, for that is just what the proponent of the eternal past claims. Craig cannot claim that such a view is absurd because an infinite cannot be added to, for he admits that there is one type of infinite that can be added to, and it just happens to be the very type of infinite claimed by the proponent of an eternal past. Finally, the claim that the entire temporal series itself must be formed as an infinite series by successive addition if individual members can be added to the series commits the fallacy of composition. It does not follow from the fact that individual members of a series have the property of being formed as part of an infinite series by being added to the series that the series set itself has the property of being formed as an infinite collection by successive addition.

A temporal series, by nature, can indeed be added to one member at a time, but it does not follow that an infinite temporal series is *formed as an infinite series* by such addition. Thus, premise 2.2 is ambiguous with respect to infinite series. It could mean that

---

13. Craig and Smith, *Theism, Atheism, and Big Bang Cosmology*, 34.

> 2.1* An infinite temporal series of events is formed *as an infinite temporal series* by successive addition.

On the other hand, it may be construed that

> 2.1** An infinite temporal series of events has been formed and is such that it can be added to by successive addition.

Premise 2.1* is false, while premise 2.1** may be true depending on the meaning of "has been formed." Now it is clear that if "has been formed" means anything like (a) "has been created at some first time," then it must be false because no one, not even God, can create a beginningless infinite temporal series of events having a first event. However, if "has been formed" means (b) "exists" or "has been created by God by forming events in each temporal moment of a past without beginning," then premise 2.1** is possibly true. It is indeed possible to add to a temporal series that has a transfinite number of members, but it is not possible to "form the series" *as an infinite series* by addition. However, if premise 2.1** in sense (b) is true, then premise 2.2 is necessarily false with respect to the transfinite order type w + n, where n is any finite number. That is, if the infinite temporal series of events is in fact formed as an actual infinite *in the sense that God has created it by forming events in each successive temporal moment of an eternal past*, then there is a series that is an actual infinite that is constituted as a temporal series by successive addition. This series is temporal in the sense that each moment is preceded by a prior moment and followed by a successive moment, but it is not infinite by virtue of the fact that each moment is succeeded by another moment; rather, it is infinite in virtue of the fact that there is no beginning to the series of succession.

Premise 2.2 also confuses the properties of a potential infinite with an actual infinite. C&C argue:

> In order for us to have "arrived" at today, existence has, so to speak, traversed an infinite number of prior events. But before the present event could arrive, the event immediately prior to it would have to arrive; and before that event could arrive, the event immediately prior to it would have to arrive; and so on *ad infinitum*. No event could ever arrive, since before it could elapse there will always be one more event that had to have happened first. Thus, if the series of past events were beginningless, the present event could not have arrived, which is absurd![14]

---

14. NMC, 156.

Indeed, the scenario painted by C&C is absurd because it does not accurately characterize the nature of the infinite past and its relation to the present. Just what does it mean to "traverse" an infinite time or to "arrive" at the present? If *traverse* means to pass through or complete a temporal series beginning with an event and ending with an event—as I believe the term implies—then the infinite past cannot be traversed in this sense.[15] However, the argument then would not apply to the infinite past since the infinite past has no beginning term. In fact, this seems to be the meaning of "traverse" implied in C&C's argument. Note first that C&C treat the past once again as a well-ordered infinity that has a first member—the first member of this set is the present event and we begin this set by counting backwards into an infinite past. We begin the thought experiment proposed by C&C by thinking of the present event, and then regress to the event before that, and then the event before that, *ad infinitum*. Since we begin with the present event, the infinity is merely potential and is in fact never completed. In fact, it is no infinity at all but merely an open-ended finite series. Since no matter how long we count we cannot complete the infinite past, C&C conclude that the past cannot be infinite. But counting backward again treats the actual past without beginning as a set that has a beginning term (i.e., the present event).

There is a way, and perhaps only one way, to create an actual infinite by counting or marking each successive moment, and that is to have been counting in each moment of existence of the eternal past as it occurred. Thus, the argument is a *non sequitur*, for it does not follow from the fact that the past is infinite that it cannot "reach" the present because there has been an infinite time in which to do it! Nor does it follow that no event could ever arrive because there will always be one more event that theoretically had to happen first. All that follows is that there is in fact an event that preceded the present event, and an event before that, and so on.

---

15. Nicholas Everett faults the Kalam argument based upon *traversing, counting, moving across,* and *completing a task* because it presupposes an "empirical interpretation of 'pairing' and 'correlating' [that] is out of place when we are considering infinite sets." See Nicholas Everett, "Interpretations of God's Eternity," *Religious Studies* 34, no. 1 (1998): 29. Richard Sorabji also criticizes the "traversal argument" on several grounds. Richard Sorabji, *Time, Creation and the Continuum* (Ithaca, N.Y.: Cornell University Press, 1983), 219–24.

In another article, Craig protests that his traversal argument does not implicitly presuppose a beginning term. He says,

> It is not obvious to me that to say a beginningless infinite series cannot be traversed means that it has no first member. The best I can make [of this] claim is that the notion of traversal entails a beginning point, so that a series with no beginning point cannot be traversed. But such a construal of traversal seems clearly wrong. A man who just finished counting all of the negative numbers, for example, has 'traversed' a beginningless, infinite series. To traverse a series means just to cross it or pass through it one member at a time. Hence, I am quite at a loss to understand how the Kalam Cosmological Argument begs the question by assuming implicitly that the past has a beginning point.[16]

But this protest of surprise isn't really a response at all. C&C implicitly assume that the series of past events has a starting point by asking us to imagine the past as a series that begins with the present event as the first term of a regress and counting backwards. They give us a well-formed infinite series when they must give us an example of a not-well-formed series that has no beginning term and terminates in the present. Moreover, the very activity of counting assumes that a beginning number has started a count. However, let's take C&C at Craig's word that to traverse means to "cross" or "pass through" a series one member at a time. If that is all that traverse means, then there is no reason why an infinite series cannot be formed by successive addition in this sense, for all it means is that an infinite time has been "crossed" or "passed through" in an infinite number of days or years, each of which has been passed through one member at a time. There is nothing absurd or impossible about that.

C&C suggest that the infinite past is like the task of completing a countdown of negative numbers and ending at 0, which seems impossible. And why is it impossible? If one has existed in every moment of the infinite past, he could have counted a number for each past moment because there is a one-to-one correspondence between the past times and the past numbers counted. That, of course, is not impossible. Yet C&C counter,

> But that only pushes the problem back a notch: how could an infinite series of moments elapse sequentially? If the past is actually infinite,

---

16. Craig, "Graham Oppy and the Kalam Cosmological Argument."

then why did one not finish his countdown of the negative numbers yesterday or the day before, since by then an infinite series of moments had elapsed? No matter how far along the series of past moments one regresses, one would have already completed his countdown.[17]

But there really is no problem at all. Our (finite) experience of counting includes the necessity that we begin counting with some number, but that is not the case if we set up the thought experiment correctly. There is confusion in the example suggested by C&C that is important to note. First, they suggest that the countdown ends with zero. Yet they say that the counter is regressing as he counts down, which suggests that the counter has begun at zero and is counting down the negative numbers backwards. But if we follow the example suggested by C&C in a way that actually reflects the infinite past, then there is no beginning to the counting. If there is no beginning to the counting, and in each new moment the counter counts a new number, it follows that the counter could have counted all of the negative numbers ending with zero, for there would then be a one-to-one correspondence between the infinite number of times in the past and each act of counting. Say that in fact I had been counting for all eternity. What follows is that I would have finished counting an infinite number of terms yesterday, and when I counted one more today I would have finished counting an infinite number of terms again today. As Wes Morriston argues in response to a similar argument by Craig:

> It is true that yesterday the infinite counter would have counted *infinitely many* numbers. Indeed, it is true that on any day during his count he would have counted infinitely many numbers. But it does not follow that on any day prior to today he has *finished* his count. Why? Because he was counting down to *zero*, and on no day prior to today had he reached zero. Yesterday, he had only reached −1, the day before he had reached −2, and so on. So there is no reason to conclude that the man has "always already" finished the countdown to zero.[18]

Again, Craig's response suggests that clearing up the confusion in the argument makes matters worse for the proponent of an infinite past:

> If we were to ask why the counter would not finish next year or in a hundred years, the objector would respond that prior to the present year an infinite number of years will have already elapsed, so that by

---

17. NMC, 157.
18. Wes Morriston, "Must the Past Have a Beginning?" *Philo* 2, no. 1 (1999): 5–19.

the Principle of Correspondence, all the numbers should have been counted by now. But this reasoning backfires on the objector: for, as we have seen, on this account the counter should at any point in the past have already finished counting all the numbers, since a one-to-one correspondence exists between the years of the past and the negative numbers.[19]

Yet Craig makes a modal error here. Craig (and C&C in their article in NMC) asserts that the infinite counter necessarily must have finished counting "all" of the negative numbers prior to today. The fact is that a person counting for an infinite number of years could have reached zero yesterday, but it is not necessarily the case. Remember, the concept of "number" is equivocal when speaking of infinite numbers. The counter could also have reached −10 or −1,528 yesterday, or any other finite number. The infinite set of negative numbers consisting of {n... −13, −12, −11}, where there is no beginning term and ends in −11, or the set with no beginning term and ends in −1,528, or any other finite number for that matter, can also be put into a one-to-one correspondence with all past years because the number of terms in each of these sets is infinite. Thus, it is simply false that the counter must have finished counting all of the negative numbers prior to today. C&C confuse "all negative numbers" with "infinitely many negative numbers." The two sets are not necessarily the same. Yet Craig's argument works only if, necessarily, the counter must have counted all negative numbers by today. The argument is simply modally confused.

C&C are equally mistaken that an actual infinite past cannot be added to. Let's say that the counter finished counting yesterday with −11. That means that today he could count −10 and he will have added one term to the actual infinite. So an actual infinite can be added to. What about when he reaches 0—won't he have used all of the negative numbers? No matter, let him begin counting with 1 the next day, and 2 the day after, and so forth. Because all of the negative numbers can be put into a one-to-one correspondence with all negative and positive numbers together, continuing with positive numbers is continuing to count with the same order of infinity having cardinal number $\aleph_0$ and the order type ω_0.

---

19. William Lane Craig, "The Existence of God and the Beginning of the Universe," *Truth: A Journal of Modern Thought* 3 (1991).

But doesn't that leave some number in the infinite set unassigned? No. As Quentin Smith explains,

> To the objection that this [counting of negative numbers] leaves some previously past event without a negative number assigned to it there is the following response: Let us call the time before some instance of the above described reassignment t1, and the time of reassignment t2. At t2 there is a past event belonging to the collection of past events that had not belonged to this collection at t1. However, at t2 there is not a greater number of events belonging to this collection than at t1, for the addition of the one event at t2 to the infinite collection that had existed at t1 results in a collection the same number of members as the collection that existed at t1, this number being $\aleph_0$. This is true because $\aleph_0$ plus 1 equals $\aleph_0$. Consequently, since there are $\aleph_0$ past events at both times, and since there are $\aleph_0$ negative numbers, there is no past event at either time that is unmatched with a negative number.[20]

However, I want to point out a feature about counting that seems counterintuitive because our finite experience dictates that we must begin somewhere to begin counting. If an infinite or eternal counter has been counting without beginning, he need not start with any given finite number. When speaking of an infinite counter who counts without beginning, we define counting as merely a *synthetic act of marking new events by a count number*, and then it can make sense to think of each past event to correspond to an act of counting—and that is all that counting means when infinite series are involved. It seems that if I am counting that I must begin somewhere, and if I use "all" the negative numbers and reach 0 that somehow there are no more numbers to use. However, this argument confuses "all" when speaking of infinite, for there is no time at which there are not "more" numbers that can be assigned to mark any given event. (Remember, in this context, "more" means only "*can be placed in a one-to-one correspondence*".) An infinite counter can use all of the even and positive numbers in any order that he chooses to mark the one-to-one correspondence between past events and numbers. So long as no number is used twice, the correspondence of infinite sets holds. Thus, today I could use number 1,247,367,987,653 and tomorrow the number –3, and I can mark the days with any numbers that

---

20. Quentin Smith, "Infinity and the Past," in William Lane Craig and Quentin Smith, *Theism, Atheism, and Big Bang Cosmology* (Oxford, England: Clarendon Press, 1993), 85.

I wish to count as long as I don't use a number twice. The reason for this is that whichever finite number is used to add to an infinite is entirely arbitrary because they all have the same effect—a finite number added to an infinite number is always an infinite number.

This last point also answers the argument presented by J. P. Moreland and adopted by Francis Beckwith and Stephen Parrish, that the problem with having no beginning is that no one could even start counting:

> [A]ssume that someone had been counting toward zero from negative infinity from eternity past. If a person goes back in time from the present moment, he will *never* reach a point when he is finishing his count or engaging in the count itself. This is because at every point, he will have already had an infinity to conduct the count. As Zeno's paradox of the race course points out, the problem with such a situation is not merely that one cannot complete an infinite task; one cannot even start an infinite task from a beginningless situation.[21]

Now it is clear that the task of counting does not *begin* at some point if it has been taking place from all eternity. But that is no impediment for a person who lives in each moment of an eternal reality from marking by synthetic succession each new moment (assuming that moments are discrete). But surely the problem with a beginningless eternity cannot be the fact that it cannot have a beginning. Zeno's point from the race paradox is that Achilles cannot complete the journey because he cannot begin it. He cannot begin it because to do so he must complete one of the tasks that make up the journey; he must first complete another task and thus have already begun. But the claim that the past has no beginning cannot be refuted by arguing that a beginningless past could never begin—for that is just what the proponent of an infinite past claims.

4.0 A Beginningless Multiverse and Infinity

It is also important to see that the infinity arguments made by C&C do not apply to a beginningless universe of the type posited by the chaotic inflationary or quantum vacuum theories of cosmology. Let's take the chaotic inflationary theory first. According to this theory,

---

21. Quoted in Francis Beckwith and Stephen Parrish, *The Mormon Concept of God: A Philosophical Analysis* (Lewiston, N.Y.: The Edwin Mellen Press, 1991), 59.

our local space-time universe began a finite time ago. However, our local bubble universe is not all that there is. It is possible, and in fact predicted by the chaotic inflationary theory, that our universe arose from a prior universe that is not spatio-temporally continuous with our local universe.[22] This prior universe gave rise to our universe in the sense that it constitutes the conditions from which the singularity arises and from which our own local universe originated. Let's say that each bubble universe within the multiverse constitutes an epoch of a discrete space-time continuum. However, because a singularity or Big Bang event constitutes the beginning of any particular bubble universe, it follows that there is no continuous time metric between any two space-time epochs. This theory also predicts that the prior universe did not have the same initial constants as our local universe, and thus it is possible that there is no continuous time metric that is shared between the two epochs. In fact, there may be infinitely many separate bubble universes given chaotic inflationary theory.[23] However, each of these bubble universes has its own time metric that is shared by no other. Each has a beginning and possibly an end. Each is finite in the past. Nevertheless, the number of bubble universes in the multiverse may be infinite. However, because they are discontinuous spatio-temporal epochs, they do not constitute a *series* of any sort. There are no equal intervals of time that are shared between them. None of the infinity arguments presented by C&C (nor any that Craig has produced on his own) apply to an infinite number of discontinuous realities that do not form a series. All series of events in the chaotic inflationary theory are merely finite in duration. Thus, it is possible that the multiverse has always existed even though each of the bubble universes has only a finite past.[24] Moreover, it is possible that the multiverse has always existed even if, *arguendo*, any of the arguments made by C&C were sound.

Suppose that there had always existed a quantum vacuum of the type conceived in many current inflationary theories of cosmology. In

---

22. Rem B. Edwards, "How Process Theology Can Affirm Creation *Ex Nihilo*," *Process Studies* 29, no. 1 (2000): 82.

23. See Andrei Linde, "The Self-Reproducing Inflationary Universe," *Scientific American* (Nov. 1994); "The Inflationary Universe," *Physics Today* 40 (1987): 61; and *Physics Review* 59 (1999); John D. Barrow, *Impossibility* (Oxford, England: Oxford University Press, 1998), 164–74; M.J. Rees, *Before the Beginning* (New York: Simon & Schuster, 1997).

24. John Barrow, *Impossibility*, 171–72.

this vacuum, there are innumerable events that occur within the limits of the Heisenberg Uncertainty Principle. None of these events are causally or temporally related to one another. They occur at random, and there is no time-metric to measure their proximity to one another.[25] Indeed, each of these events constitutes its own space-time universe in the sense that there is simply no causal or space-time continuum obtaining to place them in relation to one another. There is no beginning to this vacuum condition—it is simply the lowest energy state possible in the physical world. Such a reality must be regarded as quiescent in the sense that no events give rise to a series of events until the vacuum decays into a false vacuum creating the energy from which the Big Bang derived. Craig has admitted, correctly in my view, that the infinity arguments do not apply to a quiescent universe (i.e., a physical reality having no events).[26]

What Craig fails to address is how any of the arguments he (or he and Copan) presents could apply to the quantum vacuum. All of his arguments assume the existence of a well-formed infinite series. That is, a series that has *consecutive terms*, or has a *next term* after any selection of terms, like {1/2, 1/4, 1/8, 1/16, 1/32 . . .}. Because the quantum vacuum does not have a next term after any selection of terms, it is not a well-formed series. Indeed, it is simply no series at all but only unconnected random events—the ultimate description of chaos. Nevertheless, it is an eternal reality that has no beginning. Craig admits that the infinity arguments cannot demonstrate the existence of the universe out of nothing given the possibility of a quiescent universe: "*Creatio ex nihilo* would not then be proved, but as I employ it the *kalam* cosmological argument's primary aim is to support theism, not *creatio ex nihilo*."[27] However, it is not just a quiescent universe that escapes the arguments, but also any reality that is not continuous. Therefore, the infinity arguments also do not apply to a multiverse that has no beginning and has always existed as a quantum vacuum.

---

25. Alan H. Guth, *The Inflationary Universe* (New York: Addison Wesley, 1998), 167–87, 245–52; Timothy Ferris, *Coming of Age in the Milky Way* (New York: William Morrow, 1988), 349–66.

26. Craig, "The 'Kalam' Cosmological Argument and the Hypothesis of a Quiescent Universe," 104–8.

27. Ibid., 106–7.

Perhaps it could be argued that even if the events in the quantum vacuum do not constitute a well-formed series, they nevertheless still form an infinite *collection*. Or, even if the bubble universes does not constitute a spatio-temporally continuous reality, they still create a collection related in some sense to the cause-effect relation—in the sense that a new universe can be explained by conditions in the prior universe. Nevertheless, our concept of "cause-and-effect" derives from our experience in this spatio-temporal epoch. Look at the arguments presented by C&C. The second argument is based on a *series* that is formed by successive addition. A mere collection of random events that are not additive to one another won't work. Certainly the events of the quantum vacuum do not form anything by successive addition. Further, since the bubble universes posited in the chaotic inflationary theory do not constitute spatio-temporally related realities, it is difficult to see how the notion of addition as a series can be applied. It is also difficult to see how premise 1.1 of the first argument could be supported, because none of the supposed absurd stories apply to discontinuous realities. None of the thought experiments like Hilbert's Hotel could apply to either the vacuum or the bubble universes because they cannot be, as unrelated events, manipulated, reversed, halved or emptied the way the rooms in Hilbert's Hotel are. Thus, even if the arguments given to show that an actually infinite series were somehow sound, they don't apply to the multiverse envisioned in the chaotic inflationary theory.

5.0 Logical Possibility and the Uncreated Universe

C&C don't claim that a contradiction in first order logic can be derived from the proposition that the universe is not created and thus without a beginning. What they claim is that the idea is absurd. They thus claim that the notion of an infinitely old universe is metaphysically impossible—that is, there is no possible world in which such a universe can exist. Yet all C&C really mean by "logically impossible" is that they think the notion of an actual infinity is absurd even though they cannot show an outright contradiction in the notion. I find nothing absurd at all about the notion of an actually infinite past, though the results of transfinite mathematics are strange, given my expectations based upon experiences with finite realities. However, while the results of transfinite numbers and the concept of an infinite universe may be strange, they are not any stranger than the notions of quantum mechanics or the theory of relativity. We have learned from scientific breakthroughs that the universe is a strange place that often conflicts with our expectations and experience. Indeed, we encounter realities that are so strange that we can't even accurately picture them. A universe where an event is simultaneously a particle and a wave, or a reality that literally does not have both position and momentum at once, or space that bends and curves, or clocks that run faster and slower depending on the inertial frame of reference of the observer are at least as strange as anything we encounter dealing with infinities. C&C seek to exploit this strangeness to convince us that a universe that is eternal is simply absurd, but once the behavior of transfinite numbers and infinite realities is grasped, they are not strange but exciting and mind-expanding.

If the eternal universe is really impossible, let me ask just how old it is *logically possible* for the universe actually to be? Is there some largest number than which C&C would claim the actual universe could not be older? Of course not. The reason why C&C will not give us a largest number for the possible age of the universe is obvious—there is no such largest number at which the universe could not be older.

This recognition is no trivial matter, for it follows from the fact that there is no largest number that the set constituting the number of times at which it is logically possible that the universe actually existed has the same properties as the set of all negative numbers. Consider a thought experiment. Let's say that I have a time machine that will let me visit any time in the past at which it is logically possible that the universe *actually* existed. There may be physical barriers to the number of times that I can visit—for example, I may not be able to traverse a Big Bang event. If I cannot travel back in time past the circumstances obtaining in the early local universe, then the number in the set of past moments that I can visit is *physically* limited. However, since I believe that time travel is physically and nomologically impossible anyway, I am not speaking of natural or physical possibility. Because I want to talk about *logical possibility* and not merely what is permitted by natural laws, let me stipulate that my time machine can survive any Big Bang event. Moreover, I am not asking about whether visiting a moment is merely logically possible, but in visiting any past moment at which it is logically possible that the universe actually existed. Is there some limit to the number of times that I could visit in which it is logically possible that the physical universe *actually existed*?

Let's say that I set the clock in the time machine so that every 30 seconds I visit a past year in geometric progression to the geometric power beginning with a year two years ago. So I first visit 2 years ago in the first 30 seconds, and then I visit 4 to the fourth power (4^4) years ago after 60 seconds, and then I visit 16 to the sixteenth power years ago after 90 seconds, and so forth. After a mere ten minutes, I have visited times well older than the time of the Big Bang—about 6.6 billion years ago. But it is logically possible that the universe is older than that. After a mere hour, I have gone so far into the past that if all the 0s (just the size of the zeros on this page) needed to write the number were written on a normal piece of paper, they would fill more than the volume of the entire known universe! And yet I can still travel back in time, because for every time I pick, it is logically possible that the universe actually existed at that time. Imagine how far back I have gone after just one day. The point of this thought experiment is that there is no largest number, and so no limit to the times I could visit. No matter how far back in time I go, it is always logically possible that the world actually existed at that time.

Now let's modify the thought experiment just a bit. Let's say that instead of choosing a time further and further into the past, all I do is randomly choose various moments in the past to visit. When deciding a past time to visit, I am presented an array of possibilities from which to choose. I want to limit my choices to those times or moments in the past when it is logically possible that the world actually existed. Now let's ask the crucial question: Just how large is *the set of past times* from which I can choose to visit at which it is logically possible that the universe actually existed? A moment's reflection will show that this set is unlimited and in fact has the same properties as the complete set of real numbers—the members of this set can therefore be put into a one-to-one correspondence with the completed set of real numbers, which is infinite. The set of real numbers has $\aleph_0$ members. It follows that the number of past times at which it is possible that the universe actually existed has $\aleph_0$ members. Thus, the set of past times that are possible for me to visit and at which it is logically possible that the universe actually existed is also infinite.

Let's call *the set of past times at which it is logically possible that the universe actually existed* set *Sp*. The argument is as follows:

3.1 The members of the set *Sp* can be placed into a one-to-one correspondence with the members of the set of real numbers.
3.2 Sets whose members can be placed into a one-to-one correspondence with one another have the same number of members.
3.3 The set of real numbers has $\aleph_0$ members.
3.4 Therefore, set *Sp* has $\aleph_0$ members.

This argument is valid. Moreover, the premises seem unassailable. The only real possible question is whether the members of set *Sp* can be placed into a one-to-one correspondence with the set of real numbers as asserted by 3.1. Now it is clear that if I *begin* to visit past times, the set of times that I will have actually visited will always be finite. However, I am not inquiring about the set of times I can actually visit *by beginning to visit past times* but how large is the set of past times from which I can choose to visit? It is this set of past times *Sp* that I *could choose to* visit that has $\aleph_0$ members. Because the set is unlimited, it is logically possible that the world has always actually existed.

Moreover, there is in fact a way that I could visit an infinite number of times. If I had always been visiting times as they occurred without a beginning, then I will have visited an infinite number of times. Thus, it is not the time machine that allows me to visit the infinite number of times from which I could choose; rather, only by visiting each time as it actually occurs could I ever visit an infinite number of past times. Only one type of being can visit all of the times in an infinite past—an eternal being that actually existed in each of those times.

C&C reject this argument. They state,

> Ostler thinks that because the number of possible worlds with longer and longer finite pasts is unlimited, therefore there is a possible world having an infinite past. This is logically fallacious as reasoning that because one can count higher and higher finite numbers without limit, therefore there must be an infinitieth number.[28]

Yet C&C have misstated and misconstrued the argument. First, nothing in my argument suggests that *the set of past times* at which it is

---

28. NMC, 159. I provided a preliminary draft to Craig that did not contain the second step of the argument, and this failure on my part may have led to confusion about what my argument actually was.

logically possible that the universe actually existed contains a *particular member* that occurred an infinite number of moments ago. I am not arguing for a set of possible worlds that has longer and longer finite pasts as C&C claim. Indeed, my argument no more suggests an infinitieth number than the set of real numbers being infinite implies that there is an infinitieth real number. Any particular past time is, in fact, a finite number of intervals away from the present. But C&C themselves commit the fallacy of composition by suggesting that if the individual members of the set of past times are all finite, then *the set* of all past times *Sp* must also be finite! Because I argue that the *set of past times* has the property of infinity rather than any of its individual members, C&C simply manufacture a fallacy where there is none, and by so doing they commit the very fallacy of composition that they attribute to my argument.

Moreover, note that I say nothing about possible worlds semantics in my argument. Rather, what I argue is that the set of past times at which it is logically possible that the universe actually existed has the same properties as the complete set of negative numbers. The negative numbers can be placed in a one-to-one correspondence with the times it is possible that the universe actually existed. It follows that the *set* of past times at which the world actually exists also has an infinite number of members. I am not arguing that there is a possible world that has the property of having always existed. Instead, I am making a modal claim that is true in *all* possible worlds. In every possible world, the set of past times at which it is possible that the world actually existed is infinite. My argument shows that it can be demonstrated that it is logically possible that the world has no beginning because the set of past times at which it is logically possible that the world actually existed is infinite.

Finally, it should be noted that because this arguments deals with the times at which it is logically possible that the world actually existed, it bypasses concerns about whether the infinity arguments must be *a posteriori* (empirical) or can be merely *a priori*, that is, whether a reality exists in the actual world as an empirical or *a posteriori* question that is decided by experience, and not merely by whether we have a concept of it. C&C want to discuss the ontological status of infinities in the real world and not merely their conceptual status. Indeed, they reject the Platonic view that numbers and mathematical entities are real. If they admitted the Platonic view, then they would have to admit that not merely are infinities logically consistent, but also that infinities also *actually occur*. Indeed, it seems that there is in fact evidence that infinities actually occur in the real world because infinities turn up in standard quantum mechanical equations that give accurate predictions of quantum effects in the real world. Yet because C&C deal with actual infinities rather than with conceptual infinities, it is confusing to see how they can reach any conclusions based on a discussion of concepts and thought-experiments rather than empirical data.[29] My argument does not attempt to establish that infinities actually do or do not occur in the real world but instead demonstrates that it is logically possible that the world has always existed.

6.0 Conclusion

Copan and Craig have not given us any reason to believe that an eternal reality is either physically or logically impossible. The first argument commits the fallacy of equivocation. None of the supposedly absurd stories applies to the eternal universe. The second argument has two false premises. Those who believe in an infinite past do not claim that it can be formed by successive addition; in fact, they claim that it is in the nature of such realities that the concept of formation by successive addition doesn't apply. Thus, premise 2.1 is false. Moreover, the notion that it is impossible to add to an actual infinite is simply in error. Thus, premise 2.2 is also false.

Even if the arguments were sound, *per impossibile*, they would not apply to discontinuous spatio-temporal epochs such as those posited by the chaotic inflationary and quantum vacuum theories of cosmology. However, these theories must be considered to be speculative metaphysics rather than empirical science. I am speaking of possibilities, opening new horizons for consideration rather than dogmatically asserting that reality is actually structured as these theories predict. However, the recognition that it is logically possible that the world has al-

---

29. See the discussion in Graham Oppy, "Reply to Professor Craig," Sophia 34, no. 2 (December 1995), 15–29; "Craig, Mackie, and the Kalam Cosmological Argument," Religious Studies 27 (June 1991): 189–97; John Taylor, "Kalam: A Swift Argument from Origins to First Cause?" Religious Studies 33, no.2 (167–79); John L. Mackie, "The Miracle of Theism" (Oxford, England: Oxford University Press, 1982).

ways existed is not insignificant. It shows that it is not possible for the arguments suggesting otherwise to be constructed successfully.

16

Lehi's Opposition Theodicy

Dennis Potter, *Utah Valley University*

In 2 Nephi 2:11 the Book of Mormon prophet Lehi makes the claim that it is necessary that there is an opposition in all things. Among the examples of necessary oppositions he provides is the dichotomy of good vs. bad (i.e., evil). It might be natural, then, to look to Lehi's comment as the ground for a possible response to the argument from evil.[1] If the existence of good necessitates the existence of evil, then it may be impossible to have the best possible world without also having evil present in that world. If so, then an omnipotent God could be exonerated for allowing a world with evil.

The purpose of this paper is to examine this suggestion—I will call it *the opposition theodicy*. In this chapter I will not attempt to discover what Lehi actually had in mind, nor will I explore how evil might be a necessary condition for good due to the former's instrumental use in building character. The latter is the so-called soul-building (or soul-making) theodicy and this latter approach has been thoroughly discussed in the literature.[2] My task here, by contrast, is to find a more logically fundamental manner in which the good/evil opposition is necessary and, hence, to discern whether it is a competitive theodicy.

Opposition

In order to examine the opposition theodicy we must first analyze the possible meanings of the word "opposition" and its cognates. The word "opposition" is ambiguous. Just considering some examples of opposites

---

1. This is a well-known argument against God's existence. One version of the argument is as follows: If God exists, then he is omnipotent and omnibenevolent. An omnipotent being can do anything that is logically possible and an omnibenevolent being would want to make the world the best possible. This world is not the best possible world. Therefore, there is no God.

2. John Hick, *Evil and the God of Love* (San Francisco: Harper, 1978).

we see that the meaning of the word is different in different cases: black/white, good/evil, long/short, true/false, alive/dead, liberal/conservative, right/left, image/negative, force/resistance, offense/defense.

Some of these pairs are typically understood to be *absolute* oppositions (i.e., the terms of the opposition refer to mutually exclusive properties). For example, in classical logic no statement is both true and false. Although absolute oppositions may be mutually exclusive sets of properties they need not be exhaustive. Black and white are not the only colors, but nothing is both black and white in the same respects. Not everything is alive or dead. Some things are not alive and not dead, since they never were alive.

Some of these pairs of opposites are *relative* oppositions. A relative opposition arises from the fact that one pole of the opposition has its property by being related to the other pole. Being long or short is a matter of perspective. 26.2 miles is a relatively short distance if you are on an airplane, while relatively long if you are on foot. One cannot say something similar of true or false, alive or dead.

Some of these pairs involve an opposition between agentive forces, (i.e., *opposition of opponents*). In a particular football match, Manchester United is the opponent of Chelsea. Lex Luther is the opponent of Superman. Being opponents is something that may be relative to a certain time or even a certain aspect. Players on Manchester United that vote Labour are political opponents of their teammates that vote Conservative.

There are also other possible characteristics that determine different types of opposites such as *polarity* and *direction*. The complete exploration of all of the senses in which things can be opposites must be left to another paper. Here, I will focus on relative and absolute oppositions.

Necessity

In addition to understanding the potential meanings of the word "opposite" we must get clear on the potential meanings of the word "necessary." There is a lot to say about all the different kinds of necessities that I cannot examine here. However, for my purposes it is important to make two points. First, if the necessity involved in the opposition theodicy is something less than logical necessity, then the opposition theodicy cannot be used to preserve God's omnipotence. Indeed, the latter is usually defined in terms of logical possibility and thus God cannot be limited by anything but logical necessity. So, unless the coexistence of good and evil is logically necessary, then the necessity of their coexistence is not an explanation of the existence of evil. In the latter case, an omnipotent God could have created a world with good and without evil, logically speaking.

Second, there is a distinction between linguistic necessity and objective necessity. This is neither the same as the distinction between logical necessity and metaphysical necessity nor between *de re* and *de dicto* necessity. Linguistic necessity arises from the syntactic features of the language. The fact that it is necessary that all bachelors are unmarried is a linguistic necessity. It is a necessary truth because of the features of our language and not due to anything about the way the world is. Some have argued that logical necessity is a type of linguistic necessity. If logical necessity is a type of linguistic necessity, and if the good/evil opposition is logically necessary, then the existence of good and evil would arise from the features of our language. Good and evil, therefore, don't have objective reality; they are just a part of the conceptual framework we impose on the world. Such a conclusion would seem too relativistic for a typical Mormon theist.

In contrast with linguistic necessity, objective necessity is necessity that arises from the nature of the world. Objective necessity does not arise from the features of language. Linguistic necessity is similar to (but not exactly the same as) what David Hume referred to as knowledge based on Relations of Ideas: linguistic necessity is based on language alone, while Hume's Relations of Ideas depend on the relationships between and among human ideas alone. Objective necessity is similar to (but not exactly the same as) what Immanuel Kant claimed was synthetic *a priori*: its necessity depends on the way the world is and not just the way language is structured. Kant's synthetic *a priori* truth, though necessary, depends on the structure of appearance and not merely on how we talk.

So, given that interpreting opposition necessity as linguistic necessity yields relativism, it seems to follow that the advocate of the opposition theodicy must take logical necessity to be objective necessity. That is, logic must be a reflection of the very basic structure or general features of reality. I will return to these points below.

Logic of the Opposition Theodicy

We need to clarify the logic of the assertion that opposition is necessary in all things. In this most general form, it's hard to see what this might mean. Does it mean that everything that exists must have an opposite? It seems odd to say that some things have an opposite. For example, what would be the opposite of a bicycle? Perhaps a very large SUV?

Fortunately for our purposes we do not have to decide what it means to say that there must be an opposition in all things. Instead, we can simply entertain the claim that evil must exist for good to exist, and perhaps good must exist for evil to exist. But should we refer to good and evil with a name or with a predicate? If e refers to evil and g refers to good, then we have a statement of the form $[(\exists x)x=e \leftrightarrow (\exists x)x=g]$. But this feels like an odd way to put it. It says there is something that is identical to the Evil if and only if there is something that is identical to the Good. I suppose if e and g are mass terms then this might make some sense. But if so, then there is a quantity of stuff that is evil just as there is a quantity of stuff that is, say, water. Also, the claim that good and evil are "stuffs" makes it seem very implausible for them to be mutually necessary.

I think that it is more likely that good and evil are intended to be predicates. If so, then we have a statement of the form $[(\exists x)Gx \leftrightarrow (\exists x)Ex]$. A potential problem with this formulation of the claim is that it could be true if the amount of evil is far outweighed by the amount of good. In fact, such a claim is consistent with there being one instance of evil and millions of instances of good—call this the *minimal evil possibility*. If this is the logical force of the claim, then it is not clear how it would work as a basis for a theodicy for a world in which there are certainly many instances of evil actions and/or events.

To avoid the minimal evil possibility, one might say that there must be the same quantity of evil as there is of good. Formalizing this statement would be very complicated, and furthermore is unnecessary, since this Manichean proposal contradicts traditional Christianity. Christians claim that God is far more powerful and much greater than anything that might be evil. God's goodness is of a higher quantity than the quantity of any evil.

Instead, perhaps there is an instance of evil corresponding to (or opposing) every instance of good, where nothing is indicated about the quantities of these goods and evils. This claim has the following logical structure: $(\forall x)(Gx \rightarrow (\exists x)Ex)$. This proposal also seems odd once we think about its consequences. It entails that as I do good in the world then I thereby bring evil into the world as well, since without my good deed there would have been no necessity for the particular evil that opposes my action. The strangeness of this proposal for the logic of the opposition claim evades many because they often explain the opposition theodicy with an analogy with physics: for every action there is an equal and opposite reaction. But it seems that if we take this analogy seriously then we end up with a world in which we can hardly hope to increase the good without also increasing evil.

So, in trying to determine the logical form of the basic claim of the opposition theodicy it seems like we have a problem concerning the quantity of evil required for a particular quantity of good. Either we claim that the evil necessary for good is not enough to cover the evils in the world, or it's too much. I do not claim that there is no possible solution to this problem. But I see none forthcoming.

Relative and Absolute Oppositions

Let's suppose that we can find some way to make sense of the logical form of the claim that evil is necessary for good. If so, then this claim is supposed to be plausible because good and evil are opposites of some sort. But what sort?

J.L. Mackie considers the possibility that good and evil are opposites of the relative sort. He says:

> Perhaps the suggestion is that good and evil are related in much the same way as great and small. Certainly, when the term "great" is used relatively as a condensation of "greater than so-and-so," and "small" is used correspondingly, greatness and smallness are counterparts and cannot exist without each other. But in this sense greatness is not a quality, not an intrinsic feature of anything; and it would be absurd to think of a movement in favour of greatness and against smallness in this sense. (Presumably, one could think of a movement in favor of goodness and against evil). Such a movement would be self-defeating, since relative greatness can be promoted only by a simultaneous promotion of relative smallness. I feel sure that no theists would be content to regard God's goodness as analogous to this—as if what he supports were not the *good* but the *better*, and as if he had the paradoxical aim that all things should be better than other things.[3]

---

3. J. L. Mackie, "Evil and Omnipotence," *Mind* 64 (1955): 204.

So, Mackie's argument against the relative understanding of the good/evil opposition is that good and evil are not really analogous to opposing terms that are relative. He employs the greater/smaller opposition to show this. Being relative, greatness and smallness are not based on intrinsic features of the objects so designated. So, although it is true that the *concepts* of greater and smaller logically must exist in conjunction (if they exist at all), it seems to be a necessity that is based on a feature of our language rather than a feature of the world. In other words, it's a linguistic rather than an objective necessity. And, to repeat an earlier point, if the good/evil opposition is merely linguistically necessary, then good and evil would not be necessary features of the world, just necessary features of talking about it.

One might argue that the relative character of the greater/smaller opposition is compatible with its being based on something objective. Indeed, it's the objective size of objects that makes one greater than another. Yet, it would be strange to say that the existence of an object of one size requires the existence of some object of another size. And this seems to imply that the *necessity* of the greater/smaller opposition is not based on the actual sizes of the objects of the universe.

Perhaps the problem here is our choice of analogy (i.e., comparing good/evil to greater/lesser rather than better/worse). Preference utilitarianism claims that some consequences are better than others (which are worse) based on our preferences regarding those consequences. According to this view, actions can be related to each other by virtue of the preference of one over another. Preference does not have to be the kind of thing that could be reduced to an objective non-relative feature of the world (the "preferential" equivalent of objective size). I might just prefer chocolate to vanilla without chocolate having more of a certain quantity that thereby makes it preferable to the vanilla. So, on the utilitarian view, the good/evil opposition would be relative in our sense: it is reduced to the better/worse opposition. And, unlike the greater/smaller opposition, the better/worse opposition (based on preference) might not be reducible to some set of non-relative objective properties and/or relations.

The question is whether preference can be construed as an objective feature of the world. However, it seems to me that preference is a paradigm case of something that is subjective. So, this route to making sense of the opposition theodicy entails a subjectivist approach to ethics. Mormons who take this route in defense of the opposition theodicy might decide to bite this bullet. However, on one popular Mormon view, God himself is subject to moral laws. It is not clear how such a view would be reconciled with a subjectivist construal or moral language.

To sum up the last few paragraphs, it would seem that there is more to the suggestion that the good/evil opposition is more relative than Mackie allows. The idea that the concept of preference is at the heart of the better/worse (a.k.a. good/evil) opposition seems to have some plausibility. However, it also appears to involve a meta-ethical theory that many Mormons would find implausible or problematic.

Suppose that the good/evil opposition is *absolute*. It is absolute just in case there is a property corresponding to good and one corresponding to evil and they are mutually exclusive. On this view, one might assert that actions, rather than consequences, are good or evil. One can understand the goodness/evilness of actions in terms of a deontological approach. According to the deontological approach, actions that are mandated by moral law are good and ones that contravene moral law are evil.

On the deontological view, good and evil are based on real features of the world insofar as they arise from the relational properties that actions have to certain laws. The question is whether the fact of the existence of good actions necessitates that there are evil actions. It is not clear why there must be some actions that contravene moral laws if there are some actions in conformity with it.

Perhaps one could argue that there must be the possibility of actions that contravene a moral law for there to be some actions which conform to it. It is plausible to say that someone must be able to break the rules in order to be able to obey the rules. However, this only establishes that the possibility of evil is necessary for actual good. And that does not help to explain the existence of actual evil in the world. Of course, it is natural to say that free will explains the fact that evil is not just possible but actual. If so, then this seems to dovetail with the "free will defense," as advocated by theists such as Alvin Plantinga. As with the soul-building theodicy, much has already been written about the free will defense, whereas my interest here is whether the opposition theodicy constitutes a viable and *unique* alternative answer to the problem of evil.

Sticking with the absolute reading of the good/evil opposition, we might suggest that good is a property and evil is just the privation of good (i.e., the property of not having goodness). Perhaps one would argue that if nothing lacks a property then nothing has the property either. But, as Mackie points out, it doesn't seem logically impossible for everything that exists to have the same property. Indeed many would say that it is not logically impossible for there to be only one thing. If so, then by a trivial implication everything would have at least one property in common. Alternatively, if one argues that there must be difference at the foundation of anything that exists then it would seem that one must deny Christian Theism. Indeed, God is supposed to be capable of existing alone and is ontologically simple. His creation (that which is other than God) is not necessary but an act of will.

Conclusion

The foregoing arguments, though preliminary, suggest the following: if an understanding of the good/evil opposition involves some characteristics that clearly ground it in an objective reality (such as when it is interpreted absolutely) then it is unlikely to be a necessary opposition. Alternatively, if an understanding of the good/evil opposition involves necessity, it is not clear that this necessity will be based on something objective. It seems that our alternatives are that it is a linguistic necessity *or* that it is based on a non-linguistic fact (preference) that is nevertheless subjective. The former makes the fact that God cannot eliminate evil similar to the fact that he cannot contravene the laws of logic. On this view, then, the existence of evil is a result of the way we talk about the world merely. This, I think, is an unsavory implication of the opposition theodicy.

The idea that moral language is based on something subjective such as preference is more attractive (to me) and makes sense of the good/evil opposition's irreducibly relative character without forcing us to conclude that the necessity involved is merely linguistic. But preferences are themselves subjective, and theists typically prefer moral realism to moral subjectivism. Also, Mormons have an additional reason to reject moral subjectivism due to their unique views concerning the nature of God.

Another possibility is that there is an irreducibly relative interpretation of the good/evil opposition that is based on something objective. But my considerations above suggest that if the good/evil opposition is based on something objective, then it is reducible to a non-relative opposition (and hence does not involve the right kind of necessity). A final possibility is that the good/evil opposition is absolute but that we have yet to understand its character. And that would mean that we have yet to really understand the nature of the opposition theodicy.

17

All's Well that Ends Well: Evil, Eschatology, and Love in F. W. J. Schelling and David L. Paulsen

James M. McLachlan, *Western Carolina University*

I doubt David Paulsen remembers, but in the summer of 1985, when I was a part-time faculty member at BYU, he gave me a ride to the bus. While en route we discussed philosophers William James and Friedrich Schelling. I had recently heard him talk about James and Joseph Smith, and the possibility of shipwreck with a finite God, so I brought up the notion of a type of pantheism I had found in Schelling that was an alternative to James's finite deity. In James's deity there seemed to be a genuine risk of failure (meaning that God's purposes could theoretically be thwarted), but Schelling's deity did not face such a genuine risk. David questioned if authentic freedom was compatible with a metaphysical guarantee that both the world would work out and that God's purposed would *necessarily* be fulfilled. For the last 23 years I've thought about his question and this chapter is essentially my response.

This conundrum is an old one in religion, and Christian religion in particular. Historian Jeffrey Burton Russell discussed it in the second volume of his history of evil in the Western tradition.[1] There, he asserts that we commonly try to solve the problem of evil in one of two ways. One way is the temptation toward monism.[2] Here, all events are ultimately caused by God. In allowing that God has all power we inevitably subtract from divine goodness. In such cases God becomes the omnipotent God of the theological tradition that finds its culmination in John Calvin's doctrine of double pre-destination. The Russian

---

1. Jeffrey Burton Russell, *Satan: The Early Christian Tradition* (New York: Cornell University Press, 1981), 17.
2. Monism is the theory that denies the distinction or duality between matter and the mind or between God and the world.

Orthodox philosopher Nikolai Berdyaev thought that the great contribution of Calvin's horrible doctrine to Christian thought was to reduce omnipotence to an absurdity.[3] Similarly, Reverend John Hagee memorably expressed the vulgar version of Calvin's hyper-omnipotence: God raised up Adolf Hitler to bring about the Holocaust to get the Jews back to Israel so we could have Armageddon. It was all part of the plan.[4]

But we can also go the other way toward dualism or pluralism and reduce God's power to save God's goodness. Here, we can fall into the difficulty of having too weak a God, one that knows just enough, and who has just enough power to muddle through. There is biblical support for either position: there is a God that hardens Pharaoh's heart in order to show his power, and whom Isaiah says bestows both good and evil on the world (Isa. 45:7). There is also a God who, after seeing the violence of the world, repents of having made humanity, tries to kill Moses because he hadn't circumcised his son, bargains with Abraham about Sodom, and so on. The problem is lessened but still persists in LDS scripture. Joseph Smith's translation of the Bible takes away God's responsibility for hardening Pharaoh's heart, but numerous passages still remind us of God's power, and that things will ultimately align with God's will.

Each side of the debate has its means for interpreting the difficult passages that don't support its position. This seems to be the way that God is often presented in scriptural traditions of the West, whether Jewish, traditional Christian, Islamic, or LDS. In the biblical tradition, for example, depending on the writer (and sometimes even on the moment) God is presented as knowing the future completely, or not knowing what will be done; as inviting repentance and knowing whether we will repent; demanding that Pharaoh let the people go and then hardening his heart (Ex. 10:1, 20); or calling for Israel to repent yet making their ears heavy and their hearts fat (Isa. 6:9–10).

In the introduction to his classic text on process theodicy, *God, Power, and Evil*, David Ray Griffin noted the difficulty of arguing about divine foreknowledge and power using the scriptural tradition: "It can be

---

3. Nicolas Berdyaev, *The Destiny of Man*, trans. Natalie Duddington (London: Geofrey Bles, 1937), 24.

4. In Sam Stein, "McCain Backer Hagee Said Hitler Was Fulfilling God's Will," *Huffington Post*, May 21, 2008, http://www.huffingtonpost.com/2008/05/21/mccain-backer-hagee-said_n_102892.html (accessed May 8, 2012).

cited by defenders of absolute divine determinism as well as advocates of creaturely freedom vis-à-vis God. The passages that are relevant to the topic are legion."[5] The problem is that the scriptural tradition, written and created through many authors, is, like the human heart, wider and broader than what a strict systematic consistency concerning these questions will allow. It should be no surprise that these tensions also exist in the LDS tradition. For although in his "Inspired Translation" of the King James Bible Joseph Smith altered the story of Pharaoh so that God did not harden Pharaoh's heart but rather the Pharaoh hardened his own heart, there are still many instances where God's coercive power is manifested.[6] David Paulsen and I both fall, I think, on the "lessen God's power" side of the tension between monism and dualism/pluralism, but the question is always how one describes the tensions and addresses the problems that arise when we try to resolve them. In a recent presentation, "Searching for an Adequate Theodicy: David Griffin and Mormon Thought,"[7] David Paulsen has shown that he does not want to go as far as process theology in eliminating the coercive power of God, thereby positing a God of merely persuasive power—or, as Berdyaev so cleverly put it, a God, that from the point of view of coercion, "has less power than a

---

5. David Ray Griffin, *God, Power, and Evil: A Process Theodicy* (Philadelphia: The Westminster Press, 1976), 31.

6. Joseph Smith endeavored a re-reading or "translation" of the King James Version (KJV) of the Bible on which he worked for years but never completed. Smith softened passages like Isaiah 6:9 to read; "And he said, Go, and tell this people: Hear ye indeed but *they* understand not, and see ye indeed, but *they* perceive*d* not." Notice that the addition of the "they" and the change of "perceive" to the past tense places the responsibility for action on the human subjects. They refused to hear or perceive because of the hardness of their hearts. This emphasis on the freedom of the human being in relation to God is made even more clearly in Smith's re-reading of Exodus 14. This passage in the KJV reads that God would harden or had hardened Pharaoh's heart so that he would not let the Hebrews go, thereby allowing God to demonstrate His power by bringing on the many plagues that would result in the death of the first born and the destruction of Pharaoh's army. Smith changed each of these "I will harden" statements to "Pharaoh will harden" or the "Egyptians will harden." Thus, for Smith, God does not, perhaps cannot, coerce the human heart. See "Joseph Smith's 'New Translation' of the Bible," ed. Paul A. Wellington (Independence, Mo.: Herald House Publishing, 1970), 123, 198.

7. David L. Paulsen, "Searching For an Adequate Theodicy: David Griffin and Mormon Thought," paper presented at the Members' Seminar, Highlands Institute for American Religious and Philosophical Thought, Highlands, North Carolina, June 17, 2009. Unpublished copy in author's possession, used with permission.

policeman."[8] Paulsen's contention here is certainly in line with scripture, where even in LDS scripture God is apparently physically coercive, even though God never coerces the human heart.[9]

These tensions between the nature of God's power and love are uniquely and creatively reflected upon in the work of early process and personalist[10] thinker F. W. J. Schelling. I will argue in this essay that Schelling offers real possibilities for Mormons who want to think about issues of divine power, human freedom, evil, and eschatology. I will also engage some of David Paulsen's writings on these same subjects, particularly his "Joseph Smith and the Problem of Evil";[11] "The God of Abraham, Isaac, and William James";[12] and the above-mentioned essay on process theodicy and eschatology, "Searching for an Adequate Theodicy." My essay will in large part be appreciative of Paulsen's work, but also charitably critical of several of the positions he has taken. By exploring the conceptual areas where Schelling's and Paulsen's work intersects, I am returning in a more reflective and expansive fashion to the significant question that Paulsen raised in our discussion about Schelling so long ago.

Schelling: The Absolute and Finite God

In what Schelling scholars call the middle period of his thought, Schelling departs from the more traditional notion of pantheism that had made him famous among the Romantics due to his *The System of*

---

8. Nikolai Berdyaev, *Dream and Reality: An Essay in Autobiography*, trans. Katherine Lampert (New York: Macmillan, 1950), 177. Berdyaev points out that the term "power" should not even be applied to God at all, as power arises out of social and political contexts that are then erroneously applied to God.

9. Among numerous examples, see Jacob 7:14–15, Doctrine and Covenants 5:3, and the Alma 14 narrative, which definitely imply that God could use coercive power if he so desired.

10. Personalism is a philosophical system of thought that maintains the primacy of the human or divine person on the basis that reality has meaning only through the conscious mind.

11. David L. Paulsen, "Joseph Smith and the Problem of Evil," *BYU Studies* 39, no. 1 (2000).

12. David L. Paulsen, "The God of Abraham, Isaac, and William James," *The Journal of Speculative Philosophy* 13, no. 2 (1999).

Transcendental Idealism and *Philosophy and Religion*.[13] In 1809 he published *The Essay Concerning the Essence of Human Freedom and Related Matters*. This essay's publication appeared the same year as the death of his wife Caroline and is concerned primarily with the question of theodicy. It is perhaps the greatest work on theodicy to come out of German idealism, a philosophical movement that emerged in the late eighteenth and early nineteenth centuries, and one obsessed with the question of the problem of evil. The failure of Schelling's early systems to adequately express his intuition of human freedom led him to the 1809 essay on freedom, which Martin Heidegger called "One of the most profound works of German, and thus of Western philosophy."[14] Despite the Teutonic hubris of this statement, others share Heidegger's recognition of the importance of this essay. Holocaust philosopher Emil Fackenheim, for example, has noted that among Western philosophers only Schelling really deals with the idea of radical evil.[15]

I believe it is generally in harmony with LDS teachings that God must be both finite and infinite: finite in order to understand the anxiety of suffering and to be able to authentically love; and infinite in order to be able to comprehend the whole of reality. I think that one way to think about God as both finite and infinite is to distinguish between God as a personal being and God as the impersonal absolute. Several philosophers in the twentieth-century have attempted this in various ways, including personalist philosophers such as Edgar Sheffield Brightman and process thinkers like Alfred North Whitehead. Such a solution is also found in the seventeenth-century German mystic Jacob Böehme and in some of the nineteenth-century romantics that expanded and rationalized Böehme's visions: Franz Von Baader and F. W. J. Schelling. I find a similar solution to the problem in some early Mormon thinkers as well. Here, intelligence is the primal ground or (infinite) absolute and personal (finite) beings develop from this ground. Consider the following description of the Mormon understanding of God from early twentieth-century LDS leader, Charles W. Penrose:

---

13. See F. W. J Schelling, *The System of Transcendental Idealism* trans. Peter Heath (Virginia: University of Virginia Press, 1978 [1800]); *Philosophy and Religion* trans. Klaus Ottman (Spring Publications, 2010 [1804]).

14. Martin Heidegger, *Schelling's Treatise: On the Essence of Human Freedom*, trans. Joan Stambaugh (Athens: Ohio University Press, 1985), 2.

15. Emil Fackenheim, *To Mend the World: Foundations of Future Jewish Thought* (New York: Schocken Books, Inc., 1982), 234.

But, if God is an individual spirit and dwells in a body, the question will arise, "Is He the Eternal Father?" Yes, He is the Eternal Father. "Is it a fact that He never had a beginning?" In the elementary particles of His organism, He did not. But if He is an organized Being, there must have been a time when that being was organized.... This spirit which pervades all things, which is the light and life of all things, by which our heavenly Father operates, by which He is omnipotent, never had a beginning and never will have an end. It is the light of truth; it is the spirit of intelligence. If you see a living blade of grass you see a manifestation of that Spirit which is called God. If you see an animal of any kind on the face of the earth having life, there is a manifestation of that Spirit. If you see a man you behold its most perfect earthly manifestation. And if you see a glorified man, a man who has passed through the various grades of being, who has overcome all things, who has been raised from the dead, who has been quickened by this spirit in its fullness, there you see manifested, in its perfection, this eternal, beginningless, endless spirit of intelligence.

Such a Being is our Father and our God, and we are following in His footsteps. He has attained to perfection.... This spirit cannot be fully comprehended in our finite state. It quickens all things.[16]

What Penrose describes here is an experience of the ultimate in both a personal and impersonal form. For God, there was a time—before God existed as a person—when being was organized. But, "This spirit which pervades all things, which is the light and life of all things, by which our heavenly Father operates, by which He is omnipotent, never had a beginning and never will have an end." This is an ultimate that advances from an impersonal to a personal form, an unusual development in the history of religious thought. In traditional theism the eternal personal being exists in eternity, outside of space and time. Similarly, in many Eastern and mystical traditions the eternal impersonal absolute exist in eternity, transcending time and space. Here, we have a personal form of God the eternal Father and an impersonal form as Spirit and Intelligence. The personal form exists in time and space, and, as we will see (unlike in most Eastern and mystical traditions), this personal being is an improvement or a fulfillment of an impersonal absolute. Yet it is the structure of existence that implies the mutual inter-

---

16. Charles W. Penrose, November 16, 1884, *Journal of Discourses*, 26 vols. (London and Liverpool: LDS Booksellers Depot, 1854–86), 26:23–24.

dependence of all finite beings—and particularly personal ones—that will provide an absolute moral law that constitutes existing individuals.

Act One:
Joseph Smith, Schelling, and the Positive Fall

For David Paulsen, one of the pillars of Joseph Smith's solution to the problem of evil is the rejection of creation *ex nihilo* and the absolute transcendent God, existing in blissful eternity, that creation *ex nihilo* protects.[17] This implies a rejection of the traditional notion of omnipotence. God is not completely transcendent of the world because God struggles with the pre-existing chaos, bringing it to order.

Nevertheless, Penrose and other Mormon writers of his time, like James Talmage, still used the terms "omnipotence" and "omniscience" to describe God. But creation from chaos requires that omnipotence and omniscience be redefined. We no longer have the story of a transcendent being outside of space and time possessing all power and knowledge, resulting in the world's total dependence on that being for its existence. Omnipotence and omniscience now mean that God possesses all *possible* power and knowledge. God's power is limited by the freedom of other independent beings and God's knowledge is limited by time. The future does not yet exist; thus, God knows all that is but God cannot know what is not. Creation comes to mean creation from chaos, forming order from pre-existent disorder.

This idea of creation from chaos is older than the theological doctrine of creation from nothing.[18] Creation from nothing became such a

---

17. Paulsen, "Joseph Smith and the Problem of Evil," 55–56. This paper was expanded in David L. Paulsen and Blake T. Ostler, "Sin, Suffering, and Soul Making: Joseph Smith and the Problem of Evil" in *Revelation, Reason, and Faith: Essays in Honor of Truman G. Madsen*, eds. Donald W. Parry, Daniel C. Peterson, and Stephen D. Ricks (Provo, Utah: Foundation for Ancient Research and Mormon Studies, 2002), 237–84.

18. The idea of creation from chaos is older in Western religions than ideas of creation ex nihilo which Gerhard May, a theological proponent of ex nihilo creation, argues does not appear until the second century. See Gerhard May, *Creation Ex Nihilo: The Doctrine of 'Creation from Nothing' in Early Christian Thought*, trans. A. S. Worrall (Edinburgh, Scotland: T&T Clark, 1994); Jon Levenson, *Creation and the Persistence of Evil: The Jewish Drama of Divine Omnipotence* (Princeton, N.J.: Princeton University Press, 1994); and David Ray Griffin, "Creation Out of

powerful part of Western theological traditions because it protected the unchanging perfection of the classical deity. The problem with the classical understanding of deity *is* the problem of evil, seen most acutely as the problem of innocent suffering. How can an omnipotent, omniscient, and omni-benevolent being allow such occurrences as the Holocaust and disease when that being has the capacity to prevent them, or a least the foresight not to create the conditions for such things in the first place? Remember, in the classical sense, God, in his perfection, did not need the world. This was Ivan Karamazov's famous question, which has always been a source of both struggle for the faithful and an endless debate for philosophers and theologians. Paulsen notes that this is not a problem for Joseph Smith because Smith rejected the notion of creation *ex nihilo* and the notion of God that it protected. In his appreciation of this position Paulsen has often favored William James's idea of a "finite" God. In his 1999 article on James, Paulsen quotes with appreciation James's idea of the adventure of the creation. James holds that belief in a finite god is pragmatically richer than belief in an absolutely unlimited God because it provides greater impetus to our moral endeavors:

> I am going to make a world not certain to be saved, a world the perfection of which shall be conditional merely, the condition being that each several agent does its own "level best." I offer you the chance of taking part in such a world. Its safety, you see, is unwarranted. It is a real adventure, with real danger, yet it may win through. It is a social scheme of co-operative work genuinely to be done. Will you join the procession? Will you trust yourself and trust the other agents enough to face the risk? [19]

James's and Paulsen's God is not the totally transcendent deity of the tradition. But, as Paulsen points out in his essay on David Griffin's theodicy, traditional theists like Stephen Davis question whether such a God is strong enough to solve the problem of evil because he cannot guarantee the final victory of good, value, and meaning over evil and the absurd.[20] Paulsen cites James's famous "chess game analogy"

Nothing, Creation Out of Chaos, and the Problem of Evil" in *Encountering Evil*, 2nd edition, ed. Stephen T. Davis (Louisville, Ky.: Westminster and John Knox: 2001), 108–44.

19. William James, *Pragmatism* (Cambridge, Mass.: Harvard University Press, 1975), 139. Quoted in Paulsen, "The God of Abraham, Isaac, and William James," 124.

20. Paulsen, "Searching for an Adequate Theodicy."

as a means to protect both compatibilist freedom and providence. In it the master always beats the novice, "And the victory infallibly arrives, after no matter how devious a course."[21] Though the analogy seems to work whether God is playing chess with the devil or with me, Davis's question lingers over whether it works if God is playing against the brute meaninglessness of the universe. And the universe, of course, is an incredibly complex and changing organism. This, I think, is a far more difficult question for a finite God and it is not immediately clear, as James noted in *Pragmatism*, that such a God can triumph over meaninglessness. James, nonetheless, thought the risk was worth it. Though I must admit that, along with William James and David Paulsen, I would prefer such a God to the classical deity for the same reasons James gives above, I think we recognize the need for a God who is down here in the dirt fighting the fight with us. At least that God is in the mix with the rest of us. Schelling, on the other hand, tried a slightly different tack: a very unique form of pantheism.

By the time Schelling wrote his *Freedom* essay in 1809 he had left behind the more traditional pantheism of his earlier works that had endeared him to the Romantic artists. Instead, Schelling attempted a pantheism distinct from Spinoza's mechanical pantheism, which had activated the pantheism controversy that had rocked German thought in the debate between Friedrich Jacobi and Moses Mendelssohn.[22]

As Dale Snow has noted, in the *Freedom* essay Schelling "shattered the assumptions that had provided the framework for his earlier thought."[23] Schelling moved away from the monism of *The System of Transcendental Idealism*, *Philosophy and Religion*, and *Philosophy of Nature*. In this essay Schelling became a personalistic thinker. Here he sought

---

21. William James, "The Dilemma of Determinism," in *The Will to Believe and Other Essays in Popular Philosophy* (Cambridge, Mass.: Harvard University Press), 138. Quoted in Paulsen, "The God of Abraham, Isaac, and William James," 127.

22. See F. H. Jacobi, *Die Hauptschriften zum Pantheismusstreit zwischen Jacobi und Mendelssohn*, ed. H. Scholz (Berlin, Germany: Reuther and Riechard, 1916) for an overview of all relevant texts in the dispute between Jacobi and Mendelssohn. For a more general (and contemporary) treatment of the controversy and the intellectual context out of which it was born, see George di Giovanni, *Freedom and Religion in Kant and His Immediate Successors: The Vocation of Humankind, 1774–1800* (Cambridge: Cambridge University Press, 2005).

23. Dale E. Snow, *Schelling and the End of Idealism* (Albany: State University of New York Press, 1996), 181.

to draw out the consequences of a philosophy that does justice to the opaque and irrational elements of the person's experience of reality. Central among these is the experience of freedom. In the experience of freedom there is something that cannot be rationalized, an "irreducible remainder." Jan Olof Bengtsson correctly notes that what Schelling attempts in the *Freiheitsschrift* (Freedom essay) is a "pantheism of freedom" that is built on a new understanding of the relation between creative freedom and necessity.[24] Schelling seeks to replace the epistemologically charged concept of the subject with the living personality. He thought the problem with Spinozan pantheism was its mechanism and determinism. He said of Spinoza, "He treats the will, too, as a thing, and then very naturally proves that in its working it must in every case be determined by another thing, which in turn is determined by another, and so forth endlessly. Hence the lifelessness of his system."[25] Schelling thought that "we have to 'penetrate above the general to personality. For 'reason and law do not love, only the person can love and to love.'"[26] This movement is key for everything that will follow. Schelling thinks much like Lehi in 2 Nephi 2 in the Book of Mormon—that the absolute is dead without opposition and difference, and thus without plurality.

Schelling's view is based on the image of an initial groundlessness at the beginning of the development of Being. God is involved in the destiny of the world and is affected by the suffering and love that develop here. As the absolute, God is the Eternal Nothing, the eternal One, and the impersonal ultimate. Schelling borrows a term from the seventeenth-century German mystic Jacob Böehme to describe this basis—the *Ungrund*, or the groundless. In Schelling this is the absolute, the source of freedom that is at the basis of all that is. As the absolute, God is not really worthy of worship because God as the one is the nothing that precedes the personal God.[27]

---

24. Jan Olof Bengtsson, *The Worldview of Personalism* (Oxford: Oxford University Press, 2005).

25. F. W. J. Schelling, *Philosophical Inquiries Into the Nature of Human Freedom*, trans. James Gutmann (Chicago, Ill.: Open Court, 1936), 22–23; *Sämmtliche Werke*, edited K.F.A. Schelling, I Abtheilung Volumes 1–10, II Abtheilung Vols. 1–4, (Stuttgart: Cotta, 1856–61,) 7:349.

26. Schelling, *Werke*, xi, 566, 569–70.

27. Böehme gives a nice description of this in his commentary on creation from chaos and the Book of Genesis:

> When I consider what God is, then I say, He is the One; in reference to the

God as the One is nothing. Without the creature, without nature, without real others there is no determination about God; there is nothing to say about God. God is not will, not body, not space. If one called such a being perfect it would have to be the perfection of perfect vagueness, perfectly boring, and perfectly empty. This vagueness, this boring oneness is, of course, also bliss. It is like the vague, boring, meaningless statements uttered by so many American politicians. We find nothing to disagree with because there is nothing there. If they were actually to say or do something then conflict would arise. The only name that can be given to it is the Absolute, *The Ungrund*, or the abyss without bottom. It is an abyss in which one can find neither foundation nor a reason for things, where not even God finds his foundation. In creating the world God creates God as well. The basic difference between Böehme and Schelling and the previous Christian mystics of the NeoPlatonic tradition is that Schelling did not regard the Absolute primarily as Being but as Will. The will and desire to be something makes the Absolute dynamic. But it also makes the beginning of things not something to which we would wish to return.

We might compare Schelling's thought here with 2 Nephi 2, which provides us an outline of a basic eschatology of Mormonism. 2 Nephi 2 reflects a movement from an unconscious or dead unity in either Eden, the pre-mortal existence, or the unity of the primal chaos before God's creative acts, to an alienated conflictual multiplicity of this world, and finally to a freely chosen conscious unity in multiplicity or sociality of love in both this world and the world to come (D&C 130:1–2). But it is clearly the case that the plurality of the world, with all its conflict, is superior to the serenity of the One:

---

creature, as an eternal Nothing; as an eternal Nothing; he hath neither foundation, beginning, no abode; he posesseth nothing, save only himself: he is the will of the abyss; he is in himself only one; he needeth neither space, no place; he begetteth himself in himself, from eternity to eternity; he is neither like no resembleth anything; and hath no peculiar place where he dwelleth; he is the will of the wisdom; the wisdom is his manifestation. Cited in Jacob Böehme, *Mysterium Magnum*, vol. 1, 3rd ed., trans. John Sparrow (Hermetica Press, 2007), 2.

The key notion here in relation to Mormonism (and that is different from the Western theistic tradition and Eastern traditions) is that this is not a perfection. God lacks reality. God lacks love.

For it must needs be, that there is an opposition in all things. If not so, my firstborn in the wilderness, righteousness could not be brought to pass, neither wickedness, neither holiness nor misery, neither good nor bad. *Wherefore, all things must needs be a compound in one; wherefore, if it should be one body it must needs remain as dead, having no life neither death, nor corruption nor incorruption, happiness nor misery, neither sense nor insensibility.*

Wherefore, it must needs have been created for a thing of naught; wherefore there would have been no purpose in the end of its creation. Wherefore, this thing must needs destroy the wisdom of God and his eternal purposes, and also the power, and the mercy, and the justice of God. (2 Ne. 2:11–12, emphasis added)

The problem with the eternal bliss of the One is that it is dead. Thus, it may be unified but it is a dead perfection. It is the opposition of all things that makes joy—indeed, persons themselves—possible. This is a movement from the serenity of oneness to the difficulties and richness of the world. Both Schelling and Joseph Smith read the Genesis narrative as a "positive fall" that opens a future richer relation with God and others while simultaneously also opening the possibility of greater suffering. Schelling's point is that it is easy to love the general, conceptual foundation. It would be easier for God to love the Platonic ideal of humanity than it would be for God to love the many of us, sometimes obnoxious, human beings. Likewise, it is easier for *us* to love ideals than it is for us to love concrete human beings.

Father Zosima says as much to Madame Khokhlakov in *The Brothers Karamazov*: "And if you reach complete selflessness in the love of your neighbor, then undoubtedly you will believe, and no doubt will even be able to enter your soul."[28] Only an active love of concrete others makes real love possible. It is easy to love "humanity;" humanity is an abstraction. Loving concrete persons who are other than us, and who limit our fantasies is more difficult. Schelling made this movement from the egoistic bliss of vague plurality and love into a general metaphysical principle.

Schelling's analysis of the birth of God as the ideal person begins with the break from the general, from the absolute, which is undifferentiated. God moves from the ground to existence, from the chaos of possibility to actuality. These are Schelling's two dialectical opposites:

---

28. Fyodor Dostoevsky, *The Brothers Karamazov*, trans. Richard Pevear and Larissa Volkhonsky (New York: Farrar, Straus, and Giroux, 1990), 56.

the will of love and the will of the basis. The move to the actuality of plurality is also the positing of limitation and finitude that is essential to personality. One is limited by the other and the existence of the other is what creates the possibility of love:

> The being of the ground of that which exists can only be that which comes *before* all ground, thus, the absolute considered merely in itself, the non-ground. But, as proved it cannot be this in any other way than in so far as it divides into two equally eternal beginnings, not that it can be both *at once*, but that it is in each *in the same way*, thus in each the whole, or its own being. *But the non-ground divides itself into the two exactly equal beginnings, only so that the two, which could not exist simultaneously or be one in it as the non-ground, become one through love, that is, it divides itself only so that there may be life and love and personal existence.*[29]

The groundless divides itself into "two equally eternal beginnings." Although this sounds like the wildest of metaphysical speculations about the origin of being and God, Schelling's description here hinges on his idea that we know God through our own experience of freedom. Our actions exist in relation to situations that limit us. God's freedom is similar.

Schelling is making a concrete phenomenological observation about human freedom as an irreducible remainder, as something that is left over after any analysis. There is something about the origin of decision that despite out best efforts at analysis remains irreducibly opaque. To analyze freedom completely would be to analyze it away. For example, in LDS terms why does Alma choose to change his heart in the abyss of his suffering and grab hold of the name of Christ? Why does Korihor remain in rebellion even in his despair? Why does Satan choose to rebel out of self-love, while Christ chooses to follow his Father out of love? We have no final answer to these questions though each of us understands them to a certain extent because we have also made choices. This choice is the establishment of order in the world. Schelling calls freedom the irreducible remainder. It is the chaos at the basis of everything, the unreasonable out of which reason is born:

> The world as we now behold it, is all rule, order and form but the unruly lies ever in the depth as though it might again break through, and order and form nowhere appear to have been original, but it seems as

---

29. F. W. J. Schelling, *Philosophical Investigations into the Essence of Human Freedom*, trans. Jeff Love and Johannes Schmidt (Albany: State University of New York Press, 2007), 69–70; *Werke*, 7:408; emphasis added.

though what had initially been unruly had been brought to order. This is the incomprehensible basis of the reality of things, the irreducible remainder that cannot be resolved into reason by the greatest exertion but always remains in the depths. Out of this, which is unreasonable, reason in the true sense is born.[30]

Schelling's metaphysical attempt in the *Freedom* essay is to explain that the origin of God as personal and the human experience of freedom is the one and the same central principle that connects deity, humanity, and Being. Schelling claimed God *is* the absolute, but as the absolute ground of being God is also self-identical. However, the notion of God as absolute is prior to, but also inferior to, God as person. God as person is also finite; the ideal of the person presupposes an Other. These two terms—the absolute ground and the existent becoming—best express the two sides of divinity. Schelling sees these two moments as the key elements of the divine self-consciousness: God is conditioned, but through the act of decision and creation God becomes a person.

Schelling argued that all personal existence must be conditioned. This would be like the divine eternal spirit that Penrose describes above. Persons must exist in relation to others. They are finite in relation to each other, but infinite as they participate in freedom. Thus, Schelling actually argued for a three-part notion of the person and God as the ultimate person. First, God as the ground, as potential, as will, as vagueness, as bliss, is the absolute. Second, God as actual existence is finite in that God has actualized possibility in the creation of the world, an action that creates the self and the other: "Each organic individual is something which has become, has its being only through another, and to this extent it is dependent in terms of becoming, but not at all in terms of being."[31] Schelling argued that God could only reveal Godself in beings that resemble God—beings that must also make decisions: "The procession of things from God is a self revelation of God. But God can only reveal himself to himself in what is like him, in free beings acting on their own, for whose Being there is no ground other than God but who are as God is."[32] Thus, things once created are alive in themselves, and Schelling claims that they have divinity in them: "He speaks, and they are there" means that to speak is to speak to another.

---

30. Schelling, *Philosophical Investigations*, 29; *Werke*, 7:359–60.
31. Schelling, *Philosophical Investigations*, 18; *Werke*, 7:346.
32. Schellling, *Philosophical Investigations*, 18–19; *Werke*, 7:346

God requires humanity.³³ But this evolution includes a third moment of reflection. God must be conscious of Godself as ground, conscious of its product, and conscious of the relationship to its product. So God as conscious of the world incorporates the world without annulling the distinction between God and the world.³⁴

The process theologian Joseph Bracken has pointed out that the true unity of human consciousness in Schelling is not unity as the dialectical principle as opposed to individual existence, nor is it the ground of the divine being. It is, rather, the inscrutable act of free choice, whereby the individual determines the relation between the unity or the will to love, and self-existence, the will of the basis, and thus becomes spirit.³⁵ An individual either becomes good spirit in the imitation of God or evil in rebellion against God. In either case the ground of human existence is not a dialectical principle but a free choice. The power of the free choice is constantly being exercised, and either confirms or changes the relation between unity and self-existence within human consciousness. Bracken calls this a dynamic principle of balance. This is the implicit paradigm for both human and divine freedom in the *Freedom* essay. In personality, however, one of the two principles is subordinated and not eliminated, thereby creating a differentiated unity, the person. But notice that it is the human being that makes the decision both about which principle is subordinated and how either the will of love or the will of the basis will be subject to the other. Thus, each human being by her decision constitutes her self-consciousness as personality or spirit.

Schelling argued that human freedom is "the power of good over evil."³⁶ Hence, the individual must constantly take a stand in relation to

---

33. Schelling already approached this position in his early work, for example in *The System of Transcendental Idealism*. Like Luigi Pirandello's *Six Characters in Search of an Author*, trans. Edward Storer (New York: E.P. Dutton, 1922), Schelling likens God to a playwright who is not outside his work but in it.

But if the playwright *were to exist* independently of his drama, we should be merely the actors who speak the lines he has written. If he does not exist independently of us, but reveals and discloses himself successively only through the very play of our own freedom, so that without this freedom even he *would not be*, then we are collaborators of the whole and have ourselves invented the particular roles we play. See also *Werke*, 3:602.

34. Schelling, *Philosophical Investigations*, 98; *Werke*, 7:399.

35. Joseph Bracken, *Society and Spirit: A Trinitarian Cosmology* (Selinsgrove, Penn.: Susquehanna University Press, 1991), 95.

36. Schelling, *Philosophical Investigations*, 23–24; *Werke*, 7:352.

the two competing principles. Nicolas Berdyaev said that the inability in humanity to balance ground and existence was the source of the two types of evil. The first type—in which self-love is emphasized—would be egoism as the chaos and hell of disorder. The scriptural example of this would be the double-minded man who is unstable in all his ways (James 1:8). This is probably the way that most of us are sinful: we cannot commit to another; we cannot genuinely promise; we repeatedly follow our whims. Schelling and Berdyaev are closer to a Kantian notion of freedom for duty here than simply freedom from compulsion. If the double-minded man merely follows his inclinations, his inclination for compassion changes to his inclination for comfort. He is unable to really actualize anything, just as Dostoevsky's underground man is unable to become anything, because he cannot decide among the vortex of possibilities. This is the chaos of the ground where nothing is ever actualized. Here all order is lost in possibility.

The second source would be the total loss of possibility in order. In this case reason is reduced to mechanical reproduction.[37] The scriptural example of this is Satan's desire for the metaphysical coercion of humankind. Here, possibility is eliminated through the elimination of choice. For Schelling, however, this would also be a denial of the reality of freedom and would require intense violence in order to enforce the fantasy; thus, Satan is a "liar from the beginning" (D&C 93:25).

For Schelling, in human beings as well as in God, the possibility of doing evil must exist. Since, for Schelling, moral evil is grounded in egoism (which is a possibility of selfhood) then selfhood thus carries with it the potentiality of evil. Because Will is more primordial than Being, Schelling's God is not ontologically made to choose good but wills to do so. Each person is her act. As a person, God is God's decision. But like everything else, selfhood also has in it the possibility of greatest good because love can only be realized between persons. Evil does come to be through selfhood but only a selfhood in apostasy, which cuts itself off from love. In Alma 42, the assertion that should mercy rob justice God would cease to be God could be similar to Schelling's argument about God. Logically and metaphysically, God could choose to coerce us into God's kingdom. Mercy could rob justice—but God would then cease to

---

37. Nicolas Berdyaev, *Freedom and the Spirit*, trans. Oliver Clarke (New York: Schribner's, 1935), 168–69.

be God. Ethically and existentially this is impossible not because God could not do such an act but rather because God would not do it.

Act Two: Freedom and the Inner Necessity

The self-positing of the individual person in relation to God and others is the foundation of the essence of a person. Schelling thinks that this stance determines the meaning of the entire history of the person and that this determination does not occur in time. The fundamental choice is always mythologically portrayed as prior to time. Think, for example, of the Adam and Eve story mythologically; their time is before the Fall and thus outside of time. Time and history begin with the Fall:

> Man, even if born in time, is indeed created into the beginning of the creation (the *centrum*). The act, whereby his life is determined in time, does not itself belong to time but rather to eternity: it also does not temporally precede life but goes through time (unhampered by it) as an act which is eternal by nature. Through this act the life of man reaches to the beginning of creation; hence through it man is outside the created, being free and eternal beginning itself. As incomprehensible as this idea may appear to conventional ways of thinking, there is indeed in each man a feeling in accord with it as if he had been what he is already from all eternity and had by no means become so first in time.[38]

Mormons should find the claim Schelling makes in this passage both attractive and repellent. It may be attractive because Schelling claims that the roots of humanity are in eternity, at the beginning. Like God humanity is rooted in the freedom of the groundless *Ungrund*. The "come into being" is again related to God and to others. One could say that God calls us into being from the impersonal depths of the *Ungrund*. This is an interesting claim that differs from either of the usual ways that Mormons have thought about the pre-existence of intelligence(s). It is not like B. H. Roberts's and Truman G. Madsen's view[39] of eternal personalities, nor like Bruce R. McConkie's view that there is a kind of

---

38. Schelling, *Philosophical Investigations*, 51; *Werke*, 7:385–86.
39. See B. H. Roberts, *The Truth, the Way, the Life: An Elementary Treatise on Theology: The Masterwork of B. H. Roberts*, ed. Stan Larson (San Francisco: Smith Research Associates, 1994), 282–83; Truman G. Madsen, "Eternal Man," in *Five Classics by Truman G. Madsen* (Salt Lake City: Eagle Gate, 2001), 18–19.

primordial soup from which God creates persons.[40] Schelling's idea, like Böehme's, is of a decision to be. God calls us into Being. The decision to be is ours; it is at the basis of our being. In some ways it resembles Brigham Young's claim that the sons of perdition would be recycled back into primal element.[41] Schelling thinks that persons, divine and human, only exist in relation to others. To break completely all relations to others—which is like . . . to murder to get gain— is to lose personhood. It is to return to the no-thingness of the groundless *Ungrund*. In a way it combines features of both Roberts's and McConkie's views that the person is eternal in that she is rooted in a primal choice, but the choice of relation to the other is what makes her an individual. Schelling's conception of freedom as an irreducible remainder comes into play again here. Since Being is analyzable by reason, that which precedes Being, freedom, remains opaque to reason. There is something about the origin of choice that cannot be reduced to reason. This is the part of Schelling's claim Mormons may find repellent.

The following statement almost seems to undercut everything Schelling has said about freedom: "As incomprehensible as this idea may appear to conventional ways of thinking, there is indeed in each man a feeling in accord with it as if he had been what he is already from all eternity and had by no means become so first in time." He argues that we are free and make our own decisions, but that these are based on one decision that does not take place in time. When or where else could it take place? The key seems to be when he says that strange phrase: "it does not precede life in time but occurs (untouched by it) as an act eternal by its own nature." It is as if the fundamental question about who we are takes our entire life to genuinely ask—as if the meaning of the story is only revealed eschatologically at the end of the story when it has been present in the entire time. What could this mean?

Consider those difficult passages in the scriptures where we are told that Satan was a liar from the beginning or that Judas was Perdition. Following Kant, Schelling seems to say that since Freedom is the *noumenon*,

---

40. Bruce R. McConkie, *Mormon Doctrine*, 2nd ed. (Salt Lake City: Bookcraft, 1966), 386–87.

41. Brigham Young, June 12, 1859, *Journal of Discourses*, 7:174. See also John A. Widtsoe, "Who Are the Sons of Perdition?" in *Evidences and Reconciliations* (Salt Lake City: Bookcraft, 1987), 212–14; John A. Widtsoe, *Rational Theology* (Salt Lake City: Signature Books, 1997), 79.

"thing-in-itself," the highest reality, then it must also be eternal—and so we in our ability to choose are also eternal and beyond time. This is the source of David Paulsen's crucial question: have we simply fallen back into traditional theism's need to argue for things that simply seem incommensurate with genuine freedom and yet at the same time insist that God knows from eternity what we will do? Paulsen and James present us with the clear alternatives: an open universe that admits of the possibility of shipwreck and a closed universe in which all things are predestined. Schelling, like many religious people, is either seeking a middle way or—like many religious people—wants the contradictory goods of a free and open future with absolute security. This is the joy of the formulaic Hollywood romance: we know that at the end it will be inevitable that the couple gets together, but we want them to freely get there. But of course, the Hollywood romance is pure fantasy.

Schelling writes, "That Judas became a traitor to Christ, neither he nor any creature could alter; nonetheless he betrayed Christ not under compulsion but willingly and with full freedom."[42] This is a difficult question, and at this point it seems quite "un-Mormon" except for the fact that, like other Christians, we seem to want it both ways. Ask the typical Mormon whether God has perfect foresight about the future and whether we are completely free. They will likely respond affirmatively to both questions. This includes some LDS philosophers. Besides throwing up our hands and calling it a mystery, how can we think about this?

The Schelling scholar and religious existentialist Gabriel Marcel wrote about the ambiguity in human life in his play *A Man of God*.[43] At the end of the play the "hero," a Protestant pastor, wants desperately for God to tell him whether he is a good man. Marcel is working on the idea that we don't really know our intentions and therefore God can't judge them. The Russian science fiction fantasy film *Stalker*, by the Russian director Andrei Tarkovsky, illustrates this. In the film there is a room at the center of a place called "the zone" where your deepest wish will be fulfilled. A Stalker (a guide through the Zone) goes there in order to resurrect a dead friend. Instead, he receives incredible wealth. He then kills himself because the room has revealed what he has suspected

---

42. Schelling, *Philosophical Investigations*, 51. *Werke*, 385–86.

43. Schelling, *Philosophical Investigations*, 51. *Werke*, 385–86. *God, Ariadne, the Funeral Pyre: Three Plays with a Preface On the Drama of the Soul in Exile* (London, England: Secker and Warburg, 1952).

all along: that he is really not a good person, only greedy. The point here relates to Alma's notion of the mighty change of heart. How is conversion possible in relation to Schelling's statement that this is a choice made in eternity? Schelling claims that it is a mistake to understand this as a pre-destination. How then do we make sense of such a choice?

Accident and unity have always been a major problem in explaining the human condition. Predestination is an effort to conserve God's omniscience and providence while still preserving human freedom. But, says Schelling, the founders of the doctrine did not consider the "eternal act contemporaneous with creation" that constitutes what is partially made by us. Rather, they place the action wholly in the hands of the arbitrary decision of God. Thus, they destroyed the root of freedom.[44]

So Schelling asserts that he too declares a predestination, but in an entirely different way. Schelling thinks that this takes care of the question of why one man acts properly while the other man acts despicably: "For the question presupposes that man is not initially action and act and that he as a spiritual being has a Being which is prior to, and independent of, his will, which, as has been shown, is impossible."[45] So how are we to think of this? He says we are our acts, but also that our acts in time reveal who we are. As we move from eternity, which is the rotary motion of indecision, we move into time. Thus the decision creates time. It is the meaning of time. This naturally requires some explanation. Allow me to use some examples from the scriptures.

Alma, Korihor, and Judas. When I was a young missionary, reading the Book of Mormon for the first time, the story of Korihor struck me as just plain unfair. Admittedly, Korihor was a rotten guy. He was the Ayn Rand capitalist of his age who believed, like John Gault, that every man "fared in this life according to the management of the creature; therefore every man prospered according to his genius, and that every man conquered according to his strength" (Alma 30:17). But Alma the younger had also been a rotten guy and believed much the same. Both were granted signs from heaven. One, after enduring much suffering, repented and became a leader of the church. The other went out and was "trodden down, even until he was dead" (Alma 30:59). Alma must have seen—or at least he *should* have seen—his younger self in this other self-centered rebel. What is the difference? From Schelling's perspective this was a

---

44. Schelling, *Philosophical Investigations*, 52–53; *Werke*, 387–88.
45. Schelling, *Philosophical Investigations*, 53; *Werke*, 388.

choice taken in eternity and acted out in time, but what does that mean? It seems to mean that the "eternal" meaning of both Alma's and Korihor's lives are determined in time. The decision is eternal. In other words, had Korihor changed his heart the way Alma did this would have been the eternal meaning of his life. A vital part of Alma's story was that he had been "the vilest of sinners" and had repented and become a leader of the faithful. Consider this in relation to John Widtsoe's eternalist conception of human destiny in *A Rational Theology*:

> Likewise, the destiny of all the spirits sent to earth, is the same. Man has ever moved towards eternal life. All new information, every addition of knowledge has moved him onward, toward perfection and a vision of greater happiness. True, since all men have free agencies, individual wills express themselves in different ways, and no two spirits are therefore at precisely the same point on the upward road. Some are far ahead, some lag behind, each and all according to individual effort. However, throughout the vast eternities, all who are conscientiously moving upward, though it be ever so slowly, will in time reach a point which is absolute perfection to our mortal conceptions. Then, all will seem as if precisely alike. Whether or not we reach a given point at the same time, all men have a common destiny. As far as the destiny of man is concerned, all are alike.[46]

Now, Widtsoe is probably not intending the same thing as Schelling in the way he discusses eternity in this passage. But I think we can read Widtsoe through Schelling and produce an interesting interpretation of them both. In the above story of Alma and Korihor in the Book of Mormon, Alma is qualitatively different, and his entire life becomes different from Korihor's life because a choice—a mighty change of heart—determined his being. Widtsoe says that it is the destiny of all humanity to achieve perfection, so let's say that after his death Korihor arrives in Spirit Prison, where, after much suffering and remorse, he experiences a mighty change of heart and decides to love his fellows at least as much as himself. Because we live in a relational world he accepts the temple work that was done for him, loves, marries, and, though far behind Alma, goes on to eternal perfection. Now, because of his change of heart the meaning of Korihor's entire existence—though he was "the vilest of sinners"—is now different. And here is the potential sticking point: he was always the Korihor who attains perfection.

---

46. Widtsoe, *Rational Theology*, 126.

This is the meaning of the story from eternity. What makes Widtsoe's "destiny" different from pre-destination under this Schellingian reading is that Korihor and Alma had something to do with the decision. It is the one big decision into which the whole of one's life takes meaning.

Act Three:
Is There a Metaphysical/Eschatological Guarantee of God's Victory Over Chaos and a Return to Unity?

What is the metaphysical guarantee in Schelling that I find is more helpful for thinking about Mormon theology than William James's notion of the finite God? I think the key is Schelling's eschatology, which finds its expression in those negative statements made by Brigham Young and John A. Widtsoe about what happens to people who are even more rotten than Alma and my version of Korihor. Satan, Cain, and the fallen angels have decided from eternity to be self-centered believers so that they can "murder to get gain." They believed that we "fared in this life according to the management of the creature; therefore every man prospered according to his genius, and that every man conquered according to his strength" (Alma 30:17). In other words, they believed something that was a lie from the beginning. Evil is a denial of the reality of the relational character of the world. As such, when it completely denies relation, it ceases to be.

Schelling's eschatology resembles Lehi's eschatology because both begin with a primordial indifference—what Schelling calls the *Ungrund* and Lehi the "compound in one"—that remains dead. The first movement from such indifference is the progression into finite personal beings. As finite beings we have many choices, but the great ethical choice is between turning inwardly toward ourselves or turning outwardly toward God and others. There are billions of ways of actualizing this choice, but as Widtsoe puts it, in attaining this perfection of goodness, "Then, all will seem as if precisely alike."[47] For Schelling this concludes in love. Love is not the antithesis, nor the indifference of the groundless—although the groundless seems to imply the unity of love without the distinctions necessary to it. The groundless absolute divides itself so that life, personal existence, and love may come to be. Love can

---

47. Ibid., emphasis added.

only exist where there is some passion, some relation to another, and some need of one person for another:

> For love is neither in indifference nor where opposites are linked which require linkage for their Being, *but rather this is the secret of love, that it links such things of which each could exist for itself, yet cannot exist without the other.*[48]

The perfection that Widtsoe speaks of is for Schelling the final defeat of evil through the subordination of the selfish but individualizing passions of the will to love. The final and complete decision dissolves the basis and the person establishes herself as an enduring being in the blessed community. The longing is dissolved when all that is true and all that is good is elevated into consciousness. All that is evil is relegated to the depths of consciousness where it remains a potentiality and can never become an actuality. This is the subordination of everything to spirit. The two bases are now one.[49]

So how does evil end? Does the creation have a final purpose at all, and why is that purpose not attained immediately? Why do we have to suffer? Why doesn't perfection just exist from the beginning? For Schelling the only possible answer to this is that God is not merely "Being" (which is eternity) but a life, and life is tragic in that it is subject to development. One consolation in all this is that, as the mathematician and philosopher Alfred North Whitehead wrote, "God is the great companion—the fellow-sufferer who understands."[50] It is only a God

---

48. Schellling, *Philosophical Investigations into the Essence of Human Freedom*, 50; *Werke*, 408. In his aphorism on the philosophy of nature Schelling says,

> This is the secret of eternal Love—that that which would fain be absolute in itself nonetheless does not regard it as a deprivation to be so in itself but is so only in and with another. If each entity were not a Whole but only a part of the Whole there would be no Love: Since each is a Whole and nonetheless does not exist and cannot be without the other—thence there is Love. (Schelling, 115)

49. Schelling describes this final victory over evil as the final victory of love:

> Above spirit, however, is the initial non-ground that is no longer indifference, (neutrality) and yet not the identity of both principles, but rather a general unity that is the same for all and yet gripped by nothing that is free from all and yet a beneficence acting in all, *in a word, love, which is all in all*. (Schelling, *Philosophical Investigations into the Essence of Human Freedom*, 70; *Werke*, 3:408)

50. Alfred North Whitehead, *Process and Reality: An Essay on Cosmology,*

who suffers as we suffer that can justify the suffering of the universe, a notion Schelling believed was central to all religions and spiritual traditions from ancient times. God is a part of the suffering that is the tragedy of existence. Schelling thought that humanity has a basic intuition of the development of history revolving around the notion of a suffering Deity:

> Without the concept of a humanly suffering God, on which is common to all mysteries and spiritual religions of earliest time, all history would be incomprehensible; scripture also distinguishes periods of revelation and posits as a distant future the time when God will be all in all things, that is when he will be fully realized. God freely submitted himself to all this too, in the very beginning, when, in order to become personal, he divided the light and the world of darkness. For being is only aware of itself in becoming. To be sure, there is in being no becoming; in the latter, being is itself rather posited as an eternity; but in actualization, there is necessarily a becoming. All history remains incomprehensible without the concept of a humanly suffering god, a concept that is common to all mysteries and spiritual religions of ancient times.[51]

Schelling says our scriptural traditions speak of a time in the future when God will be all in all. He means that the meaning of the world is like the meaning of a life that comes to love and is realized in love. Heaven can only be realized over a period of time, through choices that separate the possibilities of good and evil, love and selfishness. Only when selfishness is separated out does it cease to exist. Christ is the great Western example of this. He emptied himself of selfishness by giving himself as a sacrifice for others. This is what Dostoevsky's Zosima says: the purpose of the creation is for the Good to be differentiated from the evil and brought into actuality, and that evil be cast out into non-being.

Conclusion: Tragedy vs. Instrumentalism

The Schellingian vision that I have tried to explain here in relation to Mormon eschatology is a comedy (in the literary sense) that is deeply entwined with tragedy. Suffering is an unavoidable part of love

---

corrected edition, eds. David Ray Griffin and Donald W. Sherburne (New York: Free Press, 1979), 351.

51. Schelling, *Philosophical Investigations into the Essence of Human Freedom*, 66; *Werke*, 403.

and existence for God and all creatures. But the final victory of love is guaranteed. It may take a long, long, long, long time but God is forever and ceaselessly on the job. The Book of Mormon prophesies that Christ "will take upon him death, that he may loose the bands of death which bind his people; and he will take upon him their infirmities, that his bowels may be filled with mercy, according to the flesh, that he may know how to succor his people according to their infirmities" (Alma 7:12). The last phrase here is significant for God, who must come to know what it is to suffer in the body, which is something we all can only learn just by being here.

David Paulsen quotes the above passage from Alma in his critique of David Griffin's process theodicy. From the Schellingian perspective I think there is a difficulty with the alternative soul-making eschatology that Paulsen presents, in which suffering is seen as instrumental in the development of humans toward becoming like God. While I agree this can be the case, I cannot hold with Paulsen that there is a necessary purpose to suffering. It is a part of the condition of creatures, but most of us are not ennobled by it. The primary problem with Paulsen's defense of instrumentalism in Mormon scripture and his claim that the world is a veil of soul-making is that it only covers a tiny portion of the suffering of the sentient beings that have inhabited this world since the beginning. It says nothing about the suffering, for example, of deformed babies who seem to gain little from their brief experience here, or for the billions of human lives that have endured a nasty, brutish, and short existence here and then pass on to the next world.

I think that Paulsen can actually respond to my objection here by saying that in Mormon doctrine all beings must become corporeal to move on to the next step in existence. It may be that children who are only here briefly have done what they have to do in obtaining a body, but even this does not explain why some suffer so intensely while others do not, or even why the distribution of suffering is so grossly inequitable. But even apart from human suffering, no "veil of soul-making argument" can explain the useless suffering of the billions and billions of non-human creatures who have inhabited this world; surely it cannot be that the suffering of these beings has an instrumental justification. It does not seem to render them more compassionate, and it seems wrong to say that they suffer so that humans can develop compassion, just as it is wrong to say that children starve in some far away land so that the well-fed can begin to feel compassion.

I prefer Schelling's, Whitehead's, Griffin's, and I believe Lehi's contention that this veil of tears where we "might" have joy is merely the harsh world into which we are thrown along with God, which we try bit by bit to improve. Our common hope is that God and love can become All in All.

Appendix
List of Publications

*Indicates co-authors who were students of Paulsen during the research and writing of the publication.

"Comparative Coherency of Mormon (Finitistic) and Classical (Absolutistic) Theism." Ph.D. diss., University of Michigan, 1975.

"Divine Determinateness and the Free Will Defense." *Analysis* 41, no. 3 (1981): 150–53.

"The Logically Possible, the Ontologically Possible, and Ontological Proofs of God's Existence." *International Journal for the Philosophy of Religion* 16, no. 1 (1984): 41–49.

"Must God be Incorporeal?" *Faith and Philosophy* 6, no. 1 (January 1989): 76–87.

"Early Christian Views of a Corporeal Deity: Origen and Augustine as Reluctant Witnesses." *Harvard Theological Review* 83 (1990): 105–16.

"Harmonization of Paradox." In *Encyclopedia of Mormonism*, Vol. 1, edited by Daniel H. Ludlow, 402–3. New York: MacMillan, 1992.

"Evil." In *Encyclopedia of Mormonism*, Vol. 2, edited by Daniel H. Ludlow, 477–78. New York: MacMillan, 1992.

"Omniscience, Omnipotence, and Omnipresence." In *Encyclopedia of Mormonism*, Vol. 3, edited by Daniel H. Ludlow, 1030. New York: MacMillan, 1992.

"Temptation." In *Encyclopedia of Mormonism*, Vol. 4, edited by Daniel H. Ludlow, 1468–69. New York: MacMillan, 1992.

"Reply to Kim Paffenroth's Comment." *Harvard Theological Review* 86 (1993): 235–39.

"Review of Francis J. Beckwith and Stephen E. Parrish, The Mormon Concept of God: A Philosophical Analysis." *The International Journal for the Philosophy of Religion* 35 (1994): 118–20.

"The Doctrine of Divine Embodiment: Restoration, Judeo-Christian, and Philosophical Perspectives." *BYU Studies* 35, no. 4 (1995–96): 6–94.

"Must God be Incorporeal?" In *Mormon Identities in Transition*, edited by Douglas Davies, 204–9. London: Cassells, 1996.

"Theology." In B. H. Roberts, *The Truth, The Way, The Life: An Elementary Treatise in Theology*, edited by Jack W. Welch, 619–32. Provo, Utah: BYU Studies, 1996.

Roberts, B. H. Foreword to *The Mormon Doctrine of Deity: the Roberts-Van Der Donckt Discussion*, v–xxvii. Salt Lake City: Signature Books, 1998.

"The God of Abraham, Isaac and (William) James." *The Journal of Speculative Philosophy* 13, no. 2 (1999): 114–46.

With Dennis Potter*. "How Deep the Chasm? A Reply to Owen and Mosser's Review." *The FARMS Review of Books* 11, no. 2 (1999): 221–64.

"The Seventy's Course in Theology." In *Encyclopedia of Latter-day Saint History*, edited by Arnold K. Garr, Donald Q. Cannon, and Richard O. Cowan, 1093. Salt Lake City: Deseret Book Company, 2000.

"Review of Roger Olson, The Story of Christian Theology." *BYU Studies* 39, no. 4 (2000): 185–94.

"Joseph Smith and the Problem of Evil." *BYU Studies* 39, no. 1 (2000): 53–65.

With Eric Madsen*. "Review of Al Ghazali: The Incoherence of the Philosophers." *BYU Studies* 40, no. 4 (2001): 263–68.

"The God of Abraham, Isaac and (William) James." In *Colloquium: Literature and Belief*, edited by Richard H. Cracroft, Jane D. Brady, Linda Hunter Adams. Provo, Utah: BYU Press, 2001.

With Ari D. Bruening*. "The Development of the Mormon Understanding of God: Early Mormon Modalism and Other Myths." *The FARMS Review of Books* 13, no. 2 (2001): 69–109.

With Blake T. Ostler. "Sin, Suffering and Soul-making: Joseph Smith and the Problem of Evil." In *Revelation, Reason and Faith: Essays in Honor of Truman G. Madsen*, edited by Donald W. Parry, Daniel C. Peterson, and Stephen D. Ricks, 237–84. Provo, Utah: Foundation for Ancient Research and Mormon Studies, 2002.

"A General Response to The New Mormon Challenge." *The FARMS Review of Books* 14, no. 1/2 (2002): 99–111.

With Carl W. Griffin*. "Augustine and the Corporeality of God." *Harvard Theological Review* 95, no. 1 (2002): 97–118.

"Reviews of John Sanders, The God Who Risks, and Clark Pinnock, et. al., The Openness of God." *BYU Studies* 42, no. 3/4 (2003): 110–23.

With Matthew G. Fisher*. "A New Evangelical Vision of God: Openness and Mormon Thought." *FARMS Review of Books* 15, no. 2 (2003): 417–43.

"Are Mormons Trinitarians?" *Modern Reformation* 12, no. 6 (November/December 2003): 40–43.

"The Search for the Cultural Origins of Mormon Doctrines." In *Excavating Mormon Pasts: The New Historiography of the Last Half Century*, edited by Newell G. Bringhurst and Lavina Fielding Anderson, 27–52. Salt Lake City: Greg Kofford Books, 2004.

"Joseph Smith and the Problem of Evil." *BYU Magazine* (October 2005): 37–38.

"Joseph Smith and the Problem of Evil." In *Praise to the Man: Fifteen Classic BYU Devotionals About the Prophet Joseph Smith, 1955–2005*, 151–67. Provo, Utah: BYU Publications, 2005.

With Brent Alvord*. "Joseph Smith and the Problem of the Unevangelized." *FARMS Review of Books* 17, no. 1 (2005): 171–204.

"Divine Embodiment: The Earliest Christian Understanding of God." In *Early Christians in Disarray: Contemporary LDS Perspectives on the Christian Apostasy*, edited by Noel Reynolds, 239–94. Provo, Utah: Brigham Young University Press, 2005.

"The Redemption of the Dead: A Latter-day Saint Perspective on the Fate of the Unevangelized." In *Salvation in Christ: Comparative Christian Views*, edited by Roger Keller and Robert Millet, 263–98. Provo, Utah: Brigham Young University Religious Studies Center, 2005.

"Joseph Smith Challenges the Theological World." *BYU Studies* 44, no. 4 (2005): 175–212.

"Joseph Smith Challenges the Theological World." In *The Worlds of Joseph Smith*, edited by John W. Welch, 175–212. Provo, Utah: Brigham Young University Press, 2006.

"Are Christians Mormon? Reassessing Joseph Smith's Theology in his Bicentennial." *BYU Studies* 45, no. 1 (2006): 35–128.

With Cory G. Walker*. "Work, Worship and Grace." *The FARMS Review of Books* 18, no. 2 (2006): 83–177.

With Clark H. Pinnock. "A Dialogue on Openness Theology." In *Mormonism in Dialogue With Contemporary Christian Theologies*, 489–553. Macon, Ga.: Mercer University Press, 2007.

"Polemics, Apologetics and the Fruits of Dialogue." In *Mormonism in Dialogue With Contemporary Christian Theologies*, 10–18. Macon, Ga.: Mercer University Press, 2007.

With Donald W. Musser*, eds. *Mormonism in Dialogue With Contemporary Christian Theologies*. Macon, Ga.: Mercer University Press, 2007.

"The Reverend Dr. Peter Christian Kierkegaard's 'About and Against Mormonism' 1855." *BYU Studies* 46, no. 3 (2007): 100–156.

"Joseph Smith and the Trinity: An Analysis and Defense of a Social Model of the Trinity." *Faith and Philosophy* 25, no. 1 (January 2008): 47–74.

"What Does It Mean to be a Christian? Soren Kierkegaard and Joseph Smith." *BYU Studies* 47, no. 4 (2008): 55–91.

"Open and Relational Theology: An Evangelical in Dialogue with a Latter-day Saint." *BYU Studies* 48, no. 2 (2009): 51–110.

With Roger D. Cook* and Kendel J. Christensen*. "The Harrowing of Hell: Salvation for the Dead in Early Christianity." *Journal of the Book of Mormon and Other Restoration Scriptures* 19, no. 1 (2010): 56–77.

With Brock M. Mason*. "Baptism for the Dead in Early Christianity." *Journal of the Book of Mormon and Other Restoration Scriptures* 19, no. 2 (2010): 22–49.

With Jacob Hawken* and Michael Hansen*. "Review of Jesus Was Not a Unitarian." *BYU Studies* 49, no. 3 (2010): 158–69.

With Martin Pulido*. "'A Mother There': A Survey of Historical Teachings about Mother in Heaven." *BYU Studies* 50, no. 1 (2011): 70–126.

With Kendel J. Christensen* and Martin Pulido*. "Redeeming the Dead: Tender Mercies, Turning of the Hearts, and Restoration of Authority." *Journal of the Book of Mormon and Other Restoration Scriptures* 20, no. 1 (2011): 28–51.

With Kendel J. Christensen*, Martin Pulido*, and Judson Burton*. "Redemption of the Dead: Continuing Revelation after Joseph Smith." *Journal of the Book of Mormon and Other Restoration Scriptures* 20, no. 2 (2011): 52–69.

With Hal Boyd*. "The Mormon Understand of God." In *The Oxford Handbook of Mormonism*. Edited by Phillip Barlow and Terryl L. Givens. Oxford University Press, forthcoming.

With Judson Burton* and Benjamin B. Brown*. "The Mormon Theistic Worldview." In The Routledge World of Mormonism. Edited by Carl Mosser and Richard Sherlock. New York: Routledge, forthcoming.

With Ari Bruening* and Benjamin B. Brown*. *The Earliest Mormon Understanding of God (1829–1844): Modalism and Other Myths*. Salt Lake City: Greg Kofford Books, forthcoming.

Are Christians Mormon? Reappraising Joseph Smith's Theology. Farnham, UK: Ashgate Publishing, forthcoming.

Contributors

JACOB T. BAKER is a doctoral student in Philosophy of Religion and Theology at Claremont Graduate University. He teaches philosophy at Brigham Young University and Utah Valley University.

DANIEL S. BARRON is an MD/PhD student at the University of Texas Health Science Center at San Antonio. He is a former research assistant of David Paulsen at Brigham Young University.

FRANCIS J. BECKWITH is Professor of Philosophy and Church-State Studies at Baylor University. He is the author of *Politics for Christians: Statecraft as Soulcraft*, *Return to Rome: Confessions of an Evangelical Catholic*, and a co-author of *The New Mormon Challenge: Responding to the Latest Defenses of a Fast Growing Movement*.

BRIAN D. BIRCH is Professor of Philosophy and director of the Religious Studies Program at Utah Valley University. He is a founding editor of *Element: The Journal for the Society of Mormon Philosophy and Theology* and serves on the board of directors of *Dialogue: A Journal of Mormon Thought*. He is also the editor for the new PERSPECTIVES ON MORMON THEOLOGY series from Greg Kofford Books.

CRAIG L. BLOMBERG is Distinguished Professor of New Testament at Denver Seminary. He is the author of *The Historical Reliability of the Gospels*, *Jesus and the Gospels*, and co-author of *A Handbook of New Testament Exegesis* and *How Wide the Divide? A Mormon and an Evangelical in Conversation*.

DOUGLAS J. DAVIES is Professor in the Study of Religion in the Department of Theology and Religion at Durham University. He is the author of *An Introduction to Mormonism*, *The Mormon Culture of Salvation*, and *Emotion, Identity, and Religion: Hope, Reciprocity, and Otherness*.

STEPHEN T. DAVIS is the Russell K. Pitzer Professor of Philosophy at Claremont McKenna College. He is the author of *Disputed Issues: Contending For Christian Faith in Today's Academic Setting*, *Christian*

Philosophical Theology, and editor of *Encountering Evil: Live Options in Theodicy*.

JAMES E. FAULCONER is Professor of Philosophy, Richard L. Evans Chair for Religious Understanding, and Associate Director of the Wheatley Institution at Brigham Young University. He is the author of *Romans 1: Notes and Reflections, Faith, Philosophy, and Scripture*, and co-editor of *Appropriating Heidegger, Transcendence in Religion and Philosophy*, and *Latter-day Saints and Contemporary Issues* (forthcoming with Greg Kofford Books).

JAMES M. MCLACHLAN is Professor of Philosophy and Religion at Western Carolina University. He is co-editor of *Discourses in Mormon Theology: Philosophical and Theological Possibilities*. He specializes in and writes about process theology, personalism, Schelling, and Mormon studies.

ROBERT L. MILLET is Professor of Ancient Scripture and Emeritus Dean of Religious Education at Brigham Young University. He is the author of *A Different Jesus? The Christ of the Latter-day Saints, Grace Works*, and co-author of *Bridging the Divide: The Continuing Conversation between a Mormon and an Evangelical*.

CARL MOSSER is Assistant Professor of Biblical Studies at Eastern University. He is a co-editor of *The Gospel of John and Christian Theology* and a co-author of *The New Mormon Challenge: Responding to the Latest Defenses of a Fast Growing Movement*.

DONALD W. MUSSER is Professor Emeritus of Religious Studies and Hal S. Marchman Chair of Civic and Social Responsibility at Stetson University. He is a co-editor of *Mormonism in Dialogue with Christian Theologies* (with David Paulsen), *New and Enlarged Handbook of Christian Theology* (with Joseph Price), and *An Introduction to the Bible: Revised Edition*.

LYNDSEY NAY graduated from Brigham Young University with an MA in Linguistics and a BA in English Language. She enjoys studying sociolinguistics, including language policy and planning and world Englishes. Currently, she is happily raising a family of boys.

BLAKE T. OSTLER is an attorney and independent scholar residing in Salt Lake City, Utah. A former student of David Paulsen, he is the author of the multi-volume series EXPLORING MORMON THOUGHT (the fourth volume is forthcoming from Greg Kofford Books).

PAUL OWEN is Associate Professor of Greek and Religious Studies at Montreat College. He is the author of *The Long Winter: One Man's Journey through the Darkness of Foster Care*, co-author of *Who Is the Son of Man? The Latest Scholarship on a Puzzling Expression of the Historical Jesus*, and is a co-author of *The New Mormon Challenge: Responding to the Latest Defenses of a Fast Growing Movement*.

CLARK H. PINNOCK (1937–2010) was Professor of Systematic Theology at McMaster Divinity College. He is the author of *Most Moved Mover: A Theology of God's Openness, Flame of Love: A Theology of the Holy Spirit*, and co-author (with John Sanders and others) of *The Openness of God: A Biblical Challenge to the Traditional Understanding of God*.

DENNIS POTTER is Associate Professor of Philosophy at Utah Valley University. A former student of David Paulsen, he specializes in and writes about philosophy of religion, philosophy of logic, and Mormon studies.

JOSEPH L. PRICE is the Genevieve Shaul Connick Professor of Religious Studies at Whittier College. He is the co-editor of *New and Enlarged Handbook of Christian Theology, A New Handbook of Christian Theologians*, and co-author of *Tillich (Abingdon Pillars of Theology)*, all with Donald Musser.

JOHN E. SANDERS is Professor of Religious Studies at Hendrix College. He is the author of *The God Who Risks: A Theology of Providence, Does God Have a Future? A Debate on Divine Providence*, and a co-author (with Clark Pinnock and others) of *The Openness of God: A Biblical Challenge to the Traditional Understanding of God*.

JOHN W. WELCH is Robert K. Thomas Professor of Law at Brigham Young University and editor-in-chief of *BYU Studies*. He is the author of *The Sermon on the Mount in the Light of the Temple*, and editor of *Opening the Heavens: Accounts of Divine Manifestations, 1820–1844*, and *The Worlds of Joseph Smith: A Bicentennial Conference at the Library of Congress*.

Subject Index

A

A Grief Observed, 262
A Marvelous Work and a Wonder, xxviii
A Theology of Liberation, 141
Abinadi, 122–23
Abraham, 35, 45
Abrahamic faiths, 35
absolute, the, 328–40
absolutism, 101 note 21
activism, social, 137–38
Adam, 122
  and Eve, 335
  curse, 119
Adam-God, 122
Adams, Marilyn, xxxi, xxxv
Adams, Robert, xxxi, xxxv
Added Upon, 91
Adventist, 79
Alston, William, 60
Althaus-Reid, Marcella, 140
American Philosophical Association, 211
Ammerman, Nancy, 76–77
An Approach to the Book of Mormon, xxvii
Anabaptist, 113
Anderson, Nephi, 91
Anderson, Robert D., 166 note 51
"Anglo-American Finite Theism," 33–34
Anselm, 47, 235
anthropomorphism, 214, 216–17. *See also* God.
Antinomianism, 153 note 15
Apocrypha, 190
apologetics, xxix, xxxii
Apostle's Creed, 95, 176
Appleby, Peter, xxxi
Aquinas, Thomas, 58 note 33, 144, 229, 236, 253
Arianism, 125–27
Aristotle, 58, note 33, 241, 246
Arius, 126 note 36
Arminianism, 72, 181
art, 249
Articles of Faith, 176
Articles of Faith (book), xxviii

Athanasius, 125, 258
atheism, 3–4, 10–14, 18, 20–21, 28–33
  30–31, 58
atheology, 48–58, 57 note 30
A-theory of time, 284–85
atonement, 119, 174, 181, 270, 272
Augustine, 2, 74, 217, 258
Authenticity
  American, 72–73
  Mormon, 72
  religious, 69–71, 74, 80–92

B

baptism, 76
  infant, 118–20
Barth, Karl, 41, 42 note 16
Basic Christian Communities, 134–35
Bauckham, Richard, 16–17
Bavinck, Herman, 61
Bayle, Pierre, 59
Bebbington, David, 73, 174–75
Beckwith, Francis, xxxiv, xxxvi, 299
bedazzlement, 248–49
being, 250
  equivocal, 236
  univocal, 236, 245
Being, 43, 101, 235
belief
  basic 60–62, 64
  religious, 96, 98–99
  warranted, 64 note 50
Benedict XVI, 108, 190
Bengtsson, Jan Olof, 328
Bennett, Clinton, 149
Benson, Ezra Taft, 190
Berdyaev, Nikolai, 320–22, 333–34
Bergera, Gary James, 157, 162
Bible, 65. *See also* Joseph Smith Translation of the Bible.
  interpretation, 194
  King James Version, 177
Big Bang, 300–301, 303–4
Bill of Rights, 99

Biola University, xxxix
Bitton, Davis, 161, 163
blacks, 106
blessings, patriarchal, 69, 84–92
Bloesch, Donald, 231
Blomberg, Craig L., 36
Bloom, Harold, 158
Blue Twilight, 37
Böehme, Jacob, 323, 328
Book of Mormon, xxvii, 24, 55–56, 72, 79, 82–83, 95, 109, 111–20, 122, 124, 152, 161, 168, 177, 190, 192
born-again, 69–70, 72–73, 76–78, 86
Bouillard, Henri, 144
boundary marking, 82–83
Bracken, Joseph, 333
Bradford, Gerald, 55
Brandon, S. G. F., 156–57
Brettler, Marc, 205–6
Brigham Young University, xxvi, xxxiv–xxxv
Brightman, Edgar Sheffield, 33, 323
Bringhurst, Newell, 156
Brothers Karamazov, 330
Brown, Robert McAfee, 132, 132 note 2, 138, 141–42
B-theory of time, 284
Buddha, 160
Buddhism, 78
Bundy, Walter E., 165
Burned-over District, 153

C

calling and election, 267
Calvin, John, 61–62, 153, 319
Calvinism, 61, 72, 268
Campbell, Joseph, 168
Cantor, Georg, 278–83
Cardenal, Ernesto, 135
Carter, Jimmy, 104
Catholic Church, 113, note 11, 115, 133 note 4
Catholic, Evangelical, 171
Catholicism, 74, 76, 78, 80, 92, 96–98, 106, 190–91
celestial kingdom, 75
Celsus, 163
cessationism, 189
Chamberlin, William, 1
chaotic inflationary theory, 278, 299–300

charity
 Christian, 104, 143
 theology as, xii, xiii
Christianity, 15, 28, 30, 42–44, 47, 62–63, 72, 95, 101, 103, 173, 186
 apostate, 82
 Hellenization of, 218
 liberal, 174
 traditional, 97–99, 105, 109 note 2
Christology, 124 note 30, 126, note 35, 180
Church of Jesus Christ of Latter-day Saints, 35, 50, 83
Church
 false, 114–16
 great and abominable, 115
Claremont Graduate University, 50
Clement of Alexandria, 258
cognitive linguistics, 195
Colossians, Epistle to, 43
Community of Christ, xxvii, 35
complementarity thesis, 68
confirmation, 76
Confucius, 244, 244 note 19
Congregational Church, 79
consubstantial, 123
contestation, 36 note 4
conversion, 74, 80, 83, 175
Copan, Paul, 277–307
corporeality, divine, 216–21, 227–34. See also God.
Council of Fifty, 157
Council of Latin American Bishops, 133
Craig, William Lane, xxxiv, 277–307
Creation
 ex nihilo, 21, 126 note 36, 235, 246, 277, 301
 from chaos, 101 note 18, 325
creeds, 103–4, 144, 176
Crimes and Mysteries of Mormonism, xxviii
cross, 175
Cusa, Nicholas, 258, 273

D

Davies, Douglas J., 23 note 51
Davis v. Beason, 71
Davis, Matthew S., 269
Davis, Stephen, 49, 53, 326–27
de Chardin, Pierre Teilhard, 43
Dead Sea Scrolls, 126
Dean, William, 76

Decker, Ed, 255, 271
Declaration of Independence, 99
defeater, 64–67, 68 note 62
deification, 180, 184, 255–75
deism, 47
democracy, 99, 103. *See also* government.
DesCamp, Mary Therese, 204–5
dialogue, 36, 45
    intra-Christian, 133, 145–46
    Mormon-Christian, x, xi, xli, 38–39, 43, 45, 50, 110, 131–32, 145–46, 189, 193, 227
Dilley, Frank, 33
divine materiality, 219
divinization, 259
Doctrinal Commentary on the Book of Mormon, 55
Doctrine and Covenants, 24, 95, 99, 177, 190
doctrine
    Catholic (dogma), 54
    Evangelical, 187
    Mormon, 48, 52, 172, 218
Doctrine of Deification in the Greek Patristic Tradition, 256
Dostoevsky, Fyodor, 334, 342
dualism, 320–21
Dulles, Avery, 52
Dupre, Wilhelm, 79

E

Eastern Orthodox, 267
Ebeling, Gerhard, 70–71
Eddy, Mary Baker, 268
Ehrenreich, Barbara, 137
Elijah, 150
elohim, 16, 17
Elyonic Monotheism, 128–29
embodiment
    divine, 22, 216–21, 223–24, 227–34
    and Evangelicals, 231
    pastoral argument for, 220–221
    perception, 233
    and philosophers, 233
England, Eugene, 24 note 54, 159
Enoch, 91
Ephraim, 86, 88, 91
epistemology, 68
equivocation, fallacy of, 289, 307
Erickson, Millard, 194
Eschatology, 329, 342–44

Essay Concerning the Essence of Freedom and Other Matters, 323
Essenes, 113, 126, 159
Essentials in Church History, xxviii
eternal progression, 22, 75, 184, 216
eternalism, 21
ethics. *See also* morality.
    deontological, 315
    subjectivist, 314
Eucharist, 92
Evangelicalism, 69–70, 72, 74–75, 80, 83, 86, 104, 107–8, 174–92
    African-American, 77
    Calvinist, 195
Evans, Bette Norvit, 71
Eve, 335
Everett, Nicholas, 30, 294 note 15
evidence, 60, 66, 8
evidentialism, 58, 60
evil, 309–17, 319–44
    argument from, 309
    minimal evil possibility, 312
    as necessary, 313, 315
    as predicate, 312
    problem of, 319, 323
    radical, 323
exaltation, 22, 75, 88, 96, 185, 265, 274
experience
    Mormon, 79–80
    transcendental, 248

F

Fackenheim, Emil, 323
faith, 52, 58, 71, 75, 143
    and reason, xxviii, xxxii
Fall, 74, 221
    positive, 330
families, eternal, 263
FARMS Review of Books, 69
Faulconer, James, 52–53, 57 note 30, 213 note 3
fideism, 47, 58–63, 68
    moderate, 59
    radical, 59
    Wittgensteinian, 59
finitism
    Anglo-American, 3
    Mormon, 101
    theological, 21

First Presidency, 23
First Vision, 75, 80, 83, 114, 152, 178, 215–16
Firstborn, 266
Flew, Antony, 58–59
Fluhman, Spencer, 182
Ford, David, 51
foreknowledge, divine, 193–94, 320
Forsberg, Clyde, 79 note 36
Foster, Lawrence, 158, 166
foundationalism, 61
Foxe's Book of Martyrs, 115
Fredriksen, Paula, 17–18
free will, 179
free will defense, 315
freedom, 97, 331–40
Freemasonry, 60, 79 note 36, 164
Frye, Northrop, 71
fundamentalism, 73, 177–78

G

gender, divine, 22
General Conference, 240
Genesis, 45
Gentiles, note 23
Gethsemane, 157, 181
Gift of the Holy Ghost, 63
Gilkey, Langdon, 37–38, 43–44
glossolalia, 83 note 43
Gnostics, 42, 220
God. *See also* theism, theology.
    attributes of, 19, 30–31, 264, 270
    being of, 245
    body of, 124–25
    children of, 257
    conceivable, 243
    Creator, 237
    decisions of, 334
    face of, 203
    the Father, 121–29
    finite, 268, 319, 326
    goodness of, 312, 319
    image of, 215
    immaterial, 211–15
    incorporeal, 213–15, 221–25
    influence of, 243
    invisible, 215, 221–22
    material, 212, 216–21
    Mormon attributes, 23–24, 29
    the Mother 23, 28 note 65
    mutability, 23
    and mutual relationality, 205
    name of, 14, 22
    nature of, 103, 128, 239
    omnipotence, 223, 310–11, 320, 325,
    omnipresence, 222–23
    omniscience, 193, 325
    ontologically simple, 316
    passibility, 228
    personhood of, 324
    Schelling on, 327–34
    the Son, 121–29
    and suffering, 342
God, Power, and Evil, 320
Godhead, 111, 122, 124. *See also* Trinity.
    hypostatic union, 124 note 30
    modalism, 120 note 19
Godmakers, 255
gods, 121, 124
    council of, 126
    head of, 121–22
    plurality of, 22
    polytheistic, 26–27
gold plates, 113–14
Good Samaritan, 112
gospel, 70, 115, 135, 173
government, 100
grace, 69–70, 80, 111, 181
Graham, Billy, 80
Great Apostasy, 37, 173, 218
Great Awakening, 72
Griffin, David Ray, 33, 320–21, 326, 343
Griffin, John Howard, 137
Groesbeck, Jesse, 167
Gutierrez, Gustavo, 133–45

H

Hagee, John, 320
Happiness, 241
Harrison, Milman, 77
Hasidism, 153
Hatch, Orrin, 172
Heavenly Mother. *See* God, the Mother.
Hegel, G. W. F., 158
Heidegger, Martin, 249, 323
Heisenberg Uncertainty Principle, 301
hell, 184
henotheism, 17. *See also* gods.

Henson, Richard, xxxi
heroic monomyth, 168
Hilbert's Hotel, 285–90, 302
Hinckley, Gordon B., 224, 241, 274–75
Hinduism, 25–26, 78
history, LDS, 71
Hoffmann, Melchior, 113
Holifield, Brooks, 47
Holland, Jeffrey R., xxxvii, 191
Holy Ghost, 83, 87, 92, 124
    Gift of, 63
Holy Spirit, 62, 64–65, 67, 75–76, 82, 120, 122–24, 183, 213, 221, 260, 266
    gifts of, 37
Holy Spirit of Promise, 263
Homer, 6
homoousios, 126–27
Horbury, William, 16
How Wide the Divide? 36
Howsepian, A. A., 29
Huff, Benjamin, 53–54
Hume, David, 58 note 33, 311
Hurtado, Larry, 16–17
Huss, John, 153
Hutchinson, Anne, 153
Hyde, Orson, 81
hymns, 110 note 4

I

idealism, German, 323
identity, corporate, 80, 82–83
idolatry, 215, 252, 254
illiteracy, in Latin America, 138–39
image schemas, 196–201, 204
immaterialism, divine, 211–15
    arguments in favor of, 221–25
impoverishment, 134–35
In Search of Jesus, 149
incarnation, divine, 59, 230
    theories of, 161–62
inclusivism, religious, 43
incorporeality, divine, 213–15, 221–25
infinite
    actual, 283–307
    infinities, 278–83
    potential, 283–84, 293
    series, 278–307
    sets, 278, 285
    temporal regress, 284

intelligence, 75, 99–100, 126 note 35, 335
intelligences, 21 note 46, 121 note 23, 252
interfaith, 36
Irenaeus, 258
Islam, 13, 28, 78, 103
Israel, 86, 88–89, 153
    tribes of, 84

J

Jackson County Temple, 90
Jackson, Kent P., 10 note 9, 112–13
Jacobi, Friedrich, 327
James, William, 2, 33, 77–78, 147, 248, 319, 326, 340
Jantzen, Grace, 233
Jefferson, Thomas, 155, 158
Jehovah, 92, 179 note 29
Jerusalem Temple, 11
Jesus, 43–45, 74, 76, 80, 82, 87–90, 111, 113–14, 119–20, 123, 147–70, 175, 224, 246, 256, 260–61, 270–71, 273
    historical, 151–52
    Lamb of God, 114–15, 118
Jesus the Christ, xxviii
Jewish, 86
John Paul II, 190
John the Beloved, 114
Johnson, Joel H., 86, 88
Johnson, Susan Ellen, 88, 89
Joseph of Egypt, 86
Joseph Smith Translation of the Bible, 177, 214 note 4, 320–21, 321 note 6
Judaism, 13, 15–17, 28, 35, 42–43, 116–17, 153
Jung, Carl, 168
justice, 103–5, 132, 143–46

K

Kabala, 160
Kalam infinity arguments, 277–307
Kallistos of Diokleia, Bishop, 259
Kant, Immanuel, 158, 311, 336
    synthetic a priori, 311
Kantian freedom, 334
Kaplan, Abraham, xxxi
Karamazov, Ivan, 326
Karkkainen, Veli-Matti, 257
Kavasilas, Nicholas, 273

Keller, Roger R., 179 note 29
Kelly, J. N. D., 125
Kennedy, John F., 96–98, 98 note 6, 107
Key to the Science of Theology, 49, 270
Kierkegaard, Peter, xii
Kierkegaard, Soren, xii–xiii, 59, 147
King Follet Discourse, 22 note 47, 25, 84, 121 note 25, 180, 239, 263–64
Kingdom of God, 72, 75, 146, 260
Kingdom of the Cults, 172
kingdoms of glory, 184
Knowing Brother Joseph Again, 163
knowledge, 47, 68
    scientific, 58

L

Lakoff, George, 202
Lamanites, 86
Latin American Liberation Theology: The Next Generation, 141
Law
    eternal, 100
    moral, 99–103
    natural, 100, 106
LDS Church Education System, ix note 1
Lectures on Faith, 23, 49 note 7, 256, 263, 266
Lehi, 309, 328
Levinas, Emmanuel, 237–38, 247, 250–51
Lewis, C. S., 102, 184, 230, 261–62
liberation theology, 132–46, 132 note 2
    and liturgy, 134
liberty, religious, 98, 105
Light of Christ, 62–63, 244
Linker, Damon, 99–103
literalism, biblical, 194, 214, 217
Locke, John, 58 note 33
logos, 124 note 30
Lossky, Vladimir, 260, 273
love
    final victory, 342–44
    metaphysical principle, 330
    Schelling and, 330–31, 340–41
Lucado, Max, 255, 264
Luther, Martin, 74, 153, 185, 272

M

Mackie, J. L. 30, 313
Madsen, Truman, x, 1, 220, 335
Mandeans, 35
Mandler, Jean, 196–97
Manicheanism, 113
manifest destiny, 77, 92
Marcel, Gabriel, 251, 337
Marion, Jean-Luc, 236, 236 note 2, 247–50, 251 note 34
Maritain, Jacques, 97
marriage, 106
    celestial, 266
Marshall, Ian Howard, 151
Martin, Walter, 171–72
Martineau, Aurelia, 91
Martineau, James Henry, 85–93
Martineau, Lee Edward, 91
Martineau, Nephi, 90
Marty, Martin E., 36, 39 note 10, 43, 49
Martyr, Justin, 43
martyrs, 115
Mary, 179
Masonry. *See* Freemasonry.
materialism, divine, 212, 216–21
mathematics
    finite, 278
    successive addition, 290–99
    transfinite, 288
Mavrodes, George, xxxi, xxxiii–xxxiv, 16 note 38, 173 note 7
May, Gerhard, 325 note 18
McBride, William, 84
McCann, Dennis, xxxvii
McConkie, Bruce R., 265, 335
McConkie, Joseph Fielding, 55
McDonald, Brett, 125, 178
McKim, Donald, xxxvii
McMurrin, Sterling, x, xxxi, 1, 100, 102
Medellin conference, 134–44
Meier, John, 149
Mendelssohn, Moses, 327
Mere Christianity, 102
"Messiah Puzzle," 150, 170
metaphor
    and the Bible, 204–7
    complex, 198–99
    conceptual metaphor theory, 195–209
    and God, 202–7
    and Mormonism, 207–9
    primary, 198

traditional metaphor theory, 199 note 13, 201–2
metaphysics, Mormon, 102
Methodism, 73
Midgley, Louis, xxix, 49 note 7, 51, 54–55
Mill, John Stuart, 33
Millet, Robert, xxxix, 55, 70
mind/body problem, 212
Miracle of Theism, 30
Miracles, 261
missionary work, LDS, 77, 80
modalism, 120 note 19
money-digging, 164
monism, 319, 319 note 2, 321
monism, 321
monotheism, 3–4, 10, 13, 13 note 31, 16–21, 23–25, 30, 34, 42, 122, 124, 126–27. *See also* God.
Monson, Thomas S., 108
Montanism, 113
Morain, William, 167
Moral Majority, 77
morality. *See also* ethics, law.
  agents, 73
  in Mormonism, 99–103
  natural, 101
More, Henry, 11–13, 30, 32
Moreland, J. P., 299
Mormon, 119
Mormon Culture of Salvation, 69
Mormon Spirituality, 71
Mormon studies, 50–51, 109
Mormon Tabernacle Choir, xxxvii, 132 note 1
Mormonism in Dialogue with Contemporary Christian Theologies, 36, 132
Mormonism, 14, 18, 21, 49, 68, 72–73, 75–76, 84, 89–90, 95, 100
  and Christianity, xxxiii
  Church of Jesus Christ, 188
  Evangelical, 171–92
Mormonism, the Islam of America, xxviii
Mormons, 44
Morris, Thomas, 161
Moses, 150
Mosser, Carl, xl
Mother in Heaven. *See* God, the Mother.
Mother in Israel, 89 note 60
Mouw, Richard, xxxix, 171, 268
multiplicity, ontological, 329

multi-theistic, 122 note 28. *See also* gods.
multiverse, 299–302
Muntzer, Thomas, 113
Murray, John Courtney, 97
Musser, Donald, xxxvi–xxxvii, xli, 70, 132
mutability, 23

N

National Association of Evangelicals, 172, 176–88
National Council of Churches of Christ, 35
naturalism, 21–22
nature, divine-human, 22
necessity, 310–11
  linguistic, 311, 314, 315
  necessity, logical, 310–11
  objective, 311, 314, 316
Neibaur, Alexander, 160
neighbor, love of, 104
Nellas, Panayitos, 273
Nelson, N. L., 242–45
Nestorianism, 124 note 30
New Jerusalem, 90
New Mormon Challenge, xl, 277
New Right, 77
Nibley, Hugh, xxvii, 48
Nicene Council, 125
Nicene Creed, 95, 103, 120, 176
Nicene Fathers, 126 note 36, 127
Nickel and Dimed, 137
Niebuhr, Richard, 74
No Man Knows My History, xxviii
noetic structure, 60–61 note 39
numbers
  finite, 279–307
  inductive, 280–81, 280 note 4
  infinite, 279–307
  ordinal, 281
  transfinite, 279–83
Nyssa, Gregory, 258

O

Ogden, Shubert, 52
Olasky, Marvin, 104
omnipotence, 223, 310–11, 320, 325,
omnipresence, 222–23
omniscience
  divine, 325

dynamic, 193
Ontological Argument, 47 note 2
Open theism, 194–95, 228
Opening the Heavens, 152
opposition, 309–10
　absolute, 310
　non-relative, 317
　relative, 310
oppression, 139
Oppy, Graham, 30–31
ordinances, 75, 82, 89, 182
Origen, 2
original sin, 221 note 23
Orthodox Church, 80
Ostler, Blake, 120 note 20, 129 note 49
Owens, Lance, 164
Oxford Dictionary of the Jewish Religion, 13

P

Pace, Amanda Ellena, 84
Pace, Ann Webb, 84
Pace, James, 84
paedobaptism, 186
Pannenberg, Wolfhart, 233
pantheism, 12, 31, 319, 327–28
Parrish, Stephen, 299
passibility, 228
past
　eternal, 293
　infinite, 277–307
Paulsen, Audrey Lucille (Lear), xxx
Paulsen, David Erik, xxxi
Paulsen, David L., ix, xi, xiii, xxv–xliii, 1, 33–34, 36, 38–39, 50, 69, 70, 93, 109, 125, 131–32, 147, 170, 173, 173 note 7, 178, 191–93, 211, 215, 227, 319, 321–22, 325–27, 336–37, 343
　academic career, xxxviii–xxxix
　Brigham Young University, xxxii
　childhood, xxvi
　collaborations with students, xlii
　dissertation, xxxii
　family, xxx note 11, xxxii–xxxiii
　graduate school, xxxi–xxxii
　law school, xxviii–xxx
　marriage, xxx
　military and mission, xxvi–xxviii
　Mormon Evangelical Consultation, xxxix–xl

　Richard L. Evans Chair for Religious Understanding, xxxvi–xxxvii
　seminary teacher, xxix–xxx
　Society of Christian Philosophers, xxxiii–xxxvi
　undergraduate studies, xxviii–xxx
　valedictorian, xxix
Paulsen, Helga Mae, xxvi
Paulsen, Kjersten, xxxi
Paulsen, Leif, xxxi
Paulsen, Ntanya, xxxi
Paulsen, Patrick, xxxii
Paulsen, Ray, xxvi
Paulsen, Trinyan, xxxi
"Pearls," 85
Penrose, Charles, 121 note 25, 220, 323–24
Pentecostal Church, 189
perichoresis, 24 note 29, 123
personalism, 322 note 10
persons, Schelling and, 332–34
Peterson, Daniel, 29
phenomenology, 248–50
Phillips, R. Douglas, 48
Philosophy and Religion, 322
philosophy, Greek, 217–18
Pinnock, Clark, xli
Plan of Salvation, 91
Plantinga, Alvin, 60–66, 315
Plantinga, Cornelius, 178
Plato, 218 note 15, 220
Platonism, 217
pluralism, 320–21
　metaphysical, 21
　religious, 37–44
pneuma, 214
politics, 97–99
Polkinghorne, John, 233
polygamy, 71, 86, 90, 105
polytheism, 3–4, 10–14, 16 note 38, 18–21, 25–28, 34, 125, 126 note 36. *See also* gods.
poor, 104, 135–45
　advocacy for, 141
　solidarity with, 135, 138–42
　systemic, 140
Pragmatism, 327
Pratt, Orson, 1, 25, 120–21, 122 note 28
Pratt, Parley P., 1, 48, 62, 81–82, 169, 270
predestination, 319, 338
pre-existence, 91, 126–27, 180

Subject Index 361

Price, Joseph, xxxvii
priesthood, 80–83, 85–86, 88–90, 107
process
   theism, 14, 33
   theodicy, 343
   theology, 321
prophet, 102, 106
"Prophet Puzzle," 150, 170
Proslogion, 47
Prosperity Gospel, 77
Protestant, 95
   Conservative, 77
   Evangelical, 36
purgatory, 185
Puritanism, 268

Q

quantum vacuum theory, 278, 301–2
Quest For the Plausible Jesus, 158
Quinn, D. Michael, 157, 164
Qumran, 126

R

Radical Orthodoxy, 236
Rahner, Karl, 43
Rand, Ayn, 338
Rational Theology, 49, 339
rationalism, 58, 63, 68
rationality, 64–67, 68 note 62
Rauschenbusch, Walter, 155
Read, Waldemer, xxxi
Reagan, Ronald, 104
reason, 49, 58, 65, 68, 68 note 61, 103, 144, 336
rebirth, spiritual, 69–78, 82, 84, 92
redemption, 9
Reformation, 96
Reformed Epistemology, 60–67
Reimarus, Hermann Samuel, 157
relations, transcendent, 248
relativism, theological, 37
religion, 98
   taxonomy of, 10–14, 30
Reorganized Church of Jesus Christ of Latter Day Saints. *See* Community of Christ.
restoration, 37–38, 63, 70, 73, 75–77, 82–84, 188, 191
resurrection, first, 89

revelation, 37, 41, 43, 48–52, 56–57, 68, 68 note 61, 145, 237
revivalism, 72–73, 113
Richards, Willard, 79
Rigdon, Sidney, 81, 152
Riley, Woodbridge, 165, 167
Roberts, B. H., 1, 24, 121, 122 note 28, 159, 240, 267, 335
Robinson, Stephen E., 36, 184, 231
Robson, Ken, 99
Romney, Mitt, xlii, 95–96, 98 note 6, 103, 106
Rowe, William, 32
Roy, Steven, 194
Russell, Bertrand, 279, 291
Russell, Jeffrey Burton, 319
Russell, Norman, 256

S

sacraments, 80
salvation, 75, 78
sanctification, 183
Satan, 113
Schelling, Friedrich, 319–44
Schonfield, Hugh, 160–61
School of the Elders, 263
Scott, Brandon Bernard, 153
Scotus, John Duns, 49, 236, 245, 253
Second Awakening, 72
Second Comforter, 87
Second Coming, 75, 90
Second Great Awakening, 113
Second Temple Judaism, 9 note 22
Second Vatican Council, 43, 54, 97, 134, 144, 171, 189
Secular Fundamentalism, 55
secularism, 77, 98
self-consciousness, 333
sensus divinitatus, 61–62, 64
Seventh-day Adventist, 171
sexuality, divine, 22, 28
Shandy, Tristram, 286–87 note 10
Shipps, Jan, 150, 158, 163
Sikhism, 78
sin, 63
Sjodahl, Janne M., 271
skepticism, 47
Smith, George Albert, 121 note 25
Smith, Hyrum, 90, 271
Smith, John, 85, 88

Smith, Joseph, Jr., xxxviii–xxxix, 24–25, 35, 37, 72, 75, 79–82, 84, 88 note 56, 90, 96, 99–100, 110–14, 120–22, 125, 147–70, 173, 188–90, 215–16, 221, 229 note 6, 238, 245, 251 note 38, 262–65, 268–69, 274, 325, 330
Smith, Morton, 163–64
Smith, Quentin, 298
Smith, Warren Cole, 105–6
Smith, William J., 87, 89
Smith, William Robertson, 93
Snow College, xxvi
Snow, Dale, 327
Snow, Lorenzo, 180, 270
Sobrino, Jon, 145, 155
social Trinitarianism. *See* Trinity.
Society of Christian Philosophers, 211
Socrates, 153
Sorabji, Richard, n. 15, 294
Sorenson, Ted, 97
soteriology, 185
soul-building, 309, 315
soul-making eschatology, 343
Spinoza, Baruch, 327, 328
spirit body, 213
Spirit Prison, 339
spirit, 214 note 5
spirituality, 71, 93
    Evangelical, 73
    Mormon, 72, 83
Stalker, 337
Standard Works, 72
Stoics, 42
Stott, John, 271
Stravopoulos, Christoforos, 259–60
subjectivism, moral, 316
succession, apostolic, 80
suffering, 341. *See also* evil.
    instrumental, 343
Sweetser, Eve, 204–5
Swinburne, Richard, 30, 231
System of Transcendental Idealism, 322

T

Talmage, James, 325
Tarkovsky, Andrei, 337
teleology, 102
temple, 76
Ten Commandments, 105

Tennyson, Alfred North, 192
Teología de la liberación—Perspectivas, 134
Tertullian, 59, 227 note 2
testimony, 82
"Testimony of Eight Witnesses," 82–83
"Testimony of Three Witnesses," 82
theism
    Christian, 66–67, 316
    classical, xxxii, 14, 29
    etymology, 4–5
    finite, 33
    invention of, 10–14
    Jewish, 8–9
    Mormon, 1–34
    taxonomy, 3–4
    traditional, 101
theodicy, 323
    opposition, 309–17
theological method, 142–45
theology, 51–52, 98, 128, 144
    academic, 141
    American, 47
    Christian, 41, 48, 56, 147, 241
    classical, 143
    dogmatic, 52–54, 56
    finitistic, 147
    liberation, 132–46, 132 note 2
    monosystematic, 54
    Mormon, 49, 51–52, 99, 101, 106, 127, 147, 213, 238
    narrative, 56
    philosophical, 50
    polysystematic, 54
    post-liberal, 51 note 12
    practical, 56
    revelational, 53, 57
theology, systematic, 49, 51 note 12, 53, 55
Theology: A Very Short Introduction, 51
theomorphism, 230, 254
theory
    academic, 169
    moral, 101
theos, 5–10, 16
theosis, 256, 258–59
Thomas, George, 72
Tillich, Paul, 32, 39–44, 131, 144–45
Timaeus, 33
tithing, 77
transascendance, 251–54

transcendence
  divine, 235–54
  Mormonism, 235–54
transfinite set logic, 278
Trinity, 59, 109, 120–29, 178, 193
  ontological, 129
  social, 125–29, 178
tritheism, 27 note 63, 125, 128. *See also* godhead, gods, polytheism, Trinity.
truth, 44, 132, 144–45
Trypho, 163
TULIP, 183 note 45, 186
Twelftree, Graham, 163 note 42

U

universalism, 42
universe
  infinite, 302
  uncreated, 302–7
University of Chicago, xxix, 132
University of Michigan, xxxi
University of Utah, xxxi
unpardonable sin, 79
Utah State University, 50
utilitarianism, 314

V

Vajda, Jordan, 271
Values
  moral, 100
  Mormon, 191
van Aarde, Andries, 167
Vermes, Geza, 153
Victoria, Queen, 81
visions, 84, 114

Vogel, Dan, 161
Von Baader, Franz, 323

W

Wahl, Jean, 251
Walker, Cory, 69
Wallis, Jim, 104
Ware, Bruce, 194
Warren, Rick, 108
Weber, Max, 162
Welch, John, xxxviii
Wesley, John, 74, 153
Westminster Confession, 103, 176
When Faiths Collide, 36
Whitehead, Alfred North, 323, 341
Whitney, Orson F., 240–41, 246
Widtsoe, John, 24, 339–41
Widtsoe, John, 49
Willard, Dallas, 255
Williams, Delores, 141
Winter, Dagmar, 158
witnesses, Book of Mormon, 111
Wittgenstein, Ludwig, 51 note 12
Wolterstorff, Nicholas, xxxv, 60, 66
Word of Wisdom, 75
works-righteousness, 181, 185, 272
World and the Prophets, 48
worlds, possible, 306
Wright, N. T., 256

Y–Z

Young, Brigham, 24, 85, 122, 169, 263, 336, 340
Zeno's Paradox, 299
Zion, 76, 85–86, 91

Scripture Index

Old Testament

Genesis 1:1 – 121
Genesis 1:27 – 215, 257
Genesis 3:8 – 213
Genesis 4:1–16 – 105
Genesis 5:22–24 – 203
Genesis 6:6–7 – 213
Genesis 8:1 – 217
Genesis 11:5 – 213
Genesis 18:21 – 204
Genesis 21:17 – 213
Genesis 32:30 – 213–14
Exodus 2:23 – 204
Exodus 6:6 – 213
Exodus 10:1 – 320
Exodus 10:20 – 320
Exodus 14 – 321
Exodus 20:2–17 – 105
Exodus 20:4 – 215
Exodus 24:10 – 213–14
Exodus 32:7–14 – 217
Exodus 33:11 – 203, 213
Exodus 33:18–23 – 204, 214
Exodus 33:20 – 213–14
Exodus 33:23 – 213
Numbers 6:24–26 – 203
Numbers 11:1 – 213
Numbers 11:23 – 204
Numbers 12:2 – 213
Numbers 12:8 – 203
Numbers 16:22 – 264
Numbers 22–24 – 112
Numbers 23:19 – 224
Numbers 27:16 – 264
Deuteronomy 1:21 – 203
Deuteronomy 4:12–23 – 215
Deuteronomy 4:24 – 217
Deuteronomy 4:34 – 213
Deuteronomy 7:19 – 213
Deuteronomy 24:19–22 – 104
Deuteronomy 29:20 – 213
Deuteronomy 29:28 – 217
Deuteronomy 30:14 – 204

Deuteronomy 32:11 – 206
Deuteronomy 32:18 – 206
1 Samuel 15:29 – 224
2 Samuel 22:47 – 217
1 Kings 8:27 – 214, 222
1 Kings 22:19–23 – 113
2 Chronicles 16:9 – 213
Psalms 11:7 – 214
Psalms 13:2 – 203
Psalms 14:2 – 204
Psalms 14:2 – 114
Psalms 14:3 – 114
Psalms 17:8 – 217
Psalms 18:15 – 213
Psalms 18:9 – 213
Psalms 20:1 – 204
Psalms 22:11 – 203
Psalms 24:6 – 203
Psalms 26:28 – 204
Psalms 34:8 – 204
Psalms 35:22 – 203
Psalms 36:7 – 217
Psalms 38:21 – 203
Psalms 42:4 – 203
Psalms 44:2 – 213
Psalms 44:3 – 213
Psalms 51:55 – 221
Psalms 53:2 – 204
Psalms 57:1 – 217
Psalms 61:4 – 217
Psalms 82:6 – 259
Psalms 89:13 – 213
Psalms 91:4 – 217
Psalms 96:7–10 – 9 note 23
Psalms 102:19 – 204
Psalms 104:29 – 203
Psalms 139:4 – 194
Psalms 139:16 – 194
Prov.erbs 31:8–9 – 104
Isaiah 2:2–4 – 9 note 23
Isaiah 6:1 – 230
Isaiah 6:5 – 214
Isaiah 6:9–10 – 320
Isaiah 19:21–25 – 9 note 23

Isaiah 25:6–8 – 9 note 23
Isaiah 29:10–11 – 114
Isaiah 29:13 – 114
Isaiah 40:12–26 – 215
Isaiah 42:14 – 228
Isaiah 42:7 – 115
Isaiah 45:7 – 320
Isaiah 46:5 – 224
Isaiah 49:15 – 206
Isaiah 55:8–9 – 224, 235
Isaiah 56:6–7 – 9 note 23
Isaiah 58:6–10 – 104
Isaiah 61:1 – 115
Isaiah 66:1 – 222
Isaiah 66:23 – 9 note 23
Jeremiah 1:9 – 230
Jeremiah 3:17 – 9 note 23
Jeremiah 22:13–16 – 143
Jeremiah 35 – 112
Ezekiel 1:26 – 230
Daniel 12:3 – 9 note 24
Hosea 11:8 – 228
Hosea 11:9 – 224
Amos 7:7 – 230
Amos 9:11–12 – 9 note 23
Micah 4:1–5 – 9 note 23
Zechariah 2:11 – 9 note 23
Zechariah 14:16 – 9 note 23

New Testament

Matthew 5:2–11 – 9 note 24
Matthew 5:48 – 257
Matthew 6:9 – 264
Matthew 8:8–9 – 204
Matthew 13:43 – 9 note 24
Matthew 16:13 – 148
Matthew 18:10 – 214
Matthew 19:26 – 152, 192
Matthew 25:31–46 – 104
Matthew 26:64 – 151
Mark 3:22–24 – 165
Mark 6:5 – 224
Mark 7:21–23 – 204
Mark 13:32 – 224
Mark 14:62 – 151
Luke 2:46–47 – 158
Luke 10:25–37 – 112
Luke 10:27 – 104
Luke 10:29–37 – 104
Luke 12:12 – 74
Luke 22:44 – 181
Luke 22:67 – 151
John 1:14 – 208
John 1:18 – 214
John 1:32 – 214
John 3:5–6 – 74
John 3:16 – 208
John 4:24 – 213, 214 note 4
John 5:37 – 214
John 6:51 – 217
John 10:34 – 259
John 13:34 – xiii
John 16:28 – 151
John 17:20–23 – 129
John 17:21–24 – 123 note 29
John 17:22 – 9 note 24
John 18:20 – 151
John 20:22 – 74
Acts 7:48–50 – 214
Acts 9:4–5 – 151
Acts 17:24 – 222
Acts 17:24–25 – 214
Romans 1:16 – 267
Romans 2:7 – 9 note 24
Romans 5:2 – 9 note 24, 233
Romans 5:12 – 221
Romans 6:5 – 9 note 24
Romans 8:13 – 74
Romans 8:14–17 – 208, 257
Romans 8:15 – 247
Romans 8:18–30 – 9 note 24
Romans 12:18 – 104
1 Corinthians 3:16 – 74, 204
1 Corinthians 8:5–6 – 121
1 Corinthians 15 – 213
1 Corinthians 15:42–55 – 9 note 24
1 Corinthians 15:35–36 – 233
2 Corinthians 3:17–18 – 257
2 Corinthians 3:18 – 9 note 24, 215
2 Corinthians 4:16 – 221
2 Corinthians 12:1–4 – 114
Galatians 4:5–6 – 208
Galatians 5:16 – 74
Galatians 5:25 – 74
Galatians 6:1 – 188
Ephesians 4:13 – 129
Ephesians 4:22–24 – 221
Ephesians 4:24 – 215

Philippians 3:21 – 9 note 24
Colossians 1:15 – 214, 215, 221
Colossians 2:9 – 124
Colossians 3:10 – 215, 221
2 Thessalonians 2:14 – 9 note 24
1 Timothy 1:17 – 214, 221
1 Timothy 3:16 – 150
1 Timothy 6:16 – 221, 224
2 Timothy 1:10 – 9 note 24
Hebrews 2:10 – 9 note 24
Hebrews 4:15 – 264
Hebrews 11:8 – 45
Hebrews 12:9 – 264
Hebrews 12:14 – 214
James 1:8 – 334
James 1:26–27 – 104
1 Peter 1:3–4 – 9 note 24
1 Peter 1:23 – 9 note 24
2 Peter 1:2–4 – 257
2 Peter 1:4 – 233
1 John 3:1–2 – 257, 263
1 John 3:9 – 207
Revelation 1:10–20 – 114
Revelation 4:1–2 – 114
Revelation 10:8–10 – 114
Revelation 19:7 – 208
Revelation 21:22 – 90
Revelation 22:3–4 – 214
Revelation 22:4 – 203–4

Book of Mormon

1 Nephi 1:2 – 117
1 Nephi 13 – 115
1 Nephi 13:5 – 115
1 Nephi 13:5–6 – 218
1 Nephi 13:20–29 – 116
1 Nephi 13:23–29 – 118
1 Nephi 13:24 – 117
1 Nephi 13:29 – 115
1 Nephi 13:32 – 115
1 Nephi 13:34–35 – 173 note 8
1 Nephi 13:41 – 23, 122
1 Nephi 14:3 – 116
1 Nephi 14:3–4 – 115
1 Nephi 14:7 – 115
1 Nephi 14:10 – 115
2 Nephi 1:10 – 23
2 Nephi 2 – 328–329
2 Nephi 2:4–8 – 182

2 Nephi 2:11 – 209
2 Nephi 2:11–12 – 330
2 Nephi 2:26 – 252 note 41
2 Nephi 4:20–21 – 261
2 Nephi 10:24 – 182
2 Nephi 27:10 – 23
2 Nephi 31:19 – 182
2 Nephi 31:20 – 267
2 Nephi 31:21 – 122
Jacob 7:14–15 – 322 note 9
Mosiah 1:4 – 117
Mosiah 3:5 – 23
Mosiah 3:7 – 181
Mosiah 3:12 – 182
Mosiah 3:17–18 – 23
Mosiah 3:21 – 23
Mosiah 5:2 – 23
Mosiah 5:3 – 23
Mosiah 5:15 – 23, 265
Mosiah 15:1–5 – 122–23
Mosiah 26:15 – 265
Mosiah 26:17 – 265
Mosiah 26:19–20 – 265
Mosiah 28:4 – 23
Alma 2:14 – 182
Alma 7:12 – 343
Alma 11:22 – 23
Alma 11:26–29 – 23
Alma 11:44 – 123, 270
Alma 14 – 322 note 9
Alma 30:17 – 338, 340
Alma 30:44 – 23
Alma 30:59 – 338
Alma 40:8 – 23
Alma 42 – 334
Helaman 3:21 – 266
Helaman 12:1 – 23
Mormon 7:7 – 124
Mormon 8:23 – 119
Mormon 9:19 – 23
Mormon 9:32 – 117
Ether 2:8 – 23
Ether 3:16 – 214 note 5
Ether 3:25–26 – 23
Moroni 4–5 – 110 note 4
Moroni 7:48 – 261
Moroni 8 – 118–19
Moroni 8:3 – 23
Moroni 8:18 – 23

Doctrine and Covenants

Doctrine and Covenants 5:3 – 322 note 9
Doctrine and Covenants 10:53–54 – 188
Doctrine and Covenants 14:7 – 267
Doctrine and Covenants 19:16–19 – 181
Doctrine and Covenants 20:17 – 23, 269–70
Doctrine and Covenants 20:19 – 23
Doctrine and Covenants 20:28 – 23, 270
Doctrine and Covenants 29:21 – 218
Doctrine and Covenants 50:5 – 267
Doctrine and Covenants 53:7 – 267
Doctrine and Covenants 61:1 – 23
Doctrine and Covenants 76 – 184
Doctrine and Covenants 76:5 – 255
Doctrine and Covenants 76:20 – 152
Doctrine and Covenants 76:53–58 – 263
Doctrine and Covenants 76:54 – 266
Doctrine and Covenants 76:58 – 267
Doctrine and Covenants 76:69–86 – 246
Doctrine and Covenants 76:88 – 263
Doctrine and Covenants 88:15 – 245 note 20
Doctrine and Covenants 93:25 – 334
Doctrine and Covenants 107:4 – 23
Doctrine and Covenants 109:14–15 – 266
Doctrine and Covenants 109:27 – 270
Doctrine and Covenants 109:77 – 269
Doctrine and Covenants 121:32 – 25, 121
Doctrine and Covenants 130:1–2 – 329
Doctrine and Covenants 130:3 – 124
Doctrine and Covenants 130:22 – 124, 213, 215, 231, 264
Doctrine and Covenants 131:7 – 214 note 5, 252 note 40
Doctrine and Covenants 132:18–20 – 25
Doctrine and Covenants 132:19 – 263
Doctrine and Covenants 132:19–20 – 270
Doctrine and Covenants 132:20 – 263, 271
Doctrine and Covenants 132:37 – 25
Doctrine and Covenants 132:49 – 265
Doctrine and Covenants 134:1 – 100
Doctrine and Covenants 134:3 – 100
Doctrine and Covenants 134:5 – 100

Pearl of Great Price

Moses 2 – 124
Moses 2:27 – 257
Moses 6:8–9 – 264
Moses 6:57 – 264
Abraham 3:8 – 121
Abraham 3:16–17 – 121
Abraham 3:18 – 251 note 38
Abraham 3:19 – 121
Abraham 4 – 124
Abraham 4–5 – 25
Joseph Smith—History 1:5 – 155
Joseph Smith—History 1:5–12 – 113
Joseph Smith—History 1:14 – 114
Joseph Smith—History 1:19 – 114
Joseph Smith—History 1:21–25 – 158
Joseph Smith—History 1:25 – 152
Joseph Smith—History 1:33 – 148
Joseph Smith—History 1:51–52 – 114
Article of Faith 9 – 52

Apocrypha

2 Esdras 12:27 – 117
2 Esdras 14 – 116–117

Also available from
GREG KOFFORD BOOKS

Perspectives on Mormon Theology Series

Brian D. Birch and Loyd Ericson,
series editors

(forthcoming)

This series will feature multiple volumes published on particular theological topics of interest in Latter-day Saint thought. Volumes will be co-edited by leading scholars and graduate students whose interests and knowledge will ensure that the essays in each volume represent quality scholarship and acknowledge the diversity of thought found and expressed in Mormon theological studies. Topics for the first few volumes include: revelation, apostasy, atonement, scripture, and grace.

The *Perspectives on Mormon Theology* series will bring together the best of new and previously published essays on various theological subjects. Each volume will be both a valued resource for academics in Mormon Studies and an illuminating introduction to the broad and sophisticated approaches to Mormon theology.

"This is My Doctrine": The Development of Mormon Theology

Charles R. Harrell

Hardcover, ISBN: 978-1-58958-103-6

The principal doctrines defining Mormonism today often bear little resemblance to those it started out with in the early 1830s. This book shows that these doctrines did not originate in a vacuum but were rather prompted and informed by the religious culture from which Mormonism arose. Early Mormons, like their early Christian and even earlier Israelite predecessors, brought with them their own varied culturally conditioned theological presuppositions (a process of convergence) and only later acquired a more distinctive theological outlook (a process of differentiation).

In this first-of-its-kind comprehensive treatment of the development of Mormon theology, Charles Harrell traces the history of Latter-day Saint doctrines from the times of the Old Testament to the present. He describes how Mormonism has carried on the tradition of the biblical authors, early Christians, and later Protestants in reinterpreting scripture to accommodate new theological ideas while attempting to uphold the integrity and authority of the scriptures. In the process, he probes three questions: How did Mormon doctrines develop? What are the scriptural underpinnings of these doctrines? And what do critical scholars make of these same scriptures? In this enlightening study, Harrell systematically peels back the doctrinal accretions of time to provide a fresh new look at Mormon theology.

"*This Is My Doctrine*" will provide those already versed in Mormonism's theological tradition with a new and richer perspective of Mormon theology. Those unacquainted with Mormonism will gain an appreciation for how Mormon theology fits into the larger Jewish and Christian theological traditions.

Discourses in Mormon Theology: Philosophical and Theological Possibilities

Edited by
James M. McLachlan and Loyd Ericson

Hardcover, ISBN: 978-1-58958-103-6

A mere two hundred years old, Mormonism is still in its infancy compared to other theological disciplines (Judaism, Catholicism, Buddhism, etc.). This volume will introduce its reader to the rich blend of theological viewpoints that exist within Mormonism. The essays break new ground in Mormon studies by exploring the vast expanse of philosophical territory left largely untouched by traditional approaches to Mormon theology. It presents philosophical and theological essays by many of the finest minds associated with Mormonism in an organized and easy-to-understand manner and provides the reader with a window into the fascinating diversity amongst Mormon philosophers. Open-minded students of pure religion will appreciate this volume's thoughtful inquiries.

These essays were delivered at the first conference of the Society for Mormon Philosophy and Theology. Authors include Grant Underwood, Blake T. Ostler, Dennis Potter, Margaret Merrill Toscano, James E. Faulconer, and Robert L. Millet

Praise for *Discourses in Mormon Theology*:

"In short, *Discourses in Mormon Theology* is an excellent compilation of essays that are sure to feed both the mind and soul. It reminds all of us that beyond the white shirts and ties there exists a universe of theological and moral sensitivity that cries out for study and acclamation."
-Jeff Needle, Association for Mormon Letters

Rube Goldberg Machines: Essays in Mormon Theology

Adam S. Miller

Paperback, ISBN: 978-1-58958-193-7

"Adam Miller is the most original and provocative Latter-day Saint theologian practicing today."

—Richard Bushman, author of *Joseph Smith: Rough Stone Rolling*

"As a stylist, Miller gives Nietzsche a run for his money. As a believer, Miller is as submissive as Augustine hearing a child's voice in the garden. Miller is a theologian of the ordinary, thinking about our ordinary beliefs in very non-ordinary ways while never insisting that the ordinary become extra-ordinary."

—James Faulconer, Richard L. Evans Chair of Religious Understanding, Brigham Young University

"Miller's language is both recognizably Mormon and startlingly original.... The whole is an essay worthy of the name, inviting the reader to try ideas, following the philosopher pilgrim's intellectual progress through tangled brambles and into broad fields, fruitful orchards, and perhaps a sacred grove or two."

—Kristine Haglund, editor of *Dialogue: A Journal of Mormon Thought*

"Miller's Rube Goldberg theology is nothing like anything done in the Mormon tradition before."

—Blake Ostler, author of the EXPLORING MORMON THOUGHT series

"The value of Miller's writings is in the modesty he both exhibits and projects onto the theological enterprise, even while showing its joyfully disruptive potential. Conventional Mormon minds may not resonate with every line of poetry and provocation—but Miller surely afflicts the comfortable, which is the theologian's highest end."

—Terryl Givens, author of *By the Hand of Mormon: The American Scripture that Launched a New World Religion*

Modern Mormonism: Myths and Realities

Robert L. Millet

Paperback, ISBN: 978-1-58958-127-2

What answer may a Latter-day Saint make to accusations from those of other faiths that "Mormons aren't Christians," or "You think God is a man," and "You worship a different Jesus"? Not only are these charges disconcerting, but the hostility with which they are frequently hurled is equally likely to catch Latter-day Saints off guard.

Now Robert L. Millet, veteran of hundreds of such verbal battles, cogently, helpfully, and scripturally provides important clarifications for Latter-day Saints about eleven of the most frequent myths used to discredit the Church. Along the way, he models how to conduct such a Bible based discussion respectfully, weaving in enlightenment from LDS scriptures and quotations from religious figures in other faiths, ranging from the early church fathers to the archbishop of Canterbury.

Millet enlivens this book with personal experiences as a boy growing up in an area where Mormons were a minuscule and not particularly welcome minority, in one-on-one conversations with men of faith who believed differently, and with his own BYU students who also had lessons to learn about interfaith dialogue. He pleads for greater cooperation in dealing with the genuine moral and social evils afflicting the world, and concludes with his own ardent and reverent testimony of the Savior.

Exploring Mormon Thought Series

Blake T. Ostler

IN VOLUME ONE, *The Attributes of God*, Blake T. Ostler explores Christian and Mormon notions about God. ISBN: 978-1-58958-003-9

IN VOLUME TWO, *The Problems of Theism and the Love of God*, Blake Ostler explores issues related to soteriology, or the theory of salvation. ISBN: 978-1-58958-095-4

IN VOLUME THREE, *Of God and Gods*, Ostler analyzes and responds to the arguments of contemporary international theologians, reconstructs and interprets Joseph Smith's important King Follett Discourse and Sermon in the Grove, and argues persuasively for the Mormon doctrine of "robust deification." ISBN: 978-1-58958-107-4

Praise for the *Exploring Mormon Thought* series:

"These books are the most important works on Mormon theology ever written. There is nothing currently available that is even close to the rigor and sophistication of these volumes. B. H. Roberts and John A. Widtsoe may have had interesting insights in the early part of the twentieth century, but they had neither the temperament nor the training to give a rigorous defense of their views in dialogue with a wider stream of Christian theology. Sterling McMurrin and Truman Madsen had the capacity to engage Mormon theology at this level, but neither one did."
—Neal A. Maxwell Institute, Brigham Young University

www.ingramcontent.com/pod-product-compliance
Lightning Source LLC
Chambersburg PA
CBHW060549230426
43670CB00011B/1744